Prelude to the Final Solution

Prelude to the Final Solution

The Nazi Program for Deporting Ethnic Poles, 1939–1941

Phillip T. Rutherford

UNIVERSITY PRESS OF KANSAS

© 2007 by the University Press of Kansas

Published by the University Press of Kansas (Lawrence, Kansas 66045), which was
organized by the Kansas Board of Regents and is operated and funded by Emporia State
University, Fort Hays State University, Kansas State University, Pittsburg State University,
the University of Kansas, and Wichita State University

Library of Congress Cataloging-in-Publication Data

Rutherford, Phillip T.
Prelude to the final solution : the Nazi program for deporting ethnic
Poles, 1939–1941 / Phillip T. Rutherford.
p. cm. — (Modern war studies)
Originally presented as the author's thesis (doctoral)—
Pennsylvania State University.
Includes bibliographical references and index.
ISBN-13: 978-0-7006-1506-3 (cloth : alk. paper)
1. World War, 1939-1945—Deportations from Poland. 2. Holocaust,
Jewish (1939-1945)—Poland. 3. Germany—Politics and government—1933-1945.
4. Poland—Ethnic relations. 5. Poland—History—Occupation, 1939-1945.
I. Title.
D810.D5R85   2007
940.53′180899185—dc22
2006032778

British Library Cataloguing-in-Publication Data is available.

Printed in the United States of America

10 9 8 7 6 5 4 3 2 1

The paper used in this publication meets the minimum requirements of the American
National Standard for Permanence of Paper for Printed Library Materials Z39.48-1992.

For my parents, Phillip and Lou Carolyn Rutherford

Contents

Acknowledgments

Like many first books, this one began as a dissertation. I am profoundly grateful to the members of my doctoral committee—namely, Geoffrey Giles, Jackson Spielvogel, Robert Proctor, and Richard Page—for their suggestions and support during the initial stage of this project. I also wish to thank the entire faculty and staff of the Department of History at the Pennsylvania State University. I am indebted to Professors William Pencak, Paul Harvey, Benjamin Hudson, and Gary Cross for their exceptional instruction; to Darla Franks for putting up with me so patiently over the years; and to Karin Weaver for her gentle attempts to keep me in line and, even more important, for her invaluable assistance during those moments when the meaning of a German word or phrase eluded my grasp.

My research was made possible by extensive support from the Pennsylvania State University and the Visiting Scholars Program of the Center for Advanced Holocaust Studies at the U.S. Holocaust Memorial Museum (USHMM) in Washington, D.C. As a member of the Summer Research Workshop for Scholars at the USHMM in 1999 and as a Charles H. Revson Foundation Fellow in 2002, I enjoyed the counsel and encouragement of many outstanding historians, including Alexander Rossino, Isabel Heinemann, Hilary Earl, Simone Gigliotti, Robert Kuwalek, Wendy Lower, Geoffrey Megargee, Martin Dean, Gerhard Weinberg, and Dan Inkelas. Special thanks must go to Peter Black, the senior historian at the Center for Advanced Holocaust Studies. His careful reading of my manuscript and penetrating commentary proved instrumental in the completion of this work.

I am indebted to a number of archivists and librarians in the United States and Poland. I wish to thank the archival specialists at the USHMM and the National Archives and Records Administration in College Park, Maryland, for their help with technical questions. Maciej Cholewiński of the Archiwum Państwowe-Łódź, Stefan Olejniczak of AP-Poznań, and Michalina Wysocka of Instytutu Pamięci Naradowej in Warsaw have my gratitude for their assistance during my attempts to negotiate the document collections under their management. I owe an enormous debt of thanks to Bożena Michalska, the reference librarian at the Bibliotek Uniwersytecka Mikołaja Kopernika in Toruń, Poland, for her many hours of help.

My thanks also go to the graphic arts whiz Jamie Meecham for designing the maps; to Maren Read, photo archivist at the USHMM, for her assistance in procuring photographs; and to John Delaney, my former colleague at Kutztown University, for his recommendations and reassurance as I revised my manuscript.

Many friends—far more than I can mention here—have watched my back over the years. I tip my cowboy hat to "The Roadgraders," Chuck Holden, Bryan Grove, Steve Knox, and Jake Frederick; to my oldest and dearest friend, Peter Weed; and to Joanna Ciechanowska, who single-handedly saved both my health and my sanity during my year as a high school English teacher in Toruń between 1991 and 1992. Here's to all the others as well.

Most of all, I wish to thank my parents, Phillip and Lou Carolyn Rutherford, and my doctoral supervisor and friend, Dan P. Silverman. To my parents, I owe my existence, decades of love, decades of support, and decades of patience and understanding. Words cannot express my appreciation for the guidance, encouragement, praise, and criticism that Dan Silverman has offered since our first meeting in the fall of 1992. Above all else, his willingness to share his time, his energy, and his unrivaled knowledge of European history made this book possible.

Selections from Chapters Three, Four, and Five are reprinted in slightly revised form with permission from *Central European History* 36, no. 2 (2003): 235–273. The views or opinions expressed in this book and the context in which the images are used do not necessarily reflect the views or policy of, nor imply approval or endorsement by, the U.S. Holocaust Memorial Museum.

Abbreviations

AA	Arbeitsamt (Labor Office)
AGK	Archiwum Głównej Komisji Badania Zbrodni Hitlerowskich w Polsce—Instytutu Pamięci Naradowej (Archives of the Main Commission for the Investigation of Nazi Crimes in Poland—Institute of National Remembrance)
AK	Ansiedlungskommission (Colonization Commission)
APB	Archiwum Państwowe Bydgoszcz (State Archive Bydgoszcz)
APL	Archiwum Państwowe Łódź (State Archive Łódź)
APP	Archiwum Państwowe Poznań (State Archive Poznań)
BDC	Berlin Document Center
DAI	Deutsches Ausland-Institut (German Foreign Institute)
DGFP	*Documents on German Foreign Policy*
DVL	Deutsche Volksliste (German Ethnic Registry)
EG	Einsatzgruppe (Operational Group)
EK	Einsatzkommando (Operational Detachment)
EWZ	Einwandererzentralstelle (Central Immigration Office)
EWZ-L	Einwandererzentralstelle-Litzmannstadt (Central Immigration Office–Litzmannstadt)
Gestapo	Geheime Staatspolizei (Secret State Police)
GG	Generalgouvernement
GPO	Generalplan Ost (General Plan East)
HSSPF	Höhere SS- und Polizeiführer (higher SS and police leader)
HTO	Haupttreuhandstelle-Ost (Central Trust Agency for the East)
IMT	International Military Tribunal
NARA	National Archives and Records Administration
NSDAP	Nationalsozialistische Deutsche Arbeiterpartei (National Socialist German Workers Party)
NSV	Nationalsozialistische Volkswohlfahrt (Nazi Welfare Agency)
OdB	*Ostdeutscher Beobachter*

OKW	Oberkommando der Wehrmacht (Armed Forces High Command)
OMV	Deutscher Ostmarkverein (German Eastern Marches Association)
Orpo	Ordnungspolizei (Order Police)
RBD	Reichsbahndirektion (Reich Rail System Directorate)
RfR	Reichsstelle für Raumordnung (Reich Office for the Organization of Space)
RFSS	Reichsführer-SS (Reich leader of the SS)
RG	Record Group
RKF	Reichskommissariat für die Festigung deutschen Volkstums (Reich Commission for the Consolidation of German Nationhood)
RKFDV	Reichskommissar für die Festigung deutschen Volkstums (Reich Commissioner for the Consolidation of German Nationhood)
RM	Reichsmark
RmdI	Reichsministerium des Innern (Reich Ministry of the Interior)
RSHA	Reichssicherheitshauptamt (Reich Security Main Office)
RüI	Rüstungsinspektion (Armament Inspectorate)
RuS	Rasse- und Siedlungsamt (Race and Settlement Office)
RuSHA	Rasse- und Siedlungshauptamt (Race and Settlement Main Office)
SA	Sturmabteilung (Storm Troops)
Schupo	Schutzpolizei (Municipal Police)
SD	Sicherheitsdienst (Security Service)
Sipo	Sicherheitspolizei (Security Police)
SS	Schutzstaffel (Protective Squads)
SS-AS	SS-Ansiedlungsstab (SS Resettlement Staff)
TWC	*Trials of War Criminals before the Nuernberg Military Tribunals under Control Council Law no. 10*
UFZ	*Ursachen und Folgen von deutschen Zusammenbruch 1918 und 1945 zur staatlichen Neuordnung Deutschlands in der Gegenwart*
USHMM	U.S. Holocaust Memorial Museum
UWZ	Umwandererzentralstelle (Central Emigration Office)
UWZ-L	Umwandererzentralstelle-Litzmannstadt (Central Emigration Office–Litzmannstadt)
UWZ-P	Umwandererzentralstelle-Posen (Central Emigration Office–Posen)
VoMi	Volksdeutsche Mittelstelle (Ethnic German Liaison Office)
ZBA	Zentral Bodenamt (Central Land Office)

German and Polish Place-Names

Allenstein	Olsztyn
Breslau	Wrocław
Bromberg	Bydgoszcz
Danzig	Gdańsk
Gotenhafen	Gdynia
Kattowitz	Katowice
Krakau	Kraków
Thorn	Toruń
Warschau	Warszawa
Zichenau	Ciechanów

REICHSGAU WARTHELAND
Regierungsbezirk Posen

Birnbaum	Międzychód
Gostingen	Gostyn
Grätz (Neutomischel)	Grodzisk (Nowy Tomyśl)
Jarotschin	Jarocin
Kolmar	Chodzież
Kosten	Kościan
Krotoschin	Krotoszyn
Lissa	Leszno
Obernick	Oborniki
Posen	Poznań
Rawitsch	Rawicz
Samter	Szamotuły
Scharnikau	Czarników
Schrimm	Śrem
Schroda	Środa
Wollstein	Wolsztyn
Wreschen	Września

Regierungsbezirk Hohensalza

Dietfurt	Żnin
Gasten	Gostynin
Gnesen	Gniezno
Hermannsbad (Nessau)	Ciechocinek (Nieszawa)
Hohensalza	Inowrocław
Konin	Konin
Kutno	Kutno
Leslau	Włocławek
Mogilno	Mogilno
Schubin	Szubin
Warthbrücken	Koło
Wongrowitz	Wągrowiec

Regierungsbezirk Litzmannstadt

Kalisch	Kalisz
Kempen	Kępno
Lask	Łask
Lentschütz	Łęczyca
Litzmannstadt (Lodsch)	Łódź
Ostrowo	Ostrów Wielkapolski
Schieratz	Sieradz
Turek	Turek
Welungen (Welun)	Wielun

Rivers

Warthe	Warta
Weichsel	Wisła (English: Vistula)

SS Ranks and Approximate U.S. Army Equivalent

Reichsführer-SS	General of the Army
SS-Oberstgruppenführer	No equivalent
SS-Obergruppenführer	General
SS-Gruppenführer	Lieutenant General
SS-Brigadeführer	Major General
SS-Oberführer	Brigadier General
SS-Standartenführer	Colonel
SS-Obersturmbannführer	Lieutenant Colonel
SS-Sturmbannführer	Major
SS-Hauptsturmführer	Captain
SS-Obersturmführer	First Lieutenant
SS-Untersturmführer	Second Lieutenant
SS-Sturmscharführer	Sergeant Major
SS-Hauptscharführer	Master Sergeant
SS-Oberscharführer	Technical Sergeant
SS-Scharführer	Staff Sergeant
SS-Unterscharführer	Sergeant
SS-Rottenführer	Corporal
SS-Sturmmann	Private First Class
SS-Mann	Private

Source: George Browder, *Foundations of the Nazi Police State: The Formation of Sipo and SD* (Lexington: University Press of Kentucky, 1990), 250–251.

Introduction: An Invincible
Ostwall of Flesh and Blood

The first days of November 1939 were somewhat hectic for Arthur Greiser, but they must have been altogether satisfying. Recently appointed by Adolf Hitler to serve as the Nazi governor and senior Nazi Party officer of the Warthegau, a new eastern province of the Greater German Reich carved from the shattered remains of conquered Poland, Greiser was formally inaugurated in the *Gau* (district) capital of Posen on the morning of Thursday, 2 November. In a solemn ceremony conducted by Reichsminister of the Interior Wilhelm Frick, he received his commission and gave his thanks in the swastika-bedecked throne room of the city's castle, once the residence of Kaiser Wilhelm II. The message to the Poles was clear: the Germans had returned to rule the territory they considered their own.

The inauguration itself was over, but Greiser had little time to rest. That afternoon, after visiting the graves of ethnic Germans supposedly murdered by Poles during the September campaign, Greiser and his guest of honor, Frick, toured Posen and then reviewed a parade of Hitler Youth (Hitlerjugend) and the League of German Girls (Bund deutscher Mädel) that wound its way through the city.[1] Three more days of state functions and celebrations followed. The festivities culminated on Sunday, 5 November, which was officially proclaimed "The Day of Freedom in the Warthegau." Prominent members of the new Nazi administration spoke before mass rallies held throughout the province. Greiser, for his part, delivered a lengthy speech in the town of Schroda, the place of his birth.

Arthur Karl Greiser was born in 1897, when Schroda was in the Prussian province of Posen. He grew up in the vicinity, receiving his schooling at the Königliches Humanistisches Gymnasium in Hohensalza, one of the larger cities in the province, and apparently never strayed far from home until the outbreak of

World War I. With the declaration of war in August 1914, Greiser left school without a diploma to volunteer for service in the German marines. He first saw action on the western front as an artillery observer but eventually became a navy pilot, ending the war as the commander of a naval fighter wing based in Flanders.

Germany's defeat and the peace settlement that followed left a deep and lasting impact on Greiser's psyche. Not only had his four long years of soldiering come to naught, the Treaty of Versailles had left him homeless. Ninety percent of the province of Posen, an area that included the capital city and his hometown of Schroda, was detached from Germany and handed over to the new Polish republic. Burning with resentment over his nation's humiliation and the loss of his homeland, Greiser chose to continue the fight. He joined the Freikorps (Free Corps) unit Grenzschutz Ost immediately after the armistice and spent the next three years battling Polish irregulars along Germany's new eastern frontier. After nearly seven years in uniform, he finally returned to civilian life in May 1921.² The land of his youth now in Polish hands, Greiser settled in the Free City of Danzig, still bitter about the outcome of the war and bearing a strong personal grudge against the Poles.

It is not surprising that Greiser soon became involved in right-wing politics. A World War I veteran, a Freikorps alumnus, and a diehard German ethnonationalist who was fervently anti-Polish and fanatically anti-Versailles, he possessed the classic characteristics of the 1920s *völkisch* agitator. He joined the decidedly völkisch German Social Party in 1922 and two years later founded the Danzig chapter of Stahlhelm, the German veterans' organization. The latter alone made him a fairly prominent figure in local right-wing circles, but political notoriety did not entail financial success. Throughout the twenties, Greiser's economic situation was precarious at best. At one time a salesman, at another the captain of a tourist boat in Danzig harbor, he was evidently between jobs when he joined the Nationalsozialistische Deutsche Arbeiterpartei (NSDAP; National Socialist German Workers Party) in 1929.³

Greiser quickly ascended the ladder of the local party organization. By the end of 1930, the same year he joined the Schutzstaffel (SS; Protective Squads), he was already deputy Gauleiter of the city, second only to Albert Forster in the Danzig NSDAP, as well as the leader of the Nazi faction in the Danzig Volkstag (Parliament), where he immediately gained renown for his outspoken attacks on Poles and Marxists. His political star continued to rise. In 1933, he became vice president of the Danzig State Senate. One year later, after the Nazis gained full control of the city government, he was elected Senate president, a position he retained until the outbreak of World War II. In the interim, Greiser played a major role in the *Gleichschaltung* (meaning "coordination" or, in this context, "Nazification") of Danzig, a process that left the city's institutions thoroughly Nazified well before the region was reincorporated into the Reich on 1 September 1939.[4]

A reserve officer in the German navy, Greiser was initially slated for a naval commission during the Polish campaign. But in late August 1939, just as he was about to take command of a ship, he learned via a radio message from Hermann Göring that Hitler had a more important mission for him.[5] Thus, instead of going to sea, Greiser headed inland, back to the area where he had spent his youth. Accompanied by a large contingent of German soldiers, he arrived in the city of Posen on the morning of 13 September to assume leadership of the civil administration of the entire province.[6] When the military government in occupied Poland was dissolved on 26 October 1939, Greiser, who had been promoted by Heinrich Himmler to the rank of SS-Gruppenführer just two days earlier, became both Gauleiter (senior National Socialist party leader in the Gau) and Reichsstatthalter (Reich governor) of his native district, making him the senior party and state official in the largest and economically most significant of Germany's new eastern *Reichsgaue* (Reich districts).[7]

After a two-decade absence, returning to Schroda on 5 November 1939 as the new Nazi lord of his home territory must have been a bittersweet moment for Arthur Greiser. Upon his arrival, the Bürgermeister (mayor) of the town immediately escorted him to the simple house where he had been born, now adorned with garlands and swastika pennants. From there, they proceeded down streets lined with welcoming ethnic Germans to the Schroda town hall. Before a large crowd of Nazi officials and local Germans who had gathered in the assembly room, Greiser gave his Day of Freedom address. The speech offered a telling glimpse into the future of his new domain, then termed Reichsgau Posen but unofficially called the Warthegau.

Greiser opened with a nostalgic look back at his early childhood in Schroda, framing his memories in standard Hitlerian idiom about the "struggle for survival" and "might makes right." Such Social Darwinist rhetoric served as a bridge into the heart of his address. Just as his own life had been a struggle for survival, so was the life of the *Volk*. The innate heroic capacity of the German people, a capacity that emerged in its full glory with the outbreak of World War I, prepared them well for that struggle, but the weakness of their leaders, coupled with parliamentarianism and capitalistic greed, destroyed the unity of the people and resulted in the disintegration of the Reich. The creation of an independent

Polish state, then, was not the result of any heroism on the part of the Poles but rather the consequence of German weakness. But now things had changed, he asserted, and a new Germany had arisen:

> This Germany of power and strength now stands here in the land of Posen and will—this the world can believe—never again budge from [this place]! ... Here a new generation stands, a young generation of power, hardened by a life of struggle in the storm of steel of the Great War, in the privations of economic and psychological destitution, and in National Socialism's hard campaign for the unity of the German people. Our generation has forgotten nothing and is ready to draw every conclusion—even the most extreme conclusions—from the lessons of the past.

For Greiser, the lessons of the past embodied far more than those weaknesses that had led to the loss of Posen in 1918. He went on to emphasize the mistreatment and murder of Germans at the hands of the Poles, at that time the very staple of Nazi anti-Polish propaganda, and admonished his audience never to forget these base atrocities. Their memory, he said, "must burn as an eternal warning in the hearts of your children," a warning that commanded all Germans to "remain hard—be crusaders!"

Indeed, though the "shackles of Versailles" had been eliminated and Posen was once again free of the Polish yoke, by no means was the struggle over. "With unwavering hardness," Greiser ordered his listeners, "you should continue the fight of the German soldiers who liberated you and finally made this German national soil the holy and inviolable possession of a rising German master race." He summed up the nature of the fight to come in his final sentence: "We must ensure that here in the Warthegau [we] erect an eastern wall of living human beings with vigilant minds and loyal hearts, ready to seize the plow with strong fists and once again make the mark of decent German [farmers] on the land."[8] What the creation of this "*Ostwall* of flesh and blood" meant for the native, non-German inhabitants of the Warthegau, primarily the non-Jewish population, is the focus of the pages that follow.

The defeat of Nazi Germany—something Arthur Greiser could not have imagined possible in those heady days of late 1939—marked not only the end of German rule east of the Oder River but also the beginning of the end of the German presence itself. Millions of Germans fled west before the advancing Red Army in the spring of 1945; the remainder, millions more, were driven west in the aftermath of the war. The expulsion of the Germans from what soon became the People's Re-

SS-Gruppenführer Arthur Karl Greiser, the Gauleiter and Reichsstatthalter of Reichsgau Wartheland. Photo by Heinrich Hoffmann, Hitler's court photographer and the "official" photographer of the Nazi Party. (U.S. Holocaust Memorial Museum [USHMM], courtesy of the National Archives and Records Administration, College Park, Maryland, USHMM Photo Reference Collection: WS 20379)

public of Poland brought with it the cessation of decades of often-bitter nationality conflict between Germans and Poles in the Prussian Eastern Marches. Born out of the partitions of Poland in the late eighteenth century and exacerbated by the rising tide of ethnic nationalism that swept Europe as the nineteenth century progressed, German-Polish friction escalated dramatically with the foundation of the Second Reich in 1871 and continued virtually unabated until the collapse of Germany's position in the East in 1945. The "battle for nationality" in Germany's Polish territories, a struggle that perpetuated the long-standing German preoccupation with the "Polish Question," went far to shape the character of *Polenpolitik* (Polish policy) throughout the Imperial and Nazi periods. Perceiving the Poles as politically, culturally, and demographically threatening, the governments of both the Second and the Third Reich sought to "Germanize" their Polish provinces in an attempt to integrate the Prussian East firmly within the structure of the German ethnoterritorial nation-state.

The Germanization schemes of Imperial and Nazi Germany embodied a wide range of legalized discriminatory measures aimed at undermining Polish national consciousness and cultural autonomy. But by far the most striking element of Polenpolitik during both periods was the effort to restructure the ethnogeography of regions under German control. Imperial and Nazi authorities, striving to tighten their grip on Germany's eastern provinces, endeavored to increase the German population of the area at the expense of the Polish. Through the cultural Germanization of Poles, German colonization, the expropriation of property owned by Poles, and the expulsion of Poles from the Prussian East, Otto von Bismarck and the statesmen of the Wilhelmine era attempted, in vain, to tip the ethnic balance in Germany's favor. Hitler and his National Socialist "experts" on population policy studied, adopted, and radicalized these very measures in their own pursuit of a racial "New Order" in annexed western Poland.

Proceeding from the conviction that any lasting conquest of lebensraum for the German people necessitated a comprehensive Germanization of captured territory, the National Socialist regime launched a mammoth exercise in *Volkstumspolitik* (population policy) in the autumn of 1939; it was devised to restructure the ethnogeography of occupied Poland, particularly the western regions officially incorporated into the Reich. This complex demographic project entailed two interrelated forced population movements: the mass expulsion of Poles and Jews from annexed territory and the mass resettlement of hundreds of thousands of *Volksdeutschen* (ethnic Germans) from eastern and southeastern Europe in their place.[9] Poles and Jews were to be dispossessed without compensation and deported eastward to the Nazi-administered Generalgouvernement, and their property was to be reallocated to the incoming Germans. Via these measures, the Nazis reasoned that annexed western Poland would shed its foreign character within a matter of years, a racial metamorphosis that would make this long-contested territory totally and unambiguously German for all time.[10]

As originally framed, Nazi Germanization schemes demanded the complete elimination of Poles and Jews from the incorporated eastern territories, and given the fact that virtually the entire Jewish population of the region was dispossessed, deported or ghettoized, and eventually killed, the Jews certainly emerged in the long run as the primary victims of the operation. But this horrific truth should not obscure the conspicuous anti-Polonism of Nazi Volkstumspolitik during the initial phase of the occupation. From September 1939 until the exigencies of war compelled the Nazis to terminate the "evacuations to the East" in March 1941, nearly half a million individuals were deported from annexed territory to the Generalgouvernement. The vast majority of these deportees were ethnic Poles. Though the elimination of the Jews in the region was—and remained—a fundamental goal of the Nazi regime, other issues considered more pressing than the "Jewish Question" made Poles the primary candidates for deportation from 1939 to early 1941.[11]

Most investigations of National Socialist population policy in annexed western Poland highlight either the bureaucratic mechanisms surrounding the repatriation and resettlement of Volksdeutschen or the connections between Germanization schemes and the emergence of the "Final Solution" to the Jewish Question.[12] This study concentrates instead on the anti-Polish aspects of Nazi Volkstumspolitik in the incorporated territories, specifically Reichsgau Wartheland, the province in which the deportation campaign was most energetically waged. It examines the evolution of Nazi deportation policy from September 1939 to March 1941, as well as the foundation, development, and gradual rationalization of the elaborate deportation system established in Wartheland during the period in question. In doing so, it underscores the enduring tension between the regime's anti-Polish ideological goals and the hard realities of the German war economy. Historians of the Final Solution generally agree that the ultimately genocidal dictates of Nazi Jewish policy prevailed over all rational economic considerations,[13] but can the same be said of the less murderous, though nonetheless decidedly zealous, dictates of Nazi Polenpolitik in the incorporated territories? This works seeks to provide an answer to that question.

As the *Schwerpunkt*, or main focus, of the "battle for nationality" in annexed Polish territory, Reichsgau Wartheland deserves special attention. The administrative district encompassed the former Prussian province of Posen lost at the end of World War I, as well as a large swath of territory—which included the industrial center of Łódź (renamed Litzmannstadt in 1940)—carved from what was once Russian Poland.[14] After the borders of the province were finalized on 9 November 1939, Wartheland was 45,000 square kilometers, making it the largest Gau in the Reich; it boasted 4.5 million inhabitants, including 3.96 million Poles, 327,000 Germans, and 366,000 Jews, the latter residing primarily in Łódź and its environs.[15] Its senior official, Gauleiter and Reichsstatthalter Arthur Greiser, was a true believer in the Nazi weltanschauung and a stalwart proponent of Germany's so-called historical mission in the East. He sought to transform his jurisdiction into the "parade ground of practical National Socialism," a purely German and economically robust "model *Gau*," as quickly as possible. Such an objective called for the rapid and ruthless elimination of all "foreign elements" native to the district, but this was to be no simple enterprise. Of the regions annexed to the Reich, the Warthegau had the largest Polish population and by far the most Jews. But the province's vast number of Jews notwithstanding, "the authorities on the spot in the Warthegau," as historian Ian Kershaw suggests, "did not, in fact, reckon that they would have too much difficulty in tackling the 'Jewish Question'": "The view prevailed that the real problem was Polish, not Jewish. At the onset of the occupation, the Jews were seen by the Warthegau leadership as a sideshow. The main issue in the Warthegau was thought to be less the 'Jewish' than the 'Polish Question.'"[16]

If the real problem was thought to be Polish, it was because Poles outnumbered Jews (as well as Germans) in the region by more than ten to one and, perhaps even more important, because of the Nazis' "sense of historical mission" and their priorities at that time. As Christopher Browning, the prominent historian of Nazi Jewish policy, rightly points out, the Nazis' "Jewish problem" had, of course, grown by leaps and bounds with the conquest of Poland, but "it is important to remember that in their own minds they now had a Polish problem and a *volksdeutsch* problem of immense magnitude, and the attempt to solve all three simultaneously would often necessitate an ordering of priorities."[17]

The overriding priority of Nazi ethnopoliticians operating in Wartheland from the autumn of 1939 to the spring of 1941 was the rapid resettlement of multitudes of Volksdeutschen from eastern and southeastern Europe, and this priority determined the sequence, tempo, and character of the four major deportation actions carried out during that period and examined in the pages ahead. In the year following Hitler's well-known decree "for the consolidation of German nationhood" of 7 October 1939, Germany concluded resettlement treaties with a number of east European nations, leading to the mass exodus of several hundred thousand ethnic Germans from the Baltic Republics, Nazi- and Soviet-occupied eastern Poland, and southeastern Europe (Bessarabia, Bukovina, and Dobruja). This flood of immigrants, virtually all of whom were bound for the new Reich provinces of annexed western Poland to serve as human building blocks in the Germanization of the region, required housing and employment. It would come primarily at Polish expense.

As the first wave of Volksdeutschen, Baltic Germans from Estonia and Latvia, arrived in the fall of 1939, the Nazis were still deeply involved in the process of eliminating any political opposition—real, potential, or imagined—in conquered territory. As many as 50,000 Polish citizens, including members of the Polish intelligentsia and ruling class, Poles considered anti-German, and roughly 7,000 Polish Jews, had been executed by SS-Einsatzgruppen (Operational Groups) and the Wehrmacht during and immediately following the September campaign.[18] Those nationally, politically, and racially "dangerous" Poles who survived this initial onslaught made up the bulk of the individuals expelled from Wartheland during the first two organized deportation actions, the 1.Nahplan (First Short-Term Plan) of December 1939 and the Zwischenplan (Interim Plan) of February and March 1940, both of which were initiated primarily to "create space" for the Baltic German immigrants. The next two actions, the 2.Nahplan of April 1940 through January 1941 and the 1.Teilprogram (First Phase) of the 3.Nahplan, initiated in February 1941 but suspended the following month, targeted those whose homesteads were needed for incoming Germans from eastern Poland and southeastern Europe. Because these immigrants were predominantly farmers and because very few Jews owned farms, Polish farmers were evicted and deported to accommodate them. Nearly 300,000 individuals—the overwhelming majority of whom were ethnic Poles—were evacuated from Wartheland during the course of these four operations. It was this self-imposed "volksdeutsch problem," then, coupled with the perceived need to rid annexed territory of individuals considered to pose a political, national, or racial threat to the consolidation of German nationhood, that forced the Polish Question to the forefront of the *Volkstums-kampf* (battle for nationality) in the East.

As the Germanization of annexed western Poland encompassed questions of both race and space, it is not surprising that responsibility for its implementation fell into the hands of the SS, the guardian of National Socialist ideology. On 7 October 1939, nine days after the fall of Warsaw, Hitler appointed Reichsführer-SS (RFSS) Heinrich Himmler to oversee the massive resettlement and deportation program envisioned for the East. Immediately thereafter, Himmler assumed the title Reichskommissar für die Festigung deutschen Volkstums (RKFDV; Reich Commissioner for the Consolidation of German Nationhood), a new executive position from which he, aided by his subordinates in the Reichskommissariat (Reich Commission) of the same name, was to coordinate both the immigration of Volksdeutschen and their resettlement in Reich territory. Himmler entrusted the task of "eliminating the influence of ethnically harmful alien populations that constitute a danger to the Reich and ethnic German community" to the Reichssicherheitshauptamt (RSHA; Reich Security Main Office), led by his right-hand man, SS-Gruppenführer Reinhard Heydrich.[19] The administrative apparatus that planned and carried out the deportation of ethnically harmful alien populations from the incorporated territories soon began to take shape within Heydrich's jurisdiction. At the center of the deportation system was the Umwandererzentralstelle (UWZ; Central Emigration Office), a bureau of the Nazi Sicherheitspolizei (Sipo; Security Police) originally based in Posen, the capital of the Warthegau. Founded in November 1939 as the Staff for the Evacuation of Poles and Jews to the Generalgouvernement, the UWZ was to become the leading agent of what I call "destructive Germanization" in Greiser's model Gau. In the execution of deportation policy, the UWZ was "Sipo's principal instrument of terror,"[20] and thus, the history of the UWZ and its activities in Wartheland from 1939 to early 1941 constitutes the bedrock of this investigation.

During the period under review, the UWZ concentrated its destructive Germanization efforts primarily on the non-Jewish population of Wartheland. Nevertheless, the removal of Jews—Nazi racial enemy number 1—was, from the very onset of the occupation, a ruling racial-political principle of Warthegau authorities, one that would eventually override all other aspects of National Socialist Volkstumspolitik in annexed Poland and occupied Europe as a whole. Though the specifically anti-Jewish aspect of Nazi population policy was temporarily set aside in pursuit of more immediate anti-Polish, pro-volksdeutsch objectives, the resolution of the Jewish Question was never far from the minds of the perpetrators. Likewise, it should not be far from the mind of the reader.

In his collection of essays entitled *The Path to Genocide*, Christopher Browning contends that when Hitler ordered his subordinates to pursue the wholesale destruction of European Jews in the midsummer of 1941, "what they were being asked to accomplish was at the time totally unprecedented. At this stage every step was uncharted, every policy an experiment, every action a trial run ... Murder was in the air; many avenues were being explored, but little was settled other than at least Himmler and Heydrich now knew what they were looking for—a way to kill all the Jews of Europe."[21]

With respect to its lethal conclusion—the systematic, industrialized extermination of millions of individuals—the perpetrators' mission was indeed unprecedented: never before had a nation attempted to eradicate an entire ethnoreligious group of human beings as a matter of governmental policy, using all means at its disposal to do so. But to assert that "every step was uncharted, every policy an experiment, every action a trial run" is far too strong a statement. For not only was the Final Solution to the Jewish Question dependent upon the creation of a streamlined system of mass murder, it was also predicated upon the efficiency of the police dragnet and the methodical transport of masses of human beings to the killing grounds of eastern Europe. Although the Nazis may have not resolved the specifics of the killing process at the time Hitler issued his order, they were, without question, already seasoned practitioners of search, seizure, and transport. Well before the decision to pursue the Final Solution had been made and well before the first Jewish transports rolled to Chełmno and Bełżec in the winter of 1941–1942, the National Socialists had, through trial and error, mastered the "science" of human roundups, the expropriation of property, and the shipment of human cargo en masse to the East. Without this valuable experience, gained primarily by the UWZ and primarily at the expense of the Polish population of Wartheland during the four deportation actions examined in this work, it is safe to assume that the Nazis' war of annihilation against the Jews of Europe would not have gone as smoothly and swiftly as it did.

The relationship between National Socialist resettlement and deportation policies between 1939 and 1941 and the subsequent annihilation of the Jews has been underscored in a number of recent works by leading historians of the Holocaust and the Third Reich.[22] Forcefully arguing that the decisions and actions culminating in the systematic murder of European Jews should be examined and understood not in isolation but within the broad context of Nazi New Order policies in eastern Europe, these groundbreaking studies—above all Götz Aly's *"Final Solution": Nazi Population Policy and the Murder of European Jews* and Christopher Browning's *The Origins of the Final Solution: The Evolution of Nazi Jewish Policy, September 1939–March 1942*—have greatly enhanced our knowledge of the numerous factors that led the Nazi regime to launch the Final Solution in the second half of 1941. Before the appearance of these works, the expulsions carried out in Poland during the first nineteen months of the occupation received little attention in either American or Western European historical scholarship on the Nazi period. Although valuable (if brief) overviews of the UWZ and its activities could be found within a number of sweeping investigations of Nazi wartime Polenpolitik,[23] the few detailed examinations of the subject were limited to works by Polish historians published in the Polish language.[24] None of these earlier works, however, recognized the importance of the expulsions as a stepping-stone along the "twisted road to Auschwitz."[25] The authors of the recent publications mentioned here should therefore be commended not only for advancing compelling new insights into the genesis of the Holocaust but also for stimulating scholarly interest in a heretofore little-studied aspect of National Socialist racial and occupational policy in eastern Europe.

Of all the works on the Holocaust and Nazi Volkstumspolitik in occupied Poland, Aly gives the UWZ by far the best treatment. Making good use of Polish archival materials, he is the first Western scholar to present an administrative history of the agency, tracing its activities from its foundation in November 1939 to the Wannsee Conference of January 1942.[26] Aly centers his investigation on policy as it applied to Jews, arguing (as do Browning and Hans Mommsen)[27] that the Nazis considered expulsion a viable solution to the Jewish Question until at least the late spring of 1941. His main contention is that the extermination of the Jews should be seen as but one—albeit vital, most horrendous, and most murderous—component of a larger policy aimed at the racial reorganization of eastern Europe. That thesis represents an important contribution to our understanding of the Nazi mind-set and the decision-making process that led to the Final Solution.

This work reformulates the study of Nazi population policy by emphasizing, instead, the striking anti-Polish character of the Third Reich's crusade to Germanize annexed western Poland in general and Reichsgau Wartheland in particular. In this respect, it differs from Aly's study, as well as from other recent works on Nazi population policy. It also differs in another fundamental way. The Nazi regime carried out four organized deportation actions in the incorporated territories between December 1939 and March 1941. The latest investigations of the expulsion program generally incorporate each of these in their respective analyses of the ebb and flow of anti-Jewish policy, yet they largely fail to scrutinize the intricacies of the individual actions themselves in any real detail.[28] In contrast, the pages that follow provide an in-depth examination of the four deportation actions in question. They explore the day-to-day activity of the UWZ in the Warthegau, highlighting the logistics of each operation, the limitations of each, and the lessons the Nazis learned from each. They trace the perpetrators' apprenticeship at the school of mass population transfers, an educational experience that had a profound and devastating effect on the native non-German population of Wartheland and ultimately proved instrumental to the expeditious destruction of European Jewry. In sum, this volume presents both an exploration of the wartime ordeal of Poles—an important chapter of twentieth-century European history that has often been neglected or even ignored by historians of the Third Reich and World War II—and also a prehistory of the Holocaust.

I

The "Polish Question" in German Thought and Action, 1830–1918

History loomed large in the minds of Nazi occupation authorities—Arthur Greiser included—as they planned their resettlement and deportation campaign. The examples set by Prussian and Imperial German officials during their own Germanization programs in Poland had a significant impact on the development of Nazi Polenpolitik after the invasion of September 1939. The lessons of the earlier era were put to destructive use by the National Socialists, and this hard fact makes necessary a brief examination of the Polish Question in German thought and action during the nineteenth and early twentieth centuries.

The German province of Posen, renamed Wartheland by the Nazis, was the main battleground of German-Polish ethnic struggle from the second partition of Poland in 1793 onward.[1] Strategically positioned between agrarian East Prussia and the industrial region of Upper Silesia and a relatively short march from Berlin, Posen was long considered a vital component of the Prussian-German border network in the East. Control of the province markedly shortened the lines of communication and trade between Königsberg and Danzig in the north and Breslau and Kattowitz in the south, and Posen's fertile soil provided Prussia with a ready supply of grain, lumber, and other agricultural goods. Military and economic interests, then, dictated the necessity of German rule. Prussian staff officer Carl von Grolman, the provincial commander of Posen during the 1830s, expressed this conviction unequivocally in a memorandum of March 1832: "This land [Posen] is so intimately part of the Prussian State that every idea of separation from that State must be looked upon as high treason, and every loyal son of the Fatherland must devote the last ounce of his strength not merely to retain this land for

Prussia, but also to make it loyal, that is to say German."[2] Although Grolman viewed the Polish Question not so much as a problem of ethnic nationality as one of Prussian state security, his suggestions for retaining this land for Prussia reflect a tendency that came to define German Polenpolitik in the decades to come.[3]

Grolman, like many a German statesman of the Prussian and Imperial eras, regarded the Polish nobility and clergy as the greatest threats to Prussian security in the eastern provinces. These two groups, the most influential in the Polish community, were thought to use their positions to bolster Polish national consciousness and to compel the Polish Catholic masses to resist foreign domination. This conviction was reinforced by the November Insurrection of 1830 in Russian Poland, an uprising in which many Posen Poles, egged on by the gentry and the clergy, took part. Fearing a similar confrontation in their own Polish provinces, Prussian officials perceived a need for preemptive action against potential agitators. Grolman believed that the Prussian state could undermine the influence of the nobility over the "slovenly, inoffensive" Polish peasantry through the compulsory purchase of their estates, a policy that would eradicate the material basis of a significant portion of the Polish leadership. Purchased lands would, in turn, be parceled out to German peasant colonists. Settled in groups, or "clusters," these German farmers would provide Prussia with a secure footing in the East.[4]

Grolman's recommendations were not immediately followed in practice, but they were in spirit. During his tenure as Oberpräsident (roughly meaning "high president") of Posen (1830–1841), E. H. Flottwell resolved to merge his province "inseparably" with the Prussian state, a policy that called for the "inner fusion of the two nationalities" residing there.[5] Flottwell, by no means alone in his thinking, proceeded from the standpoint that the merits and achievements of German Kultur far surpassed those of Polish culture. Despite the Polish demographic edge in the province—the Poles composed over 60 percent of the population throughout the nineteenth century and beyond[6]—the German cultural edge could be used to recast the Poles in the image of good Prussians. Sufficient exposure to the glory, prosperity, and discipline of Prussian-German civilization would eventually win over the recalcitrant Poles and lead them to abandon their nationalistic aspirations. The "inner fusion" of the German and Polish nationalities would come at the expense of Polish cultural autonomy, or as Flottwell put it, "through the decisive predominance of German culture."[7]

The Oberpräsident's Prussianization policy entailed the active promotion of the German language in his jurisdiction. He made German the official and exclusive language of the internal affairs of Posen's civil administration and provided state funds to invigorate German-language secondary education. Flottwell also made efforts to replace Polish officials, both bureaucratic and ecclesiastical, with Germans. Taking aim at the influential Polish clergy, he closed down all remaining monasteries in Posen, founded two new theological institutions, staffed them with Germans, and filled the teaching posts of existing Catholic seminaries with Germans as well. The Polish landed aristocracy also felt Flottwell's sting. In legislation of 1833 and 1836, he revoked the nobility's right to appoint *Landräte* (county commissioners) and rural police officers and gave these positions to his own men instead. And in an action more or less in keeping with Grolman's recommendation, Flottwell set up a state fund to purchase bankrupt Polish estates, a move with the express goal of increasing "the number of intelligent and politically dependable manor-holders in the province."[8] These estates, as well as tracts of royal Prussian domain land, were sold exclusively to German buyers, many of whom came from outside Posen Province. Though inner fusion was their purported goal, these measures sent a clear message to the Poles that they were but second-class subjects of the Prussian king.[9]

The ascension of Friedrich Wilhelm IV to the Prussian throne in 1840 marked the end of Flottwell's so-called reforms. A personal friend of several prominent members of the Polish landed aristocracy, the new Prussian king recalled Flottwell in 1841 and not only put an end to his discriminatory policies vis-à-vis the Polish nobility but also issued a series of decrees guaranteeing the right to use the Polish language in both civil administration and public schools.[10] Still, the impact of Flottwell and of Grolman as well on future German Polenpolitik should not be underestimated. Flottwell's Prussianization policy and Grolman's anti-Polish writings provided a wellspring of inspiration for Otto von Bismarck during his own campaign against the Polish population of Posen in the years following German unification in 1871.[11]

The thaw in Prussian-Polish relations was short-lived. The revolutionary turmoil of 1848 witnessed the creation of the Polish National Committee in Posen, a move spearheaded by the Polish nobility, intelligentsia, and clergy, whose principal aim was "the independence of the whole of Poland" from foreign rule. The restoration of an independent Poland was initially backed by German liberal nationalists who believed it was required for the unification of Germany on a liberal-democratic basis, but the idea soon lost German support when it became clear that German and Polish interests were simply incompatible. Upon weighing the prospect of Polish control of Posen, one German delegate at the Frankfurt Assembly asked whether it was right "if a million Germans should live as naturalized foreigners under a people of lesser cultural content?"[12] The answer was, of course, absolutely not. Although the Assembly drew up legislation that extended the linguistic, cultural, and local self-administrative rights of Poles, the question of the restoration of a Polish state was pushed to the side, and eventually, the delegates voted to incorporate the entire province of Posen into a unified Germany. All of these plans came to naught, however, for by the summer of 1849, the German revolutionary movement had been crushed by the counterrevolutionary backlash of the revitalized Prussian monarchy.[13]

A major consequence of the unsuccessful revolutions of 1848 was a deep and ever-widening gulf between Germans and Poles in the Prussian East. The majority of Germans living in the region had no wish to live under Polish rule and had rejoiced at the reassertion of Prussian monarchical authority. The events of 1848 and 1849, moreover, went far to strengthen the ever-present anti-Polish sentiment among Prussia's leadership. Through their revolutionary activity, the Polish nobility and clergy had confirmed, once and for all, that they were irreconcilable enemies of Prussia and that no amount of exposure to German culture would change them. As long as they held sway over the Polish masses, the dream of Polish independence would remain alive and the Poles would remain a potentially lethal thorn in Prussia's side. In the aftermath of 1848, the Prussian government began to conclude that only the ruthless suppression of Polish nationalism—only the *Ausrottung* (extirpation or extermination) of Polish society as a "politically distinctive formation within the Prussian state"—would eradicate the Polish menace and lead to a comprehensive Germanization of the Prussian East. Oberpräsident of Posen Eugen Puttkammer expressed this growing sentiment in 1851: "[The Polish national movement] is and will remain an element hostile to the Prussian government, no matter what form in which it may choose to appear. To conciliate it is impossible. To extirpate [*ausrotten*] it is inhumane (as well as impossible; at least it would take generations to do so). Therefore, nothing remains but to confine it energetically to the subordinate position it deserves."[14]

Though Puttkammer rejected Ausrottung (literally speaking) as inhumane, the term was used more and more frequently (and more and more literally) in anti-Polish rhetoric as the years passed. This new and uncompromising resolve paved the way for Bismarck's radicalization of Polenpolitik in the decades to come.

IMPERIAL GERMAN POLENPOLITIK: ENTER BISMARCK

The Polish Question was an issue that troubled Otto von Bismarck well before he was appointed Prussian minister-president in September 1862. Writing in the revolutionary year of 1848, Bismarck, then politically obscure but already an outspoken foe of the Polish cause, expressed his views in a scathing editorial attacking German liberal sympathy for the Polish national movement: "The national evolution of the Polish element in Posen," he declared, "can have no other sensible goal than preparing the restoration of an independent Polish state." Any reconstruction of Poland at the expense of West Prussia and Posen would "sever the best sinews of Germany," and "millions of Germans would fall prey to Polish arbitrariness"; the Poles were an "implacable enemy" of Germany, and in light of this hard fact, "only a German who allowed himself to be guided by tearful compassion and impractical theories," he implied, could think otherwise.[15] He was more blunt in a letter to his sister in 1861: "Flay the Poles until they despair for life! I have all sympathy for their position, but if we wish to endure, we can do nothing but extirpate them ... It is not the wolf's fault that God created him as he is, but nevertheless we kill him whenever we can."[16]

Despite his harsh rhetoric, Bismarck was not calling for the physical annihilation of the Poles; rather, he sought the eradication of their distinctive national and cultural identity. And when it came to flaying the Poles, he almost certainly had the aristocracy and clergy, not the Polish peasant masses, in mind.[17] Like many of his Prussian contemporaries, Bismarck regarded the Polish nobility and clergy as the brains behind the Polish national movement; barring aristocratic-clerical agitation, common Poles were deemed a loyal and docile lot, sincerely grateful for the socioeconomic and cultural advantages of Prussian citizenship. Moreover, as long as one could "teach them that it is nice to wash oneself and that one should not [steal] things," Polish peasants were a "well-behaved people" and, unlike the rebellious nobility and clergy, ripe for Germanization.[18] Although there was little new in Bismarck's views on the Polish Question, the policies he would pursue after 1871 as the "Iron Chancellor" represented a new and energetic phase of German Polenpolitik.

With the foundation of the Second Reich in January 1871 came the official incorporation of Posen into the German nation-state. The geopolitical entity known after 1871 as Germany had hitherto been a patchwork of independent states, all with distinctive socioeconomic, political, and cultural traditions.[19] Regional particularism abounded. Life in the agrarian East, its economy dominated by large Junker estates, differed markedly from that in the western industrial regions of the Ruhr and the Rhineland and from that on the small family farms of the south and southwest. The reserved, militaristic order of Prussian society contrasted sharply against the gemütlichkeit of Bavaria. And as historian Mary Fulbrook points out, "The linguistic watersheds between Bavarian, Swabian or Frisian" and "the religious chasm between Protestants and Catholics, served to render Germany as a place of pattern and great variety."[20] Noticeably absent was a cohesive German national identity. A Prussian generally still considered himself or herself first and foremost a Prussian, a Westphalian a Westphalian, a Thuringian a Thuringian, and so on. Germany, then, was largely an artificial creation, a nation imposed on the disparate masses from above by the superiority of Prussian arms. Bismarck and other statesmen of the Second Reich sought to overcome the problems of regional particularism and cultural fragmentation by demanding an exclusive but altogether ill-defined German (or, one might argue, Prussian) national character for the empire. Germanization, in this sense, would promote cultural uniformity and serve to integrate the various and dissimilar regions under Reich authority into the new German nation-state. If the problem of integration was acute in terms of Bavaria, Baden, or Württemberg, it was more so with respect to the predominantly Catholic and predominantly Polish-speaking province of Posen.

Demands for the cultural unification of the German Empire, coupled with Prussia's long-standing hostility toward the perseverance of Polish national consciousness within its borders, brought about an all-out state-sponsored campaign against "Polonism" in the Prussian East. Imperial Germanization policies, launched by Bismarck and pursued by his successors, entailed a vigorous assault on both the cultural and the economic life of the Polish population of Posen. Excluding a brief period of conciliation during the chancellorship of Leo von Caprivi (1890–1894), this two-front attack stands out as the defining characteristic of German Polenpolitik during the four and a half decades spanning the foundation of the Second Reich and the outbreak of World War I. But not only did this cultural-economic war against the Poles fail, it also backfired. Far from undermining Polish national consciousness, the Germanization campaign only served to unite the Poles and consolidate their sense of ethnonational identity.

The opening round of the German war against Polish culture came in the midst of a much larger conflict that rocked the Imperial political establishment during the 1870s: the struggle between the Protestant Prussian-German state and the Catholic Church. The summer of 1871 witnessed the inauguration of the *Kulturkampf*, the "struggle for culture" waged until 1879 by Bismarck and his National Liberal supporters against the church and its influence in German domestic affairs. Bismarck and the Liberals saw Catholicism as an obstacle to German political-cultural unity and social progress. They held that the church—an archaic and superstitious institution ruled by the ultramontane Vatican—represented a divisive element in the German body politic, subverting the loyalty of German Catholics to the Kaiser by demanding their allegiance to a foreign religious leader. Branded *Reichsfeinde* (enemies of the Reich), Catholics were subjected to persecution, and their institutions were suppressed. The Kulturkampf did not bode well for the Poles. By and large, to be Polish was, and still is, to be Catholic. Catholicism and Polish national consciousness were, and remain to this day, indissolubly linked. Polish society, then, embodied a two-fisted threat to *Deutschtum* (roughly meaning "German nationhood): loyalty to a foreign religious leader and loyalty to a foreign nationalistic ideal.

The most blatantly anti-Polish legislation implemented during the struggle for culture dealt with education and language. In an effort to eradicate the influence of the Catholic Church in educational affairs, the Prussian Landtag's Schulaufsichtsgesetz (School Supervision Law) of 1872 placed all schools, both public and private, under state supervision. School inspectors were to be state appointees, not church officials, which particularly affected the Polish-speaking regions of the Reich where the post of school inspector was usually held by a Polish priest. The measure was perhaps meant to do just that; indeed, Bismarck himself intimated that an underlying motive for the codification of the law was the pressing need to combat, as he put it, "the Polonizing influence of the clergy in schools."[21] Another swipe at the clergy came with the May Laws of 1873. This legislation dictated that all clerical officials in the Reich had to hold German citizenship and a German university degree and had to pass a state examination in German history and culture. Hundreds of Polish priests lost their ministries as a result, and some were imprisoned for opposition. The May Laws were soon followed by a decree, aimed at Posen in particular, that made German the official language of instruction for all subjects in elementary and secondary schools with the exception of religion and hymn singing, both of which could still be taught in Polish but only in grades one through three. Perhaps the hardest blow to the Polish language was delivered by the Official Language Law of 1873. This edict made German the sole official language of Posen. All discourse associated with public administration, the courts, and political institutions was to be conducted in German; the right to use Polish when dealing with official bodies, guaranteed even during the Flotwellian era, was revoked. In light of these harsh measures, the anti-Polish thrust of the Kulturkampf seems to have been much more than an inadvertent side effect of the campaign against the Roman Catholic Church.[22]

By the end of 1879, the Kulturkampf had run its course. Realizing that he needed the support of the Catholic Centre Party as a counterweight to the Socialists in the Reichstag, Bismarck called off the struggle for culture and made amends with the church. Nevertheless, the anti-Polish legislation remained in effect, and additional discriminatory measures leveled at Polish cultural life were to follow in the years to come.[23] These measures, combined with the impending economic war against the Poles, only served to perpetuate and heighten the friction between Prussian Poles and the Reich government that had redoubled during the Kulturkampf.

The struggle for culture, particularly when measured in terms of its impact in Prussian Poland, had clearly not worked in the interests of the Reich. The Catholic Centre Party, established to defend the interests of the church in German affairs, had grown in members, power, and seats in the Reichstag and had gained significant support among Polish Catholics. The church had become more, not less, involved in the Polish national movement. And perhaps most important, the Kulturkampf had imposed a certain sense of political unity, previously missing, across the broad spectrum of Polish society, leading to the extension of the Polish national movement both socially and geographically; it spread beyond the ranks of the clergy and aristocracy to the Polish peasantry and the growing Polish urban proletariat and beyond Posen and West Prussia to Upper Silesia and the Baltic coast.[24]

The Prussian government's attack on the material basis of Polish life began in the mid-1880s against the backdrop of a recent shift in the demographic and socioeconomic character of the eastern provinces that seemed to endanger Germany's hold on the Prussian East. The industrialization of central and western Germany, in full swing since about 1850, had triggered an exodus of laborers, primarily Germans but a significant number of Poles and Jews as well, from the agrarian East. In search of economic opportunity in the factories and mines to the west, the majority settled in Saxony, Brandenburg, the Ruhr, and the Rhineland. The *Ostflucht* (flight from the East) picked up speed in the two decades following German unification, a trend that helped to tip the ethnic balance in Prussian Poland, particularly in Posen, even more in favor of the Poles. Statistics compiled by William Hagen indicate that the Polish population of Posen grew at a rate of 15 percent, from 966,000 to 1,112,650, between 1871 and 1890, while the German population increased by only 7 percent, from 556,000 to 594,000, during the same period. The Jewish population, by contrast, decreased significantly, falling by 28 percent, from 62,000 in 1871 to 44,300 in 1890.[25] As Germans and Jews moved west from the cities and villages in the eastern provinces, Poles moved in from the countryside not just to take their houses and apartments but also to take their jobs. This internal migration led to the rapid development of a Polish middle class and urban proletariat—both previously negligible—and with it, a substantial growth in the economic power of Prussian Poles. Many German farmers also migrated to the West. The Ostflucht of Germans from rural areas left a vacuum in the ranks of the region's agricultural labor force, a group essential to the economic vitality of the great Junker estates. These Germans, too, were replaced by Poles, many of whom had come from Austria and Russian Poland as low-wage, seasonal workers but had remained on the German side of the border permanently. The high birthrate among these "foreign" Poles, as well as their declining death rates, due largely to the higher standard of living on German estates relative to those in Austria and Russia, went far to contribute to the numerical increase of Prussian Poles during the period in question.[26] These factors, coupled with the recent spread of Polish nationalistic sentiment, rendered the age-old Polish Question all the more complex.

Alarmed by "the retreat of German nationality," both economically and demographically, from the Prussian East, Bismarck and his Imperial cohorts launched a new anti-Polish campaign in 1885 that lasted virtually unabated until the outbreak of World War I.[27] This phase of Polenpolitik, marked by a series of measures aimed at undermining Polish economic life while simultaneously increasing the German population of the East at Polish expense, represents the climax of Imperial efforts to Germanize Prussian Poland. It was during this period that Grolman's earlier proposals for German colonization and the compulsory purchase of Polish estates, as well as Flottwell's policies of the 1830s, came to fruition. It was also this period of Imperial Polenpolitik that provided Hitler and the National Socialists with a wealth of inspiration for their own pursuit of a New Order in occupied Poland after the September campaign of 1939.

Ushering in the new anti-Polish campaign was Bismarck's executive order of March 1885 calling for the expulsion of some 30,000 Russian subjects, primarily Polish agricultural workers, then residing in Prussian territory. The expulsion of resident aliens from Prussia had been proposed by Bismarck as early as 1872, but due to pressure by the Junkers, who did not want to lose their pool of cheap

Polish farmworkers, no action had been taken. By 1885, however, the perceived
need to combat Polish demographic gains took precedence, at least temporarily,
over Prussian agrarian interests. "Despite our acknowledgement of agriculture
as the most important industry of all," Bismarck reasoned, "we still consider it
a lesser evil for a few areas to have a shortage of labor than for the state and its
future to suffer."[28]

The resulting deportations, which continued until the end of 1887, cannot be
viewed as strictly anti-Polish. Of the 32,000 Russian and Austrian nationals expelled from the Prussian East between 1885 and 1887, about 9,000 were Jewish
traders and artisans.[29] But the remainder were primarily Polish agricultural laborers, many of whom had lived in Posen and West Prussia for a generation. This
situation provoked strong opposition from the Junkers, but Bismarck remained
adamant. In speeches before the Reichstag in December 1885 and January 1886,
he declared that government had the duty "to protect the German nationality, in
its continuance and in its development, against any injury by foreign elements ...
Polish nationalism and Polish propaganda were the reason for the expulsions."
The alien Poles had to go, he said, "because we have enough of our own."[30] The
expulsions, which were never repeated during the Imperial era, did little to alter
the demographic balance in the Prussian East, and the Junkers continued to rely
on Polish labor from Austria and Russia, but the deportations of some 32,000
individuals did sow the seeds for additional state intervention in the ethnic composition of Prussian Poland.[31]

It did not take long for the seeds of state intervention to sprout. On 26 April
1886, the Prussian Landtag passed the Ansiedlungsgesetz (Settlement Law), an
act that brought, in the words of historian Robert L. Koehl, the beginning of "a
state policy, very definitely self-conscious and planned, directed toward changing
the population composition by nationality of certain areas of the Prussian kingdom."[32] The Settlement Law established the Royal Prussian Ansiedlungskommission (AK; Colonization Commission), an independent agency headquartered
in the city of Posen and directly responsible to the king of Prussia. Its mission
was officially defined as "the strengthening of the German element [of Posen and
West Prussia] against Polonizing tendencies."[33] Bismarck's definition was more
direct and to the point: the purpose of the AK was "to put it bluntly, to expropriate the Polish nobility" and thus end "the cancer-like spread of Polonization" in
the Prussian East.[34]

Formulated by Christoph von Tiedemann, head of the Bromberg Regency
in Posen Province, the Settlement Law was based on the assumption that the

government could capitalize on the economic weakness of members of the Polish landed aristocracy—then suffering, like their German counterparts, due to chronically low grain prices—by buying out as many as possible. Purchased estates would be subdivided into small agricultural holdings and parceled out to German peasant farmers brought in from the West. It was reasoned that such an action, which clearly reflected the earlier Polenpolitik of Grolman and Flottwell, would not only help to counter the Ostflucht but also would undermine the political power of the Polish nobility and foster the Germanization of the eastern provinces.[35]

At the time of its creation in 1886, the Colonization Commission received a 100 million mark endowment meant to sustain its activity for a period of twenty-five years. But colonization proved to be more expensive than initially envisaged. In 1896, the AK received an additional 100 million marks, another 150 million in 1902, and yet another 225 million in 1908. A final 100 million mark endowment was approved in 1912.[36] Despite the generous funding and equally generous expenditures, by no means did the work of the AK live up to the German government's lofty expectations. That is not to say, however, that the program was a complete failure. By the end of 1897, the commission had managed to purchase 96,190 hectares of estate property and an additional 1,500 hectares of peasant holdings.[37] On purchased land, it settled 1,342 German families from the West, as well as 999 families already residing in Posen and West Prussia.[38] Yet these apparent gains must be measured against Polish land purchase and settlement during roughly the same period. Two Polish settlement organizations, the Bank Ziemski (Land Bank) and the Spólka Rolinków Parcelacyjna (Farmers' Parceling Society), were established in 1888 and 1894, respectively, to counter German colonization efforts. Between 1888 and 1896, the Land Bank purchased some 30,000 hectares of farmland, on which it settled 1,073 Polish families; the Parceling Society acquired an additional 13,500 hectares by 1900.[39] And much to the chagrin of German authorities, both the AK and the Polish counterprograms acquired more and more land as time passed not from insolvent Polish estates but from Germans. Of the total property secured by the Colonization Commission between 1891 and 1897, fully 59.5 percent was purchased from bankrupt Germans. During the next four years in Posen alone, the Polish purchase of German farmland outstripped the German purchase of Polish land by over 16,000 hectares. All of this buying and selling drove up the price of land, enticing a growing number of profit-seeking Germans but not nearly so many profit-seeking Poles to liquidate their property, whether they were bankrupt or not.[40] The Poles, moreover, tended to sell their land to Polish parceling agencies, but Germans were not so choosy, selling their property to the highest bidder, be that a German association or not.[41]

The campaign "to strengthen the German element" in the East also experienced setbacks that originated not among the Poles but within the Imperial government itself. In 1890, Wilhelm II dismissed the aging Bismarck and replaced him with the more liberal-minded Leo von Caprivi. Caprivi's brief tenure as German chancellor and Prussian prime minister witnessed a temporary relaxation in anti-Polish policy. Though the Settlement Law remained in effect, the new chancellor passed legislation in 1890 and 1891 that created several special regional commissions to assist all aspiring farm owners, regardless of their nationality, in acquiring small homesteads on a *Rentengüter* (quitrent) basis. As a result, a number of Poles secured farms through German channels, something that directly contradicted the objectives of the Settlement Law and the mission of the AK.[42] This move was not the only paradoxical action on the part of the Caprivi administration in its approach to the Polish Question. Bowing to the pressure of Junker elites who were in desperate need of cheap labor, Caprivi relaxed the tight eastern-border restrictions imposed by Bismarck in 1885 and allowed Prussian authorities to issue short-term work visas, good from April to November, to foreign workers. Once again, Polish laborers from Austria and Russia entered Prussia in droves, and their number rose steadily as the years passed. By 1906, well over half a million people were coming to Prussia each year in search of jobs. By 1914, on the eve of World War I, 365,000 alien workers were employed in the Prussian agricultural sector alone; of these, 290,000 were Austrian and Russian Poles.[43] Despite the nationalistic demands "to be rid of alien Poles" and their "Polonizing tendencies," Junker economic interests prevailed, and "foreign" Poles remained an integral part of the Prussian agrarian workforce.

THE ARRIVAL OF THE HAKATISTS

Caprivi's lenient Polenpolitik provoked strong opposition among German nationalists and elements of eastern Prussia's German middle class who were troubled by Polish economic and demographic gains. Out of this discontent arose the first important nongovernmental nationalist pressure group with a specifically anti-Polish agenda. Founded in 1894 and known after 1899 as the Deutscher Ostmarkverein (OMV; German Eastern Marches Association), this organization played a key role in the formulation of Imperial Polenpolitik during the years preceding Germany's loss of Posen and West Prussia in 1918. The basic tenets of the OMV platform were particularly proto-Nazi, embodying essentially the same ideas that steered National Socialist anti-Polish policy from September 1939 onward. The Hakatists,[44] as OMV members were known, held that "Poles have at no time been faithful and loyal Prussian citizens"; that they deserved the partitions and foreign rule because of their own ineptitude; and that Germans, as the champions of culture and prosperity in the East, had a moral and historical right to the region.[45] But the OMV did grudgingly recognize the extent of recent Polish triumphs in the "battle for nationality" and realized, unlike Grolman, Flottwell, Bismarck, and others, that the Polish nationalistic threat was not confined to the clergy and nobility. The Polish people as a whole—peasants, workers, and the middle-class included—represented a menace to Germany's position in the East. Long underestimated, the Polish challenge demanded immediate and concerted emergency action.[46]

OMV nationalists held that as long as hordes of Austrian and Russian Poles were allowed to enter Prussia each year, the Germanization of the Eastern Marches was all but impossible. Polish seasonal workers were cheap. Their presence depressed wages for all, causing more and more Germans to desert the region, and since the Poles brought with them a lower standard of living and a way of life incompatible with that of "good" Germans, German farmworkers from the West were reluctant to settle in Posen and West Prussia. The Junkers therefore were forced to rely on these "undesirables" because so few German laborers were available.[47] This problem was never resolved. Even the founding members of the OMV, all of whom owned large estates in Posen, employed Polish seasonal workers, leading the Pan-German writer Arthur Dix to observe somewhat sarcastically that "the very men who are trying with all their might to combat the Polish population native to their own land are bringing in Slavic laborers en masse from abroad."[48]

Still, the Hakatists continued to proclaim that "large estates Polonize," blocking the expansion of the German peasantry and depriving the eastern towns of German clientele.[49] All hopes to reverse the Ostflucht and eradicate the need for Polish labor were pinned on the colonization program. German peasant colonization was central to the Hakatist faith. The organization was an enthusiastic supporter of the Settlement Law, and through tireless lobbying, it helped to secure an additional 250 million marks for the AK in 1898 and 1902 and also brought pressure on the Hohenlohe administration to end Caprivi's policy of allowing regional settlement commissions to offer land to Poles on an equal basis with

Germans. The Poles nevertheless continued to keep pace with the Germans in land purchases and settlement. The OMV demanded action. In 1904, the editor of *Die Ostmark*, the monthly periodical of the OMV, wrote: "It is a fact that the successful work of the Polish parceling associations in the Eastern Marches has brought about a situation that cannot possibly be tolerated any longer. To appropriate 350 millions for the Colonization Commission and then to permit unrestricted subdivision of estates by the Polish banks is like hitching one horse before and one horse behind the same wagon."[50]

It was reasoned that two methods could be employed to counter Polish settlement activity. The first, regarded as drastic and never seriously considered because it violated traditional property rights, was simply to forbid the sale of German property to Poles. The second was to enforce restrictions on the use of land once it had fallen into Polish hands. The latter method, then, seemed the more viable policy, and its implementation became the pet project of the OMV.[51]

The chancellorship of Bernhard von Bülow (1900–1909) marked the heyday of Imperial German anti-Polish policy. The Polish Question, in Bülow's view, was the foremost domestic problem confronting the Second Reich, and throughout his tenure, he served as the outstanding spokesman for German nationalists and proponents of Germany's "mission in the East."[52] Bülow's aggressive anti-Polish stance created a governmental atmosphere congenial to OMV demands. In January 1904, the OMV sent a memo to the Prussian government demanding an end to the unrestricted subdivision of eastern estates and the enactment of legislation that would empower German officials to deny building permits to Poles in cases where property improvement would be detrimental to the mission of the AK. The latter proposal found a receptive audience. Two months later, the Prussian Landtag passed a law that required anyone who wanted to construct or remodel a building in Posen or West Prussia to produce a voucher from the Oberpräsident before receiving a permit to do so. This move was intended to prevent Poles from erecting houses and barns on parceled land, and therefore, it met the OMV's demands, at least in part. Since Poles would neither be able to take up residence on newly purchased property nor improve existing farms, it was reasoned that the law would curb the activity of the Polish settlement organizations and compel more Poles to sell out to the AK.

The law, however, did not have the desired effect. Polish land banks responded by purchasing either entire German farms with preexisting buildings or parcels of land that could be incorporated into adjacent Polish farms. As both methods generally targeted bankrupt or profit-seeking German peasants, they directly contradicted the goals of the colonization program. The Building Voucher Law, moreover, further exacerbated Polish nationalism. By attempting to thwart the common Polish peasants' desire to improve their economic conditions, the law made them all the more conscious of their second-class status and all the more susceptible to Polish nationalistic agitation.[53]

If Prussian authorities and the OMV were vexed by the glaring failure of the law of 1904, the twentieth annual progress report of the Colonization Commission, submitted to the Prussia Diet in 1906, displeased them more. The AK report made clear that the twenty-year history of struggle for the soil was by no means a story of unqualified German victories. German colonization had been both painfully slow and extraordinarily expensive. During the first two decades of its activity, the AK had managed to purchase 325,000 hectares of land, on which it had settled 12,000 German families. But this apparent success was largely offset by Polish counteractivity. From 1900 to 1904, Polish settlement associations had acquired 25,000 more hectares from Germans than the AK had bought from Poles. Furthermore, fully two-thirds of all property purchased by the AK between 1886 and 1906 had come from Germans, not from Poles; in 1906 alone, 90 percent of all land procured was originally German.[54] The obvious shortcomings of the colonization program, coupled with the recent failure of the Building Voucher Law, set the stage for the high-water mark of Imperial anti-Polish legislation, the Expropriation Act of 1908.

At the end of 1906, the OMV, the Pan German League, and other German nationalist groups began calling for the outright expropriation of Polish estates for the purpose of German colonization. The directors of the AK, also convinced that the success of their program now hinged upon state-seizure of Polish property, took up the cause in 1907. In the fall of that year, Bülow, backed by Wilhelm II, introduced a bill to the Prussian Landtag demanding that the state extend its rights of eminent domain and expropriate Polish estates by government fiat. After much debate, the bill passed by a slim majority (143 to 111) in March 1908. The Expropriation Act, however, was saddled with a number of restrictions, including a clause that not only placed a 70,000 hectare cap on the amount of private land that the AK could seize but also confined any expropriation to very specific regions of Posen and West Prussia.[55] Still, the law was the most radical anti-Polish legislation of the Imperial era. It violated the right to private property, guaranteed by the Prussian constitution, of a substantial portion of Prussia's own population. "Not even in Russia," the Austrian ambassador in Berlin complained, was such a ruthless measure used against national minorities.[56]

Domestic and foreign opposition to the Expropriation Act prevented its immediate application. The Progressive and Catholic Centre Parties, as well as an
influential minority of Prussian Conservatives, denounced the law and refused to
support it. It was also condemned by the Austrian Reichsrat and provoked serious criticism in the British and French presses. Facing opposition at home and
abroad, Bülow never invoked the act, apparently believing that the mere threat
of dispossession would convince the Poles to see reason and resign themselves to
German rule.[57] But German nationalist groups, spearheaded by the Hakatists,
demanded the expropriation of Polish estates and continued to do so with growing fury over the next four years. In 1912, the Bürgermeister of Posen urged the
administration of Bülow's successor, Chancellor Theobald Bethmann-Hollweg, to
make immediate use of the law, pointing out that the AK land reserve had diminished to only 15,000 hectares, down from 52,000 in 1908.[58] Nationalistic pressure
eventually compelled Bethmann-Hollweg's government to act. In October 1912,
four Polish estates totaling 1,900 hectares were confiscated. Though this did little
to increase the holdings of the AK, it placated the nationalists, at least temporarily. But outside of nationalist circles, the move met with widespread disapproval. It was attacked by the Socialists and Catholic Centrists in the Reichstag,
prompting a vote of censure in 1913, and the Habsburg regime reacted with equal
disdain. The expropriations also provoked massive Polish demonstrations in the
eastern provinces, further radicalizing the Polish opposition to the German government. The political fallout reinforced Bethmann-Hollweg's determination to
avoid expropriation in the future. The act was, in fact, never invoked again.[59]

On the eve of war in 1914, the Bethmann-Hollweg administration made a
last-ditch effort to energize the colonization program. In March of that year,
Bethmann-Hollweg submitted a draft of a new Parceling Law to the Prussian
Landtag. It proposed that district presidents in the East be given the right to
veto the sale and subdivision of any estate if such an action conflicted with the
mission of the AK, something demanded by the OMV since the early 1900s. The
draft also suggested that the AK be granted license to intervene and assume the
role of purchaser in the sale of any landholding of 10 hectares or more, providing
that the property in question was needed for colonization and had not been in
the seller's possession for ten years or more.[60] Such legislation held mighty potential. Its implementation could have ultimately led to a German victory in the
struggle for the soil, preventing the further subdivision of German estates, frus-
trating Polish efforts to acquire additional property, and dramatically increasing
the holdings of the AK. But the proposed law was never enacted. War loomed on

the horizon, and the German government was forced to turn its attention to the international arena.

WARTIME FANTASY: *LAND OHNE MENSCHEN*

The outbreak of World War I in 1914 may have extinguished the colonization program in reality, but a series of grand German victories on the eastern front, resulting in the capture of huge sections of Russian Poland and Russia's Baltic provinces, fired the imaginations of German nationalists with visions of a monumental annexationist and colonization project in the East. Invigorated by the defeat of the Russian army at Tannenberg in the autumn of 1914, the upper echelons of the Reich government seized upon this dream as well.

In the early months of the war, nationalistic visionaries embraced a plan that called for the annexation and Germanization of a "Polish Frontier Strip" running from Łódź in the south to Suwałki in the north, along the Rivers Warthe, Narev, and Vistula, a scheme that would push the German border farther east into Russian "Congress Poland." According to the plan, which was formulated by Berlin professor Ludwig Bernhard in August 1914, the new Frontier Strip would be consolidated—Germanized—through a large-scale colonization program. German peasant colonists from the West would be settled in the region en masse, providing the basis for a future increase in population. Such resettlement would help to ensure the permanent conquest of the territory, and beyond that, it would also create a "Germanized frontier wall," a human barrier separating Prussian Poles from their Russian and Austrian brethren and shielding the German heartland from the "Slavic menace" to the east.[61]

The Germanization of the proposed Frontier Strip entailed much more than peasant colonization. To radical German nationalists, as well as to the Reich government itself, the war seemed to offer the opportunity to resolve the Polish Question once and for all. The Frontier Strip plan, code-named *Land ohne Menschen* (Land without People), reflected this widespread sentiment. Side by side with German colonization, the scheme foresaw the deportation of hundreds of thousands of Prussian Poles, primarily those from Posen. Radical nationalist groups, most notably the OMV and the Pan German League, brought pressure upon the government to pursue the mass expulsion plan, apparently with some success. A series of letters exchanged in late 1914 between Ludwig Bernhard and Alfred Hugenberg, a prominent Pan-German and later minister of both agriculture and economics in Hitler's first cabinet, indicates that Chancellor Bethmann-Hollweg was favorably disposed to the idea of Polish evacuations. In December 1914, Bernhard informed Hugenberg, who regarded Land ohne Menschen as Germany's paramount objective of the war, of Bethmann-Hollweg's supportive attitude: "No doubt you have heard that the *Land ohne Menschen* idea has made an impression on the Chancellor. Ganse [president of the AK] has been ordered to provide the evacuations with a legal rationale."[62]

A few weeks later, Bethmann-Hollweg commissioned Friedrich von Schwerin, the völkisch-nationalist Regierungspräsident (president of the [regional] government) of Frankfurt-Oder, to work out a detailed strategy for the realization of the Frontier Strip plan. Schwerin responded with two extensive reports, submitted in March and December 1915, in which he outlined the principles for a new German *Ostpolitik* (eastern policy):"The present war offers the opportunity, perhaps for the last time in world history, for Germany to assume in a decisive way its colonization mission in the East ... It must not be deterred by words; rather it must be engaged with resolute action; it calls [for us] in time to get accustomed to the idea of a resettlement of large masses of people."[63]

Schwerin recommended that German annexations should not be limited to the proposed Frontier Strip: they should also encompass the Russian provinces of Lithuania and Courland to the northeast. The Germanization of these annexed territories would ensue through a massive colonization program, much like the one proposed by Bernhard, though more far-reaching to include not only colonists from the interior of Germany, but Volksdeutschen from western Russia as well. Bethmann-Hollweg was evidently pleased with these suggestions; Schwerin soon became his chief adviser on all questions concerning annexation and colonization in the East.[64]

The summer offensive of 1915, during which German and Austrian armies overran all of Russian Poland, brought about a fundamental change in German Polenpolitik. Now that millions of Russian Poles were in Germany's sphere of influence, the Reich government began to reconsider its long-standing opposition to the re-creation of a Polish state. After a year of deliberation, the regime moved to reinforce its position in the East by announcing on 15 November 1916 the establishment of a semi-independent kingdom of Poland within former Russian territory. In essence a satellite of Germany, the kingdom would fall under German military and economic jurisdiction and, as a matter of course, German political control. Coupled with the proposed annexation of the Frontier Strip, Courland, and Lithuania, this Polish buffer state between the Prussian East and

Russia would serve as a vital component of Germany's eastern border defenses.[65] The creation of the Kingdom of Poland would also facilitate the resolution of Germany's Polish problem, providing a convenient dumping ground for Poles expelled from Posen, West Prussia, and the Frontier Strip.[66]

Land ohne Menschen seemed within reach, but the exigencies of war, culminating in Germany's defeat in 1918, forestalled the implementation of the resettlement and deportation program. What is more, the Polish state that emerged after World War I was anything but a German satellite. Still, the dream of a German colonial empire in the East and that of a purely German Eastern Marches remained alive. It was left to a later generation of German nationalist politicians to attempt once again to turn dreams into reality.

THE LOSS OF THE PRUSSIAN EAST AND ITS AFTERMATH

The collapse of the Second Reich and its subsequent dismemberment at the hands of the victorious Allied powers transformed Germany's Polish Question from an issue of domestic policy to one of foreign policy. An autonomous Polish nation, a concept that had induced acute trepidation in the hearts of German nationalists since the early nineteenth century, reappeared on the map of Europe in the aftermath of Germany's defeat. Poland's rebirth came largely at German expense. The thirteenth of Woodrow Wilson's "Fourteen Points," the document on which the armistice of November 1918 was based, promised that "an independent Polish state should be erected which should include the territories inhabited by indisputably Polish populations, which should be assured a free and secure access to the sea, and whose political and economic independence and territorial integrity should be guaranteed by international covenant."[67]

The Treaty of Versailles, signed in June 1919, made good on this promise. Some 90 percent of the province of Posen, 66 percent of West Prussia, and a substantial portion of Upper Silesia were detached from Germany and formally integrated into the new Republic of Poland. Danzig, a major Baltic seaport at the mouth of the Vistula, was proclaimed a "free city" and placed under the administration of the League of Nations. The resulting "Polish Corridor," which ran along the left bank of the Vistula and incorporated the eastern half of West Prussia, made East Prussia a German island, separated from the Reich proper by hundreds of square kilometers of now Polish-controlled territory. According to 1919 estimates, these territorial losses left 2,132,000 ethnic Germans under Polish

jurisdiction, and another 308,000 were marooned in the narrow confines of Freistadt Danzig.[68] Bismarck's prediction, expressed in 1848, that the re-creation of
an independent Poland would "sever the best sinews of Germany," leaving millions of Germans victim to "Polish arbitrariness," had, in the minds of many—indeed most—German citizens, come to pass.[69]

By any measure, the loss of much of the Prussian East represented the ultimate failure of Imperial German Polenpolitik. The struggle for the soil had ended
not in a heroic German victory but in a crushing German defeat. But even if one
disregards Germany's forced withdrawal from the Eastern Marches between 1918
and 1919 and considers only the Second Reich's prewar efforts to Germanize
Prussian Poland, it is clear that the actual achievements of Imperial Polenpolitik
were minimal. Far from eradicating Polish national consciousness and cultural
autonomy, Germany's long-standing anti-Polish stance, laced with Teutonic hubris and ethnocentric nationalism, had only reinforced the Poles' desire to shake
the foreign yoke and reestablish a state of their own. Despite the enormous efforts
and equally enormous expenditures of the Ansiedlungskommission to wrest land
away from the Poles and settle German peasant colonists in the eastern provinces,
the German population had increased only slightly, leaving the ethnic balance
decidedly in favor of the Poles.[70] The creation of new Polish farms by Polish
settlement organizations kept pace with and largely canceled out the AK's pains
to create new German farms. All told, both the ratio of Polish to German farmers
and the relative proportions of Polish- and German-owned farmland remained
virtually unchanged in the province of Posen throughout the nearly three decades
of the colonization program's existence.[71] Germany's struggle for the soil had
been in vain. Twenty-eight years of AK activity and the outlay of almost 1 billion
marks failed to restructure the ethnogeography or foster the Germanization of
the Prussian East. It seems that the Imperial colonization program failed primarily because the cost of purchasing Polish estates was simply beyond the means of
the Reich, but even if the Colonization Commission had managed to secure the
land it needed, it is unlikely that it could have convinced hundreds of thousands,
if not millions, of Germans, who enjoyed a relatively high standard of living in the
West, to move east. The radical World War I plans may have eliminated both of
these obstacles, but the collapse of the German war effort in 1918 precluded their
implementation. Two decades would pass before a Land ohne Menschen scheme
could be truly put to the test.

For the statesmen of the short-lived Weimar Republic, the Polish Question
was essentially an issue of territorial revisionism, not one of Volkstumspolitik.

Most of the region that their Imperial predecessors had endeavored for so many years to Germanize was no longer under German control. Not wishing to live under Polish rule, nearly half of those Posen and West Prussian Germans who eventually found themselves citizens of the Republic of Poland—some 592,000 people—had immigrated west by the end of 1921.[72] Although violations, both real and alleged, of the "minority rights" of those Germans who chose to remain on the Polish side of the frontier provided the Weimar government with a ready supply of ammunition in its diplomatic and propaganda campaign against the new Polish state, territorial questions weighed foremost on the minds of Weimar statesmen and radical German nationalists alike.[73]

The outright robbery, as they saw it, of Germany's eastern provinces was an injustice unprecedented in European history. If, by 1926, the German government had come to accept that Poland was not simply a *Saisonstaat* (roughly meaning "temporary state") but a very real and long-term player in European international politics, it still refused to accept, as historian Harald von Riekhoff argues, "Poland's postwar territorial composition where it interfered with German claims."[74] Germany's incessant demands for the return of its lost territories, coupled with the intense anti-Polonism propagated in the German press, German schoolbooks, and within the ranks of the emasculated German army,[75] prevented any genuine thaw in German-Polish relations throughout the fifteen-year history of the Weimar Republic. Despite occasional attempts at reconciliation after 1927, primarily on the initiative of Polish statesmen, no real compromise between the two governments was ever reached. Indeed, "as long as Germany retained her territorial claims and exploited every available opportunity to conduct her revisionist campaign before the international forum," Riekhoff writes, "Poland, associating revision with the prelude to a fourth partition, feared for her national existence. The barren political and emotional climate of this elementary conflict prohibited the growth of an effective reconciliatory settlement."[76]

Ironically, it was left to Hitler, one of the most outspoken and fanatical critics of the Treaty of Versailles and a leading herald for the reannexation of the Prussian East during the 1920s and 1930s, to forge a reconciliation—albeit a temporary one—between Germany and Poland through the conclusion of the "ten-year" German-Polish nonaggression pact of 1934.

OLD DREAMS, NEW RESOLVE

In September 1939, Germany's Polish Question once again became an issue of
domestic population policy. When the hour for action chimed once again on
the ethnographic front in the Eastern Marches of the Reich, National Socialist
Volkstumspolitik "experts" did not have to look far for inspiration. They merely
turned to the examples, both positive and negative, set by their predecessors.
Imperial German Polenpolitik had clearly been a failure, but nevertheless, its
principles and procedures and even its obvious lack of success went far to determine Nazi policies. The Imperial Germanization schemes for peasant colonization, the expropriation of Polish property, and the expulsion of Poles from the
eastern provinces of the Reich had remained fresh in the minds of militant German nationalists and völkisch ethnopoliticians. Following the reconquest of West
Prussia and Posen in 1939, the National Socialists revitalized these very measures
in their own quest to strengthen the German element in the East. But they also
radicalized these very methods dramatically, broadening them in scope, sever-
ity, and ideological extremism. As evinced by their actions in occupied Poland,
Hitler and his henchmen acknowledged the viability, at least in theory, of many
aspects of Imperial anti-Polish policy, but they also recognized the overall failure
of the Second Reich's Polenpolitik. In the 1920s, Hitler, for his part, had criticized
Imperial policy for its forbearance and "half-measures";[77] after the invasion of
September 1939, he and his regime acted accordingly. As Koehl puts it, "It was as
if Hitler were going to show what the Royal Prussian Colonization Commission
should really have done from 1886 on."[78]

It seems clear that prewar Imperial Germanization policy influenced Hitler
and the National Socialists, but the Land ohne Menschen proposal developed
during World War I did so even more. The similarities between the Second Reich's
wartime plans and future Nazi Ostpolitik are so striking that a connection seems
undeniable. In the pages that follow, it will become evident that the Nazis embraced the concept of a Germanized Frontier Strip, both as "a bulwark against
Slavdom" and as a human barrier encapsulating Prussian Poles behind an Ostwall of Germans. They seized upon the idea espoused by Friedrich von Schwerin
of resettling the vast ethnic German population of Russia in the eastern provinces
of the Reich. And proceeding from Hitler's maxim that "Germanization can only
be applied to *soil* and never to *people*,"[79] the Nazi regime abandoned—or at least
attempted to abandon—the Imperial policy of Germanizing ethnic Poles and

implemented, instead, the extremist solution advocated in Ludwig Bernhard's Land ohne Menschen plan of deporting hundreds of thousands of Poles to the East, dumping them en masse in their own satellite kingdom of Poland—the Generalgouvernement.

Though Imperial and Nazi Germanization policy certainly differed in magnitude, intensity, and ideological assumptions, it seems reasonable—though some historians would disagree—to speak of a basic continuity in Polenpolitik between the Second Reich and the Third Reich.[80] Bismarck and his successors, as well as the radical nationalistic pressure groups and population planners of the Imperial era, bequeathed to Hitler and the National Socialists the vision of a Germanized Prussian East and a strategic design for its realization. And what is more, the anti-Polish words and actions of statesmen and prominent figures of the Second Reich lent a degree of respectability to the xenophobic trends present in German society, leading many "good" Germans to accept the notion that Poles could never be reliable members of the national community and to embrace the conviction that the Polish Question demanded resolute governmental action. In summing up his analysis of Imperial Polenpolitik, German historian Hans-Ulrich Wehler writes:

> One can scarcely avoid detecting the genesis of later ideologies and policies, including the need for "living space," Germany's "civilizing" mission, and its imperialism in the East. Yet the contradiction within this policy could be seen in the way that the Poles were treated as "enemies of the Reich." The laws which operated to the detriment of those citizens of the state who spoke a different language had a double-edge to them. They helped prepare the way for dismantling the "state based on the rule of law" and its constitutional principles by the use of legalized methods sanctioned by the state itself. They also encouraged a situation in which discrimination against minorities came to be accepted. Expulsion and expropriation, social ostracism and a "Germanizing" repression, all played a part in the Wilhelmine Empire. Had it not been for the acceptance of such public injustices, the path towards the violent events of a latter period could never have been made so smooth so soon.[81]

As we well know, the social acceptance of "public injustices" in German society had ramifications far beyond the geographic confines of the Prussian East and far beyond the conceptual framework of the Polish Question. Indeed, this conciliatory attitude toward "legal" discrimination against minorities, a public mind-set that became the norm in the years following the *Machtergreifung* (seizure of power) of 1933, may well be the most significant legacy of Imperial German Polenpolitik.

2

"Racial Reshuffling" in the East: The Genesis of the Program

Despite Poland's vast population of Slavic and Jewish "undesirables" and despite its obvious importance as a stepping-stone to lebensraum in the East, the National Socialist regime had developed only rudimentary plans for the country and its inhabitants before September 1939. These plans amounted to little more than Hitler's widely known commitment to reannex former German territory lost at the end of World War I, as well as short-term "security measures" aimed at neutralizing any opposition to German rule through mass arrests and executions. But a blueprint for the racial reorganization of Poland, an operation that soon became the defining element of Nazi Polenpolitik, did not exist prior to the invasion.

Though there were certainly fiercely anti-Polish factions within both the Nazi leadership and the German military and rampant antipathy toward Poland and its inhabitants in German society at large,[1] Hitler himself had surprising little negative to say about Poland in the years preceding the diplomatic crisis of 1939 that led to the outbreak of World War II. That is not to say, of course, that he rejected the popular demand for the return of Germany's lost eastern provinces or the widespread völkisch conviction that Poles had no place in the German ethnoterritorial nation-state. He revealed his opinion on these matters in a swipe at the Second Reich's Germanization policy written in 1928, a passage that also foretold, somewhat eerily, of National Socialist policies to come:

> The *völkisch* state ... must under no conditions annex Poles with the intention of wanting to make Germans out of them someday. On the contrary, it must muster the determination either to seal off these alien racial elements so that the blood of its own

people will not be corrupted again, or it must without further ado remove them and hand over the vacated territory to its own national comrades.[2]

The striking similarity between this early political statement and future Nazi policies notwithstanding, it would be far-fetched to suggest that Hitler's ramblings represented a concrete blueprint for Nazi Polenpolitik. His statement did, however, show that the dream of a purely German Eastern Marches was still alive in völkisch-nationalist circles well after the collapse of the Second Reich, and alive it would remain.[3] But at this time, the reacquisition and comprehensive Germanization of lost territory did not necessarily entail the wholesale destruction of the Polish state. The Poles, anti-Russian and anti-Bolshevik to the core, could prove useful allies in a future war of conquest against the Soviet Union. Moreover, if Hitler could forge some sort of mutually beneficial agreement with Poland—be it ephemeral or not—he could potentially break a vital link in France's alliance system vis-à-vis the Reich. Such practical diplomatic concerns, not the ideological fantasy of a grandiose Land ohne Menschen scheme, dictated Hitler's policy toward Poland during the first years of his rule, and his actions indicated as much.

After several months of negotiations, Germany and Poland concluded a non-aggression pact on 26 January 1934, representing the Nazi regime's first diplomatic agreement with a major European state. The ten-year, renewable pact—a treaty "that seemed to reconcile two countries most Europeans thought irreconcilable"[4]—worked to both parties' advantage. The Poles, alarmed by the recent move of France and the USSR toward rapprochement, feared that the French might eventually call for Russian involvement in Polish affairs. The agreement with Germany therefore diminished the hitherto critical importance of the Franco-Polish alliance and granted Poland room for maneuver. Furthermore, since the accord paved the way for the end of the German-Polish trade war, which had raged since the days of Weimar, it was economically advantageous for the impoverished and underdeveloped Polish republic, still reeling, like all European countries, from the impact of the Depression. For Hitler, the conclusion of the nonaggression pact not only removed the threat of a two-front Franco-Polish preventive war against his new regime;[5] it also reinforced his shaky image as a man of peace. Though Hitler did not renounce Germany's claim to the lost Prussian East, he did promise that this long-standing grievance would not be redressed by force. Rather, all problems, both present and future, between

Germany and Poland would be dealt with through direct negotiations. And although the Poles had, during the course of the diplomatic exchanges, brushed aside any suggestion that they might one day take part in a move against the Soviet Union, Hitler apparently still believed that Poland would sooner or later become a loyal German satellite and bow to German wishes.[6]

One might argue that for Hitler, the German-Polish agreement was little more than a manifestation of "the Leninist maxim," as British historian A. J. P. Taylor puts it, "of taking a man by the hand, preparatory of taking him by the throat."[7] Indeed, when it became clear in 1939 that Poland would never play the role of German marionette, Hitler did, of course, take Poland by the throat—and strangled it. But despite the fact that the Reich and the Polish republic never became truly comfortable bedfellows in the years prior to the war, relations between the two remained, for the most part, amicable. Germany backed Polish demands for the annexation of the Cieszyn region of Czechoslovakia in 1938, Hermann Göring often went on hunting trips to Poland and even wrote the introduction to the German edition of Jósef Piłsudski's works, and pro-Polish books could be printed in Germany until as late as 1939.[8] Polish statesmen, in turn, remained passive when Hitler renounced the Versailles Treaty's limitations on the German armed forces in 1935, and although they agreed to cooperate with France in devising a response to the reoccupation of the Rhineland in 1936, they most likely did so knowing that none would actually take place.[9]

In the German minority residing in Poland, Hitler showed little interest. Though he evidently regarded the Polish Volksdeutschen as a potential forward base for ambitious foreign policy machinations in the distant future—indeed, he ultimately used the "minority question" as one of the pretexts for the attack on Poland in September 1939—he did not see them as group worth preserving for its own sake.[10] There was, moreover, virtually nothing in the way of public discourse in high political circles about a move to reannex lost territory until the autumn of 1938 and no talk whatsoever about a policy of racial reorganization in eastern Europe.

Hitler's attitude toward Poland changed markedly in late 1938. With Austria, the Saar, and the Sudetenland now officially incorporated into the Reich, the Rhineland remilitarized, and German rearmament in full swing, Germany's strategic position had been greatly enhanced. The last of the Reich's outstanding grievances regarding the Versailles settlement lay in the East beyond the German-Polish frontier, and Hitler felt that the time was now ripe to squeeze some concessions out of the headstrong Poles. He did not, however, go as far as to demand the return of the Polish Corridor, Upper Silesia, and the lost districts of Posen Province. Rather, his demands, handed to the Poles in that wake of the Munich Crisis in September and October 1938, were limited to the surrender of Danzig and the construction of a railway and a highway through the Corridor connecting East Prussia to the Reich proper; in exchange, he offered a German guarantee of Poland's borders and Polish partnership in a common front against the Soviet Union via collaboration with members of the Anti-Comintern Pact. The Poles flatly rejected these proposals, and the five-year thaw in German-Polish relations was all but over. Soon after Poland received the March 1939 British guarantee of assistance in the event that the country's sovereignty was "clearly threatened," Hitler renounced the nonaggression treaty and issued Case White, the initial contingency plan for the invasion. By the launch of the campaign on 1 September 1939, German objectives were no longer restricted to the reacquisition of Danzig and an extraterritorial highway through the Corridor but rather called for the reannexation of the Prussian East in its entirety and the total destruction of the Polish republic.[11]

Even though Hitler and the Nazi leadership had, by the late summer of 1939, committed themselves to the violent reacquisition of western Poland, no specific plans for the racial reorganization of the East had been developed by the time of the invasion. It was only during the course of the Polish campaign—in a mood Christopher Browning terms "the euphoria of victory"[12]—that a scheme for "racial reshuffling" in occupied Poland began to take shape. The remainder of this chapter surveys the events, factors, and decisions that led to the launch of the Nazi resettlement and deportation campaign in eastern Europe. It traces the gestation of Nazi plans in the late summer and early autumn of 1939 by examining Hitler's views on the matter, as well as orders and memoranda emanating from a number of National Socialist agencies and individuals involved in Polish affairs. An investigation of the sources in question reveals that a number of disparate bureaucratic considerations and political objectives coalesced within a few short weeks to give birth to the massive exercise in Volkstumspolitik that followed. Foreign policy ambitions, state-security interests, economic concerns, and racial-ideological goals, all of which had previously developed along more or less separate and distinct political tracks, converged in late September 1939 and became intertwined, prompting the Nazi regime to inaugurate the great demographic project in the East. What follows, then, is an attempt to explain a rapid-fire process of political fusion, an ad hoc synthesis of governmental initiatives that unleashed a veritable crusade to Germanize the Eastern Marches of the Reich.

UMSIEDLUNG: FROM CONCEPTION TO BIRTH

One could consider the signing of the German-Soviet nonaggression treaty on 23 August 1939 as the moment of conception for the resettlement-expulsion program. Although no plans yet existed for a policy of "ethnic redistribution" in eastern Europe, the treaty did establish the groundwork for the political conditions in which the mass population transfers could take place. The Molotov-Ribbentrop Pact served Hitler's immediate foreign policy goals, giving him Soviet neutrality while Germany smashed Poland and the guarantee of future cooperation while the Wehrmacht turned its attention to the West. But there was a price. The Secret Additional Protocol to the treaty promised Stalin not only a share of the Polish prize but also free rein throughout much of eastern Europe: Finland, Latvia, Estonia, and Bessarabia, as well as eastern Poland beyond the Narev-Vistula-San line, were all declared Soviet spheres of influence. Control of western Poland and Lithuania, a much smaller region by comparison, would fall to Germany. This arrangement, which amounted to a partition of eastern Europe, ensured the destruction of "Versailles Poland," but it did not necessarily offer a final solution to the Polish Question. Whether the preservation of an independent, residual Polish state was in the interests of Germany and the USSR was a question that remained open. The existence of such a state, as well as its exact borders, were matters that could be resolved, so the agreement stated, "only in the course of further political developments."[13]

   The Molotov-Ribbentrop Pact greatly strengthened Germany's immediate military-strategic position, but it also generated long-term political ramifications that prompted a shift in long-standing Nazi policy. Although the treaty placed the majority of ethnic Germans then living under Polish jurisdiction within the region set aside for Nazi control, hundreds of thousands of eastern European Volksdeutschen remained outside of Germany's sphere of influence, including 78,000 in the Baltic Republics, 81,000 in Bessarabia, and some 150,000 in eastern Poland.[14] The traditional National Socialist approach to the German minorities abroad was to use them as trump cards in negotiations with foreign governments, exploiting the issue of "national self-determination" championed by Wilson at the Paris Peace Conference in 1919 to justify aggression and expansion. This strategy had proved effective during the Sudeten Crisis of September 1938. Staring war in the face, the Western powers surrendered at Munich to Hitler's demands for the immediate annexation of the Sudetenland, the mountainous region of western

Czechoslovakia then inhabited by approximately 3 million ethnic Germans. The Nazi regime had recently employed the same political tactics against Lithuania, leading to the peaceful reannexation of the Memelland, along with its estimated 60,000 Germans of former Prussian citizenship, on 22 March 1939.[15] But Hitler's need to maintain good relations with Stalin while he prepared for war with the West precluded the immediate use of the eastern European Volksdeutschen as diplomatic leverage against the Soviet Union. He would now have to limit temporarily the revisionist policy of uniting ethnic Germans with the Reich through annexation and pursue a policy of immigration instead. The decision to withdraw the Volksdeutschen from the Soviet sphere of influence would not come for several weeks, but after 23 August 1939, a reversal in Nazi policy toward ethnic German minorities in the East was necessary. The impending political about-face would set in motion the wheels of resettlement, something that would exacerbate and expand the brutal process of destructive Germanization, a procedure under way within the first days of the Polish campaign.

If the German-Soviet treaty of 23 August laid the diplomatic foundation for constructive Germanization initiatives in occupied Poland, the parallel track leading to the mass expulsion of Poles and Jews originated in arrangements and decisions made a few weeks earlier. On 31 July 1939, SS-Gruppenführer Reinhard Heydrich, the chief of the Nazi Sicherheitspolizei (Sipo; Security Police) and the Sicherheitsdienst (SD; Security Service), concluded a formal agreement regarding security measures during the forthcoming Polish campaign with Colonel Eduard Wagner, the general quartermaster of the German army. The agreement simply stated that Einsatzgruppen, special mobile detachments of SS security policemen and SD agents, would be responsible for "the suppression of all anti-Reich and anti-German elements in enemy territory behind the fighting troops."[16] The full implications of this phrase, however, were not made known to the upper echelons of the German military until 22 August, the day Hitler met with his high command at Obersalzberg to discuss the objectives of the September campaign. Several contemporary accounts of this conference survive, including the notes of Franz Halder, chief of the General Staff, as well as an unsigned memorandum found after the war by the Nuremberg prosecution in the files of the Oberkommando der Wehrmacht (OKW; Armed Forces High Command).[17] According to these reports, Hitler announced that relations with Poland had become unbearable and that the time had come to strike. He explained in no uncertain terms that the campaign was to be one of annihilation; the Polish nation was to be destroyed, its "living forces" (*lebendige Kräfte*) eliminated: "It is not a question of reaching a specific line or a new frontier, but rather the annihilation of the enemy, which must be pursued in ever new ways ... Execution: Harsh and remorseless. We must steel ourselves against humanitarian reasoning!"[18]

To Hitler, the elimination of Poland's living forces signified far more than the destruction of the Polish army. Polish intellectuals, political leaders, the clergy, and the landed gentry, who by virtue of their positions and prestige might provoke unrest and undermine German authority (just as they had supposedly done in the Imperial era), were to be exterminated. Although the accounts just mentioned make no explicit reference to the "neutralization" of the Polish ruling class, Hitler certainly discussed the subject at the meeting. One participant, Field Marshal Fedor von Bock, later reported that the Nazi leader had explained that "things would be done of which the German generals would not approve. He did not therefore wish to burden the army with the necessary liquidations, but ... would have them carried out by the SS."[19]

Hitler's mandate for direct action against the Polish leadership and intelligentsia represented, in effect, Reichsführer-SS (RFSS) Heinrich Himmler's ticket for admission into the arena of race and resettlement policy in occupied Poland. From this springboard, Himmler would expand SS activity in conquered territory dramatically over the next several months. Beginning with the "necessary liquidations" Hitler had ordered, the SS functioned, without rival, as the spearhead of the Nazi New Order in the East, and occupied Poland for all intents and purposes quickly became an "SS state."[20]

Three days after Hitler's 22 August conference, Himmler ordered Reinhard Heydrich to establish a special section, code-named Tannenberg, within the Sipo main office in Berlin.[21] From there, Heydrich rapidly organized five Einsatzgruppen, each subdivided into Einsatzkommandos (operational detachments) of 120 to 150 men, to carry out Hitler's instructions. One such task force was assigned to each of the five German armies that would participate in the invasion of Poland. All commanders and most officers were members of the SD.[22] Though legally subordinate to the Wehrmacht, the Einsatzgruppen received their operational orders from Heydrich via the main office of the security police.[23] As a result, the military could exercise little control over the SS death squads, whether during the campaign or after the conclusion of hostilities on 5 October.

In the early morning of 1 September 1939, Hitler unleashed his war machine on the Republic of Poland, giving Europe its first bitter taste of blitzkrieg. As German forces progressed at breakneck speed, overrunning the entire western half of the country in twelve days, the SS task forces began their grim work of *politische*

Flurbereinigung (political housecleaning) in newly conquered territory. Working from lists of "anti-Reich and anti-German elements" compiled by Sipo and the SD before the invasion, Heydrich's five Einsatzgruppen, reinforced by two more death squads formed during the first week of hostilities as well as three regiments of SS Death's Head units temporarily removed from concentration camp service,[24] shadowed the advancing German troops and executed their mission with murderous proficiency. "Special police duties" were aimed, first and foremost, at the Polish intelligentsia, the clergy, and the nobility, but they also targeted Jews and any "politically-unreliable individuals" who might oppose German authority.[25] Hundreds were rounded up and summarily shot within the first days of the occupation. By 8 September, Heydrich could boast of 200 executions daily.[26] The shootings increased dramatically in number as the region under Germany's control expanded. Assisted by as many as 40,000 members of the Volksdeutsche Selbstschutz, "self-defense" units of ethnic Germans native to Poland, and, even more important, by the German Wehrmacht itself, the Einsatzgruppen of Sipo and the SD methodically—and with alarming speed—decimated the ranks of the Polish leadership.[27] Just three weeks into the Polish campaign at a meeting with his division chiefs and Einsatzgruppen commanders held on 21 September, Heydrich estimated that "three percent of the political leadership at most is still in the occupied territories." "This three percent," he ordered, "must also be rendered harmless."[28]

It was during the first days of Operation Tannenberg that Nazi plans for the deportation of Poles and Jews from western Poland began to emerge. Linked in no way to *volksdeutsch* resettlement, an operation not yet under consideration, the deportation schemes hatched in early September 1939 were essentially manifestations of a long-standing Nazi policy geared toward ridding Germany of all so-called undesirable elements who seemed to threaten the integrity of the German "racial community" and the security of the National Socialist state. The Jewish population of Germany had been a primary target of this policy for years. Since 1938, the Nazis had attempted to remove Jews from German territory through forced expulsion, and one could regard the plans to deport the Jewish population of western Poland—later estimated at 550,000 individuals—not as a new policy per se but as essentially an expansion of a preexisting anti-Jewish program.[29] The fate of these Polish Jews, then, was preordained; prewar racial policy dictated that they be driven from Reich territory.

Anti-Polish initiatives developed along a different path. The Nazi government had no concrete plans to deport Poles before the invasion; they initially sought "only" to neutralize the Polish intellectual, religious, economic, and political leadership and thus eliminate those who represented a nationalistic—but not necessary a racial—threat to German rule. But very soon after 1 September 1939, the regime began to move toward a policy of removing all Poles, regardless of their social or economic status, from the Eastern Marches of the Reich. The invasion had, in effect, produced a new enemy of the Nazi *Volksgemeinschaft* (community of the people). Granted, the National Socialists always considered *Judenpolitik* (Jewish policy) and *Polenpolitik* separate and distinct issues, and the Nazis never attacked the Polish Question with the same fanatical zeal that they reserved for the Jews, but as a scheme for the Germanization of western Poland materialized, anti-Jewish and anti-Polish policy steadily became more and more entwined, converging by 21 September into one comprehensive expulsion program aimed at all the supposedly undesirable elements, Jews and Poles alike. The relationship between Polish and Jewish policy would be cemented, if only temporarily, by the final and definite decision to receive and resettle the eastern European Volksdeutschen, which came several days later.

The first documented reference to mass deportations was made by Heydrich at a Sipo conference on 7 September. Security in conquered territory, particularly the Einsatzgruppen's mission, was the main topic of conversation, but Heydrich's comments revealed that the Nazi hierarchy was now committed to deporting all Jews from western Poland and was beginning to weigh the prospect of action against Poles in the region as well. "It has been decided," Heydrich told his subordinates,

> that the ruling class, which in no case may remain in Poland, will be interned in concentration camps, while for the lower classes temporary concentration camps will be established on the frontier behind the Einsatzgruppen, from where they can be immediately deported, *if the need arises,* to the remaining part of Poland ... The expulsion of Polish Jews from Germany [that is, both the *Altreich,* or old Reich, and western Poland by implication] must be carried out, including those Jews who immigrated [to Germany proper] and in the meantime acquired German citizenship.[30]

By the "remaining part of Poland," Heydrich meant those Polish territories within Germany's sphere of influence not marked for outright annexation. Although he stated at the meeting that "for [the remaining part of] Poland, no protectorate government, but rather a purely German administration is planned," one must keep in mind that the status of region had not been finalized as of 7 September.[31] Whether it would become an autonomous state or a German protectorate was still an open question, one that could be decided only through further negotiations with the Soviets. It is clear, however, that the Nazi hierarchy already regarded the region as a dumping ground for Polish and Jewish "rabble."

Within a week, Nazi deportation plans, at least those that targeted Jews, had apparently become more concrete. At a lunchtime conference on 14 September, Heydrich discussed the immense Jewish Problem in Poland with his division chiefs and intimated that a possible solution was on the horizon. "Proposals [concerning the Jewish Question]," he announced, "are being submitted to the Führer by the Reichsführer [Himmler] that only the Führer can decide, since they will also be of foreign-policy significance."[32] We do not know exactly what these proposals were, but decisions concerning Judenpolitik made over the next several days embodied a scheme for a massive deportation campaign leveled not only at Polish Jews but also at all Jews living in the Reich.[33] Whatever the exact details of Himmler's proposals, all signs suggest that some sort of large-scale demographic project was on Hitler's mind during the third week of September 1939. International events would soon lead the Nazi leader to take the first steps toward approving a policy of racial reshuffling in the East.

On 17 September, Stalin's Red Army crossed the eastern Polish frontier and, meeting little resistance, quickly advanced toward the predrawn German-Soviet line of demarcation. The Soviet invasion sealed Poland's fate. Although Warsaw held out against the Germans until 28 September and the last pocket of organized Polish resistance did not capitulate until 5 October, Poland was all but crushed by 18 September, leading Nazi propagandists to refer proudly to this short chapter of World War II as "der Feldzug der 18 Tage" (the campaign of 18 days). At this relatively late stage in the Polish campaign, the future of that remaining part of Poland, a subject that had not been addressed in diplomatic exchanges since the signing of the Molotov-Ribbentrop Pact, was still undetermined. But early in the morning of 20 September, Friedrich Werner von der Schulenburg, the German ambassador in Moscow, cabled the Foreign Ministry in Berlin to inform his superiors that Stalin no longer considered the existence of an independent "residual" Polish state desirable; the Soviet leader, he said, was now inclined simply to partition Poland between Germany and the USSR along the Narev-Vistula-San line and wanted to begin negotiations on this matter at once.[34] Perhaps it was Stalin's own "euphoria of victory" that drove him toward this more radical solution to the Polish Question.

The virtual collapse of Polish resistance, coupled with the Soviet occupation of eastern Poland and Stalin's decision regarding the remaining area, evidently boosted Hitler's growing conviction that a far-reaching resettlement and expulsion program was a viable option. He presented his plans, though still vague in design, to Walter von Brauchitsch, commander-in-chief of the German army, on 20 September, shortly after Schulenburg's telegram arrived in Berlin. "Extensive resettlement," Hitler said, would take place in conquered territory after the cessation of hostilities. Although he provided few details, he did state that former German territory would be cleared of Poles who had immigrated to the region after 1918 and that for every German moving into this territory, two people would be deported. From where these incoming Germans would originate, Hitler did not say, but he did employ the term *population exchange*.[35] In view of recent foreign policy developments, it seems likely that Hitler was now considering the possibility of "repatriating" the 150,000 ethnic German natives of Soviet-occupied eastern Poland. Within six days, the Nazi dictator would decide to withdraw not only these ethnic Germans but also the 75,000 Volksdeutschen from Estonia and Latvia.

The following day, Heydrich met with his division chiefs and Einsatzgruppen commanders to discuss the latest diplomatic and military developments, the progress of Operation Tannenberg, and the objectives of future policy. Also present was SS-Hauptsturmführer Adolf Eichmann, an individual who would soon play a leading role in the deportation campaign. Heydrich announced that, in accordance with decisions made the day before, Poland would be divided more or less in half and partitioned between Germany and the USSR. The German portion would be subdivided into two distinct regions. The former Prussian provinces lost at Versailles would be formally reincorporated into Germany. Beyond a defensive Ostwall, which would be erected along the eastern frontier of these new Reich districts, a "foreign Gau" would be established, its capital Krakau.[36] Now lying fully within Germany's sphere of influence, this remaining part of Poland could—and would—be exploited in any way the Nazi regime saw fit.

Heydrich did not address the topic of German resettlement at the conference, but he discussed at length the subject of Polish and Jewish expulsions. His comments, the first detailed description of Nazi plans for a racial New Order in conquered territory, made clear that western Poland was to be completely purged of Jews and Poles, an action that entailed, by definition, a thorough Germanization of the region, if by "eliminative" means. He unveiled a well-developed scheme for the deportation of all Jews from the Reich, which seems to indicate that Himmler's proposals presented to Hitler on or after 14 September did, in fact, amount to a blueprint for such an extensive *Judenaktion* ([anti-]Jewish action). The minutes of the meeting state:

> The deportation of Jews into the foreign Gau, expulsion over the demarcation line, has been approved by the Führer. The entire process, however, is to take place over the course of a year ... The Jews are to be assembled in urban ghettos in order to ensure better possibilities of control and later removal ... The following comprehensive directive was issued:
>   1. Jews as quickly as possible into the cities,
>   2. Jews from the Reich to Poland,
>   3. the remaining 30,000 Gypsies also to Poland,
>   4. the systematic expulsion of Jews from German territory via freight trains.[37]

Deportation plans for Poles, however, were far less precise. They existed only in general form, which suggests that the Nazi regime had only recently—perhaps only within the previous few days—come to definite decisions regarding the Polish population of what would soon be the "incorporated eastern territories." They also reveal that security measures and racial-ideological initiatives were becoming intertwined: *politische Flurbereinigung* and *völkische Flurbereinigung* (ethnic housecleaning) were finally converging into one comprehensive policy. Though Tannenberg was still in full swing and many executions were yet to come, the elimination of the Polish leadership, initially dictated primarily by questions of state security, was now considered but one component, albeit an integral component, of a larger project directed at the entire non-German population of western Poland. Evacuations, moreover, would soon displace physical liquidation as the primary means of neutralizing opposition to German rule. Heydrich's remarks insinuate as much:

> As has been repeatedly explained, the solution to the Polish problem will vary between the ruling class (Polish intelligentsia) and the lower working-class Poles. Three percent of the political leadership at most is still in the occupied territories. This three percent must also be rendered harmless and put into concentration camps.[38] The Einsatzgruppen must draw up lists in which prominent leaders are registered, along with lists of the middle-class [Poles] ... These, too, must be arrested and deported to the remaining area ... The primitive Poles will be incorporated into the labor process as migrant workers and will likewise be deported from the German districts into the foreign Gau.[39]

The problem of bringing the requirements of the German economy into harmony with the goals of Volkstumspolitik was already beginning to rear its head. Heydrich all but admitted that neither he nor his superiors knew how the regime could simultaneously exploit and expel the Polish labor force: "The Einsatzgruppen leaders ... must consider how, on the one hand, one can integrate the primitive Polish workers into the labor force and, on the other, deport them at the same time."[40] This question, as will be shown, was never resolved; it remained open throughout the entire history of the occupation.

A rudimentary plan for the evacuation of Poles and Jews was now on the table. Three political paths—*Judenpolitik*, *Polenpolitik*, and *Sicherheitspolitik* (security policy)—had merged into one sweeping policy of destructive Germanization. It would take only another dispatch from the German ambassador in Moscow to bring "constructive Germanization" into the fold. At 12:30 A.M. on 26 September, the German Foreign Ministry in Berlin received a top-secret telegram from Schulenburg in which the ambassador related the details of a meeting he had had with Stalin and V. M. Molotov the previous evening. Stalin, according to Schulenburg, had reiterated his firm opposition to the preservation of an independent Polish state and had submitted a new proposal as well: if the Reich government agreed to waive its claim to Lithuania, the Soviet Union was prepared to transfer the entire eastern Polish province of Lublin, as well as a portion of the province of Warsaw, from the Soviet sphere of influence to the German. He added that if Germany consented to this arrangement, "the Soviet Union would immediately take up the solution of the problem of the Baltic countries in accordance with the [Secret] Protocol of August 23, and expected in this matter the unstinting support of the German government." The Soviet leader, Schulenburg declared, "expressly indicated Estonia, Latvia, and Lithuania, but did not mention Finland."[41]

Stalin's remarks seemed to imply that a Soviet invasion of Estonia and Latvia, if not Lithuania as well, was imminent. Eastern Poland, with its 150,000 Volksdeutschen, was already occupied by Soviet troops. Faced with the prospect of another 125,000 ethnic Germans immediately falling under Bolshevik rule, Hitler decided, once and for all, to extract the "splinters of Germandom" from the Baltic Republics and east Poland. Eventually, he would summon all Volksdeutschen residing in the Soviet sphere of influence "home to the Reich."

Hitler's decision was driven, above all, by foreign policy considerations. Just as the ethnic Germans of Czechoslovakia, the Memelland, and western Poland had pleaded for Germany to rescue them from foreign domination, so, Hitler expected, would their counterparts in eastern Europe—and this time from Bolshevik domination at that. The Führer had come to a political crossroads. He now had to choose between preserving cordial relations with Stalin and his long-standing, revisionist policy of uniting German minority groups with the main body of the Volk through annexation.[42] Resettlement offered a way for him to save face. By withdrawing the Volksdeutschen from the East, Hitler could secure future Soviet cooperation while he turned his attention to the West and, at the same time, maintain his image as the lord protector of the German minorities of Europe.

Economic concerns probably influenced Hitler as well. In early 1937, Hermann Göring, who, as the general plenipotentiary for the Four-Year Plan, served as the Reich's economic czar, calculated that Germany was running a deficit of some 160,000 workers in the agricultural sector alone. Göring ordered Reichsführer-SS and Chief of German Police Heinrich Himmler to tackle the problem. Himmler responded by establishing his own Four-Year Plan office within his personal staff.[43] Led by SS-Oberführer Ulrich Greifelt, a Nazi technocrat whom Himmler would later appoint to direct the resettlement program, this SS Dienststelle (Service Office) worked for the next two years to ensure that Germany's labor needs were met, but despite its efforts, the overall shortage of workers had risen to approximately 550,000 by the beginning of 1939. Greifelt proposed an innovative solution for the dilemma. In a memorandum submitted to the RFSS in January 1939, he suggested that the "repatriation" of the estimated 30 million *Reichsdeutschen* (Reich Germans, that is, Germans from the Altreich) and *Volksdeutschen* scattered across the globe—whose "labor, ability, knowledge, blood, and descendants" were all at the disposal of foreign states—would go far to solve Germany's labor problems. Himmler declared the plan good on January 23.[44] German historian Heinz Höhne perhaps overemphasizes the importance of these economic concerns, implying that they, above all else, drove Hitler to act, but it seems clear that economic policy—yet another more or less distinct political matter—merged with his strategic, racial-ideological, and security considerations to generate the resettlement and expulsion campaign.[45]

Negotiations with Moscow regarding Stalin's most recent proposals were scheduled for 28 September. According to the minutes of a German Foreign Ministry conference held 26 September, the day Schulenburg's telegram arrived in Berlin, specific subjects for the forthcoming Nazi-Soviet parley now included the "exchange of populations between the areas east and west of the line of the rivers, especially the transfer of Volksdeutschen from Russian to German territory," as well as "safe-

guarding the fate of Volksdeutschen in further areas possibly to be occupied by
Russia."[46] These very matters were also on Hitler's mind. As Foreign Ministry officials worked out a strategy for the 28 September negotiations, a meeting took
place in the nearby Reich Chancellery between the Nazi leader and Birger Dahlerus, a Swedish civil engineer who had served as an unofficial intermediary between
Germany and Great Britain in the weeks before the invasion of Poland. During the
conference, held in the presence of Göring, Hitler discussed his plans for Poland,
including his decision, apparently made earlier that day, to repatriate the eastern
European Volksdeutschen. "The Führer," so the interpreter Paul Schmidt recorded,

> intended to reincorporate in the Reich the former German and former Austrian sections
> of Poland, as well as strategically important territories. Besides this there was to be a
> "reshuffling" not only by uniting once more inside the Reich by large-scale resettlement
> the scattered German minority groups, but also by effecting an adjustment between
> the thickly populated west, with a population of 140 persons per km^2—a condition that
> could not last—and the thinly populated east with a density of only 35 people per km^2.
> To carry out these great plans would require 50 to 100 years, particularly if one consid-
> ered the tremendous backwardness and demoralization in Poland ... M. Dahlerus then
> brought up the question of the Jews ... whereupon the Führer replied that if he should
> reorganize the Polish state, an asylum could also be created for the Jews. Someone had
> to see that there was order in the East [*Ostraum*] and convert the conditions of com-
> plete disorder into an orderly one ... The aim was to create a sensible regional distribu-
> tion of nationalities as well as a sensible economic structure in the Polish area.

"Germany did not want to 'swallow any Poles,'" Hitler explained; "she wanted
only security for the Reich, and borders which would provide the necessary possibilities for her provisioning and for the reshuffling of peoples."[47]
    The date 26 September 1939 was a landmark moment in the development
of National Socialist Volkstumspolitik in the East. The Nazi regime was now
fully committed to a policy of racial reshuffling; only the details of the operation
needed to be worked out, and these hinged, to no small degree, on the results of
the forthcoming negotiations in Moscow. On 28 September, just before he was to
meet with Molotov, Joachim von Ribbentrop received a message by coded telephone from State Secretary Ernst von Weizsäcker in Berlin. Weizsäcker updated
the German foreign minister on Hitler's recent decisions, stating that "Gruppen-
führer Heydrich has informed me that the Führer and Chancellor had ordered
the evacuation of Volksdeutschen from Estonia and Latvia ... it would be desir-

able to reach agreements with the Soviet Union on an orderly evacuation with safeguards for property interests."[48] With these new instructions in hand, Ribbentrop went to the bargaining table.

In the exchange that followed, the territorial demands of the Soviet Union and Germany's demands for the unobstructed evacuation of the eastern European Volksdeutschen were mutually accepted. The diplomats agreed that "the territory of the Lithuanian state falls into the sphere of interest of the USSR, while, on the other hand, the province of Lublin and parts of the province of Warsaw fall to the sphere of influence of Germany." Germany did, however, retain a strip of southwestern Lithuania bordering East Prussia, which contained the vast majority of the country's ethnic German population.[49] This arrangement worked to the Reich's advantage, eliminating—or so it seemed at the time—the need to resettle the Lithuanian Volksdeutschen.[50] Regarding the ethnic Germans of Estonia, Latvia, and eastern Poland, Molotov pledged that "the Government of the USSR shall place no obstacles in the way of Reich nationals and other persons of German descent residing in its sphere of influence if they desire to migrate to Germany or the German sphere of influence." Furthermore, the Soviet foreign minister agreed that "such removals shall be carried out by agents of the Government of the Reich in cooperation with local authorities," and he promised that "the property rights of the emigrants shall be protected."[51]

Ribbentrop had accomplished his mission: the borders of the German and Soviet spheres of influence were all but finalized, and the door to the Reich was now open for the German minority groups of eastern Europe.[52] The diplomatic groundwork for ethnic redistribution in occupied Poland was now in place. The responsibility for establishing the New Order in the East would fall to the SS.

THE RISE OF THE RKFDV

Hitler first turned to SS-Obergruppenführer Werner Lorenz, the chief of the Volksdeutsche Mittelstelle (VoMi; Ethnic German Liaison Office), to plan and conduct the resettlement operation.[53] VoMi was the logical choice: since January 1937, Lorenz's office had coordinated political and financial transactions with ethnic Germans abroad, especially those in eastern Europe, and had served as an effective medium for aiding Konrad Henlein's Volksdeutschen during the Sudeten Crisis of 1938. Lorenz had more recently been involved in a project to resettle the South Tyrolean Germans, residents of an "outpost of Germandom" that Hitler was willing to sacrifice for the benefit of German-Italian relations. VoMi's status within the Nazi power structure was somewhat ambiguous. It was originally conceived as a secret party apparatus under the control and funding of "Deputy Führer" Rudolf Hess and his NSDAP staff. In July 1938, Hitler granted VoMi state authority as well, placing it in charge of all Reich, party, and private organizations dealing with Volksdeutschen, including the distribution of state funds to ethnic Germans abroad. As a state agency, VoMi was publicly subordinate to Ribbentrop and the Foreign Ministry, but operationally, Lorenz and his office remained under the leadership of Hess and the NSDAP. The divided authority of this bastard state-party agency, coupled with Lorenz's SS connection, was exploited by Himmler to expand his own power. Through Lorenz, Himmler easily infiltrated VoMi with SS personnel, giving himself some leverage at the Foreign Ministry as well as some influence in Hess's affairs. In reality, then, VoMi had three masters—two official and one not. But the Reichsführer-SS quickly managed to inveigle supreme control of VoMi for himself.[54]

When Hitler appointed Lorenz to oversee the resettlement of the Baltic and eastern Polish Volksdeutschen, he evidently had no coherent operational plan in mind. He merely suggested that they might be accommodated in the Danzig and Posen regions.[55] The ambiguity of Hitler's orders gave Lorenz a great deal of room for maneuver, but the VoMi chief had little time to exercise his new authority. Reichsführer-SS Himmler had fully expected that he, not Lorenz, would be crowned Germany's resettlement czar, and he was clearly annoyed when the position was given to one of his subordinates instead.[56] Upon hearing of Lorenz's assignment, Himmler rushed to Hitler and protested that the resettlement program—soon to be the cornerstone of Nazi Volkstumspolitik in the East—was far too important to be in the hands of a mere SS-Obergruppenführer. The immigration and resettlement of nearly 200,000 people, reasoned Himmler, was a complex affair, requiring the coordination of many state and party agencies. Only he, as Reichsführer-SS and the chief of German police, had the authority to carry out such a mighty task. Hitler agreed. After hearing Himmler's arguments, he revoked Lorenz's appointment and gave the RFSS supreme control of the entire operation.[57] This turn of events represented a major political coup for Himmler. By capturing Lorenz's jurisdiction, the Reichsführer-SS was in a good position to prevent other branches of the German government from exerting influence in matters of racial policy, an area he considered his special field of expertise. It also allowed him to tighten his grip on VoMi; he could now control its activities within both its Foreign Ministry and its NSDAP jurisdictions much more effectively.[58] In short, Himmler's new authority enabled the SS to extend its tentacles even deeper into the power structure of the Nazi state.

On 28 September, Heinrich Lammers, the chief of the Reich Chancellery, informed Finance Minister Schwerin von Krosigk of Himmler's appointment and ordered the Finance Ministry to turn over 10 million marks in state funds to the RFSS without delay.[59] Six days later, Himmler sent SS-Oberführer Ulrich Greifelt, his liaison man with Göring's Office of the Four-Year Plan, to pick up the money.[60] Greifelt, whom Himmler soon named director of his SS resettlement bureau in Berlin, was a loyal and unassuming individual, a man the RFSS could easily control. In elevating Greifelt instead of a more prominent figure (such as Reinhard Heydrich or even VoMi's Werner Lorenz) to an important administrative position of this type, Himmler evidently hoped to concentrate all the more authority over resettlement affairs in his own hands, a power play that would enable him to dictate policy with little constraint.[61]

As the Reichsführer-SS jockeyed for position, Nazi resettlement planning moved forward. During an early morning harangue on 29 September, Hitler revealed an outline for racial reorganization in conquered Polish territory to a group of his closest associates. Rudimentary at best, Hitler's scheme was never implemented as described, but it was the Nazi leader's most definitive statement regarding his personal vision of occupied Poland, and it at least set the tone for resettlement and deportation policy in the months to come. According to Alfred Rosenberg, who recorded Hitler's comments in his diary, the Führer declared that Germany's sphere of influence would be divided into three separate "belts" of settlement: a purely German zone in the annexed territories of the west; a Polish zone immediately to the east; and beyond the Polish belt, in the region between the Vistula and Bug rivers, a zone for "the whole of Jewry," as well as all other undesirable elements residing in Reich territory. In the future, Hitler stated, Germany might gain the opportunity to move these three settlement belts even farther to the east, but only time would tell.[62] The German zone, in fact, would be shifted to the east within a few short weeks, a move that would have a profound impact on Nazi Judenpolitik and expulsion policy in general.

Heydrich met with his division chiefs later that day to clarify Hitler's plans for far eastern Poland. He explained that in area around the city of Lublin, a "nature preserve" or "Reichs-ghetto" would be created to serve as a dumping ground for all "political and Jewish elements" under the German yoke.[63] Officially assigned to Germany's share of Poland just three days before, the province of Lublin remained the principal destination of Jewish deportees in the months that followed.

However, Nazi plans for an all-embracing *Judenreservat* (Jewish reservation) in the district, seen until the spring of 1940 as a potential Final Solution to the Jewish Question, were never realized.[64] They were eventually scrapped, superseded by issues considered more pressing than the Jewish Question.

All of the decision making, political machinations, and demographic planning discussed in the previous pages took place behind closed doors. Only the upper echelons of the German and Soviet governments, leading figures within the SS and the National Socialist police establishment, and a few select foreign diplomats, such as Birger Dahlerus and Italian foreign minister Count Galeazzo Ciano, were aware of the scheme for a vast program of ethnic redistribution in eastern Europe.[65] But on 6 October, emboldened by his victorious tour of Warsaw the previous day, Hitler went before the Reichstag to unveil his plans for the New East to the German people and the world at large. After reviewing the highlights of the Polish campaign and boasting of the minimal losses suffered by the German military, he turned to the reorganization of newly conquered territory.

Hitler presented only a broad outline of the regime's plans for Poland, cloaking his discussion of future occupational policy in the language of peace. The German Reich, he proclaimed, was now in the position to tackle the problems arising from the disintegration of Poland and also the important task of eliminating international difficulties that had endangered the political and economic existence of all European states. He defined Germany's aims in its sphere of influence as follows:

> 1) The establishment of a Reich border that shall do justice to existing historical, ethnographic, and economic conditions.
>
> 2) The pacification of the entire region in the sense of creating acceptable peace and order.
>
> 3) The absolute guarantee of security not only for Reich territory, but for the entire sphere of interest.
>
> 4) The reordering, the reconstruction of economic life and transport, and along with it, the development of culture and civilization.
>
> 5) *But as the most important task:* a reordering of ethnographic relationships, meaning a resettlement of nationalities so as to yield in the end the development of better lines of demarcation [between them] than is the case today.[66]

Reiterating his purely peaceful intentions, Hitler went on to explain how the "splinter groups of Germans" spread across eastern and southeastern Europe constituted a basis for further international conflict. To preserve the peace, Germany was prepared to take action: "In the age of nationality principles and racial thought," he pontificated, "it is utopian to believe that [other countries] can simply assimilate these members of a 'high grade' people; a far-sighted ordering of European life therefore necessitates resettlements in order to remove at least some of the [potential] causes of a European conflict."[67]

The price of peace and stability in eastern Europe, particularly in terms of German-Soviet relations, was clear for all Germans to see: a reversal of time-honored Nazi volksdeutsch policy. Though Hitler, for his part, certainly regarded the forthcoming retreat of Deutschtum as only a temporary expedient, the public was led to believe the German demographic front, which had for centuries extended far beyond the eastern borders of Germany, was to be shortened and "leveled," perhaps permanently.[68] It was to be withdrawn to the new eastern frontier of the Reich, to the ramparts of the invincible Ostwall that would shield and protect the German people from the Slavic and Jewish hordes to the east.

Hitler mentioned neither Himmler's appointment nor the SS. And though he made reference to Judenpolitik, stating that Germany would attempt to forge "an arrangement and settlement of the Jewish Problem" within its overall effort to resolve "minority questions," he did not speak of the impending mass expulsions of either Jews or Poles.[69] The ruthless ethnic cleansing of conquered territory was not then, or ever, a matter for public consumption. Allegedly constructive Germanization, however, was no secret. Soon, the German press would be jam-packed with heroic tales of sacrifice and hardship, describing how the Volks-deutschen of eastern Europe had abandoned all to answer the call of their Führer. "Heim ins Reich" (home to the Reich) became a catchphrase for superpatriotism. The ethnic Germans who followed the "call of their blood" became the darlings of the Nazi propaganda machine, "noble pioneers" in the National Socialist quest for a racial utopia in the East.[70]

Himmler's appointment as settlement commissioner was not immediately divulged to the German public, most likely because his tasks, as defined by Hitler's secret executive order for the "consolidation of German nationhood" of 7 October 1939, embodied destructive Germanization measures aimed at all "foreign elements" in the eastern territories. The official description of his new assignment was first disclosed to Himmler on 29 September, the day he received a rough draft of Hitler's decree from Heinrich Lammers.[71] It evidently pleased him. After reviewing the draft, Himmler wrote back to Lammers on 4 October, saying that all was in order and suggesting no changes.[72] Still, minor amendments were made before the decree became official.

R. Walther Darré, the Nazi minister for food and agriculture, a long-time proponent of agrarian settlement, and the regime's foremost *Blut und Boden* (blood
and soil) theorist, expected to play a prominent role in resettlement affairs. Darré
saw western Poland as the potential breadbasket of Germany, and well before the
fall of Warsaw, he had drawn up a survey of Polish estates in the region and had
asked Prussian administrators to compile a list of trustworthy German farmers
who might be willing to oversee them. But as the new settlement commissioner,
Himmler would be granted supreme control over all agrarian settlement and the
redistribution of Polish farmland. Darré, then, was understandably upset when
he learned of Himmler's appointment, and he sought to secure some influence in
the resettlement program for himself.[73]

Darré wrote a letter to Lammers on 4 October, railing against Himmler and
his "uneconomic" plans for new Reich territory. "Settlement questions," he
stressed, "are not matters of inspiration or romance, but the soberest considerations of agrarian realities."[74] By "matters of inspiration and romance," Darré
was no doubt referring to Himmler's plans for SS administered settlements of
Wehrbauern (armed peasant farmers) along the new Russo-German frontier.[75]
Shortly thereafter, Darré and Himmler were told, presumably by Lammers on
Hitler's orders, to sit down together and work out a compromise. As a result, a
clause was inserted into the decree for the consolidation of German nationhood
that stated: "The tasks assigned to the RFSS with regard to the reorganization
of the German peasantry will be carried out by the Reich Minister for Food and
Agriculture following the general directives of the RFSS."[76] Nonetheless, Darré
never enjoyed much influence in the resettlement campaign. Despite the clause,
the Führer Directive as a whole gave Himmler more than enough power to make
him the veritable overlord of occupied Polish territory.

On 7 October 1939, Himmler's thirty-ninth birthday as it happened, Hitler
issued the "Order of the Führer and Reich Chancellor for the Consolidation of
German Nationhood," the secret order that constituted the formal basis for much
of the authority the RFSS would exercise in eastern Europe during the years to
come. The decree gave Himmler sweeping powers to accomplish a threefold task:
"(1) To repatriate reichs- and volksdeutsch residents abroad who are eligible for
permanent return to the Reich; (2) To eliminate the harmful influence of those
ethnically alien sections of the population that constitute a danger to the Reich
and the German Volksgemeinschaft; and (3) To form new German settlements
through the transfer of populations and, in particular, through resettling Reichs-
and Volksdeutschen returning from abroad."[77]

The scope of Himmler's new authority was vast. To carry out his duties, the RFSS was empowered to issue general orders and directives to all "existing authorities and institutions of the Reich, the states, and the municipalities, as well as other public bodies and existing settlement associations." And since the program would require the careful ordering of nationalities, Himmler was entitled "to assign certain dwelling places to the population[s] in question" and confiscate any property needed for German settlement in accordance with a law regarding the state seizure of private land for military purposes published 29 March 1935.[78] Adequate funding for the project was guaranteed: "The Reich Minister of Finance," the decree concluded, "will provide the Reichsführer-SS with the financial means necessary for putting the above measures into operation."[79] Himmler now had his mission in the East and the power and funding to realize it.

Hitler's long-standing habit of creating special positions and organizations to expedite the realization of specific political objectives had given birth to one of the most influential governmental posts in the history of the Third Reich. In effect, the decree for the consolidation of German nationhood granted Himmler not only the authority to manipulate any institution of the party and the state operating in conquered Polish territory but also the power to control the lives and property of millions of individuals, Poles, Jews, and Germans alike. In one of his first acts as chief of the resettlement program, Himmler gave himself the somewhat awkward title Reichskommissar für die Festigung deutschen Volkstums (RKFDV; Reich commissioner for the consolidation of German nationhood) and established an SS-Dienststelle of the same name (RKF) in Berlin, led by his reliable subordinate SS-Oberführer Ulrich Greifelt.[80] The RKF would coordinate the mosaic of individuals, organizations, and agencies involved in the crusade to Germanize the New East. These included VoMi, NSDAP agencies, provincial administrators, and a host of governmental ministries. Eventually, more than a dozen organizations fell, at least nominally, under the jurisdiction of Greifelt's office.

But Greifelt was able to exercise his authority for the most part only in the nominally constructive aspects of Germanization and resettlement. Destructive Germanization—"the elimination of those ethnically alien sections of the population that constitute a danger to the Reich and the German Volksgemeinschaft"[81]—was a task assigned to the Reichssicherheitshauptamt (RSHA), the vast Nazi security agency created by Himmler on 27 September 1939 and placed under the personal command of SS-Gruppenführer Reinhard Heydrich.[82] Under the RSHA umbrella, the ethnic cleansing of the new eastern provinces via organized evacuations to the East would soon begin in earnest.

THE TERRITORIAL ORGANIZATION OF OCCUPIED POLAND

The day after Hitler issued the decree for the consolidation of German nationhood, Germany officially annexed the western half of Poland. The so-called incorporated eastern territories embraced the former Imperial German provinces
of West Prussia and Posen, East Upper Silesia, and the Zichenau (Ciechanów)
region of north-central Poland. Hitler's order of 8 October, which sanctioned the
annexations, stated that the Volksdeutschen residing in these territories would
immediately become citizens of the Reich, whereas individuals of German or
kindred blood would become German nationals in accordance with certain provisions to be announced at a later date. The annexation order was supposed to
take effect on 1 November 1939, but it actually went into force on 26 October, the
day the military government in occupied Poland was dissolved and replaced by
civil administrations.[83]

East Upper Silesia and Zichenau were simply attached to preexisting German Gaue (Silesia and East Prussia, respectively); Hitler's 8 October decree created two new administrative districts, the Reichsgaue West Prussia and Posen.
Reichsgau West Prussia, soon renamed Danzig–West Prussia, encompassed the
territory of Friestadt Danzig, the Polish Corridor, and the Regierungsbezirk West
Prussia, a region detached from East Prussia and joined to the new Gau.[84] Several
Kreise (roughly meaning "counties") once part of the Prussian province of Posen,
among them Thorn and Bromberg, and two former districts of Russian Poland,
namely, Lipno and Rypin, were incorporated as well. Placed under the leadership of Gauleiter and Reichsstatthalter Albert Forster, Reichsgau Danzig–West
Prussia embraced 26,055 square kilometers of territory, 21,237 of which had previously been under Polish jurisdiction.[85] The population of the province in the
fall of 1939 was 2.15 million people, of whom 1.3 million were Poles, 817,000 were
Germans, and 23,000 were Jews.[86]

Reichsgau Posen was the largest and most economically significant of the
new eastern provinces. The Gau initially comprised most of the former Prussian
province of Posen, as well as a large swath of territory carved from what was
once Russian Poland. Several more districts of pre–World War I Russian Poland,
including the important textile center of Łódź, were attached to the province on
9 November 1939. The annexation of former Russian territory pushed the eastern
frontier of the Reich some 150 to 200 kilometers beyond the border of 1914 and
made Posen—at 43,943 square kilometers—the largest Reichsgau in Germany.

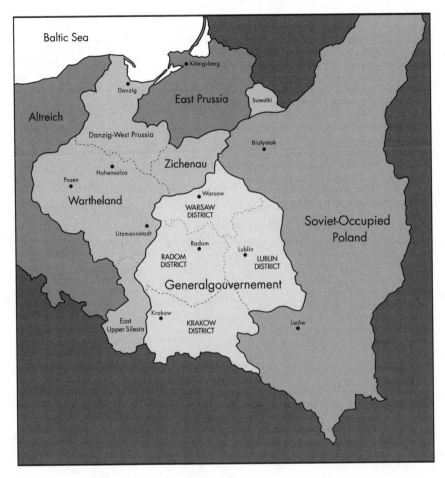

Map 1. Occupied Poland, 1939–1941

Renamed Wartheland in January 1940, the Gau had a population of 4.6 million, including 3.96 million Poles, 366,000 Jews, and 327,000 Germans.[87] Its senior official was Arthur Greiser, soon to be a major figure in the resettlement and deportation campaign.

The total area annexed to the Reich amounted to 91,974 square kilometers of territory populated by approximately 10 million people, of whom 8.9 million were Poles, 550,000 to 600,000 were Jews, and the remainder were primarily ethnic Germans.[88] Economically speaking, annexed western Poland was fully incorporated into Germany. On 20 November 1939, Hitler ordered that the *Zollgrenze* (customs border) of the Reich would extend to the eastern frontier of the incorporated territories, meaning that the German reichsmark would be the official currency of the entire region. (Beyond, in the far eastern part of Nazi-occupied Poland, the Polish zloty remained the legal tender.) But on the express wishes of RFSS Himmler, the *Polizeigrenze* (police border) would extend only to the prewar German border with Poland, the exceptions being Upper Silesia and the city of Danzig. Practically speaking, then, the new provinces remained foreign territory. They could neither be entered nor left without official administrative approval. This arrangement was most likely designed to prevent uncontrolled population movements between the Altreich, the incorporated territories, and Restpolen so as not to impede Himmler's tasks as resettlement commissioner. But it also significantly increased the overall power of the RFSS in the East, allowing him to perform his duties as RKFDV and chief of German police in the region beyond the normal confines of German civil law.[89]

Immediately to the east of the incorporated territories was the remaining part of Nazi-occupied Poland. Though not annexed, Restpolen was to be neither a protectorate nor an independent residual Polish state. On 12 October 1939, Hitler decreed that a German civil administration under the leadership of Dr. Hans Frank, a lawyer and Nazi Altkämpfer (old fighter) who held a number of influential posts within both the state and party hierarchies, would be installed in the region as soon as the military government was dissolved.[90] Designated the Generalgouvernement of the Occupied Polish Territories (after 8 July 1940, simply the Generalgouvernement), the region originally was 96,559 square kilometers in size and was home to approximately 12 million inhabitants in 1939, including roughly half of Poland's prewar population of 3 million Jews. It was initially subdivided into four administrative districts: Warsaw, Krakau, Radom, and Lublin. A fifth district, East Galicia, was attached in August 1941, increasing the size of the Generalgouvernement to 142,114 square kilometers and adding some 5 million new subjects—among them 550,000 Jews—to Frank's domain. From Wawel Castle in Krakau, the seat of medieval Polish kings, Generalgouverneur Frank lorded it over a realm that ultimately encompassed nearly 37 percent of the former Polish state.[91]

According to Hitler, who voiced his plans for the Generalgouvernement to Wilhelm Keitel on 17 October 1939, the region—though governed by Germans—was to be autonomous insofar as it would be neither a part of the German Reich nor an administrative district of the Reich. Rather, it was to be more or less a "pure colony," of use to Germany only as a dumping ground for deportees, a "reservoir" of seasonal workers, and a military buffer zone between the eastern provinces and the Soviet Union. Apart from these functions, the Generalgouvernement could, as far as Hitler was concerned, wither on the vine:

> It is not the task of the administration to turn [Restpolen] into a model province or a model state in accordance with the principles of German order; nor is it its task to reorganize the country economically and financially. The Polish intelligentsia must be prevented from forming itself into a new ruling class. The standard of living in the region should remain low; it is of use to us only as a reservoir of labor ... The accomplishment of this task will involve a hard Volkstumskampf which will not permit any legal restrictions. The methods will be incompatible with our other principles. The Generalgouverneur should give the Polish nation only minimal possibilities of life and preserve the basis for military security ... Any tendencies toward stabilizing the situation in [the Generalgouvernement] are to be suppressed. The *polnische Wirtschaft* must flourish.[92] The leadership of the region must make it possible for us to purify Reich territory of Jews and Polacks. [It may cooperate] with the new Reichsgaue only for resettlement purposes ... Shrewdness and severity in this ethnic struggle [will] spare us from having to go into battle again because of this country.[93]

"Corruption and epidemics in the Generalgouvernement," Hitler stressed, "would be the order of the day." The population of the region had but one purpose: to serve as work slaves for the Greater German Reich.[94]

One sentence, written in an unsigned memorandum regarding the 17 October Hitler-Keitel conference, summed up the overall goal of German policy in conquered Polish territory: "[Hitler] wants Greiser and Forster to report to him in ten years that Posen and West Prussia have become a flourishing German region, and Frank [to report] that the 'Devil's work' in the Generalgouvernement is finished."[95] Armed with this succinct Führer Directive, Greiser, Forster, and Frank, each with his own interpretation of Hitler's wishes, assumed control of their fiefdoms nine days later and soon began preparations to meet the ten-year deadline for the consummation of the Nazi New Order in the East.

An examination of the conception, gestation, and birth of Nazi resettlement plans reveals the ad hoc nature of the decision-making process within the National Socialist hierarchy. The genesis of the program, an operation that reflected the very core of Nazi racial ideology and lebensraum theory, was extraordinarily rapid, taking shape within six short weeks. Not yet the subject of concrete discussion when Molotov and Ribbentrop signed the agreement on 23 August 1939 that partitioned eastern Europe, a policy of ethnic redistribution emerged in rudimentary form during the course of the September campaign and by 7 October had become official policy, one that would require an enormous commitment of time, energy, and effort on the part of the Nazi regime. The key decisions leading to the decree for the consolidation of German nationhood were marked not by systematic planning or a careful calculation of racial and political objectives; they were, for the most part, a series of shoot-from-the-hip responses to recent diplomatic developments, many—if not most—of which transpired due not to the actions of Adolf Hitler and the Nazi hierarchy but rather as a result of Joseph Stalin's clever exploitation of Germany's obvious need to maintain cordial relations with the Soviet Union.

As historian Richard Breitman observes, "The whole scheme for the partition of Poland and racial stratification was haphazard and improvised, not the result of long-held convictions about the shape of the German empire in the East."[96] Though the dream of a purely German Eastern Marches certainly had deep historical roots, the actual program for resettlement and expulsion was, in a very real sense, thrown together at the last minute. It was, first and foremost, a makeshift synthesis of governmental initiatives geared toward the realization of immediate political objectives and the resolution of immediate political problems. It was essentially a by-product of the Nazi regime's need to safeguard Germany's eastern frontier, to establish security in conquered territory, to procure manpower for German industry and agriculture, and, not least, to eliminate the vast numbers of Jews and other undesirables residing in the new provinces of the Reich. But within a few weeks, an additional consideration—the housing and employment requirements of hundreds of thousands of immigrant Volksdeutschen—would become the overriding priority of Nazi ethnopoliticians and SS functionaries operating in annexed western Poland, and this concern, above all others, would determine the sequence, tempo, and character of the four major deportation actions carried out in the months to come.[97]

3

Pipe Dreams and Preparations

There may have been no blueprint for a program of ethnic redistribution in eastern Europe before the September campaign, but as soon as the smoke of battle had cleared, Poland became a playground for Nazi ethnopoliticians and supposed experts in the field of population and depopulation policy. As SS functionaries in western Poland geared up in October and November 1939 for the resettlement of the Baltic Volksdeutschen and the deportation of Poles and Jews, German macroplanners based at academic think tanks, NSDAP offices, and state agencies in the Reich proper concocted a number of elaborate schemes for the demographic and political consolidation of the new eastern territories.[1] Nazi ethnographic planning was—and remained—altogether decentralized, and the various schemes that emerged in the autumn of 1939 certainly differed in terms of scope and detail, reflecting the personal obsessions and specific bureaucratic agendas of their authors. Still, all were marked by a common völkisch spirit and an analogous set of racial-political suppositions and ideological objectives. Perhaps the most important of these early comprehensive plans for occupied Poland was the forty-page memorandum by Drs. Erhard Wetzel and Gerhard Hecht of the Racial Policy Office of the NSDAP entitled "The Question of the Treatment of the Population of the Former Polish Territories According to Racial-Political Points of View," issued on 25 November 1939.[2] The proposals introduced in this paper never became, as the framers intended, the guiding principles of National Socialist Polenpolitik, but the significance of the memo should not be underestimated. Wetzel's and Hecht's suggestions were, for the most part, in keeping with Hitler's various statements regarding German policy in conquered territory, and their report was disseminated far and wide, crossing not only the desks of the Reich governors and their district Oberpräsidenten in annexed western Poland but even that of SS-Sturmbannführer Albert Rapp, the SD officer initially in charge of the deportation of Poles and Jews from the Warthegau.[3] And although Himmler apparently brushed aside the NSDAP memorandum,[4] it most likely served as the basis for his own, strikingly similar essay of May 1940, "Some Thoughts on the Treatment of the Alien Population in the East."[5]

The NSDAP guidelines for Polenpolitik reflected the widespread euphoria of the late autumn of 1939 that followed the conquest of new lebensraum in the East. Now that Poland was soundly defeated and the "shackles of Versailles" eliminated, Wetzel and Hecht, like the authors of the other megalomaniacal programs for occupational policy developed at the time, were convinced that Germany at last had the freedom and opportunity to break the long-standing Polish grip on the Eastern Marches of the Reich. Only a "ruthless decimation" of the Polish national spirit and the Polish population, they argued, would guarantee the consolidation of German nationhood in annexed territory. Through a carefully orchestrated forced migration of peoples and a thorough Germanization of "suitable racial elements" among the native people of the East, they believed that the Nazi regime could eradicate, once and for all, the cultural, political, and demographic threat that *Polentum* (roughly meaning "Polish nationhood") represented to the German people and give the new Reichsgaue a truly lasting "German face."

The NSDAP memo presented a detailed analysis of the ethnonational structure of conquered Polish territory, as well as an overview of the practical problems associated with the institution of legal, economic, and cultural policy in the region. But the primary topics of discussion were questions of Germanization, resettlement, and expulsion. "The aim of German policy in the new Reich territories," proclaimed Wetzel and Hecht,

> must be the creation of a racially- and, therefore, intellectually-, psychologically-, ethnically-, and politically-unified German population. It follows from this that all non-Germanizable elements must be ruthlessly eliminated.
>
> This aim embraces *three interconnected tasks*:
>
> *First*, the complete and final Germanization of those sections [of the population] that appear suitable for it,
>
> *Second*, the deportation of all non-Germanizable foreign groups and
>
> *Third*, new settlement by Germans.[6]

The authors' call for the Germanization of certain sections of the Polish population was not meant to contradict Hitler's well-known maxim, voiced in *Mein Kampf*, that "Germanization can only be applied to *soil* and never to *people*."[7] A "genuine ethnic transformation" of an individual, they maintained, was possible only if the person in question was of German or Aryan-Teutonic origin. In other words, if the so-called Pole was not, in fact, a Pole but rather a German in terms of his or her racial constitution, the individual could, in certain circumstances, be "extracted" from the native population and "psychically absorbed" into German *Volkstum* (German nationhood)—re-Germanized, in effect, through linguistic, cultural, and educational initiatives. Of the estimated 6,336,000 alleged Poles in annexed territory,[8] Wetzel and Hecht calculated that approximately 1 million were candidates for re-Germanization. The remaining 5,336,000 Poles, as well as all Jews, all persons of Polish-Jewish mixed blood, and all others deemed racially undesirable, would have to be deported as soon as possible to the Generalgouvernement. The urgency of such an action became all the more apparent, they pointed out, when one considered the high birthrate among the Polish masses. In the years before the war, the Poles produced 30 to 32 children per 1,000 individuals yearly—or roughly 60,000 births per year—in the incorporated territories alone. "If the transfer of the Poles from Reich territory is not effected in a ruthless manner," Wetzel and Hecht warned, "it has to be feared that the Polish population will increase at more or less the same rate as before the war up until now."[9]

The authors' proposals regarding German resettlement in annexed territory followed the basic lines of Hitler's, as well as Himmler's, views on the matter. The establishment of a strip of German settlement, 150 to 200 kilometers wide, along the eastern frontier of the Reich provinces received first priority. This Ostwall would be populated by armed peasant farmers (Wehrbauern), who would stand as a defensive buffer against the Slavs to the east. Cleared of Poles and Jews, the cities and countryside behind the frontier strip would be gradually repopulated with Germans from the Reich and volksdeutsch immigrants from abroad. The standard of living for Germans in the incorporated territories, Wetzel and Hecht argued, should be higher than even that of Reich Germans:

> We have to grant our population [in the eastern provinces] a considerably larger living space and a broader basis for life [to ensure] the maintenance of a minimum of culture. Therefore, it is not at all necessary to move and settle an equal number of Germans in the East, at least for the time being, as the previous Polish population. The Germans in these areas, in the city as well as in the country, must have the feeling of a wider range of personal freedom for development. This will probably show in their increased birthrate.[10]

Protected by the noble Wehrbauern of the frontier strip and settled by this upwardly mobile and demographically expanding population of Germans, who had to consider themselves "the natural ruling caste in the East," the new provinces would soon become an integral part of the Reich and the "parade ground" of the National Socialist state.

According to Wetzel and Hecht, those Germans who had abandoned their property in the Prussian East and fled west after 1918 should take precedence over all other settler groups. Apart from these former residents of the eastern provinces, Nazi authorities, they declared, should give first priority to the resettlement of Baltic Germans, Volksdeutschen from the Generalgouvernement, and those from Soviet-occupied territory; the resettlement of other groups of ethnic Germans could proceed later.[11]

Baltic Germans, in fact, had been streaming into the Reich since mid-October, and the immigration of Volksdeutschen from other parts of the Soviet sphere of influence was to begin within a few weeks. On 15 October 1939, Germany concluded a resettlement treaty with Estonia, and three days later, the first ship of Estonian Volksdeutschen set sail for Germany.[12] Similar treaties with Latvia and the Soviet Union followed on 30 October and 3 November, respectively.[13] By 21 December 1939, the date the last of eighty-seven transports of Baltic Germans left Riga, 61,934 Reichsdeutschen and Volksdeutschen from Estonia and Latvia had answered the "call of the Führer."[14] An additional 128,047 ethnic Germans from Soviet-occupied Volhynia, Galicia, and the Narev region of eastern Poland would arrive in Reich territory, primarily via wagon caravans, by the end of January 1940.[15]

The agency responsible for processing these incoming Volksdeutschen was the Einwandererzentralstelle (EWZ; Central Immigration Office).[16] Established by Heydrich on 13 October 1939 and placed under the command of the SD officer SS-Sturmbannführer Martin Sandberger, the EWZ was originally based in Gdynia (renamed Gotenhafen by some romantic Nazi), the port of entry for the majority of Baltic Germans. Though officially under the jurisdiction of the RSHA, Sandberger's office was staffed by representatives from a number of governmental ministries, including the Ministries of the Interior, Health, Labor, Food and Agriculture, Finance, and Transport. Working alongside RuSHA agents, who conducted "racial screenings" of the immigrants to confirm their true ethnicity, these clerks and bureaucrats all collaborated in the naturalization of the volksdeutsch settlers.[17] According to Himmler's original plans, NSDAP Gauleiters and provincial officials were to arrange for the reception and care of the ethnic Germans, providing them with temporary housing while they awaited resettlement.[18] However, in Reichsgau Danzig–West Prussia, Himmler faced a major source of vexation, the obstinate Gauleiter Albert Forster.

Forster was no racial fanatic and no fan of the RFSS. Of Heinrich Himmler, perhaps the foremost racial ideologue in the Nazi hierarchy, Forster once remarked, "If I looked like Himmler, I would not talk about race!"[19] Himmler had to take such jabs: Forster had long been one of Hitler's close associates, joining the NSDAP in 1923 and receiving his commission as the Gauleiter of the Free City of Danzig in 1930. As a Gauleiter, he was responsible to Hitler alone and considered Danzig–West Prussia his inviolable domain. He refused to take orders from the RFSS and did his best to thwart resettlement efforts in his Gau. When the first shipload of Estonian Volksdeutschen arrived on 20 October, Forster refused to accommodate them, forcing the RKF to reroute the transport to Stettin in Pomerania. The Gauleiter complained that the Baltic Germans were, for the most part, too old; he needed vigorous young workers in his fiefdom, not invalids. But after extensive telephone negotiations with Himmler, Forster finally agreed to grant some Baltic settlers temporary accommodations in Danzig–West Prussia for the 1939–1940 winter. SS-Gruppenführer Richard Hildebrandt, who in his capacity as the Höhere SS- und Polizeiführer (HSSPF; higher SS and police leader) of Danzig–West Prussia served as Himmler's RKF deputy in the province, eventually managed to settle 12,000 Balts in Forster's territory but only with great difficulty.[20]

Largely due to Forster's intransigence, the main office of the EWZ was relocated in November 1939 to Posen, the capital of Wartheland, and the majority of the Baltic German immigrants quickly followed. There, Himmler found a senior Nazi official much more sympathetic to the RKF program: Arthur Greiser. In the months to come, it was Greiser's domain that emerged as the geographic focal point of volksdeutsch resettlement, as well as the hotbed of ethnic cleansing in the incorporated eastern territories.

LAND DER ZUKUNFT: THE WARTHEGAU

Named for the Warthe River, which ran through the heart of the province, Reichsgau Wartheland was—and as the modern-day Polish region of Wielkapolska still is—"big sky country," predominantly flat, dotted by small lakes, and crisscrossed by narrow, tree-lined country lanes. The province encompassed the major cities of Posen (Poznań), Gnesen (Gniezno), Hohensalza (Inowrocław), and Litzmannstadt (Łódź),[21] but by no means was it an urban Gau. Surrounding the countless small farming communities were fields of rye, wheat, potatoes, and sugar beets, and the region's industrial base was primarily related to agricultural activity. In the western part of the district, most farms were of substantial size, averaging 5 to 50 hectares, but in the east, relatively tiny homesteads, 48 percent of which were less than 6 hectares in total area, were the norm.[22] The rationalization and modernization of agriculture in the Warthegau, particularly in the eastern Kreise, remained the principal goal of Nazi economic policy in the province throughout the entire history of the occupation. Wartheland was to be a land of farmers, the breadbasket of the Greater German Reich.

Its leader, Arthur Greiser, was determined to make his fiefdom the *Mustergau* (model Gau) of National Socialism, the showplace of the Nazi New Order in the East. His ambition to make Wartheland a model Gau demanded the ruthless Germanization of the region, as well as massive efforts geared toward economic rationalization and the reconstruction of the district's basic infrastructure. These were to be no easy tasks, as Greiser himself readily admitted. Writing in 1942, he noted that when he took control of the Gau, the province was utterly devastated: telephone and telegraph lines were down, all bridges were destroyed, railways were in disrepair, and good roads were virtually nonexistent.[23] Hitler, for his part, was initially shocked by the state of affairs in the Warthegau. In March 1940, he told Benito Mussolini that "the most terrible conditions had prevailed [in Posen], and that there had often been moments in Poland when he had asked himself whether or not he would do better to turn back and just leave the wretched country and its even more wretched people to themselves."[24]

War damage and an underdeveloped infrastructure were not the only problems Greiser confronted. He recounted that upon his arrival in Wartheland in the autumn of 1939, he found no existing administrative basis—no personnel or organizational apparatus on which he could rely. Everything had to be created from scratch. This situation, he contended, made his province unique, unlike the other incorporated territories where preexisting German administrations only had to step in and begin governing.[25] The Nazi mission in Wartheland was further complicated by the fact that the district encompassed both former Prussian and former *Kongresspolen* (Congress Poland) territory,[26] the latter having, Greiser asserted, "a fundamentally different völkisch-economic face" than the western half of the Gau.[27] Indeed, as one National Socialist economist later observed, at the time of Wartheland's annexation, "the Polish spirit, Volk, and economy pre-

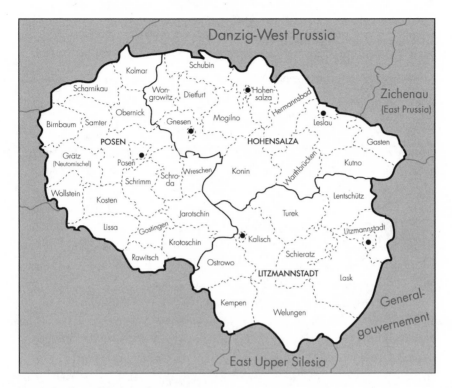

Map 2. Reichsgau Wartheland, 1941

vailed" in the eastern Kreise of the province, "creating the conditions known as the polnische Wirtschaft."[28] Former *Kongress* territory, moreover, contained the great bulk of the province's Jews, most of whom lived in Litzmannstadt and its environs. Its annexation increased the "undesirable" Jewish population of the Warthegau fourfold, swelling the number of Jews to be deported from the district by approximately 230,000.[29] The presence of so many Jews, combined with an ethnic Polish population of 3.96 million, made the Germanization of the district all the more difficult.

Despite these complications, many in the Nazi hierarchy believed that the incorporation of former Kongress territory into Wartheland was justifiable and altogether necessary for a number of reasons, among them the exigencies of volksdeutsch resettlement. As VoMi chief Werner Lorenz argued in November 1940, Posen alone could not possibly accommodate all of the tens of thousands of predominantly urban-dwelling Baltic German immigrants; therefore, the city of

Litzmannstadt was also needed for their resettlement.[30] Economic considerations also came into play. Litzmannstadt was a major industrial and textile center, one of the most significant in eastern Europe. Its annexation, coupled with that of Kutno, an important transport hub to the north of the city where five rail lines intersected, would go far to reinforce Wartheland's economic base and greatly benefit the German war economy in general.[31]

Walter Geisler, a German professor of geography who assumed a prominent position at the Reichsuniversität Posen following its foundation in April 1941,[32] later reiterated the economic advantages of this territorial addition and emphasized its military-strategic necessity as well. The former Prussian province of Posen, he maintained, had included an "unfavorable indentation" in its eastern border. The existence of this "unnatural frontier" meant that German military and economic traffic between East Prussia and Upper Silesia had been forced to take a noticeable detour to the west. Shifting the Wartheland-Generalgouvernement border to the east not only rectified this problem but also corrected Berlin's geographic position. Between 1919 and 1939, the German capital was only 160 kilometers from the Polish border, and even during the Imperial period, it lay far too close to the Russian frontier. But now that Germany had eradicated this unnatural frontier and had at last secured a "unified *Wartheraum* [Warthe space]," "the eastern region of the Reich," Geisler proudly declared, "has received a harmonious form."[33]

Though annexed western Poland was to be colonized by German settlers, by no means did the Nazi regime view the region as colonial territory. "In the word 'colonization,'" wrote the agricultural specialist Wilhelm Zoch in early 1940, "lays the concept of a demarcation between the Altreich and the new land." Such thinking, he stated bluntly, constituted "a crime to the German future." The new eastern provinces were to be completely and inexorably integrated into the Reich. These territories, Zoch contended, were not seized for imperialistic reasons; they were not meant simply to be administered as a colony by Germany and exploited economically for the Reich. Rather, they were conquered and annexed for the survival and demographic expansion of the German Volk: "It is not a question of widening the power of a rich and sated people, but rather a new conquest of urgently needed Lebensraum for a land-hungry people who otherwise would become stunted and waste away in the narrowness of their previous borders."[34]

If this lebensraum were to be permanently secured for the German people, it was not to be treated merely as a colonial appendage of the Reich. On the contrary, the Nazis held that the eastern territories were to become an essential and inseparable part of Germany, just as "German" as the Ruhr or the Rhineland. A comprehensive Germanization of the region required the physical presence of an overwhelming German majority, and volksdeutsch resettlement was to serve as the primary means to this end.

The hub of ethnic German resettlement in the incorporated territories was Reichsgau Wartheland. By mid-1941, less than two years after the launch of the program, some 300,000 Volksdeutschen from the Baltic Republics, the General-gouvernement, Volhynia, Galicia, Bessarabia, and Bukovina already resided in the Gau, though many, if not most, languished in VoMi camps awaiting placement in former Polish and Jewish homes. Greiser, at least publicly, welcomed the arrival of the immigrants. Since there was "no base of German people" in Wartheland, Germans from all over the Reich and eastern Europe were needed for "pioneer work" in his province. But within the various volksdeutsch splinter groups extracted from the East lurked a potential impediment to the creation of a model Gau. Their members were accustomed neither to the ways of the Reich nor to the regimentation and discipline of the Nazi Volksgemeinschaft. Greiser therefore envisioned Wartheland as a melting pot of immigrant groups, not in the multiethnic sense of the United States but rather as a melting pot of Germans and only Germans. Within his Gau, the immigrants would shed their past traditions and habits and undergo a process of cultural and ideological amalgamation (*Verschmelzung*): they would be coordinated as quickly as possible into the "community of the people" and unified into a homogenous working society. Through this process, the Warthegau melting pot would become, in Greiser's words, "the parade ground of practical National Socialism."[35]

But not all German soldiers were welcome on the parade ground. As RKF office chief Ulrich Greifelt asserted, "only the best" Germans could become pioneers in the East.[36] Greiser concurred wholeheartedly. In a speech delivered during the first year of his tenure as Gauleiter, he stated: "The East can only use as leading men true warriors and pioneers who are entirely consumed by their task. He who measures his position only in terms of material value has not at all grasped the fateful importance of the German East and its task for the Greater German Reich. This task: To organize this space in the East so that it receives a German face forever."[37]

The creation of a lasting German face for Wartheland necessitated the fusion of Blut und Boden. Indeed, the final goal of resettlement, Greifelt declared, "can only be the convergence of inherited German soil and the best German people into an inseparable union ... People and soil, *Volkstum* and *Raum*, belong together."[38] As many a Nazi saw it, the "best" Germans—those most suited to be trailblazers in the incorporated territories—were peasant farmers, the "life source" (*Lebensquell*) of the Nordic race.[39]

Since the regime's major economic task in the Warthegau was to make the district the *Kornkammer* (granary) of the Reich, farmers would naturally play the leading roles. During the years of the Second Reich, the province had been the breadbasket of Germany, and top Nazis all agreed it was to become so again.[40] But this would require a great deal of initiative on the part of the Nazi lords and German peasants of the region. "The fact that the Pole has used only ten percent of his soil value says absolutely nothing," Göring pontificated on 9 September 1939: "where he has used only ten percent, we will soon have use of one hundred percent."[41] If Germany were to enjoy the full economic potential, agricultural and otherwise, of its new territory, the region would have to be organized in such . a way that it became "a rich land of farmers and children, the granary of the Reich, and the blood source of the nation."[42] The small farmer was seen as the keystone of this New Order. Indeed, at least ostensibly if not in fact, a Blut and Boden mentality, propagated by Reich Peasant Führer Walther Darré since the early 1930s, guided German rural settlement and agricultural activity in the East. Theodor Oberländer, the former leader of the Bund Deutscher Osten (League of Germans in the East), an agricultural specialist, and outspoken proponent of "blood and soil" theory, argued in 1940 that one only had to study history to see that the survival, or "victory," of a people demanded the preservation of its racial purity and biological strength. For this, a nation needed a broad agrarian lower class with a strong bond to the soil and a deep feeling of community. After all, he wrote, "a people is like a forest ... it can only stand firm from its roots." Throughout history, he continued, nations had conquered empires and expanded their borders, "but all was lost if the plow did not follow [the sword], and the farmer did not grow with the soil." Oberländer's message was clear: permanent conquest was contingent upon settlement, above all on the settlement of a "soil-based, biologically strong Bauerntum [farming community]."[43]

In its own right, the creation of an agrarian utopia in the East could be considered a constructive or positive endeavor, but as the Nazis understood their mission, the garden could not be planted without pulling some weeds. Walter Geisler put it this way: "If one wants to construct, he must begin with a cleansing action, meaning that [everything] that does not fit into the new plan or opposes it must be destroyed or removed."[44] In no way did the Poles—"who live and think true to their Slavic way"[45]—fit into the new plan. Their very presence constituted a threat to Germany's grip on its newly conquered lebensraum, the purity of German blood, and the biological vigor of the German Volk. Therefore, a clean division between Germans and Poles was deemed absolutely necessary. The racial theorist Egon Leuschner of the Racial Policy Office of the NSDAP argued that a complete separation of the races was imperative not only from a völkisch standpoint but also due to matters of security, political interests, and German national pride: "The Pole, who from the musty sense of his racial inferiority, hates no other people more than the Germans, is our enemy, with whom we will never again enter into a friendly relationship."[46] Oberländer felt the same way. The Poles would have to go, for Poles and Germans could not live together in peace; their respective interests would forever remain in conflict. The assimilation of Poles was to be unconditionally rejected. If a program of assimilation were pursued, "it would contradict our racial principles, our national principles, and the meaning of our fight for new Lebensraum."[47] Another Nazi thinker pointed out that Hitler himself had said as much: "Any attempt to assimilate a foreign people into the master race through the adoption of the German language and German culture by a people of the lower race is, according to the Führer's view, not Germanization, but rather 'de-Germanization.'"

The inevitable blood mixing that would occur as a result of linguistic and cultural Germanization would only weaken the völkisch strength and biological value of the higher race.[48] Since assimilation was obviously not an option and since the Poles, with their aspirations for a nation-state of their own, would always be at loggerheads with the Germans, the Polish population of the incorporated territories would have to be eliminated, completely removed so that the German Volk could realize its full potential and consummate the long-held Nazi dream of an Aryan Garden of Eden in the East.

Though the National Socialists ultimately failed to realize their vision of a purely German Wartheland, they pursued it vigorously during the first nineteen months of the occupation. A comprehensive demographic reorganization of the Warthegau demanded resolute and brutal action, and resolute and brutal action against the non-German natives of the region quickly became the norm. Arthur Greiser would later admit (rather cryptically) that "we have in the Warthegau a somewhat different method of leadership than in the Altreich."[49] Indeed, by the time he wrote these words in 1942, most of the 366,000 Jews who had lived in Wartheland before the war were either dead, deported, or wasting away in the confines of the Litzmannstadt ghetto, and some 300,000 Poles had been driven from their homes and "evacuated" to the Generalgouvernement. Thousands of others had lost their homes but remained in the Gau as workers. An examination of the decisions and orders leading to the first wave of organized deportations follows. It concentrates on October and November 1939, the period in which "wild evacuations" were terminated in favor of a more orderly approach to destructive Germanization. By the end of the period in question, Nazi deportation efforts, initially aimed at the incorporated territories as a whole, had narrowed to Greiser's Wartheland, the Mustergau of the Third Reich.

FROM RKFDV ANORDNUNG 1/II TO THE RSHA 1.NAHPLAN

Unauthorized deportations of Poles and Jews from the incorporated territories began in mid-September 1939. These so-called wild evacuations were carried out primarily by regional authorities, local police, and detachments of the Volksdeutsche Selbstschutz (essentially, ethnic German vigilante groups), all operating on their own initiative, not in accordance with orders from above. Such actions were in no way connected to volksdeutsch resettlement or the mission of the RKF;[50] rather, they were driven largely by revenge and self-interest. With the Polish army on the run and a German victory all but certain, local Germans felt that the time was ripe to avenge the years of misery they had allegedly suffered at the hands of the Poles. The chaotic situation in the East gave them the opportunity to cleanse their turf of non-Germans, on the one hand, and the chance to seize particularly desirable Polish and Jewish property, on the other. During this period, evacuees were driven from their homes, marched or transported east, and simply dumped in the Generalgouvernement. No preparations of any kind had been made for their reception; they were left homeless and penniless to fend for themselves.

For the most part, wild evacuations emanated from Reichsgau Danzig–West Prussia. According to one Polish historian, many small cities and towns in the province lost up to 90 percent of their Polish and Jewish population as a result of these actions.[51] The bulk of the deportees, however, came from the major port city of Gdynia on the Baltic coast. Between 12 September and 26 October 1939, approximately 50,000 people—44 percent of the city's population—were expelled. At first "wild," this specific operation was sanctioned, in effect, on 11 October when Himmler ordered that Gdynia was to be cleared of Poles to create space for the Baltic Germans, due to begin arriving the following week. The population of Posen was also targeted in this directive.[52] Though the evacuations from Gdynia

SS-Gruppenführer Wilhelm
Koppe, the Höhere SS- und
Polizeiführer of Wartheland.
(Bundesarchiv-Berlin)

and Posen had, as of 11 October, become official as opposed to wild, unsanctioned deportations from annexed western Poland continued, primarily from Forster's district in the north. Finally, on 26 October, the day the German military government in Poland was dissolved and the civil administration installed, Himmler ordered a halt to all evacuations from Danzig–West Prussia and announced that he would personally inform all concerned when population transfers could resume.[53] Transports of Poles and Jews from the new provinces would soon roll again, but they would originate not from Danzig–West Prussia but only from Wartheland, the destination of the vast majority of volksdeutsch immigrants.[54]

    With the war over and the civil administration in place, the Nazi regime now took steps to rein in undisciplined forces such as the Selbstschutz and bring order to the evacuations.[55] On 30 October, Himmler issued RKFDV Anordnung 1/II, his first major directive as settlement commissioner. He ordered the expulsion of all Jews from the incorporated territories; all Congress Poles from Danzig–West Prussia;[56] and an undetermined number of particularly hostile, anti-German Poles from the new Reich provinces. The HSSPF of each province was responsible for the deportations from his jurisdiction. This initial phase of "organized" evacuations was to be concluded by the end of February 1940.[57]

Himmler's directive stated no figures concerning the number of individuals to be evacuated, but in a report submitted to Hans Frank on 31 October, SS-Brigadeführer Bruno Streckenbach, the Befehlshaber der Sicherheitspolizei und des SD (commander of Sipo and the SD) in the district of Krakau, placed their numbers at approximately 1 million. He did not distinguish between Poles and Jews.[58] It is probable that Streckenbach included 550,000 Jews, more or less the total number residing in the incorporated territories after the borders of Wartheland were finalized on 9 November 1939, in his calculation. In fact, the figure of 550,000 Jewish deportees appeared in an undated memorandum, signed by Rudolf Creutz, an SS business manager working for the RKF. Judging by its content, it was probably issued before Himmler's 30 October directive, though we cannot be certain.[59] But since neither Himmler nor Streckenbach knew at this time whether the city of Litzmannstadt with its 230,000 Jews would be annexed to the Warthegau, it is possible that the 1 million evacuees included far more Poles than is commonly acknowledged.[60] Whatever the case, plans for such an extensive *Judenaktion* would soon fall by the wayside, as would Himmler's immodest deportation objectives in general.

Immediately after Himmler issued Anordnung 1/II, the leadership of the Warthegau began preparing for the resettlement and deportation campaign. On 1 November, Arthur Greiser set up a *Gaukommissariat* (Gau commission) to arrange for the reception of the Baltic Germans immigrants. Fourteen representatives from various Gau ministries and departments sat on the committee, including officials from Transport, Labor, Finance, and Agriculture, as well as SS-Standartenführer Ernst Damzog, the Inspekteur (supervisor) of Sipo and the SD in Posen.[61] A report of unknown provenance issued the same day defined the committee's mission for the immediate future. The RFSS, it stated, had decreed that 7,500 Baltic Volksdeutschen had to be accommodated in Posen by 5 December 1939. But since preparations for the evacuations necessary to accommodate these individuals were not yet complete, Polish evictees would be assembled in a transit camp to be established on the site of a former munitions factory in Głowno, a suburb on the eastern edge of the city. There, they would be detained until they could be deported to the Generalgouvernement. The report suggested that the camp should have a capacity of 5,000 inmates. Evictions, the author stated, should proceed as follows: Poles were to be roused from their sleep at five or six in the morning, given one hour to pack, and then escorted to the camp, which would be guarded by officers of the Schutzpolizei (Schupo; Municipal Police). Evictees could retain no more than fifty zloty per person; since animals could not be taken along, all pets were to be shot on the spot! Ernst Damzog was personally responsible for approving the arrest warrants of all evacuees, among whom "all those persons designated 'enemies of the state'" were to be included. The first wave of evictions, the report concluded, would take place the following Sunday (5 November); the arrest quota for this initial house-clearing action was 100 to 150 Polish families.[62]

Christened "Lager Glowno" by the Nazis, the transit camp established on the outskirts of Posen was by far the largest in Wartheland during the first few months of the deportation campaign. The first contingent of Polish evictees, 217 people, arrived in Glowno on schedule on 5 November, and another 222 entered the camp two days later. The detainees were housed in three massive, two-story barracks with cement floors, built by a company of Wehrmacht engineers. Straw was enclosed within wooden frames to provide bedding. A lavatory, two field kitchens, a supply building, and a clinic were also on the site. But even though Lager Glowno was up and running on schedule, there were a number of serious problems in the camp. According to an 8 November report on camp conditions, more than a few individuals interned at Glowno had not been earmarked for evacuation; they had merely been visiting targeted persons, often their relatives, at the time the police arrived and thus were arrested along with their hosts.[63] The author of the report also complained that the camp was woefully lacking in basic supplies. Allowed to bring along no more than they could carry, the evictees had no opportunity to procure personal necessities such as soap, blankets, or toilet paper. These materials, as well as disinfectants, heaters, washtubs, showers, and lighting, were urgently needed. Furthermore, the camp possessed only eight table settings for 489 inmates; people were forced to eat, he said, out of empty cigarette packs. To remedy these problems, he suggested that a canteen be erected within the camp or, if this were not possible, that "reliable inmates" should be allowed to leave Glowno to purchase supplies for the others.[64] Whether these proposals were adopted or the requested supplies delivered, the record does not state.

Meanwhile, high-level Nazi functionaries met in Krakau on 8 November to discuss the forthcoming evacuations. Participants included the higher SS and police leaders of the eastern provinces and the Generalgouvernement, as well as SS-Brigadeführer Bruno Streckenbach, at that time responsible for the central planning of deportations. After opening remarks by the meeting's chairman, HSSPF Friedrich-Wilhelm Krüger of the Generalgouvernement, the podium was turned over to Streckenbach. Streckenbach explained that the need to accommodate the Baltic Germans then arriving in the incorporated territories, as well as the 150,000 Volksdeutschen who would soon begin moving west from Soviet-occupied eastern Poland, meant that "the resettlement and evacuation [measures] must be accomplished on a different basis than the Reichsführer-SS and Chief of German Police had initially intended." Though the goal of 1 million expulsions by 28 February 1940 demanded by Himmler remained on the planning table, the central priority of the operation was no longer strictly one of ethnic cleansing but rather the provision of housing and employment for the incoming ethnic Germans. This task was now to take precedence over all other considerations. The participants agreed that the inhabitants of Litzmannstadt, including its 230,000 Jews, would not be included in the evacuations, since it had not yet been determined whether the city would be incorporated into the Warthegau or the Generalgouvernement. They did, however, continue to work with the figure of 1 million deportees, suggesting that far more Poles than previously anticipated would have to be expelled to meet the quota. The transport of evacuees, scheduled to begin in mid-November, would be carried out by the *Reichsbahn* (the rail system of the Altreich and annexed territory); there would be no transport by road, since neither the guards nor the supplies necessary for a long march were available. Lastly, all Poles remaining in the annexed regions after the conclusion of the action, the officials agreed, would be examined to determine if they were in fact Poles or Volksdeutschen and whether they were "unwanted" (that is, whether they were believed to constitute a threat to the German ethnic community). The removal of these additional unwanted Poles would be completed by the beginning of 1941.[65]

By decree of Arthur Greiser, "the party member solely responsible" for the central management of all party and state authorities involved in evacuations from and resettlement in Reichsgau Wartheland was HSSPF Wilhelm Koppe.[66] Born in Hildesheim in 1896, Koppe was a good man for the job. He was highly intelligent, well educated (fluent in both French and English), and possessed a scientific mind. During World War I, he served in an engineer battalion and became an expert in mines, explosives, and bridge construction. After the war, he earned his keep as a self-employed grocery and tobacco salesman. He joined the NSDAP in 1930 and the SS in 1932. Described as "a model National Socialist in words and deeds," Koppe was active as an SS-Gruppenführer at the SD Main Office in Berlin between 1936 and 1939, but the RFSS had bigger plans for him. On 26 October 1939, he was named higher SS and police leader of the Warthegau, becoming, in effect, Himmler's personal deputy in the new province. As HSSPF and an official representative of the RKFDV, Koppe played an eminent role in the Germanization and de-Polonization of his jurisdiction.[67]

On 10 November, two days after the Krakau meeting, Koppe issued a directive calling for the expulsion of 200,000 Poles and 100,000 Jews from Wartheland by 28 February 1940.[68] As the Litzmannstadt region and its 230,000 Jews had been officially incorporated into the Gau the day before,[69] Koppe's figures represented a significant departure from Himmler's orders of 30 October, which had demanded the deportation of *all* Jews from the incorporated eastern territories. But we must keep in mind that Koppe's directive was based on the agreement reached in Krakau *not* to include the population of Litzmannstadt in the forthcoming action, Himmler's earlier wishes notwithstanding.

The purpose of the 300,000 evacuations, Koppe declared, was the "cleansing and safeguarding of the new German regions," on the one hand, and "the creation of living and work places for the immigrant Volksdeutschen," on the other; interests that did not correspond to these dual objectives were of no consequence. The security of annexed territory, he maintained, could be ensured only "if no criminal or political Polish elements at all are still present." Therefore, along with the Jews, "all members of the intelligentsia without consideration of their political attitude" and "all known politically active individuals" were to be deported. Local authorities, namely, *Oberbürgermeister* (mayors) and *Landräte* (county commissioners), were to identify "suspect" persons in their jurisdictions and submit a report to Sipo and the SD by 18 November. These officials were also responsible for organizing evictions in their districts and establishing transit camps to accommodate the deportees before their transport to the Generalgouvernement. All Jews in the Warthegau, with the exception of those residing in Litzmannstadt, and at least 2,000 Poles from each *Landkreis* (rural county) were to be expelled. Koppe stressed that local officials had to take immediate steps to replace economically vital individuals whose deportation would cause problems for the remaining population. Still, a deportee's membership in an important occupation group was in no case to constitute grounds for a disruption in the operation. Economic considerations were secondary: "Far more decisive," Koppe insisted, "is the political moment and the necessity to create adequate housing and work places for the volks- and reichsdeutsch settlers."[70]

The following day, HSSPF Koppe established two special bureaus based in Posen to coordinate resettlements and evacuations in the Gau. One, the Staff for the Local Housing and Occupational Accommodation of the Baltic and Volhynian Germans, was placed under the command of Dr. Albert Derichsweiler, also the leader of Greiser's Gaukommissariat for resettlement. The other, the Staff for the Evacuation of Poles and Jews to the Generalgouvernement, was led by SS-Sturmbannführer Albert Rapp, the chief of the SD-Leitabschnitt (roughly meaning "lead section" or "main office") in Posen. All offices of the party and state, Koppe decreed, were at the disposal of these two staffs. The RFSS-RKFDV, he asserted, expected everyone's full cooperation in the "great historical task of the consolidation of German nationhood in Reichsgau Wartheland."[71]

SS-Sturmbannführer Rapp was born in Schorndorf, Württemberg, in 1908. He held a law degree and had worked as a junior barrister and assessor before joining the SS and SD in 1937. Judged by his superiors as a good party comrade who consistently distinguished himself through his extraordinary diligence, love of action, and organizational talent, Rapp quickly rose through the ranks of the security establishment. He served in Einsatzgruppe VI during Operation Tannenberg, and after the mobile death squads were made stationary on 6 October 1939, he assumed leadership of Posen's SD Main Office. Until May of the following year, Rapp would direct all evacuations from the Warthegau. His Staff for the Evacuation of Poles and Jews, which functioned as the nerve center of Wartheland's deportation system, was renamed the Umwandererzentralstelle in April 1940.[72]

Koppe's secret updated orders concerning deportations from Wartheland issued on 12 November made clear that the forthcoming operation would focus primarily on the larger cities of the Gau where housing and employment opportunities were needed for the predominantly urban-dwelling Baltic Germans. The population of Litzmannstadt was now included in the evacuations. Still, the target figures of 200,000 Polish and 100,000 Jewish deportees remained in effect. Koppe's new directive called for the expulsion of 30,000 Poles and approximately the same number of Jews from Litzmannstadt, 35,000 Poles and all Jews from Posen, 2,300 Poles and all Jews from Gnesen, 2,300 Poles and all Jews from Hohensalza, and at least 2,000 Poles from each of the remaining Kreise in the province.[73] He ordered that plans for the evacuation of each Pole had to be prepared on an individual basis. Indiscriminate mass clearings of city sections or streets was to be discontinued, he said, since through such actions, nondangerous Poles were removed and their labor lost. To ensure that Wartheland's economy continued to run smoothly despite the evacuation measures, the HSSPF suggested

SS-Sturmbannführer Albert Rapp,
the leader of the Staff for the
Evacuation of Poles and Jews to the
Generalgouvernement, renamed the
Umwandererzentralstelle in April
1940. (Bundesarchiv-Berlin)

that local authorities work closely with commercial and industrial leaders in their
districts. Economic considerations were now beginning to move to the forefront
of deportation planning, despite rhetoric to the contrary.[74]

Armed with Koppe's various directives, Rapp and his subordinates in the
Staff for the Evacuation of Poles and Jews to the Generalgouvernement worked
feverishly to prepare for the operation, concentrating particularly on evacuation
procedures and the identification of allegedly dangerous Poles who should be
deported. "It remains decisive," wrote Rapp on 16 November,

> to evacuate every Pole who on the basis of his intellectual ability, his political influence,
> or his economic power could represent an obstruction to the penetration of Deutschtum
> in the individual Kreise ... The goal is to remove not only the Polish intelligentsia of the
> past, but also to prevent the formation of a new Polish ruling class. The sequence of the
> evacuations is to be determined by the degree of danger [the individual represents].[75]

A survey of anti-German Poles was to be carried out by the SD with the cooperation of regional Sipo offices and local civilian authorities. Crucial to the goals
of the operation was the determination of a suspect individual's political stance

as of 1 September 1939; later declarations of loyalty to Germany were to be ignored. Rapp presented a list of twenty-three Polish political parties, including the staunchly anti-German Westmarkverein (Polish Western Marches Association) and the Grosspolnischer Aufständischenverband (Greater Polish Insurgent Society),[76] whose members were to be deported without exception. Evacuees would also include writers, artists, and journalists, as well as all "criminal elements" such as beggars, prostitutes, and the "work-shy" (*Arbeitsscheue*).[77] Though certainly deemed dangerous, the Catholic clergy, Rapp declared, would not be expelled during the first wave of deportations. Rather, priests, monks, and nuns were to be interned in a monastery and evacuated all at once in a special action to be carried out at a later date.[78] "A consideration of administrative and economic factors can follow," Rapp insisted in the same memo, "only insofar as it does not affect the objectives of the operation." But he did concede that such considerations could affect the sequence of the transports, implying that the deportation of administratively and economically vital individuals could be postponed until the last phase of the action.[79] Moreover, even though he stated unequivocally in another memorandum penned 16 November that "the political goal of the evacuation measures allows no consideration of purely economic or administrative special requests," he did acknowledge that "the possibility exists" to defer the expulsion of those Poles deemed economically or administratively essential until they could be replaced by Germans.[80] Organized deportations had yet to begin, but the ideological objectives of the deportation program were already coming into conflict with hard economic realities. Rapp would soon back off even further from his stringent guidelines for evacuation.

Problems outside the realm of economics and administration also vexed the SS functionaries. A relatively high percentage of leading Poles had either moved within Wartheland or fled beyond the borders of the Gau during the past several weeks, making the apprehension of these individuals difficult if not impossible. On 13 November, Koppe had issued orders prohibiting Poles and Jews from moving from their original homes in order to facilitate their arrest and expulsion,[81] but this did nothing to aid in the capture of those already at large. Rapp therefore suggested that along with deportation lists, a "wanted persons" list should be compiled and that a small commission of officials familiar with police records regarding missing Poles and Jews should be set up and placed at the disposal of his staff.[82] The record does not state whether Rapp's proposals were implemented at that time, but in the summer of 1940, soon after he had been replaced as deportation chief in the Warthegau, a special search office was established within the UWZ system to track down and apprehend Poles who had fled the police at the time of their eviction. The results of the search office's efforts would be mediocre at best.

These problems—as well as others[83]—aside, it was economics that loomed particularly large in the minds of Nazi officials in Wartheland as November 1939 drew to a close. On the afternoon of 23 November, a conference was held in Posen to address the economic questions associated with the deportation campaign. Chaired by Rapp, the meeting's participants included the members of his staff and eight officials from agencies involved in economic policy in the Warthegau.[84] The primary topic of conversation was property registration and confiscation, but the question of exactly how political measures could be brought into harmony with the requirements of the Gau economy arose during the exchange. It was agreed, and Rapp consented, that "the deportation action may bring about no disturbances in economic life." Rapp proposed that economic leaders—factory directors, business owners, and the like—should identify those workers who, owing to their indispensability, could not be deported at the present time and then submit a list of such persons to his staff. He also suggested that if need be, local political authorities, first and foremost the Landräte, should be given the same assignment. One participant questioned whether the decision as to who was economically superfluous should be left to the Landräte; perhaps a central bureau, he said, should make such determinations. Rapp, however, rejected this idea, arguing that the matter should be the responsibility of authorities at the local level. The Landräte, he implied, had a far better grasp of the economic conditions and the needs of their jurisdictions than any central office could hope to acquire.[85] To guarantee that deportations caused no economic disruptions, Rapp soon agreed that evacuation deferments could be extended beyond Polish civil servants in Posen, which he had approved on 16 November, to other essential Polish workers in the Gau. Still, these deferments would be granted "only in the rarest of cases." The few exceptions to the rule, he stressed, received *only deferments*, never exemptions.[86] In the long run, however, the number of deferments would prove to be far more than a few.

There would be no exceptions for Jews. "For the expulsion of Jews," Koppe stated on 10 November, "economic and other points of view play no role whatsoever."[87] All Jews, regardless of their skills and economic potential, were slated for expulsion. Since a Jew's political posture was of no consequence, investigations into his or her political past were unnecessary. Sipo and the SD, moreover, did not have to bother compiling detailed lists of Jewish evacuees. Rather, a Jewish

Council of Elders in each community was responsible for submitting evacuation lists to the security establishment. And unlike the Poles, who would be assembled by Nazi functionaries in transit camps before their expulsion, Jewish deportees would be gathered together twenty-four hours before transport by a Jewish community leader and, several hours before transport, brought to an enclosed space, such as a school or synagogue, to be searched. Severe punishment awaited those who hoarded weapons or valuables. Evacuees would include all *Mischlinge* (so-called mixed breeds) of two or more Jewish grandparents. Aryan women married to Jews would be given the opportunity to divorce their husbands; if they refused, they, too, would be deported. The Nazis clearly expected the Jews to pack up and leave their homes like automatons, entrusting them with the organization of their own evictions.[88]

Eviction and evacuation procedures vis-à-vis Poles were more complicated. Before they were evicted, evacuation lists were to be verified by Volksdeutschen or reliable Poles, never by uniformed policemen. With lists in hand, these inconspicuous functionaries were to go from dwelling to dwelling to confirm that targeted individuals were still resident and had not moved or fled. If the evacuees were present, local police would soon move in with no advance warning to carry out the evictions. The Poles were allowed time to pack, generally one hour at the most.[89] They were required to stock the one suitcase they were allotted with warm clothes and blankets, food supplies sufficient for several days, eating and drinking utensils, and their passports and birth certificates. Each individual was allowed to retain 200 zloty in cash (Jews were allowed only 50 zloty, and their baggage allowance was less as well). Valuables of any type had to be left behind, as were pets, though by late November, the animal-loving Nazis had decided that instead of facing immediate execution, pets would be turned over to neighbors or animal shelters.[90] The evictees would then be marched or trucked to a transit camp to await transport to the Generalgouvernement.

Following the evictions—and this procedure applied to Jews as well—a local police leader, assisted by an *Ordensjunker* (a graduate of an elite school of the NSDAP), would enter the vacated dwelling; gather and register all valuables, such as securities, foreign currency, and jewelry; and then bring them to a central collection point. All other property, including works of art, were to remain on site, where they would be inventoried by civil servants working in the name of Hermann Göring's Haupttreuhandstelle-Ost (HTO; Central Trust Agency for the East). The inventory lists would then be turned over to the HSSPF.[91] After the inventory was complete, the gas and water would be shut off, the houses and apartments sealed, and the keys stored at a local police station. If not immediately taken over by Volksdeutschen, the homes would be guarded by the police, Selbstschutz, or reliable neighbors.[92]

At the transit camps, Poles would undergo body searches before transport. Their luggage would be searched as well. If arms, munitions, explosives, poison, or any other dangerous materials were found, the possessor would be turned over to Sipo and the SD, and his or her name would be struck from the evacuation list.[93] After receiving a warm meal, the evacuees would be loaded on transport trains. According to orders issued 22 November, each transport train was to consist of approximately thirty-two carriages, five of which were passenger cars and the rest freight wagons. Forty people would be assigned to each carriage; men and women were to be separated, though children twelve and under could remain with their mothers. The passenger cars were reserved for escort detachments and medical personnel, as well the sick and elderly. Landräte and Oberbürgermeister were responsible for providing straw for the freight wagons, milk for the babies, and a warm meal to all before departure.[94]

Ultimately responsible for delivering the deportees to their final destination was a German transport leader. Beneath him, an escort detachment guarded the evacuees during their journey. The complement of these detachments varied; one example included three gendarmerie, two Schupo officers, and twenty members of the Selbstschutz, all armed with carbines and pistols.[95] Responsibility for security on the rails was shared by the evacuees themselves. Each train had a "transport elder" whom the Germans selected from among the evacuees, and beneath him, each freight and passenger car had a "wagon elder." The former was accountable for order and security on the train as a whole, the latter for the same in each carriage. After the deportees were jettisoned in the Generalgouvernement, the empty train was to return to Wartheland immediately and pick up a new load of human cargo. The transport leaders were ordered to submit a report to Rapp's office at the conclusion of each trip.[96]

By the end of November, Rapp and his subordinates had completed their preparations for the first wave of organized evacuations. The requisite administrative machinery, so they thought, was now in place. All that was needed was the necessary order from Himmler or Heydrich to launch the operation. At that point, the SS functionaries in Wartheland apparently expected to exceed Koppe's quota of 200,000 Poles (estimated at roughly 4 percent of the Polish population of the Gau) and 100,000 Jews by 28 February 1940. Working from surveys compiled by those Oberbürgermeister and Landräte who had met Koppe's deadline for the

submission of their reports regarding deportation objectives in their respective jurisdictions, SS-Obersturmbannführer Hermann Krumey, Rapp's transport officer
and later chief of the UWZ office in Litzmannstadt, calculated on 22 November
that 409 transport trains would be needed to accomplish the mission. At approximately 1,000 deportees per train, this meant that roughly 409,000 Poles and
Jews were now candidates for evacuation. In his report, Krumey stated that the
Reichsbahndirektion (German Railway Administration) in Posen had informed
him that if no unforeseen complications arose and if a six-day rotation period for
each train were realized, the operation would be completed on schedule.[97]

These numerical objectives, however, abruptly fell by the wayside, and the
geographic focus of the entire deportation campaign in the incorporated territories narrowed exclusively to the Warthegau. On 28 November—and much to
the surprise of Nazi officials in the province—RSHA chief Reinhard Heydrich
ordered the immediate expulsion of only 80,000 Poles and Jews from Wartheland
to accommodate the approximately 40,000 Baltic German immigrants already
present in the district. All 80,000 individuals were to be deported between 1 and
16 December, a timetable that called for the evacuation of 5,000 people daily.
According to Heydrich's directive, Ernst Damzog was to determine from which
locations the deportees would originate, and Bruno Streckenbach would decide
upon suitable destinations within the Generalgouvernement. German authorities
in the Generalgouvernement, Heydrich stated, were not responsible for the accommodation of the deportees; rather, local Polish officials were to arrange for
their care. The action would apply only to Wartheland. After its completion, a
meeting would be held in Berlin at which the RSHA would formulate a *Fernplan*
(long-range plan) concerning future deportations from the incorporated territories as a whole. But for now, Heydrich noted, the primary concern was to expel a
sufficient number of Poles and Jews from the Warthegau to meet the housing and
employment needs of the Baltic Volksdeutschen at hand.[98]

Termed the 1.Nahplan (First Short-Term Plan), the seventeen-day operation
that ensued was the Nazis' first major experience in systematic mass deportations. It was the time when they cut their teeth on the process of removing people
from their homes, expropriating their property, interning them in transit camps,
and shipping them en masse east. The 1.Nahplan, however, was not without its
problems.

4

The 1.Nahplan: Logistics, Limitations, and Lessons

On 29 November 1939, two days before the launch of the 1.Nahplan, Dr. Eduard Könekamp of the Deutsches Ausland-Institut (German Foreign Institute), an academic think tank based in Stuttgart, embarked on an eleven-day research trip through the new Reich provinces to evaluate National Socialist resettlement and deportation measures in the region. Könekamp visited Posen, where he had the opportunity to witness eviction and evacuation procedures in action. He was impressed by the efficiency of the operation and included a detailed account of the process in his final report. Könekamp recounted that German policemen, armed with evacuation lists drawn up by the SD and verified by the Oberbürgermeister, approached the targeted individuals' homes in Posen at eight in the evening, announced to all occupants that they were being evicted and deported, and gave them an hour to pack. The evacuees (in this case, Poles) were allowed to bring only a suitcase, a change of underwear, blankets, food, and 200 zlotys each. At 9 P.M., they were transported to Lager Glowno. He described their arrival:

> We are standing on wet ground. Some lamps dimly light the scene. Children, risen from their sleep, are crying. We see old women, eighty to ninety years old. [We see] one man with a ribbon of the Iron Cross Second Class, a German master of a secondary school who had opted for Poland. We see [a] countess [and] women in fine furs. *Here the individual Pole, above all [members of] the ruling class, is meeting an inexorable but just fate.*[1]

The SS men stationed at the camp, he said, were helpful and performed their duty in perfect form. Fresh straw had been laid throughout the barracks. Immediately before transport to the Generalgouvernement, the evacuees were given bread, butter, and coffee, and milk was graciously distributed to the babies. The entire process, Könekamp reported with satisfaction, was marked by "straight-forward, frictionless organization."[2]

Könekamp's description and favorable evaluation of eviction and deportation procedures focused on one specific action carried out in the city of Posen at some point in early December 1939. It was also the report of an outside observer. But as SS-Sturmbannführer Albert Rapp and the members of the Staff for the Evacuation of Poles and Jews saw it, the implementation of the 1.Nahplan was, as a whole, neither straightforward nor frictionless. Granted, the 1.Nahplan began on schedule, and by 17 December 1939, National Socialist functionaries in Wartheland had managed to evict 87,833 Poles and Jews from their homes and deport them to the Generalgouvernement. To an outside observer and, as Götz Aly points out, to the victims themselves, this achievement must have seemed monumental, a reflection of the revolutionary zeal of the SS, the single-minded fanaticism of the Warthegau authorities, and the "horrible efficiency" of the Nazi bureaucracy.[3] But from the perspective of the perpetrators, even though the deportation quota of 80,000 was met and exceeded, the operation had been rife with complications and, as one SS-Sturmbannführer in Litzmannstadt put it, replete with "absolute organizational deficiency."[4] Dispatches and orders issued during the course of the 1.Nahplan, as well as Rapp's final reports submitted to his superiors after the seventeen-day action was over, indicate that Nazi officials within both the Warthegau and the Generalgouvernement had encountered difficulties at virtually every stage of the operation. At the end of this first wave of organized evacuations, it was clear to all involved that a major overhaul of Wartheland's deportation machinery was in order. The system would undergo dramatic changes in the months to come.

"ABSOLUTE ORGANIZATIONAL DEFICIENCY"

A mosaic of National Socialist agencies and authorities took part in the deportations conducted between 1 and 17 December 1939. Many of the problems associated with the operation were eventually attributed to the sheer number of individuals and organizations involved. These included Rapp's bureau, Sipo and SD officials, the Landräte and Oberbürgermeister, and the Ordnungspolizei, as well as the two railway systems in occupied Poland—namely, the Reichsbahn, which operated in the incorporated territories, and the Ostbahn, which handled transports in the

Generalgouvernement.[5] Rapp's office was responsible for the central planning and management of the operation, but the Landräte and Oberbürgermeister were effectively the leading agents of Nazi deportation policy within Wartheland during the 1.Nahplan. These local officials were entrusted with the selection of deportees, the organization of evictions, the establishment of a transit camp and the transport of evictees to it, the provision of a meal to evacuees before departure, and the outfitting of evacuations trains with straw for warmth and rudimentary equipment (specifically buckets) for sanitation. Although the local officials were often assisted by Sipo and SD officials in the identification of allegedly dangerous Poles, the remaining organizational tasks within their respective jurisdictions were ultimately their responsibility alone, and the overall success of eviction and evacuation measures at the regional level was therefore largely dependent upon their personal initiative and administrative talent.

Following instructions formulated by these local officials, the various branches of the police, reinforced by Selbstschutz detachments, carried out the evictions and guarded the evacuees before rail transport to the Generalgouvernement. Guards for the deportation trains also were drawn from their ranks. The Reichsbahn and the Ostbahn managed the transports themselves. Operating according to schedules worked out between railway authorities, Rapp's staff,[6] and Generalgouvernment officials, these two rail systems delivered the evacuees from transit camps in Wartheland to predetermined locations in Hans Frank's fiefdom to the east.[7] The jurisdiction of the Reichsbahn extended to the border of the Generalgouvernement. At stations such as Kutno and Litzmannstadt along the frontier, the transports were turned over to the Ostbahn, personnel were exchanged, and the trains proceeded to their final destinations. The process was repeated in reverse when the empty trains returned to the Warthegau. Within the Generalgouvernement, Polish and Jewish reception committees and native local officials were responsible for the accommodation of the deportees. They were to supply both food and shelter for incoming Poles and Jews, as well as medical facilities for the sick and elderly.[8] The organization of rail transport and the reception and accommodation of Polish and Jewish evacuees in the Generalgouvernement proved to be the weakest links in the expulsion process.

When the first transports left Lager Glowno on 1 December 1939, evacuation planning and procedure—as it existed on paper—appeared sound. Glowno, by far the largest transit camp in Wartheland, held approximately 2,700 inmates on the night of 30 November. Most were sent east on the first day of the action, freeing up space for thousands of additional evacuees who would arrive from Posen and its environs over the next two and a half weeks.[9] The first transport reports, however, indicated that little had gone according to plan. In a dispatch sent to Rapp's office on 7 December, Transportführer (Transport Leader) Howein, the leader of the first train to roll from Glowno, described the many problems he had encountered during his journey to and from the Generalgouvernement. His report reflected the sudden announcement of the 1.Nahplan and the ad hoc nature of its implementation.

On the afternoon of 30 November, Howein was ordered to assume command of a transport at Glowno and deliver it to Lublin. He took control of the loaded train at 11:45 P.M. and five minutes later proceeded to Posen Ostbahnhof (train station). At 12:30 A.M., the train steamed up and headed east. Upon arriving in the town of Dęblin on the far side of Warsaw later that day, Howein telephoned authorities in Lublin to request further instructions, but he received none. He was merely told to continue on to Lublin, where he would be met by appropriate officials. After a three-hour trip, the train arrived, but to Howein's surprise, no one was there to meet him. He eventually contacted the SD office in the city and learned that he and his transport would have to stand by until morning, since there was no space to accommodate his cargo. He therefore moved the train to a nearby freight station and waited.

At 3 A.M. on 2 December, Howein learned that the deportees could not be accommodated in Lublin; instead, he was to deliver them to Ostrowiec, a city some 80 kilometers to the southeast in the neighboring district of Radom. Three hours later, he left Lublin, traveled back to Warsaw, and then went on to Ostrowiec, finally arriving after numerous delays at 10 A.M. on 4 December. Howein immediately telephoned the city commissioner to announce his arrival. The commissioner, to Howein's consternation, said the transport could not be received in Ostrowiec; it was the third to appear within the last forty-eight hours, and there was no longer any housing available for the deportees. Nevertheless, after extensive negotiations with city officials, the evacuees were eventually unloaded, and at 7:30 P.M. on 4 December, Howein and his empty train left Ostrowiec and headed back to Wartheland.

Two days later, he reached Hohensalza, just 90 kilometers northeast of Posen, but he was told by railway officials that the train could go no farther (reason unstated). Frustrated to the core, Howein informed these officials that it was now their responsibility to deliver the train back to Lager Glowno. He and his escort detachment abandoned the transport, still loaded with milk jugs, buckets, and supplies, and returned to Posen. They finally arrived at 3 P.M. on 6 December, "trainless" and over six days after their departure from Glowno. In addition to these egregious problems, Howein reported that the evacuation list he had received from camp officials was incorrect: instead of 864 deportees, his transport held only 833. "Control of the actual strength of the transport upon departure from Glowno," he asserted, "was [therefore] impossible."[10]

Howein was by no means alone in his vexation. Other transport leaders confronted many of the same problems during the course of the I.Nahplan. They often found that no preparation whatsoever for the reception of evacuees had been made in the Generalgouvernement. Cooperation with local authorities therein was often poor, and accommodations for the incoming Poles and Jews were frequently unavailable; as a result, trains had to be constantly rerouted. Long delays were common due to substandard or destroyed rail lines or the unavailability of free tracks. Railway personnel, particularly Polish workers, were often unreliable as well. One transport leader reported that the coal stoker on his train, presumably a Pole, wanted to quit his post upon arrival in Warsaw and had to be forced to perform his duties.[11] Another complained that his transport, which originated from Kreis Dietfurt (Żnin), was "thoroughly overfilled." One carriage, for example, held 106 people, though there was space for only 50. He also reported that his evacuation list was incorrect; while the train sat idle in Warsaw due to mechanical failure, his escort detachment made a head count of the evacuees and discovered that 1,154, not 1,104 as specified, were actually on board. Upon reaching Mińsk Mazowiecki, his destination in the Generalgouvernement, he learned another transport of 1,000 people had arrived earlier that day; since local officials were unprepared for their reception, the evacuees were simply dumped at the station. For his part, he managed to secure an empty shed and an old army barracks for his 1,154 Poles. The return trip was equally problematic. In addition to repeated mechanical problems with his locomotive, he had trouble convincing Polish railway workers in Litzmannstadt that he needed to be routed to Leslau, the new German name for the city of Włocławek, and not Breslau, in Silesia. He suggested that place-names should henceforth be designated in both Polish and German.[12]

In an attempt to overcome these difficulties, Rapp quickly issued updated instructions to all authorities involved in the operation. The formulation of accurate transport lists, communications between the Warthegau and the Generalgouvernement authorities, and the selection of appropriate destinations had not, Rapp was forced to admit on 4 December, "functioned flawlessly." From now on, Landräte and Oberbürgermeister were to make absolutely certain that

An Ordnungspolizei (Orpo) unit conducts a winter roundup of Polish deportees. A truck stands by for transport. (USHMM, courtesy of the Institute of National Remembrance, USHMM Photo Reference Collection: WS 09985)

they provided an accurate count of evacuees to the transport leaders. Rapp also ordered stationmasters in both Wartheland and the Generalgouvernement to report precise departure and arrival times immediately after the fact to his office (preferably by telegraph, since telephone connections were unreliable), so that his transport officer could develop a workable train schedule with the Reichsbahn and Ostbahn.[13] Three days later, he also acknowledged that the employment of Polish railway personnel, though necessary, did not guarantee proper management of transports; Polish officials continuously directed trains to destinations other than those officially designated as unloading depots, acts that sabotaged the timetables worked out with central rail authorities. Henceforth, Rapp decreed, transport leaders were to have the same authority as head conductors of the Reichsbahn; they alone were responsible for ensuring that their respective trains proceeded to the proper station by the shortest route possible, and they were to allow no interference by other railway officials or any outside agency. Moreover, they were to see to it that their trains were unloaded as quickly as possible, so that they could immediately move to a new loading station in Wartheland.

Poles from Wartheland board a passenger train bound for the Generalgouvernement, presumably during the 1.Nahplan of December 1939. Several clergymen can be seen among the deportees. Members of the Orpo guard the transport. (USHMM, courtesy of the Archives of Audio-Visual Records, Warsaw, Poland, USHMM Photo Reference Collection: 06003)

This directive in effect gave transport leaders the official license to abandon Poles and Jews at stations in the Generalgouvernement, whether accommodation was available or not.[14]

But problems persisted. On 8 December, SS-Untersturmführer Strickner, a member of Rapp's staff, met with camp officials at Lager Glowno to discuss the various kinks in the deportation procedure. During the exchange, Strickner learned that some evacuation trains had been underfilled and precious space wasted. The previous day, for example, only 337 Poles had been loaded on a train that presumably had space for 1,000. Two trains were scheduled to leave Glowno the following day, but there were enough inmates in the camp to fill only one.[15] Strickner informed the camp commandant, Oberinspektor Otto, that he had to secure more "material" for future transports so that at least 1,000 Poles could be deported daily.[16] Perhaps in response to Strickner's report, Rapp sent a directive the same day to all Landräte and Oberbürgermeister in the Warthegau stating that "in order to save space and time, it is requested that the trains be fully utilized and, so far as possible, to be loaded with more than one thousand persons, in no case less."[17] The consequences of this order would lead to conflict between Warthegau officials and Generalgouvernement authorities and further complicate the latter's task of accommodating the multitudes of incoming Poles and Jews.

Transport problems aside, additional setbacks arose within a number of cities in Wartheland as local Nazi functionaries prepared for the eviction and evacuation of Polish and Jewish "undesirables." Perhaps the worst-case scenario was the situation in Litzmannstadt. On 16 December, SS-Sturmbannführer Richter, the leading SS operative involved in deportations from the city during the 1.Nahplan, drafted a report detailing the numerous problems he had experienced over the course of the preceding two weeks. The evacuation of 15,000 Poles and Jews, Richter explained, had been planned for the December operation. According to his initial orders, politically active Poles and members of the Polish intelligentsia were to make up the bulk of the deportees, but as Sipo and SD officers attempted to identify and register such individuals, they ran into a number of difficulties. Described by Richter as "good," an extensive card file on Polish intellectuals compiled by the Gestapo in early September had since disappeared.[18] A new file had been prepared, but it listed only 5,000 people, far fewer than the 15,000 required, and to make matters worse, it was found to include a number of Volksdeutschen who had to be struck from the roster. Furthermore, when the police attempted to apprehend those individuals on the list who did qualify for deportation, they discovered that nearly one-third had abandoned their homes; as a result, they managed to arrest only 2,600 people.

"Therefore, in order to fulfill the quota of 15,000 persons," Richter declared, "[we] had to fall back on the Jews." It was decided that several blocks of houses in the Jewish quarter would be cleared and the evictees placed either in a transit camp established in Radogoszcz, a suburb of Litzmannstadt, or in a Gestapo concentration camp on the outskirts of the city. The operation, which was carried out by 80 members of the Nationalsozialistisches Kraftfahrkorps (NSKK; National Socialist Motor Corps) and 650 Schupo officers on the night of 14 to 15 December, was, according to Richter, "surprisingly" successful: 7,000 Jews were apprehended within five and a half hours. All but 500 were immediately sent east on the three transports that departed Litzmannstadt on 15 December. An additional 2,000 Jews were evicted later that day and interned with those who remained. But to Richter's consternation, the numerical achievements of the operation were overshadowed by sloppy organization and a lack of cooperation on the part of city officials. The municipal government had offered little in the way of assist-

Straining under the weight of heavy packs, Jewish deportees prepare to leave Wartheland for
the Generalgouvernement. Most are women and children. (USHMM, courtesy of the Institute
of National Remembrance, Warsaw, Poland, USHMM Photo Reference Collection: WS 81221)

ance, and acting Oberbürgermeister Franz Schiffer could not even be contacted.
For the registration and body searches of the Jewish evacuees, a city official had
put a factory at the disposal of the SD, but neither the foreman nor the workers
there had been informed of the decision, and the Jews were eventually thrown
out. Richter moved the registration process to a courtyard in the vicinity, but this
also did not work out. The freezing temperatures, he explained, made it "impossible for the people with children to stand around for hours in the cold and snow
drifts; I therefore ordered that the registration and searches of the Jews should
take place in a nearby office building connected to a slaughterhouse"—an amaz-
ing show of sympathy for Jews on the part of an SS-Sturmbannführer.

All of this, Richter complained, exemplified the "absolute organizational deficiency" of evacuation measures within his jurisdiction. Although it was the
Oberbürgermeister who had ordered the deportations, he had provided virtually nothing in the way of assistance. The city government had not once in-
quired about the operation, and it had prepared no evacuation lists. Camps were

overfilled to the point where no more evacuees could be admitted. And since not all of the evicted Jews could be accommodated, sealed homes had to be reopened, a state of affairs that constituted, according to Richter, "an unbearable loss of prestige to German authorities." City officials had, he conceded, provided bread for the deportees, but they had distributed no milk for the babies, and even though he had repeatedly requested straw for the transport trains, none had been provided: "Since the transports of December 15 left in severe cold, it will have to be calculated that as a result of the lack of straw and supplies, not all transported persons, especially unweaned babies, arrived at their final destination alive." Oberbürgermeister Schiffer alone, Richter concluded, was responsible for the catastrophic situation in Litzmannstadt.[19]

Oberbürgermeister Henkel of Gnesen, a city some 50 kilometers northeast of Posen, also infuriated deportation officials, but unlike the mayor of Litzmannstadt, his noncompliance was more active in nature. Henkel's uncooperative behavior was cited by a local Ordensjunker named Walther in a report submitted to Rapp on 18 December. Henkel, Walther carped, had made no preparations whatsoever for the evacuations, and to add insult to injury, he had accused the Ordensjunker of lacking a basic understanding of the state of affairs in Gnesen, claiming that he, as Ober-bürgermeister, was better informed. But despite his claims to be all-knowing, Henkel was not aware that the Gestapo had established an internment camp in the vicinity, and even after he learned of its existence, he could not decide where to place Polish evictees before their transport. "What is entirely incomprehensible to us," Walther stated with exasperation, "is that he wants to accommodate not Poles but rather Baltic Germans in this camp[!]" Henkel also went as far as to prevent deportation functionaries from carrying out their duties. A politically active Polish teacher by the name of Gorski had been evicted and interned in the Gestapo camp. Shortly before he was to be loaded on a transport train, Walther learned that the man had, on Henkel's orders, been released and had returned to his home. Gnesen's SA-Oberführer and a detachment of Schupo officers attempted to reapprehend the Pole but to no avail. At the time Walther penned his memo, Gorski was safe in his home, solely because "the Oberbürgermeister and Regierungsrat Henkel has a different opinion." Walther ended his report with a question to himself: "I ask myself why a man, who is not a party member and whose behavior during the Baltic action borders on that of a saboteur, has been appointed to this occupational post, while an SA-Oberführer is assigned only as a figurehead."[20] Whether the Ordensjunker found an answer to his question is unknown, but no doubt much to his satisfaction, Henkel died in April 1940.[21]

THE REPORT CARD ON THE 1.NAHPLAN

The last four of the eighty transports that rolled during the 1.Nahplan left Hohensalza and Litzmannstadt on 17 December, one day behind schedule.[22] Within seventeen days, Warthegau authorities succeeded in deporting 87,833 Poles and Jews, nearly 8,000 beyond the objective set by Heydrich on 28 November. The Nazis made no distinction between Polish and Jewish deportees in their various "final" reports on the 1.Nahplan, but the majority of those ousted from the Gau where certainly non-Jewish Poles, primarily political and intellectual elites and members of anti-German political organizations. Indeed, as Rapp stated unequivocally on 26 January 1940, the fundamental objective of the 1.Nahplan was to expel "those elements of Polentum which represent an immediate danger to German nationhood."[23] Another report, issued in February 1940, asserted that the first 300,000 evacuations from Wartheland (including those under the 1.Nahplan) should target the following groups: (1) politically active Poles, (2) the Polish intelligentsia, (3) "criminal and a-social elements," (4) Congress Poles, and (5) all Jews.

The author emphasized, however, that the deportation of the first two groups was considered the most urgent.[24] How many Jews, then, were among the 87,833 deportees? We can only approximate. Christopher Browning estimates that roughly 10,000 Jews, most of whom originated from Litzmannstadt, were deported from Wartheland during the course of the 1.Nahplan. This figure is probably not far off the mark. Browning reasons that the 10,000 Jewish evacuees were not mentioned specifically in the final reports on the operation "because it was not evidence of success in deporting Jews, but rather a failure to identify and seize Polish political activists and intelligentsia." In light of the stated goals of the 1.Nahplan, Browning's reasoning seems valid.[25]

Objectives aside, a significant number of "nondangerous" Poles were deported as well. These included—but were not restricted to—individuals who owned desirable homes and businesses or who were employed in occupations needed for the 40,000 Baltic German settlers. As Dr. Könekamp insinuated in his report on evacuation procedure, one of the guiding principles of the 1.Nahplan was to evacuate Poles whose occupations mirrored those of the incoming Volksdeutschen: "If, for example, twenty German bakers arrive on a transport from the Baltics, then twenty Polish bakers in Posen [or] other parts of the Warthegau must be evacuated."[26] The actual ratio of deportees to immigrants was, of course, closer to two to one, but Könekamp did grasp the essence of the operation. Although economic considerations such as these played an important role in the design and implementation of deportation policy, security remained the number one priority. If twenty Polish bakers had to be deported, Nazi functionaries would, whenever possible, attempt to deport twenty politically active bakers, though they often failed to secure the appropriate "material" to do so. The deportation of nondangerous, economically valuable Poles that frequently resulted certainly troubled Warthegau officials, even in those heady days of late 1939. The need to maintain the region's Polish labor force would grow even more important as the German war machine turned its attention to the West in the spring of 1940, and even more so after the launch of Operation Barbarossa on 22 June 1941.

Regardless of the numerical success of the 1.Nahplan, Albert Rapp and his associates understood that the many complications, economic and otherwise, that the Nazi bureaucracy had encountered during this first wave of organized evacuations needed to be addressed. In his two final reports on the 1.Nahplan, issued 18 December 1939 and 26 January 1940, Rapp sought to impress upon his superiors the unfavorable conditions in which the operation had been carried out. He described in detail the many problems with deportation planning and procedure and leveled a litany of complaints at virtually every agency and institution involved. But despite his somewhat gloomy overview of the December expulsions, Rapp had clearly learned a great deal from the experience and was optimistic about future operations. He offered a host of suggestions for refining the deportation process, many of which were seized upon by higher officials and soon put into action.[27]

Rapp attributed much of the confusion and disorder associated with the execution of the 1.Nahplan to the adverse conditions in Poland, as well as to the acute shortage of personnel and technical materials. More workers, particularly reliable Reichsdeutschen, had been needed to staff the various administrative offices that took part in the action; more transit camps should have been established, with more guards assigned to secure them; vehicles had been in short supply; an insufficient number of typewriters and typists had been available to transcribe orders and transport lists; and so on. Furthermore, the relay of orders and transport reports both within Wartheland and between Wartheland and the Generalgouvernement had been obstructed by the ineffectiveness of the post, as well as that of the telecommunications system. This problem was especially acute in regions where the lines of communication had been damaged or destroyed during the September fighting. A courier service had been established to deliver important orders and reports, but difficulties persisted nevertheless.

Generally speaking, Rapp asserted, the police agencies responsible for the eviction of Poles and Jews and their delivery to transit camps and train stations had functioned well. But by no means had their mission been "frictionless." Many individuals slated for evacuation were not in their homes when police arrived, either because they had fled or because they had recently moved, and thus remained at large. Moreover, the transport of evictees from their homes to camps or train depots had at times been hampered by poor road conditions and by the long distances they sometimes had to march; in some rural Landkreise, the deportees had to travel 30 to 40 kilometers by foot before reaching points of departure. Rapp had attempted to overcome this latter problem by assigning a motorized police company to carry out evictions and transport in particularly remote regions of the Gau, but the former problem—the repeated failure to apprehend targeted Poles—proved far more difficult to surmount. In fact, a substantial number of Poles would continue to escape deportation in the months that followed either by fleeing at the time of eviction or by simply avoiding their homes during the hours they expected the police to arrive to arrest them. Surprisingly, this rudimentary act of resistance frustrated Nazi functionaries throughout the entire history of the deportation campaign, despite their extensive efforts to counter it.

Organizational matters handled by local authorities, such as the selection of deportees, the establishment of transit camps, and the outfitting of transports, had proceeded according to the talent and initiative of the individual Landräte, Oberbürgermeister, and their personnel. Rapp stated that although older officials of the "German-bureaucratic type" had performed well, others lacked the organizational ability and in some cases "the necessary hardness" that their work demanded. A common grievance against the provincial bureaucrats was that they repeatedly failed to provide accurate evacuation lists to the transport leaders. In many cases, the actual strength of a transport was unknown until the escort detachment performed its own head count of the deportees. If the number of deportees was less than that reported, the discrepancy may not have been due to sloppy paperwork; the missing persons may have somehow escaped. If, by contrast, the number of deportees was greater, it represented a breach of contract between Generalgouvernement and Warthegau authorities, and—if one is to take the protests emanating from Frank's realm at face value—it also created problems for Generalgouvernement officials responsible for the accommodation of the incoming Poles and Jews. Another complaint leveled at some local officials involved their failure to outfit the evacuees in an appropriate manner. Adequate rations were often not provided, nor was straw for the freight cars, and sometimes, local authorities neglected to make sure the deportees had brought along proper winter clothing for their journey. But perhaps due to the SS-Sipo-SD establishment's need to maintain cordial relations with provincial bureaucrats, public criticism was kept to a minimum.[28]

Like that of local authorities in Wartheland, the Wehrmacht's performance also varied. Rapp reported that whereas younger, "active" troops usually showed support for the operation, older soldiers were generally either passive or went as far as to demonstrate open disapproval of the action. One example of unacceptable behavior on the part of the German military cited by Rapp occurred in the town of Mogilno. There, the Wehrmacht had delayed the departure of a transport by attempting to hand over a field kitchen to the Poles aboard, even though the Landrat had supposedly already provided an adequate supply of food. This act, Rapp complained, was emblematic of the attitude of certain army personnel. Moreover, some members of the military obstructed the deportation process, both during and after the operation, by repeatedly approaching the police to request evacuation exemptions for individual Poles. This issue was apparently resolved in early February 1940 when General Walter Petzel, the military commander of Wartheland, forbade such action, asserting that it contradicted the "mandatory" attitude toward the Polish population and "shamed" the image of the Wehrmacht.[29]

These various problems within Wartheland were certainly troublesome, but in Rapp's assessment, the most injurious setbacks that arose during the 1.Nahplan were the result of poor coordination between the Reichsbahn and the Ostbahn, the intransigence of Polish railway personnel, and the organizational ineptitude—or outright opposition—of local officials in the Generalgouvernement. Detrimental to frictionless transport, he asserted, was the fact that the departure and destination railway stations lay in two separate jurisdictions, that of the Reichsbahndirektion-Posen and the Ostbahndirektion-Krakau. Consequently, a "double-planning" had been necessary, and this led to logistical complications. Transports had been slowed by long delays at stations, by logjams along the rails, and by the exchange of personnel at depots along the Reich-Generalgouvernement frontier. Moreover, Ostbahn personnel were predominantly Polish and had frequently refused to cooperate, in effect sabotaging the rapid circulation of trains.[30] Cooperation with other authorities in the Generalgouvernement had been equally problematic. On the whole, Rapp complained, they had displayed little understanding of the operation, had chosen insufficient destination stations, were inadequately prepared for the reception of transports, and had repeatedly refused to accept deportees in their jurisdictions. As a result, trains had to be constantly rerouted and often had to sit idle for days until satisfactory destinations could be identified.

Rapp's criticism reflected little concern about the enormous problems the deportations created for authorities in the Generalgouvernement and little interest in the fate of the deportees themselves. As long as the trains ran according to schedule and evacuees continued to flow en masse out of the Warthegau, he had fulfilled his personal responsibilities and was complacent. Eastern officials, of course, had an entirely different perspective. The influx of 87,833 Poles and Jews constituted an immense burden for both central and local administrations. In a 29 December dispatch to Generalgouverneur Hans Frank, a bureaucrat in the district of Krakau described the great difficulties he faced in accommodating and caring for deportees. Between 14 and 20 December, twenty transports had arrived in his jurisdiction alone, and reception capacity had been exhausted. Upon arrival, the deportees had already spent two to three days in unheated cattle cars, most of which, he asserted, had not been opened during the entire course of their journey.[31] Many deportees were forced to remain on the trains for several more days until suitable accommodations could be found. This, combined with transport delays, the extreme cold, and the appalling lack of food and supplies, often had devastating results. As SS-Sturmbannführer Richter had "calculated" on 16 December, a significant number of the freezing and ill-equipped Polish and Jewish deportees did not reach their final destinations alive.

Examples of transport deaths arising from cold and hunger are many. One Polish witness reported that a trainload of deportees from Wartheland, 70 percent of whom were women and children, had been sent east in open coal cars; half purportedly froze en route.[32] In another case, a transport arrived in Krakau after a four-day journey, and forty dead children were found onboard.[33] SS-Hauptsturmführer Mohr of the Generalgouvernement later blamed many deaths on the fact that transports habitually contained more than the prescribed number of 1,000 people. Due to the resulting accommodation problems, the deportees often had to remain on the tracks for up to eight days "without being able to attend to their needs"; on one transport alone, he stated, the extreme cold had caused 100 fatalities.[34] Even Himmler expressed some degree of sorrow over the deaths that occurred during the 1.Nahplan, though he laid the blame not on German officials but on the harsh climate in the East. During a speech before the Gauleiters and party functionaries in Berlin on 29 February 1940, he acknowledged that

> among the trains in the East, but not only in the case of evacuation [trains], it is obviously possible that [one] will become icebound, and people will freeze to death. This is possible, [and] it has unfortunately happened to Germans too. You simply cannot do anything about it, if they travel from Lodsch to Warsaw, and the train remains standing on the tracks for ten hours. You cannot make accusations against the railway or anyone else. It's just the climate there. It is regrettable for Germans, it is also regrettable for Poles, and as far as I'm concerned, even regrettable for Jews, if anyone wants to feel sorry for them[!]

Himmler went on:

> But it is neither intended nor can it be prevented, and I consider it wrong to moan and groan about it now. Whoever says, yes it is indeed cruel that the Poles were expelled from their homes in Posen within three or four days and marched out, then may I remind them that in 1919 our Germans were driven over the bridges [by the Poles] ... with thirty kilograms of baggage.[35]

His "regrets" notwithstanding, Himmler's message was clear: the evacuation of Poles and Jews—and by implication, the resettlement of Volksdeutschen—was justifiable and absolutely necessary, and it would continue despite the many fatalities and despite the probability that even Germans might die in the process.[36]

Himmler's rhetoric, as well as that of several other officials as presented earlier, gives the impression that at least as this juncture in the evolution of National Socialist ethnic-cleansing policy, the perpetrators were genuinely concerned about the welfare of their victims. In individual cases, this may well have been true. SS-Sturmbannführer Richter's comments and actions regarding the plight of Jews in Litzmannstadt seem to reveal an unfeigned sympathetic attitude toward the deportees under his wing. If his concern—and that of others—was in fact sincere, perhaps many a Nazi, including some members of the SS, had not yet gained the "necessary hardness," had not yet achieved the "mandatory" attitude toward the natives of the East, and had not yet been sufficiently "barbarized" to the point where they could ship evacuees to certain destitution and quite possibly death without a moment of reflection. But though a few individuals may well have questioned their actions, in most cases the issue was probably not so much that a substantial number of "worthless" Jews or "dangerous" Poles had died en route to the Generalgouvernement but rather that regulations concerning the outfitting of evacuation trains had not been followed, that incorrect figures had been entered on evacuation lists, and that transports had not circulated according to schedule. Sloppy paperwork and the failure to follow orders would not be tolerated in the Third Reich.

Problems considered far more detrimental to the demographic goals of National Socialist Volkstumspolitik than dead evacuees arose in the wake of the 1.Nahplan. Soon after the conclusion of the operation, Nazi functionaries in Wartheland discovered a significant number of deportees were returning to the Gau, even though that was an offense punishable by death.[37] Some returned clandestinely, but others did so with official approval. As early as 2 January 1940, the Polizeipräsident (chief of police) of Posen reported to Himmler that military authorities in the Generalgouvernement were distributing travel passes to evacuated Poles "for the purpose of retrieving belongings left behind in their private homes as well as to visit their relatives in Posen."[38] Four days later, the Landrat of Konin informed Greiser that large numbers of Poles and Jews were reappearing in his jurisdiction also, with Wehrmacht passes in hand; a large-scale and uncontrollable return of evacuees, he said, was possible, which would constitute a great danger for German authorities on both political and security grounds.[39] Rapp concurred. In the second of his two final reports on the 1.Nahplan, he brought this matter to the attention of his superiors and pointed out that it was not the fault of the Wehrmacht alone:

> The obliging attitude of many administrative offices in the Generalgouvernement towards the evacuees has had an almost catastrophic effect. An exceedingly high number of evacuees are discharged to their former homes with "vacation passes" for a duration of up to four weeks for the "settlement of personal matters," etc.... The passes were, for the most part, issued by community and Kreis authorities and Wehrmacht offices. On the one hand, the returnees pestered the Volksdeutschen assigned to their homes and, on the other, caused unrest among the entire population through their reappearance and reports ... Despite repeated protests, the Generalgouvernement was unable to do anything to stop this deplorable state of affairs [caused] by subordinate administrative offices.[40]

Indeed, Hans Frank conceded on 19 January that absolutely nothing could be done to prevent evacuees from returning to the incorporated territories, though he hoped that the temporary lull in deportations would allow his subordinates time to work out a solution to the problem.[41] But Poles and Jews continued to flow back to the West in droves. By 19 February, an official in Hohensalza could report that 20 percent of the people expelled from his district had returned, despite all police measures to stem the flow.[42] As in the case of the multitudes of Poles who continued to escape evacuation through flight, this form of resistance plagued the Nazis for the duration of the occupation.

Rapp also reported that the "true" ethnicity of many deportees had not been properly identified, a serious mistake that resulted in a discharge of so-called racially valuable blood from the Warthegau. In early January, for example, HSSPF Friedrich-Wilhelm Krüger of the Generalgouvernement informed SS officials in Wartheland that 200 "Poles" deported during the 1.Nahplan claimed that they were actually Volksdeutschen.[43] The actual number of cases, particularly in terms of those of German descent (*Deutschstämmigkeit*), was probably far greater. In his 26 January report, Rapp admitted that even though it was relatively easy to identify individuals of volksdeutsch status, German descent was far more difficult to determine. People of volksdeutsch status had deliberately "remained German" during the preceding decades: they had publicly championed Deutschtum, had sent their children to German schools, and had belonged to German political and social organizations. But many individuals of German descent had become Polonized over the years. To make matters worse, many Poles of German descent were strongly anti-German. According to Rapp's figures, 16,000 *deutschstämmige* individuals in the Warthegau belonged to chauvinistic Polish organizations; of them, 1,497, a number that included 32 political leaders, came from pure German families. Politically speaking, such persons were certainly considered undesirable, but their German blood made them candidates for reacceptance into Deutschtum. If the Germanization of the incorporated territories was to proceed rapidly, the Reich could ill afford to lose this valuable racial stock. As Wetzel and Hecht had asserted in their essay of November 1939, these individuals had to remain in the Reich and undergo the process of "re-Germanization."[44]

LESSONS LEARNED AND PLANS FOR THE FUTURE

His criticism of specific agencies and individuals aside, Rapp ultimately attributed the myriad problems that arose during the 1.Nahplan primarily to the sudden announcement of the action, the speed with which it had to be carried out, and the lack of experience on the part of those involved in its implementation. But if there was one problem that overshadowed all others, it was the sheer number of authorities and agencies that took part and the many interrelated tasks they had to perform. In a passage that seemed to echo a plea for bureaucratic centralization and a rationalization of the deportation system, Rapp asserted that the success of the 1.Nahplan in Wartheland alone had hinged upon the effective teamwork of six different organizations—namely, his Staff for the Evacuation of Poles and Jews, the local civil administrations, Sipo and the SD, the Reichsbahn, the police, and the Volksdeutsche Selbstschutz. "Complications that arose in one sector," he lamented, "directly influenced the entire course of the action, since all authorities were dependent upon one another."[45] In subsequent operations, such difficulties could be overcome, Rapp suggested, through timely organizational preparation and "sympathetic cooperation" among all agencies involved.[46]

Rapp proposed that future evacuation measures in Wartheland should once again be geared toward the broad ethnopolitical objectives that had been established in November 1939 but cast aside due to the sudden announcement and launch of the more modest 1.Nahplan. The expulsion of all anti-German Poles, all members of the Polish intelligentsia and ruling class, and all Jews should once again take precedence. These groups, in Rapp's words, embodied "a biological, a political, and a social component": "In the case of Jews, the biological moment alone is sufficient [to justify] deportation, but in the case of the Poles, either political activity against Deutschtum or a pretension of intellectual leadership must be demonstrable as well."[47]

Clearly, practical considerations were dictating a more conservative deportation policy vis-à-vis the Poles. Rapp pointed out that an unreasonably high number of Polish evacuees would be detrimental to Wartheland's economy. He conceded that in order to maintain economic productivity, deferments for essential workers had, in the past, been allowed "in individual cases," though businesses had been advised to replace these Polish employees with Germans, above all with Baltic Volksdeutschen, as quickly as possible.[48]

Evidence suggests, however, that more than a few deferments had been—and would be—granted to Poles, even to individuals who, by virtue of their position or education, constituted a potential threat to the security of the Reich. For example, on 6 December 1939, the Oberlandesgerichtspräsident (provincial high court president) of Wartheland temporarily released from evacuation all Polish judicial workers who were employed by German judicial authorities. These individuals, he said, were needed to make translations and document summaries, above all

in matters dealing with property ownership and land registry—issues obviously
fundamental to Nazi economic and resettlement policy.[49] Later in the month,
officials in Landkreis Jarotschin (Jarocin) requested deferments for Polish as-
sistants at local financial offices and Polish postal workers as well. The school
commissioner of Jarotschin went as far as to suggest that 68 (28 percent) of the
248 Polish teachers in his district should be exempt from evacuation, since these
persons, whom he listed by name, "are the most loyal and have the best command of the German language."[50] This was a surprising appeal, considering that
the SS, as the school commissioner certainly knew, viewed Polish teachers as one
of the most dangerous groups in annexed territory and had executed hundreds
during the first two months of the occupation. Other requests for deferments included—and would include in the future—petitions on behalf of Polish employees of the Staatsarchiv (State Archive) in Posen, pharmacists, survey technicians,
and public utility workers. Whether archivists and druggists were released from
evacuation is not recorded, but public utility workers (electricity, water, gas) were
fortunate enough to receive outright exemptions.[51]

The conflict between economic interests and the objectives of the Germanization program is perhaps best illustrated by the case of Polish railway workers.
Many Polish employees of the Reichsbahn were initially scheduled for deportation, yet the Nazis needed these very workers both to maintain and improve
Wartheland's infrastructure and to accomplish their ideological goals. On 1 December 1939, recognizing that the success of the 1.Nahplan was contingent upon
the smooth flow of rail traffic, Rapp ordered all Landräte and Oberbürgermeister to report immediately to the Reichsbahn exactly which Polish workers they
stood to lose through deportations. But at the same time, he forbade the deportation of all Polish railway personnel during the December operation. Rather,
their expulsion was to be postponed until the beginning of 1940; by then, Rapp
hoped, German railroad workers would be available to replace them.[52] German
railway officials, however, had different plans. On 30 December, the president
of the Reichsbahndirektion-Posen wrote a long letter to Greiser stating that as
long as no Volksdeutschen were available, he intended to employ former workers of the Polish rail system or hire new Polish employees in their stead. He also
complained that even though it had been agreed that no Polish railway personnel would be deported during the 1.Nahplan, indispensable workers had, in a
number of instances, been expelled and without prior notification; only prompt
action on the part of the Reichsbahn had ensured that the rail system functioned
properly. The president stressed that the rail system was responsible for a wide

variety of tasks vital to both Wartheland's economy and the ethnopolitical goals of the Nazi regime, namely, the deportation of Poles and Jews; the transport of ethnic German resettlers; military transports; and the delivery of food and raw materials to, from, and within the incorporated territories. As of late December, he said, the Reichsbahndirektion employed 4,200 Reichsdeutschen and 12,000 native personnel, but to carry out these multiple tasks, he needed at least 20,000 men. Further, his office had to be kept well informed about any future deportation of Polish workers, so that they could be immediately replaced either by Poles or by Germans. Chaos would otherwise ensue; the resulting disruption in rail traffic, he emphasized, would be "unbearable for the war economy and could bring the various large-scale population movements into question."[53] The Reichsbahn apparently had its way. By April 1940, it employed 33,967 Polish workers in the incorporated territories alone.[54]

One day after the last transports of the 1.Nahplan left Wartheland, Greiser took action to prevent any future disruption in the economic life of the Gau. In a strongly worded directive sent to all Landräte and Oberbürgermeister in his domain, the Gauleiter acknowledged that numerous Polish workers in the province were indispensable, since there were simply not enough Germans at hand to replace them. Therefore, he stated explicitly that "in order to make certain that vitally important economic enterprises do not come to a standstill as a result of the evacuation measures and that economic reconstruction work in the Warthegau is [in no way] impaired, indispensable workers must for the time being [be granted deferments] from all evacuation measures, so that the concerned enterprises have the opportunity to procure German replacement personnel." Greiser even went so far at to countermand arrests of Poles that had already taken place. "Indispensable workers who are already in transit camps," he ordered, "are to be released by request of the responsible Arbeitsamt."[55]

But deferments were not to be handed out indiscriminately. If a businessperson or factory owner wanted to secure a reprieve for one of his workers, he had to file an application with the local Arbeitsamt (AA; Labor Office) expressing the special knowledge, skills, and experience that the individual in question possessed and declaring that no German replacement personnel were available. The AA would then review the request and decide whether to grant the deferment. There was one caveat: anyone who "frivolously" reported that a nonessential worker was indispensable would be punished.[56]

Deferments based on economic considerations would keep a significant number of otherwise deportable Poles in the Warthegau, but as Rapp made clear on

18 December, hundreds of thousands remained candidates for expulsion. According to the twenty-nine (out of forty-one) Landräte and Oberbürgermeister who had responded to HSSPF Koppe's demand for reports concerning deportation targets in their jurisdictions, 402,000 people were identified for evacuation. This figure, based on criteria outlined in Koppe's two comprehensive directives issued in mid-November 1939,[57] included all Jews in the province, with the exception of the 230,000 residing in Litzmannstadt. Rapp calculated that after all reports were submitted, reviewed, and compared with statistical data from prewar Polish and German sources, as well as with the results of Sipo and SD investigations carried out in late 1939, the number of necessary deportations would rise to 540,000; if one included Litzmannstadt's Jewish population, the figure would grow to 680,000.[58]

Rapp conceded, however, that it was still difficult to determine the precise number of individuals to expel. Materials published before the war, particularly the Polish census of 1931, were outdated and included only the former German districts of Posen and West Prussia. Likewise, earlier attempts to reconstruct the political demography of many Kreise in Wartheland were problematic, since the number of politically active Poles had been sharply reduced by flight, shootings, and incarceration. In Gnesen, for example, there were 1,300 fewer such Poles than before the war. An accurate calculation of potential evacuees was further complicated by the diverse socioeconomic structure of the Gau. Alongside Kreise with many large estates were districts with innumerable small farms, the result of the Polish farmers' habit of parceling out land to their sons. Moreover, the landscape of former Russian Kreise in the eastern part of Wartheland was dominated by countless abnormally tiny agricultural homesteads and an extremely low standard of living. "These great structural differences," Rapp argued, "make every diagrammatic determination of evacuation numbers for the individual Kreise impossible." The approximate figure of 680,000 deportees, he said, would have to suffice for the time being.[59]

Some 80,000 Poles and Jews had already been deported. The expulsion of these additional 600,000 "undesirables," Rapp stated, would therefore require 600 transports of 1,000 persons each. An average of 3 transports daily meant that the entire operation would last six to seven months. Rapp explained that no more than 3 transports per day was possible due to the unavailability of rolling stock, and furthermore, an overly expeditious operation would not give local officials adequate time to prepare. After all, one must keep in mind, he asserted, that this impending exercise in Volkstumspolitik would not entail "an indiscriminate mass deportation"; rather, candidates for expulsion were to be identified, evaluated, and expelled on an individual basis. The mistakes of the 1.Nah-plan—specifically the evacuation of economically vital Poles, Volksdeutschen, and persons of German descent—were not to be repeated. Such a meticulous selection process would necessitate concerted action on the part of all agencies and authorities involved, and this would take a good deal of time to plan and organize.[60]

Rapp concluded his 18 December final report on the 1.Nahplan with a question for his superiors about the coming deportations from Wartheland:

> In terms of the determination of evacuation numbers, a clarification is still needed as to whether a distinction should be made between the Kreise of the former province of Posen and the regions of former Kongresspolen newly attached to Wartheland. [Should the evacuations center] on the western Kreise in order to make possible the gradual shifting of the German ethnic border [to the east] or should all Kreise be treated the same[?][61]

This very question would be addressed by RKF ethnopoliticians and Nazi experts in population and depopulation policy in the early months of 1940. Their answer, coupled with Heydrich's response to Rapp's plea for bureaucratic central-ization and a rationalization of the deportation system, would go far to determine the future course of evacuations and resettlements in the so-called Mustergau of National Socialism.

5

Volksdeutschen, Poles, and Jews:
An Ordering of Priorities

"The New Order introduced in the East, particularly the creation of the new eastern Gaue, is forcing a final solution to nationality questions," wrote Heydrich on 21 December 1939, four days after the conclusion of the 1.Nahplan. "A colonization of the German East can only be achieved," he continued, "through the simultaneous deportation of members of foreign nationality, especially the Jews still resident in this region. But the cleansing of the German East of those inhabitants of foreign nationality and foreign stock is a process that [will only] lead to serious shocks in the economic life of the eastern *Gaue* if it is not carried out according to a plan that is clearly thought out in all details."[1]

The need for fastidious deportation planning demanded immediate administrative action. In another communiqué distributed the same day, Heydrich announced the appointment of SS-Hauptsturmführer Adolf Eichmann, considered an expert on Jewish affairs and the chief of the Reichszentrale für jüdische Auswanderung (Reich Central Agency for Jewish Emigration), as his "special consultant" for all deportation measures in the East.[2] Albert Rapp's call for the bureaucratic centralization of the deportation system had been answered.

Assisted by his deputy, SS-Hauptsturmführer Hans Günther, Eichmann now seized the reins of the deportation program, managing operations from his bureau within Amt IV (Gestapo) of the Reich Security Main Office in Berlin. Initially called Amt IVR (Evacuation), his section was redesignated Amt IVD4 (Emigration and Evacuation) in early February 1940. Eichmann worked hand in hand with SS-Sturmbannführer Dr. Hans Ehlich, chief of RSHA Amt IIIES (Immigration and Settlement), renamed Amt IIIB (Volkstum) in March 1940. Ehlich was ultimately responsible for organizing the racial screening of incoming Volksdeutschen and, eventually, outgoing Poles as well. Rapp's Staff for the

Evacuation of Poles and Jews, soon to become the UWZ, fell within the respective jurisdictions of both Eichmann and Ehlich and was answerable to both.[3] Over the next three months, the deportation system in Wartheland would be fine-tuned and "rationalized," largely due to the efforts of these two men.

The details of Eichmann's career are well known. Born in 1906, he joined the Austrian SS in 1932 at the persuasion of Ernst Kaltenbrunner, later appointed head of the RSHA after Heydrich's assassination in 1942. In 1934, Eichmann volunteered for work at the central office of the SD in Berlin. He eventually gained a post in Section II/112 (Jewish Question) and became one of the chief intelligence officers involved in anti-Jewish operations. After the Anschluss in 1938, he was dispatched to Vienna to organize the expulsion of Austrian Jews. His efforts met with astounding success: within eighteen months, his agency, the Zentralstelle für jüdische Auswanderung (Central Office for Jewish Emigration), managed to drive 150,000 Jews from their homeland. Such results impressed Heydrich, prompting him to order the creation of the Reich Central Agency for Jewish Emigration in Berlin in January 1939. On 6 October 1939, Eichmann, who had in the meantime established an expulsion bureau in Prague based on the Vienna model, assumed control of the Berlin office. From this position, he organized the first experiment in systematic deportations, the so-called Nisko-Aktion of October 1939. Meant to serve as a probe "to collect experiences, in order ... to be able to carry out evacuations of much greater numbers [in the future],"[4] the operation initially targeted the Jewish population of East Upper Silesia but was immediately expanded by Eichmann to include Jews from Austria and the Protectorate of Bohemia and Moravia, all of whom would be bound for the Judenreservat in the Lublin district of the Generalgouvernement. Confident in the feasibility of this "territorial solution" to the Jewish Question, Eichmann fully expected that his probe would quickly evolve into a full-scale deportation campaign aimed at the entire Jewish population of the Altreich. But after the successful transport of only five trainloads of Jews—roughly 4,800 individuals—from Kattowitz, Märisch-Ostrau, and Vienna to a transit camp at Nisko on the San River, the operation was abruptly canceled on 19 October, primarily due to the exigencies of Baltic German resettlement.[5] As the new chief of RSHA Amt IVR, Eichmann was granted the mission he had long coveted. He would now apply his considerable experience in deportations to the ethnic cleansing of the incorporated eastern territories.[6]

Though an influential figure in the formulation of Nazi racial policy in the East, Dr. Hans Ehlich has received little attention in historical scholarship. Ehlich was born in Leipzig in 1901, was schooled in medicine, and worked as a general practitioner before the Nazi seizure of power in 1933. After the Machtergreifung, he was active in the Saxony branch of the Racial Policy Office of the NSDAP before joining the staff of the SD Main Office in 1937 as a specialist in racial hygiene and public health. Following the creation of the RSHA in September 1939, Ehlich was assigned to Amt III (Domestic SD), assuming control of the suboffice Amt IIIES. Within his jurisdiction fell questions of immigration, citizenship, and naturalization, and, as a matter of course, the racial screening of ethnic German resettlers carried out by the EWZ at VoMi camps throughout annexed western Poland.[7]

During the last weeks of December 1939, both VoMi and the EWZ were deeply involved in preparations for the reception of an estimated 120,000 ethnic Germans from Volhynia, Galicia, and the Narev region of Soviet-occupied eastern Poland.[8] Germany and the USSR, as previously noted, had signed a resettlement treaty in early November 1939 that guaranteed the emigration of these individuals from the Soviet sphere of influence.[9] According to a 4 December report by the EWZ office in Posen, German authorities expected 4,000 to 5,000 Volksdeutschen to arrive in Wartheland daily during the course of the operation, scheduled to end in late January 1940. The vast majority would enter the Reich via Litzmannstadt, where three massive VoMi camps had been established to process them.[10] In the months that followed, Litzmannstadt would become the gateway between the Reich and the Generalgouvernement—the principal reception station for incoming ethnic Germans and the primary point of departure for Polish and Jewish evacuees.

Led by SS-Obersturmbannführer Horst Hoffmeyer, VoMi resettlement teams assigned to locate and register potential resettlers entered Soviet-occupied territory on 8 December.[11] On 23 December, the first trainload of ethnic Germans reached Litzmannstadt,[12] and by 26 January 1940, the day that the last group of immigrants crossed the German-Soviet frontier at Przemyśl, 134,950 Volhynian, Galician, and Narev Volksdeutschen had "answered the call of the Führer," arriving in the German sphere of influence on 92 trains and approximately 15,000 wagons. The journey by road generally lasted from three to five days, and as a consequence of severe weather conditions and bitter cold, multitudes died along the way.[13] Himmler's reference to the many transport deaths of volksdeutsch resettlers voiced during his speech before the Gauleiters on 29 February 1940 was apparently based in fact.[14]

This chapter explores a transitional phase in Nazi deportation planning. It focuses primarily on the first three months of 1940, a period in which the regime's original plans for the immediate evacuation of the entire Jewish population of the incorporated eastern territories were abandoned in favor of a more conservative policy aimed almost exclusively at the rural Polish population of the Warthegau. In doing so, it examines a transitional deportation action, the Zwischenplan (Interim Plan) of February and March 1940, meant to create space for some 30,000 Baltic German immigrants who had not yet received housing. The steadily increasing importance of utilitarian considerations within the formulation of deportation policy will also be investigated.

THE 2.NAHPLAN: THE INITIAL BLUEPRINTS AND THEIR DEMISE

As the vast majority of the Volhynian, Galician, and Narev Volksdeutschen were peasant farmers, they would require agricultural homesteads in the incorporated territories in compensation for the property they had abandoned in the Soviet zone of occupation.[15] Since very few Jews worked in the agricultural sector, Polish farmers, by necessity, would have to make up the bulk of those dispossessed and deported to provide the new arrivals with the farms they had been promised. But as of late December 1939, Nazi authorities had clearly not yet come to terms with the absolute interconnectedness of—and the reciprocal relationship between—resettlements and deportation. On 21 December 1939, the day of Eichmann's appointment, Heydrich issued the 2.Nahplan (Second Short-Term Plan), calling *not* for the expulsion of Polish farmers but rather for the evacuation of all Jews, now estimated at 600,000, residing in the incorporated territories. Since very few Jews lived in Danzig–West Prussia, 10,000 Poles would be evacuated from Albert Forster's Gau as well. The deportation of these 610,000 individuals was to be accomplished by the end of April 1940.[16]

The geographic focus of the 2.Nahplan, as originally framed, was limited exclusively to the incorporated territories. All Jews living there were to be driven east without regard to age, gender, or, by implication, either economic productivity or economic potential. The deportations, according to Heydrich, were to sweep from the north and west toward the Generalgouvernement, but as a matter of principle, the 10,000 Poles living along the Danzig–West Prussia–Generalgouvernement border were to be evacuated first.[17] The supervisors of Sipo and the SD, serving as representatives of the higher SS and police leaders of the eastern districts, would oversee the operation. The registration of Jews was the responsibility of the Councils of Elders established by Sipo and the SD. These councils were ordered to provide exact figures concerning the age of deportees, since male Jews between eighteen and sixty would, as far as possible, be concentrated in work details upon their arrival in the Generalgouvernement. In view of the large numbers of unemployed Poles in annexed territory, Heydrich ordered that no postponement of the evacuations could take place.[18] The deportation of propertied Jews, however, could be put off until the last days of the action in order to allow adequate time to register their property; still, property registration and confiscation could in no way delay the completion of the operation as a whole. The baggage allowance for each deportee was one suitcase, a blanket, personal papers, and food for fourteen days. Before departure, German currency would be exchanged for "transport zlotys," the maximum of which was soon placed at 100,[19] and all evacuees would be carefully searched. Within the Generalgouvernement, Sipo and SD operatives were responsible for identifying and securing suitable unloading stations and supervising the distribution of transports in cooperation with native local officials charged with accommodating the deportees. The 2.Nahplan was to begin on or around 15 January 1940. Therefore, to realize the objectives of the operation by 30 April, a minimum of 5,000 people would be evacuated daily.[20]

Heydrich also stressed the new emphasis on central deportation planning in his 21 December directive. He announced that a major conference would be held at RSHA Amt IVR in Berlin on 4 January 1940, which the evacuation specialists in the incorporated territories and the Generalgouvernement were required to attend. In preparation for this meeting, those specialists from the eastern Reichsgaue were ordered to compile data specifying the exact numbers of Jews residing in individual cities and Landkreise and formulate proposals for potential loading stations within the regions in question. Those from the Generalgouvernement were to provide provisional plans for the distribution of evacuees and suggestions for unloading stations within their jurisdictions. Using these materials, Heydrich's special consultant, Adolf Eichmann, would devise a comprehensive evacuation plan that, in turn, would serve as the basis for a detailed transport plan to be worked out in cooperation with the Reich Transport Ministry.[21] As of 21 December, then, the responsibility for organizing a workable transport schedule had been removed from Rapp's agency, the Reichsbahn, and the Ostbahn and placed in the hands of higher officials based in Berlin, in an attempt to overcome the problems with rail traffic that had arisen during the 1.Nahplan. Yet despite these efforts, logjams along the rail lines in occupied Poland, as well as other complications associated with the railway system, would continue to frustrate the Nazis, just as they had in the past.

The RSHA meeting, chaired by Eichmann, was held according to schedule on 4 January. Participants included evacuation specialists from the incorporated territories, the Generalgouvernement, and the RSHA; representatives of the Economic, Transport, and Finance Ministries; and an official from the Treuhandstelle-Ost. Though Heydrich had initially placed the number of Jews to be deported at 600,000, the so-called experts had in the meantime calculated that only 350,000 Jews were candidates for deportation, a figure that included 200,000 from Wartheland (primarily from Litzmannstadt) alone.[22] Furthermore, Warthegau authorities announced that they wanted to expel 80,000 Poles immediately, to create space for the Volksdeutschen who were then arriving in droves from Soviet territory. Pushing Heydrich's original blueprint for the 2.Nahplan further to the side was Eichmann's verdict that the operation could not possibly begin on 15 January, since loading and unloading stations had yet to be identified. As soon as this issue was resolved, he would work out a final transport schedule with the Reich Transport Ministry. Eichmann added that his office would also develop a *Fernplan* (long-term plan)—to be subdivided into several *Nahpläne* (short-term plans)—for future deportations. But in light of the present organizational difficulties, the 2.Nahplan itself could not begin before 25 January.[23]

Deportation guidelines set at the 4 January conference more or less followed those of the 1.Nahplan, but they did include new stipulations regarding procedure and transport strength that were meant to remedy the many problems of the December operation and to placate authorities in the Generalgouvernement as well. To prevent deaths from freezing, women and children, whenever possible, would be transported in passenger wagons; men, however, would continue to make the journey in freight cars. Each evacuee, regardless of age and gender, would be required to bring along enough food for at least ten days. Most important, no transport was to include more than 1,000 people. "This figure," it was stressed, "is to be unconditionally observed in order to avoid difficulties with accommodation in the Generalgouvernement." The emphasis on transport strength was certainly a response to Hans Frank's recent complaints, expressed by SS-Hauptsturmbannführer Mohr at the meeting, that the transports of the 1.Nahplan had been constantly overloaded.[24] Moreover, Frank soon protested that in addition to the 87,833 evacuees he had received in December through organized deportations, 30,000 had been sent to the Generalgouvernement "illegally," evidently through so-called wild evacuations.[25] Made two weeks later, this complaint was not addressed at the 4 January meeting, but in a firm statement directed at the Generalgouvernement at the end of the month, Heydrich stressed that "since Referat IVD4 has been organized for the central management of evacuation measures, reservations [about the deportations] no longer apply."[26]

As Nazi functionaries in Wartheland prepared for the 2.Nahplan, it became increasingly clear that Heydrich's demand for the expulsion of the entire Jewish population of the district was in harmony neither with immediate security considerations nor with the exigencies of volksdeutsch resettlement. The focus of the operation therefore began to shift away from the Jews. On 6 January, one official argued that "in the case of the first evacuations, it is urgently necessary to include members of the Polish intelligentsia who are, at the same time, politically troublesome, in order to guarantee the seizure of good housing [for ethnic Germans]." Securing employment for Volksdeutschen was of crucial importance as well. He added that politically active Poles who possessed no desirable property but who did hold sought-after occupational positions should also be subject to deportation.[27] Others were pressing for evacuations in no way connected to the resettlement campaign. Dr. Karl Coulon, the leader of Wartheland's NSDAP Office for Nationality Questions (Gauamt der NSDAP für Volkstumsfragen) and Greiser's personal consultant on all matters concerning race and ethnicity,[28] viewed the continued presence of "criminal elements" in the province as intolerable. He declared on 5 January that since the social reconstruction of the Warthegau could in no way be hampered by the continued presence of such "harmful" individuals, they too had to be evacuated. As a matter of principle, he argued, those already convicted of crimes should be deported sooner than those who merely represented a potential criminal threat. Coulon did suggest, however, that members of "respectable families"—in this case, those deemed not ethnically harmful—who committed only minor crimes "out of need, desperation, or temptation" should be excluded. But ethnically harmful criminals, no matter how trivial their crimes may have been, should be deported to the Generalgouvernement without exception.[29] The movement away from Heydrich's original conception of the 2.Nahplan was accelerating.

Perhaps in response to this pressure to expand the parameters of the operation, Koppe circulated an order on 14 January stating unequivocally that "the 2.Nahplan, which is now coming into effect, embraces fundamentally only the deportation of Jews." He did concede, however, that some Poles would nevertheless have to be evacuated from Wartheland but "only insofar as [their deportation] is directly connected to the installation of Baltic and Volhynian Germans." Demands for the evacuation of "criminal" and "a-social elements" for the sole purpose of ridding the Warthegau of such individuals, he implied, could not be met at present. Koppe also reiterated the guidelines for the evacuation of Jews established at the RSHA meeting of 4 January, but he did augment them, stating that in cases where Jewish Councils of Elders could not fulfill their assigned duties (the registration and assembly of Jews before transport), evictions could be carried out in a blanket fashion, either by city quarter or in some similar manner. Evidently, given that economic considerations carried no weight in terms of Jewish deportations, this indiscriminate method of eviction, though abandoned vis-à-vis Poles, was considered legitimate. And once again, the launch date for the operation was pushed forward: "Since the previous difficulties with regard to accommodation in the Generalgouvernement still exist, it must therefore be calculated that the evacuation of the Jews cannot begin before 1 February 1940."[30]

But three days after the distribution of Koppe's directive, the 2.Nahplan—and with it, the scheme for the immediate expulsion of all Jews residing in the incorporated territories—was put on hold. Just as the need to accommodate the Baltic Germans had superseded the extensive deportation scheme developed by Rapp and his subordinates prior to the onset of the 1.Nahplan, so did the exigencies of volksdeutsch resettlement lead to the postponement—and eventual abandonment—of the plan for the comprehensive evacuation of the Jews. On 17 January, Ehlich and Eichmann announced that a brief "cleanup" resettlement and deportation operation would be implemented to create space for some 30,000 Baltic German immigrants who had not yet received housing and employment. These Volksdeutschen were then quartered in Pomerania (presumably in VoMi camps), but within a few weeks, all would be transported to Wartheland. An additional 80,000 Volhynian and Galician Germans already present or soon to arrive in the Warthegau required accommodations as well.[31] Given the necessity of an immediate deportation action to provide housing and employment for the immigrants, Ehlich and Eichmann disclosed that Bruno Streckenbach, the commander of Sipo and the SD in Krakau, had agreed to accept 40,000 evacuees from Wartheland, despite the fact that "the Generalgouverneur himself, influenced by the district chiefs, refuses to receive additional Poles and Jews." Unnerved by the arrival of so many impoverished deportees the previous December, Frank and his bureaucratic cohorts did not want to take in more, but nevertheless, Ehlich and Eichmann made clear that new transports would soon roll. The Transport Ministry, they said, had agreed to provide two trains daily for the operation; at 1,000 evacuees per train, the action would last twenty days. RSHA Amt IVR and the Transport Ministry would work out a detailed evacuation plan at a meeting to be held in Breslau on 19 January. They stressed that that the figure of 40,000 deportees should be regarded as provisional, since this number would create space for only 20,000 Volksdeutschen. But for the time being, Warthegau officials should make good use of the already approved 40,000 evacuations to secure urban homes for Baltic Germans and rural resettlement sites for the Volhynian and Galician immigrants.[32]

On 20 January, HSSPF Koppe relayed these new orders to his Sipo and SD subordinates, as well as to various civilian officials in the Warthegau. He revealed that "before the beginning of the 2.Nahplan" (an indication that, at that point, the planned evacuation of all Jews from annexed territory had merely been postponed), a "number" of Poles and Jews would be deported from Wartheland to provide accommodations and jobs for Baltic Germans. The operation, termed the Zwischenplan (Interim Plan), would primarily target the native populations of Posen, Litzmannstadt, Hohensalza, Kalisch, Leslau, and Gnesen. A branch office (*Aussenstelle*) of Rapp's bureau, which had since December evolved from the Staff for the Evacuation of Poles and Jews to the Generalgouvernement to the Office for the Resettlement of Poles and Jews,[33] had been set up in each of these cities (with the exception of Posen, where the main office was headquartered) to oversee evictions and evacuations.[34] In forceful terms, Koppe ordered that each person (meaning each Pole) slated for deportation was to be examined to determine "with the greatest accuracy" whether he or she was a member of German Volkstum; in all cases where any doubt whatsoever existed concerning the evacuee's ethnicity, that person would be excluded from the evacuations. Deferments would also be granted to individuals in German-Polish mixed marriages. Moreover, in order to prevent any disruption in the economy (particularly armaments production and other vital enterprises), the recommendations of the local Arbeitsamt had to be weighed before an individual was deported. Lastly, Koppe stressed once again that all evacuees were to be outfitted for winter travel and that no transport was to include more than 1,000 people.[35]

Koppe did not announce a launch date for the Zwischenplan. But during the course of a two-day meeting between Eichmann, Hans Günther, and SS-Hauptscharführer Siegfried Seidl, a staff member of Rapp's agency, held in Berlin on 22 to 23 January, Eichmann stated that the operation could not begin until 5 February at the earliest. Evacuations from Litzmannstadt, he said, would have to be delayed even further, a consequence of the Volhynian German resettlement program. Ten trains from the Soviet zone of influence arrived in Litzmannstadt daily, and another six left the city bound for the Altreich. The railway stations were so busy with volksdeutsch immigrants that Jews would have to be transported from Litzmannstadt westward to Posen and loaded there! Therefore, no evacuation trains could roll directly from Litzmannstadt to the Generalgouvernement before 15 February.[36] These dates, however, soon changed. On 26 and 27 January, representatives of the RSHA, the Office for the Resettlement of Poles and Jews (specifically Hermann Krumey, Rapp's transport officer), the Reichsbahn, and the Ostbahn convened in Leipzig to work out a transport schedule for the Zwischenplan. They agreed to postpone the launch of the operation until 10 February. Furthermore, owing to the intense rail traffic caused by Volhynian immigration and winter coal transports, as well as an acute shortage of locomotives and railway personnel, evacuations from Litzmannstadt could not commence before 20 February.[37] These various postponements are telling: racial politicians and security officials were—and would remain—subject to the "structural constraints" of the German rail system and the authority of the Reich Transport Ministry. Despite the vast power of RFSS Himmler and his subordinate organizations, the SS establishment simply could not bend the railway system at will to conform to its needs.

According to Himmler's orders, which Eichmann relayed to Seidl at the 22 to 23 January meeting, only Jews and Congress Poles would be evacuated from the Warthegau during the Zwischenplan. Seidl took issue with this. Congress Poles, he argued, were, for the most part, only "simple workers" who were "to an extent indispensable" economically speaking and possessed only modest housing. Their collective evacuation was therefore undesirable on economic grounds and would not fulfill the housing and employment needs of the Baltic Germans.[38] This matter was apparently never resolved, though Rapp later ordered that if the goal of 40,000 evacuees could not be met by deporting only Jews and Congress Poles, other Poles could be expelled, as long as they were members of anti-German organizations.[39] This perhaps opened the way for circumventing Himmler's orders, but we do not know. The final report of the Zwischenplan made no distinction between Congress Poles and others. All evacuees were described only as Poles, though we can—and should—assume that a significant number of Jews were deported as well.[40]

THE ZWISCHENPLAN

The Zwischenplan did, in fact, begin on 10 February 1940. Forty individual transports were reserved for the operation, at that point scheduled to run until 3 March.
As of 30 January, 4,000 to 5,000 Warthegau Poles and Jews had been evicted for
the benefit of Baltic Germans and were confined in transit camps awaiting deportation.[41] Some 35,000 to 36,000 more would be evicted and detained over the next
several weeks. Landräte and Oberbürgermeister whose jurisdictions fell within
the scope of the Zwischenplan were ordered to apprehend and intern only those
Poles whose names appeared on arrest warrants; others found in the homes of
targeted persons at the time of eviction, such as relatives or tenants, would not
be taken into custody.[42] This regulation was meant to avert the problem of mistaken arrests and internments experienced during the 1.Nahplan. Furthermore,
on the express orders of the Reichsführer-SS, no individuals of German extraction, regardless of their past political activity, were to be deported. Likewise,
all Kaschubes, Masurians, and members of similar splinter groups were exempt
from the operation on the grounds that they "have shown a pro-German attitude
and have intermingled racially with the German people." It was implied that if
deemed fit for assimilation, select persons from these groups could eventually be
"psychically absorbed" into German Volkstum, thus furthering the consolidation
of German nationhood in the East.[43]

On 6 February, four days before the launch of the Zwischenplan, Rapp presented the supposedly final evacuation plan to relevant Landräte and Oberbürgermeister, the five branch offices of his agency, and the commandant of
Lager Glowno in Posen. The plan defined the precise date, time, and point of
departure for each of the forty transports reserved for the operation, as well as
the precise date, time, and point of arrival within the Generalgouvernement. The
operation would focus primarily on Posen and Litzmannstadt: twelve transports
would originate from the former city and ten from the latter. The remaining
eighteen evacuation trains would roll from Leslau (five), Hohensalza (three),
Gnesen-Stadt (three), Kalisch (three), Mogilno, Konin, Gnesen-Land, and Dietfurt (one each). Most of the major cities in Wartheland, then, would lose at least
a fraction of their native population. Trains were to stand ready for loading at
least six hours before departure. Escort detachments would now be composed of
one transport leader, five police officials, and ten members of the Volksdeutsche
Selbstschutz;[44] the larger detachments of the past had, according to Rapp, been

"too strong." Rapp also reiterated that all evacuees had to bring along proper winter clothing and sufficient food for their journey to the Generalgouvernement.[45] Those without means would be outfitted at the expense of well-to-do deportees.[46]

The first transport of the Zwischenplan left Ostbahnhof-Posen at 2:45 P.M. on 10 February, bound for Jędrzejów in the Generalgouvernement.[47] Later that evening, German police carried out the first evictions of Posen Poles within the designated time frame of the operation. According to the police report, the evictions took place between 8:30 and 10:55 P.M. Thirty-five families of up to eight members each were arrested, given anywhere from twenty minutes to one hour to pack and vacate the premises, and then taken into custody. The police were required to note the condition of the evictees' homes in their report. Of these thirty-five dwellings, over one-half were deemed "uninhabitable."[48] Rapp's agency evidently expected such a critical evaluation. As of 20 January 1940, only 9.8 percent of those Polish and Jewish homes selected for confiscation had been judged "very good" or "good," whereas a total of 63.9 percent were declared "poor" or "uninhabitable."[49] This evaluation seems to indicate that the Nazis had already seized the highest-quality housing in Wartheland. Owing to the new influx of Baltic Germans, they were now forced to confiscate less desirable homes to accommodate them.

A VoMi representative in Litzmannstadt, however, noted soon after the launch of the Zwischenplan that within his jurisdiction, the quality of confiscated housing was quite good, especially in the city center. He added that the eviction of Poles and Jews (presumably from the center of Litzmannstadt) was proceeding as planned. Targeted individuals were then being removed block by block and thereafter allowed to dwell only in designated parts of the city.[50] Thousands of these evictees—10,000 according to the evacuation plan of 6 February—were most likely moved, or would be moved, to transit camps to await deportation to the Generalgouvernement, scheduled to begin 20 February. The others, as this VoMi agent suggested, were subject to a program of "internal resettlement" within Litzmannstadt itself. On 9 February, the Polizeipräsident of Litzmannstadt, SS-Brigadeführer Johannes Schäfer, announced that a Jewish ghetto, eventually to become one of the largest in Europe, had been established in the northern part of the city. The entire Jewish population of Litzmannstadt, he stated, would be confined in this district.[51] The area was already home to 62,000 Jews, and 100,000 more would be transferred to this 2.6 square kilometer slum quarter, known as the Bałuty ward, by 30 April 1940.[52] The southern part of the city, by contrast, was reserved exclusively for Poles. Once all Poles and Jews had been moved to their assigned precincts, the center of Litzmannstadt, so Schäfer predicted, would be free for Baltic resettlement.[53]

This moment of optimism was short-lived. VoMi officials learned on 16 February that "the question of evacuating 'good' or 'bad' housing" was no longer dependent upon the suitability of homes for Baltic German resettlement but rather hinged upon security guidelines set by authorities in Berlin. Therefore, for the time being, only "politically troublesome elements" could be evicted and evacuated. They also received word that the Generalgouvernement categorically refused to accept more than the predetermined number of 40,000 deportees, since the most recent transports had already led to severe food shortages in their regions of destination.[54] These new developments constituted a sharp thorn in the side of those responsible for the placement of Baltic Germans. Although the internal displacement of Poles and Jews within Litzmannstadt would suffice to create at least some suitable housing for Volksdeutschen, whether the evacuation of those deemed politically dangerous would do so was largely a matter of chance. VoMi's predicament was exacerbated on 5 March, the day the agency was informed that the 40,000 evacuees must now include asocial elements as well. The deportation of asocials would, so one VoMi official complained, "naturally free no homes for the Balts." Clearly, the Nazis believed that such individuals, by their very nature, lived only in substandard housing and in extreme cases, as Oberbürgermeister Gerhard Scheffler of Posen reported, even in "holes in the ground."[55]

The housing problem was certainly acute, but far more detrimental to the overall organization and implementation of the Zwischenplan was the 15 February announcement by Bahnrat Kukielka of the Reichsbahndirektion-Litzmannstadt that he could no longer guarantee the timely arrival of empty evacuation trains at loading stations in Wartheland. In a telephone conversation with Rapp's transport officer, Hermann Krumey, Kukielka disclosed that both locomotives and fuel were in short supply. Consequently, all evacuations would have to be postponed until the problem was rectified. The standstill, he estimated, would last five to eight days.[56] The Office for the Resettlement of Poles and Jews could do little but wait.

The meticulous evacuation plan that Rapp unveiled on 6 February was now in shambles. Only eleven transports of Poles and Jews had entered the Generalgouvernement before Kukielka's announcement. Nonetheless, Rapp and his cohorts would recover, resume the evacuations on 22 February, and ultimately fulfill the objectives—at least in terms of deportation targets—of the Zwischenplan. But even though the goal of 40,000 evacuees was met and slightly exceeded, the placement of all Baltic Germans in their *own* homes was not. The transport halt meant that the inmates of the transit camps spread throughout Wartheland had to remain stationary until the trains could roll again. Furthermore, evidence suggests that the standstill left the camps filled to the point where they could accept no more deportees, which temporarily impeded the Nazis' efforts to carry out further evictions. On 21 February, Koppe's RKF deputy, SS-Oberführer Hans Döring, noted that he had received word that many Baltic German families who had been installed as the trustees of former Polish property were then living with the previous owners in a "household community" (*Wohngemeinschaft*), since the Poles had not yet been removed. Döring stated that "in the interest of the consolidation of German nationhood, it is undesirable for Germans [to live in] a Wohngemeinschaft with Poles, [lest] the Germans find themselves in a position dependent upon Poles." He ordered local civilian officials, in cooperation with the SD, to evict such Poles immediately. To accommodate the evictees, the officials were instructed either to assemble several Polish families together in one building or to simply transport them to a station from which evacuation trains departed. Where exactly the Poles were to stay before their deportation if the latter option was selected was not stated.[57]

Securing employment for all Baltic Germans also proved difficult. On 7 March, Rapp—with far too much optimism—informed Eichmann that by the conclusion of the Zwischenplan, now scheduled to end 15 March, the majority of Baltic Volksdeutschen present in Wartheland would have new homes. Not all, however, would have jobs. To correct this "deplorable state of affairs," Rapp requested at least five additional evacuation transports for the Zwischenplan, implying that perhaps as many as 5,000 Balts were still without employment. These supplementary evacuations, he contended, would guarantee that every Baltic German would have a source of income.[58] Rapp's request was denied. Eichmann telephoned Posen on 11 March to report that no additional transports were available. The rail system, he explained, was swamped with heavy traffic due to the Easter holiday, and rail officials were also preoccupied with the task of developing a summer train schedule.[59] This situation left a significant number of Baltic Germans in the lurch—and many remained so, both in terms of housing and employment. As late as 31 August 1940, a Warthegau bureaucrat involved in the installation of Baltic Germans would comment: "Herr Greifelt [the leader of the RKF main office in Berlin] let it be known that he would have to consult the Reichsführer personally on the issue should final progress not be achieved in the general question of assignment of accommodation [to Baltic Germans]." But the prospects for final progress appeared bleak: "Nothing else," the official conceded, "can be done at the moment."[60] It is clear that some Baltic Germans were still unemployed and homeless long after they had followed "the call of their blood home to the Reich."

The transport halt lasted six days, from 16 February though 21 February. By 22 February, the Reichsbahn had resolved its problems, and deportations resumed. At some point during the standstill, Eichmann distributed an updated transport schedule listing the exact place, date, and time of departure and arrival for each of the remaining twenty-nine evacuation trains reserved for the Zwischenplan. In terms of loading stations, the new schedule, for the most part, mirrored the plan disseminated on 6 February. The only major difference between the two was that one transport originally allocated to Hohensalza and two initially assigned to Leslau were canceled. One of these trains was diverted to Kosten, a town south of Posen not included in the original schedule, and the other two were placed at the disposal of authorities in Posen and Litzmannstadt (one each). A few adjustments regarding unloading stations within the Generalgouvernement were made as well. Apart from these minor alterations, the remaining transports proceeded, geographically speaking, according to Eichmann's original plan.[61]

The last transport of the Zwischenplan left Posen on 15 March 1940. Despite the setbacks, Nazi authorities in Wartheland managed to deport 40,128 individuals during the operation. As stated earlier, the final report on the Zwischenplan made no distinction between Poles and Jews, describing the 40,128 evacuees simply as Poles, all of whom were deported for the purpose of "creating housing and employment possibilities for the Baltic Germans who had returned to the Reich."[62] Several hundred Jews were certainly among the evacuees, but as in the case of the 1.Nahplan, their exact numbers are unknown.[63] The absence of statistical data aside, any attempt to determine the ethnic breakdown of the deportees is complicated by the contradictory nature of orders issued both before and during the Zwischenplan. Prior to the launch of the operation, Himmler called for the deportation of only Jews and Congress Poles, but as noted earlier, VoMi agents were soon informed, apparently by the RSHA, that only "politically troublesome" individuals could be evacuated. Rapp, perhaps unaware of these instructions (though this seems unlikely), ordered on 29 February that if the goal of 40,000 deportees could not be met by evacuating *only* Jews and Congress Poles, other Poles could be deported, as long as they were members of anti-German organizations. Just a few days later, however, VoMi officials were under the impression that the evacuations would also include asocial elements. Granted, the Nazis may have considered many a Jew to be politically troublesome or asocial, but generally speaking, their reports—though obviously not the final reports on the 1.Nahplan and Zwischenplan—referred to Jews as Jews (a label that, in itself, justified evacuation), whereas the politically troublesome and asocial categories were usually reserved for individuals among non-Jewish populations. Unless new documentary evidence comes to light, we will most likely never know exactly how many Poles—Congress, politically troublesome, asocial, or otherwise—and how many Jews were among the 40,128 evacuees.

The evictions and evacuations carried out during the Zwischenplan were evidently conducted in much the same manner as those of the 1.Nahplan, though it is clear that the creation of Eichmann's bureau at the RSHA had, as intended, brought far more order to the process than previously existed. And if the various deportation guidelines issued by the RSHA and HSSPF Koppe in late January and early February were closely followed (and we can assume they were), Rapp's Office for the Resettlement of Poles and Jews played a more hands-on role than his Staff for the Evacuation of Poles and Jews had in December. Higher officials had demanded that Rapp and his subordinates pay careful attention to the precise ethnicity of the deportees in order to prevent the loss of "valuable" German blood through the evacuation of Volksdeutschen and individuals of German descent to the Generalgouvernement. They had also made clear that the deportations could lead to no disruptions in the economic life of Wartheland. The vitality of the Gau economy was to be safeguarded at all costs. During the weeks preceding the inauguration of the Zwischenplan, economic considerations loomed large in the minds of Nazi occupation authorities, and their impact on deportation policy, particularly in terms of the selection of evacuees, was far from insignificant.

ECONOMICS AND EVACUATIONS

On 5 January 1940, Greiser's adviser on nationality questions, Karl Coulon, reasserted the position, voiced time and time again by both Reich officials in Berlin and leading Gau authorities, that the impending evacuation measures could in no way impair the regime's economic mission in Wartheland. In a letter to all county and city commissioners in the district, Coulon noted that "useful agricultural workers and respectable craftsmen are of considerable importance for the reconstruction [of the Warthegau]." Such persons, he forcefully argued, should not be deported without first considering their value to the regional economy.[64] Indeed, if Wartheland was to become the breadbasket of the German Reich, a ready supply of workers, above all agricultural workers, was absolutely essential. But Polish farm labor was a hot commodity and not just in Wartheland alone. The Altreich was also in desperate need of Poles to supplement its agricultural workforce.

By the end of December 1939, 20,000 Polish workers from the Warthegau had been sent to the Altreich as migrant labor.[65] Many more were needed. At some point in early January 1940, Altreich officials demanded another contingent of Polish workers, this time 100,000 farmhands, all from Greiser's domain. The potential loss of such a large pool of labor naturally vexed Warthegau economic authorities, and on 11 January, a meeting was held in Posen to address their concerns. Those attending included Rapp, Hans Ehlich of RSHA Amt IIIES, representatives of the Reich Labor Ministry and the Arbeitsamt-Posen, and Wartheland's trustee for labor, SS-Obersturmbannführer Ernst Kendzia. Kendzia explained, in no uncertain terms, that needs of the Altreich notwithstanding, his district should not be made to suffer. "The provision of the demanded contingent of one hundred thousand Polish farm workers," he stated bluntly, "is impossible." Whereas Jews had been rounded up to participate in the autumn harvest, they were now to be evacuated,[66] making Polish manpower all the more indispensable. Kendzia even went as far as to call for a halt to all Polish evacuations. "For the time being," he declared, "the Warthegau's requisite supply of agricultural labor must be guaranteed; accordingly, the evacuations to the Generalgouvernement must be suspended."[67]

Unsurprisingly, such a radical proposal fell on deaf ears. Rapp did, however, assure Kendzia that at least for the immediate future, evacuations would target only the urban (that is, Jewish) population of the Gau. That being said, he pointed out that 12,000 to 15,000 Volhynian German families needed or would soon need accommodation, and for this purpose, Polish farms would eventually have to cleared. Still, he promised that Polish farmhands, as opposed to Polish farm owners, would not be evacuated en masse. Most farmhands could remain in Wartheland, Rapp assured Kendzia, though it should be expected that a certain percentage would have to be deported for political reasons.[68]

Rapp may have placated Kendzia's reservations about the evacuation of Poles to the East, but the Altreich's demand for Polish labor was another matter entirely. By the time the meeting adjourned, the participants had not yet resolved the issue. They merely concluded that four options existed:

1. Individual Poles could "voluntarily" emigrate to the Altreich as an alternative to deportation to the Generalgouvernment.

2. Entire Polish families could "voluntarily" emigrate to the Altreich.

3. Individual Poles could be forced into the Altreich, and their families could be deported to the Generalgouvernement.

4. "Forced emigration" could be instituted (apparently meaning that any Pole needed for labor would be apprehended and sent west and that no immediate action would be taken against his or her family).

Another meeting, Rapp announced, would be held in the near future to clarify this matter as well as other questions regarding labor allocation. Kendzia, for his part, remained adamant. Whatever policy they ultimately pursued, all authorities, he insisted, had to pay careful attention to the needs of Wartheland, *"since this Gau has great tasks."*[69]

Kendzia was not alone in his views. Hermann Göring also advocated a more conservative deportation policy vis-à-vis Poles. As plenipotentiary for the Four-Year Plan, Göring's mission was to maintain and strengthen the Reich's capacity to make war, which included attaining agricultural self-sufficiency to counter any attempt on the part of the Allies to starve Germany through a naval blockade. In his mind, this economic mission took precedence over all other considerations, matters of racial policy included. At a major conference held at Carinhall on 12 February 1940, Göring stood before Himmler, Frank, and the eastern Gauleiters and asserted that the overriding issue in all "eastern questions" was the need to bolster the Reich's war potential, particularly in terms of agricultural production. "Posen and West Prussia," he declared, "must again become the granary of Germany." Enough farmworkers, therefore, had to remain in the region, and "[they] will be for the most part Poles." All evacuation measures, Göring ordered, had to be redressed to ensure that "useful manpower does not disappear."[70] Jews were a different matter: he was not opposed to the continuation of Jewish expulsions, as long as they were carried out in an orderly and systematic manner. Göring's harangue clearly pleased Frank. The deportations had already led to a food and housing shortage in the Generalgouvernement, and any effort to minimize the number of future evacuees had his blessing. And though they obviously desired the rapid Germanization of their districts, Forster and Greiser voiced no open opposition to Göring's ruling. They merely followed his lead and boasted of the vast amounts of grain that Danzig–West Prussia and Wartheland would be able to produce in the coming months.

RFSS Himmler, however, reminded his fellow Nazis that 200,000 Volks-deutschen from the Baltic states and Soviet-occupied territories required housing and employment. During 1940, he bluntly stated, Polish farmers from Warthe-land, West Prussia, and East Prussia would be deported to create space for the German immigrants. Furthermore, some 30,000 ethnic Germans from the Lublin region of the Generalgouvernement, the area reserved for the creation of a Juden-reservat, would be moved out and resettled in the eastern Gaue, an action that would necessitate additional evacuations. He did, though, agree to postpone the planned "repatriation" of some 220,000 to 270,000 ethnic Germans from Lithu-ania, Bukovina, and Bessarabia. The RFSS did not comment on any impend-ing Jewish deportations. As Christopher Browning argues, "Himmler seemed to think that by scaling back the pace of ethnic German resettlement and indefi-nitely postponing Jewish deportation, he could sufficiently minimize disruption in both the incorporated territories and the General Government so as to continue with his cherished project, despite Frank's and Göring's objections. For Himmler at this time, the consolidation of Germany's new Lebensraum through Volks-deutsche resettlement clearly had priority over deporting Jews."[71]

Still, Himmler's matter-of-fact words show that as far as he was concerned, the deportation of Poles—even those employed in the agricultural sector—would proceed, whether Göring and Frank approved or not. And Polish deportations did, of course, continue, though by no means were economic considerations ig-nored in the process.[72]

German authorities in Wartheland did not confine their attention to the well-being of the agricultural sector alone. Other aspects of the Gau economy also warranted protection against the consequences of mass evacuations. On 24 Janu-ary, HSSPF Koppe wrote to the three Regierungspräsidenten in the Warthegau, pointing out that very few qualified craftspeople could be found among the Baltic Germans earmarked for resettlement during the impending Zwischenplan. In all cases where a position left vacant by the removal of a Pole could not be filled by a Baltic German, he ordered the local Landrat or Oberbürgermeister to work to-gether with the Handwerkskammer (Chamber of Trade) in Posen, as well as with the regional Arbeitsamt, for the purpose of "claiming" (*Anforderung*) the missing worker. This directive apparently allowed for Polish craftspeople considered vital to Wartheland's economy to be released from detention (that is, a transit camp) and granted deferments from evacuation to the Generalgouvernement.[73]

By the launch of the Zwischenplan, the exact procedure for issuing evacu-ation deferments had been established. The procedure was somewhat compli-

cated. Business owners or managers determined who among their Polish workers
were indispensable and reported their names to the local Arbeitsamt. The AA, in
turn, presented lists of such workers to the regional SD office, where they would
be reviewed to determine if any of the registered workers constituted a security
risk. The SD then returned the lists to the AA, indicating on the basis of security
considerations alone exactly who was and who was not eligible for a deferment.
After receiving the SD's ruling, the AA decided whether those deemed eligible
were indeed vital to the economic well-being of the Gau and granted evacuation
deferments on an individual basis accordingly. Businesspeople who received a
deferment for any of their Polish workers were responsible for the apprenticeship and installation of German replacement personnel within a specified time
frame set by the AA. Once the deadline had passed, they either had to release
the workers to the SD or, if no qualified replacements were available, apply for
another deferment. If the businessperson was judged not to have been at fault
for the delay and if the AA complied, the SD would grant permission for a new
deferment. As a rule, the red-tape specialists of the SD would always sanction the
deferments requested by the *Arbeitsämter* (Labor Offices) as long as the Poles in
question did not represent a threat to the security of the Gau.[74]

We have no statistical data concerning the number of evacuation deferments
issued to Poles during the Zwischenplan or, for that matter, during any of the
four major deportation operations examined in these pages. We can assume, however, that in light of the considerable amount of extant correspondence regarding
the issue, as well as the obvious lengths to which Warthegau officials went—or at
least attempted to go—to strengthen the economic vitality of their province, more
than a few deferments were granted. Though nearly 200,000 ethnic German immigrants had arrived in Wartheland by the beginning of March 1940, there were
simply not enough skilled workers and craftspeople among them to allow the Gau
leadership to renounce its Polish industrial labor force. Of the roughly 61,000
Estonian and Latvian Germans who immigrated to the Reich in the autumn of
1939, only 6,726 of those of working age found positions in industry. Nor could
many skilled laborers be found among the nearly 130,000 Volhynian, Galician,
and Narev German immigrants: just 9,968 of those of working age were previously employed in the industrial sector.[75] If the Nazi occupation bureaucracy
hoped to avoid serious shocks to the economic life of Wartheland, then the lion's
share of the Polish industrial labor force would have to remain. And remain it
did. The Polish share of Wartheland's entire workforce grew from 76 to 81 percent between April 1940 and April 1941.[76] By May 1942, Poles constituted between

80 and 90 percent of the workers in armaments production alone.[77] But even during these first months of the occupation and well before Germany faced a war of attrition on two fronts, it is clear that Warthegau authorities—or at least those with the slightest grasp of hard economic realities—understood that skilled Polish workers were far too valuable to dump without ceremony in the General-gouvernement.

THE 2.NAHPLAN REVISED

HSSPF Koppe's 20 January directive announcing the Zwischenplan had stated that the operation would be carried out "before the beginning of the 2.Nahplan," which at that time meant before the evacuation of the entire Jewish population of the incorporated eastern territories. But well before the first transport of the Zwischenplan left Wartheland, the objectives of the 2.Nahplan had changed. At an RSHA conference held in Berlin on 30 January, Heydrich declared that immediately after the Zwischenplan had run its course, an "improvised evacuation" of Polish farmers would take place to create space for the roughly 20,000 Volhynian German families who had by then arrived in Wartheland. The deportation of all Jews from annexed western Poland, as well as that of 30,000 Gypsies from Germany proper, would commence later that year but only after the Poles had been expelled. For the time being, he stated, Nazi deportation authorities should operate under the assumption that 120,000 Poles would need to be evacuated for the purpose of Volhynian resettlement, a figure based on the supposition that the ethnic German families had, on average, six to seven children each. Still, this number was to be regarded as provisional, since a certain percentage of the evicted Polish farmers would remain in the Warthegau as farmhands or would be transported to the Altreich as migrant labor. Within the context of the action, Congress Poles, Heydrich ordered, should be deported as far as possible. The evacuation of the 120,000 Poles, an operation that became known as the 2.Nahplan, was then scheduled to begin on 1 March 1940.[78]

During the 2.Nahplan, which dragged on until 20 January 1941, 133,508 individuals, primarily Polish farmers and their families, were evicted from their homes in Reichsgau Wartheland. The vast majority were deported to Frank's fiefdom east of the Vistula. Most of the others went to the Altreich as compulsory labor, and a few of "racially valuable" stock were to be assimilated.[79] By the end of the operation, the deportation system in Wartheland had expanded and evolved far beyond the quagmire of December 1939. "Absolute organizational deficiency" became largely a thing of the past.

As noted earlier, the original blueprint for the 2.Nahplan—the scheme for the evacuation of all Jews residing in annexed western Poland—was scrapped because it was simply not in harmony with the exigencies of ethnic German resettlement. Though the "elimination" of the Jews from Reich territory was and remained a fundamental goal of the Nazi regime, the Jewish Question was, for the time being, pushed aside by other issues considered more pressing. Some 120,000 Volksdeutschen required immediate accommodation and employment, both for their own well-being and for the good of the Reich economy. Since the overwhelming majority were peasant farmers, Polish farmers would have to be evicted and deported to meet their needs. Therefore, the Polish Question, now clearly and inexorably linked to the resolution of the Volksdeutsch Question, once again took precedence over the Jewish Question in the hierarchy of Nazi racial-political priorities, just as it had during the 1.Nahplan and the Zwischenplan.

In light of the Nazi regime's long-standing goal of creating a judenfrei Reich, Hitler's decision to "repatriate" the ethnic Germans may have been shortsighted, but it had been made. If not for the huge influx of eastern European Germans, the need to expel hundreds of thousands of Poles to create space for the immigrants would not have been so immediate or so pressing, and the deportation establishment would have almost certainly focused its attention on the Jews. But the Volksdeutschen were already in Reich territory and had to be accommodated. Hitler's hands-off leadership style of vaguely defining the objectives of policy and leaving his subordinates to work out a concrete plan to realize those objectives (in this case, the consolidation of German nationhood in the incorporated territories) created this complex situation that caused so many headaches among his underlings in the East. And as was his style, Hitler took no part in the various debates of January and February 1940 discussed earlier, nor does the record indicate his thoughts on resettlement questions in general. Rather, he simply let administrative Social Darwinism run its course. In the dog-eat-dog world that was the Third Reich, Himmler and his anti-Polish racial-ideological priorities prevailed at that time over Göring and his economic priorities, as well as over the practical concerns of Hans Frank.

Wartheland's Jews, therefore, remained where they were. The Litzmannstadt ghetto was sealed on 30 April 1940, trapping roughly 160,000 Jews within its narrow confines. Arthur Greiser and his Warthegau cohorts were, however, determined to clear the ghetto as soon as possible and were thus careful to emphasize its "preliminary character." According to an agreement worked out between Himmler and Frank in early April, the Germans would begin emptying the ghetto in August 1940, that is, immediately after they had finished deporting the 120,000 Poles and 35,000 Gypsies as outlined in the revised 2.Nahplan.[80] But the Litzmannstadt ghetto did not soon disappear. By the spring of 1940, it was already becoming clear to many top Nazis, even to Hitler himself, that the Lublin Reservation scheme was unfeasible.[81] A far more fantastic plan for Jewish resettlement, one focusing not on Europe but on Africa, would take shape in the coming months, and it would prove wholly illusory as well. Further complicating matters, the evacuation of the 120,000 Poles and the resettlement of the Volhynian Germans did not proceed with the alacrity originally predicted. Much to Greiser's disappointment, 1940 would not witness the resolution of Wartheland's Jewish Question.

In this context, Christopher Browning's observation comes to mind: the Nazis' Jewish problem in occupied Poland notwithstanding, "it is important to remember that in their own minds they now had a Polish problem and a *volksdeutsch* problem of immense magnitude, and the attempt to solve all three of these simultaneously would often necessitate an ordering of priorities."[82]

CHAPTER

6

The 2.Nahplan

The Balts speak Russian,
The Volksdeutschen Polish,
The Poles German,
The Reichsdeutschen are speechless.
Doggerel from the streets of Litzmannstadt, Spring 1940[1]

Under the revised 2.Nahplan, the geographic focus of resettlements and evacuations shifted from the cities of Wartheland to the countryside. Unlike the Baltic Volksdeutschen, the Volhynian, Galician, and Narev Germans were predominantly farmers and would therefore receive Polish farms in compensation for the ones they had abandoned in Soviet-occupied territory. Although Heydrich had characterized the 2.Nahplan as an improvised action, the resettlement of these Volksdeutschen and the corresponding eviction and expulsion of Poles were actually subject to considerable preparation and planning. Well before the launch of the operation, SS-Sturmbannführer Rapp's question of late December 1939 regarding future evacuations—that is, whether deportation planning should first concentrate on the western districts of the Warthegau in order to make possible a gradual shifting of the German ethnic border to the east or whether all districts should be treated the same[2]—had been addressed by ranking ethnopoliticians in Berlin. Perhaps to Rapp's surprise, the answer was "neither." Rather, they had determined that the focal point of resettlements and evacuations within the framework of the 2.Nahplan—also known as the Volhynian Action—would be the eastern Landkreise of Wartheland situated along the Reich-Generalgouvernement frontier.

The placement of the Volhynian, Galician, and Narev Germans was meant to proceed according to a set of guidelines entitled "Planning Principles for the Reconstruction of the Eastern Territories" ("Planungsgrundlagen für den Aufbau

der Ostgebiete") formulated in January 1940 by Dr. Konrad Meyer, chief of the
Main Planning Office (Planungshauptabteilung) of the RKF.[3] Meyer, an SS-Obersturmbannführer, was born in a small village near Hanover in 1901. As a university student at Göttingen in the early 1920s, he had been active in right-wing
youth organizations and became a devotee of the völkisch cause. After receiving
his Ph.D. in 1925 for research in wheat genetics, he served as a professor of farming and agricultural studies at the Universities of Göttingen, Jena, and Berlin. He
joined the NSDAP in 1932. One year later, he entered the SS and worked within
RuSHA throughout the 1930s on behalf of the German peasantry. At Himmler's
behest, Meyer joined the staff of the RKF immediately after the creation of the
organization in October 1939.[4]

As leader of the RKF Main Planning Office, Meyer oversaw a staff of ten to
twenty full-time personnel, all academic experts in the field of population policy
and spatial planning. They understood their mission as a threefold endeavor;
according to Dan Inkelas, "RKF experts set out to change the biological characteristics of the population living in conquered Poland, to replace exploitative
capitalistic practices with a sustainable agrarian economy 'organically' based on
the laws of races and nature, and to reinvigorate German culture by reuniting
peasants to the rural countryside." "The first product of the RKF planning office, the *Planungsgrundlagen für den Aufbau der Ostgebiete*," Inkelas continues,
"reflected this understanding in establishing guidelines for subsidiary agencies
and for the more detailed planning carried out by the RKF *Planungshauptabteilung* thereafter."[5]

Meyer's memorandum discussed a wide range of issues pertaining to the
Germanization of annexed western Poland, including, among others, economic
objectives, the ideal population density of the region, and the ideal physical structure of the German villages and farms therein. But practically speaking, of most
importance to Nazi officials and agencies responsible for the immediate installation of German immigrants and the immediate expulsion of native populations
was the section of the memo labeled "Settlement Zone I Order" ("Siedlungszone
1.Ordnung"), a three-page outline of Meyer's plans for German resettlement in
the New East. Meyer's vision called for a deep "belt" (*Gürtel*) of German farms
along the border of the incorporated territories and the Generalgouvernement.
Much in line with the Frontier Strip concept promoted by Imperial German authorities during World War I, this "wall of German Volkstum" would protect
and separate the new Reich provinces from the Slavic hordes to the east. The

belt of German farms would be connected to the Altreich by a broad "bridge" of German settlement running through Wartheland from west to east along the Warthe River;[6] a smaller bridge would run through the former Polish Corridor. These "West-East Axes" would divide the remnants of Polish Volkstum in the eastern Gaue, creating Polish "islands" that, Meyer implied, could be easily eradicated in the future. Larger German islands, in turn, would be established by resettling German farmers around the larger cities in the region. The islands and bridges of German Volkstum would serve as "crystallization points" from which German settlement could eventually expand. All told, the Settlement Zone 1 Order, according to Meyer's calculations, embraced 44,000 square kilometers of territory that was then populated by 4.3 million people, including 285,000 Germans. He estimated that an additional 1.8 million German settlers would be needed to realize his plan.[7]

By the beginning of March 1940, the Nazi establishment had decided that the first step toward the realization of Meyer's elaborate scheme would be the construction of the "settlement belt"—the Ostwall—along the eastern frontier of Wartheland, an objective that dictated both the geographic placement of volksdeutsch settlers and the geographic origin of Polish deportees during the initial stage of the 2.Nahplan. Greiser broadcast this plan on 1 March, stating in a directive circulated among regional officials in the eastern districts of his province that the primary goal of the forthcoming Volhynian Action was "to create a solid, impenetrable wall of German people against Polentum." On the express orders of the RFSS, 18,000 ethnic German families would be installed in twelve Landkreise, all in the eastern third of the Gau, including the six immediately adjacent to the Generalgouvernement.[8] To make room for the settlers, "only Congress Poles and 100% Nationalpolen" (the latter apparently meaning "pure-blooded Poles") would be deported. Though he did not state it explicitly, Greiser implied that those responsible for the operation were to take all necessary measures to ensure that agricultural production in Wartheland was in no way disrupted by the evacuations and resettlements. He merely asserted that "for tactical reasons, it is urgently necessary to carry out the settlement of a Kreis with Volhynian and Galician Germans in the shortest possible timeframe."[9]

Writing in late April 1940 after the 2.Nahplan was under way, Dr. Hermann Rüdiger of the Deutsches Ausland-Institut gave a more definitive statement on the relationship between agricultural productivity and evacuations, as well as a concise overview of the operation as a whole:

The initial systemless and arbitrary evacuation of Poles and Jews from the new eastern Gaue has gradually been brought into a more unified system. Today, the uppermost leading principle is [that] the evacuations and resettlements may not interrupt agricultural production as the foundation for our food supply in Reichsgau Wartheland nor disturb the Generalgouvernement as an extension of our food and armaments base. Therefore, the deportation of Poles and the resettlement of Volhynian and Galician Germans have ensued in rapid succession since the end of March. So that no work is interrupted in any single agricultural enterprise, the Pole is evacuated at night, and the Volhynian German takes over the farm the next morning. The evacuated Poles are assembled in camps, sifted through and examined, and then either come to the Altreich as farm workers or are deported to the Generalgouvernement.

Rüdiger's comments reveal that he had a firm grasp of evacuation and resettlement procedures. But at the time he penned his report, he was unaware whether the administrative machinery for "sifting through" the Polish population of Wartheland had actually been put into place: "If the 'Umwanderung-Zentrale,' planned since the beginning of March, has been established in the meantime," he confessed, "I do not know."[10]

THE UMWANDERERZENTRALSTELLE: ORIGIN, ORGANIZATION, AND OBJECTIVES

The establishment of the Umwanderung-Zentrale (Emigration Center), as Rüdiger called it, had in fact been planned since late January. At some point before the RSHA meeting of 30 January 1940, Dr. Hans Ehlich, the leader of Amt IIIES, drafted an eight-page memorandum entitled "Establishment of Central Emigration Offices." "A thorough evaluation of the whole problem of surveying the Polish population in the eastern provinces," Ehlich asserted, had led him to conclude that "a racial stock-taking of the entire Polish population is, in principle, urgently necessary for all Volkstumspolitik in the German East." The racial examination of approximately 8 million Poles (Ehlich's figure) in closed camps, he conceded, was unfeasible—the process would simply take far too long—but there was an alternative: the "stock-taking" could be carried out by Umwanderungszentralstellen (Central Emigration Offices) or Umwanderungskommissionen (Emigration Commissions) that would work hand in hand with Landräte and regional Arbeitsämter within the incorporated territories to evaluate in the field, so to speak, the Polish population of their individual jurisdictions. Due to a lack of personnel, such an operation, Ehlich admitted, could not begin until May 1940, that is, not until after the processing and resettlement of the remaining Baltic Germans, as well as the Volhynian Volksdeutschen, were complete. But before then, he contended, a partial survey could take place. Those Poles targeted for immediate evacuation could be assembled in camps before their transport to the Generalgouvernement, and while interned, they could undergo thorough racial and political examinations by the Emigration Commissions. Those found to be racially and politically suitable would be allowed to chose their destination: they could either go to the Altreich as farmworkers or be sent to the Generalgouvernement. "It is to be expected," Ehlich wrote (perhaps with a touch of sarcasm), "that the greater number of [these] Poles will no doubt report for work in the Altreich." The Central Emigration Offices or Emigration Commissions, then, would serve as a filter, sorting out the "racially valuable" Poles from the rest.[11]

The perceived need to screen the entire Polish population of the incorporated territories was driven by both ethnopolitical and practical considerations. As noted earlier, Wetzel and Hecht of the Racial Policy Office of the NSDAP had argued in November 1939 that one of the fundamental tasks of German policy in the new Reich provinces was "the complete and final Germanization of those sections [of the population] that appear suitable for it." They had estimated that 1 million Poles were candidates for re-Germanization and, with it, readmission into the collective body of the German Volk. The reclamation of this "lost German blood," it was reasoned, would facilitate the rapid consolidation of German nationhood in the East and at the same time weaken the ethnic vitality of Polentum by extracting the most valuable racial elements from the ranks of the Polish masses.[12]

Although Himmler had apparently brushed aside the NSDAP memo upon receiving it in November 1939, he clearly embraced not only its arguments concerning the re-Germanization of Poles but also the figure of approximately 1 million candidates for such a program. In his own strikingly similar essay, "Some Thoughts on the Treatment of the Alien Population in the East," written in May 1940, Himmler argued for the need to implement a racial-screening process in all of occupied Poland in order "to winnow out" racially valuable individuals from the "ethnic mishmash." Those judged worthy of re-Germanization, he asserted, should be taken to Germany proper and assimilated there. Parents of children with "good blood" would be given the choice of either giving up their offspring or accompanying them to Germany, where they, too, would become worthy members of the Volk.[13] If they chose to give up their child, Himmler reasoned that they would probably not produce any more children, and consequently, the danger that the "subhuman population of the East" might again develop a racially strong ruling class would be eliminated. The Jews would be eliminated as well: "I hope to erase totally the concept of Jews through the possibility of a great immigration of all Jews to a colony in Africa or elsewhere," wrote Himmler, a statement that indicates he was well aware that the Lublin Reservation scheme had reached a dead end.[14] A few days after writing the memo, Himmler submitted it to Hitler, who deemed it "very good and correct" and agreed that it should be distributed among the eastern Gauleiters and to Generalgouverneur Hans Frank.[15] Soon, the Nazi racial policy establishment would follow Himmler's lead and focus its attention on breaking the impasse over the Jewish Question through a massive immigration to an African colony, namely, the island of Madagascar.[16]

In a postscript to his "Thoughts," penned on 24 June 1940, Himmler stated unequivocally that since the new eastern provinces would become truly German only when every inhabitant was German, "seven-eighths [of the native population of western Poland] must continue to migrate eastward to the Generalgouvernement,"[17] and one-eighth—roughly 1 million people—would remain in annexed territory and undergo the re-Germanization process. Economic considerations could in no way obstruct this migration: "I am convinced that in the east we can get by without native Polish labor in the long run, and that we cannot and must not leave Poles in the eastern provinces even for economic reasons."[18] That being said, Himmler had, in fact, earlier acknowledged the importance of Polish workers, asserting on 20 May that racially unacceptable Poles would remain in the incorporated territories "as long as we need their labor," though he added that over the course of five to ten years, even these Poles would be deported to the Generalgouvernement "without exception or mercy."[19] But despite the convictions of the RFSS, economic considerations had, of course, already had a substantial impact of the deportation campaign. They would ultimately play a significant role in bringing the entire program to a halt in March 1941.

Himmler's statements came months after Ehlich drafted his proposal for the establishment of the Central Emigration Offices, but they reflected many of the conclusions already reached by late January 1940 regarding the necessity for a racial screening of the Polish population then living under the Nazi yoke. And although the RFSS may have believed that economic interests were of secondary importance to the goals of the Germanization program,[20] it is evident that practical economic considerations were on Ehlich's mind as he wrote his memorandum. Polish farm labor was urgently needed in the Altreich. As Ehlich saw it, that labor force should, as far as possible, be composed of racially valuable and politically reliable Poles who would not pose an ethnopolitical threat to the main body of the German Volk in the west, and this could be guaranteed only through a careful evaluation of the native inhabitants of the incorporated territories. Furthermore, Ehlich was surely aware of a recent discussion concerning the allocation of Polish farm labor that had taken place between his immediate superior, Otto Ohlendorf, the chief of RSHA Amt III, and Dr. Helmut Kaestner of the Reich Labor Ministry on 5 January 1940. Their talk led to the conclusion that a "double resettlement" of Poles had to be avoided in the future. No longer should Poles from the eastern Gaue first be deported eastward to the labor reservoir of the Generalgouvernement and then transferred back west for agricultural work in the Altreich. Rather, Poles should be examined to determine their racial suitability before deportation; those who qualified would be sent directly from the new provinces to Germany proper, a move that would streamline labor allocation by eliminating the double resettlement that had occurred in the past.[21] Ehlich envisioned his Central Emigration Offices as the judge and jury in this selection process. They would meet both völkisch and economic objectives simultaneously by ensuring a steady supply of racially valuable Polish workers for the Altreich and, at the same time, by preventing the loss of precious German blood that would invariably result from unregulated deportations.

Heydrich unveiled an abbreviated version of Ehlich's proposals at the RSHA conference on 30 January 1940. He announced that plans were in the works to create a number of Central Emigration Offices to assist in the resettlement and deportation campaign. The mission of these new bureaus, as he framed it, was to examine the entire population of the new eastern Gaue, to register each person according to "personal, racial, medical, and security" criteria, and to evaluate each individual's capacity for labor. This selection process, he said, was to begin after the three mass movements discussed at the meeting, that is, the Zwischenplan, the 2.Nahplan, and the deportation of all Jews (as well as 30,000 Gypsies) from Reich territory.[22] However, the partial survey suggested in Ehlich's memo began much sooner.

On 24 April 1940, Rapp's Office for the Resettlement of Poles and Jews was renamed the Umwandererzentralstelle (UWZ; Central Emigration Office) and placed within the administrative jurisdiction of Ernst Damzog, the supervisor of Sipo and the SD in Wartheland.[23] The responsibilities of the UWZ as eventually defined were as follows:

a) Defense of German blood before deportation through the examination of farmers and business owners earmarked for evacuation by the SS-Arbeitsstäbe [SS Work Staffs].

b) Deferment [from evacuation] of Poles employed in enterprises of strategic importance and working on the reconstruction of the Warthegau.

c) Preparation for the evacuations through the *provision of all necessary documents* as well as through close cooperation with Landrat [*sic*], Schutzpolizeibattaillon [Municipal Police Battalion], Gendarmerie, and the NSV [Nationalsozialistische Volkswohlfahrt, the leading Nazi welfare organization].

d) *Supervision* of the evacuations.

e) Transport of the evacuated Poles from the Kreise to UWZ camps in Litzmannstadt.

f) Survey, registration, distribution, and containment of the Poles [in the camps] and transport to the Generalgouvernement or the Altreich.

g) The selection of racially good Poles who [are to be] naturalized in the Altreich [during the period prior to the foundation of an independent branch office of the Rasse- und Siedlungshauptamt (Race and Settlement Main Office) in Litzmannstadt on 1 November 1940].[24]

Although the UWZ was officially under Damzog's command, it was in reality subordinate to Amt IIIB (formerly IIIES) and Amt IVD4 of the RSHA, and consequently, the most significant orders and directives regarding the fulfillment of its duties continued to come from Hans Ehlich and Adolf Eichmann.[25] Rapp stayed on as office chief of the bureau during its first week of operation under the new designation UWZ, but in late April, he was transferred to Braunschweig to serve temporarily as the region's supervisor of Sipo and the SD.[26] Shortly after Rapp's departure, Damzog announced the appointment of Rolf-Heinz Höppner, a thirty-one-year-old SS-Hauptsturmführer and lawyer from Siegmar, as the new leader of the Posen office. Judged "a very diligent and conscientious worker with good negotiation skills" by his superiors, Höppner remained the chief of the UWZ-Posen office until July 1944.[27]

Well before the creation of the UWZ was announced, its previous incarnation, Rapp's Office for the Resettlement of Poles and Jews, had taken a number of steps to put Ehlich's recommendations of late January 1940 into action. As Wartheland's Nazi functionaries and racial politicians prepared for the impending Volhynian Action in late February and March 1940, the nerve center of the deportation system shifted from Posen to Litzmannstadt. Led by SS-Obersturm-

SS-Hauptsturmführer Rolf-
Heinz Höppner, the second
leader of the UWZ. Höppner
replaced Albert Rapp as
UWZ chief in May 1940.
(Bundesarchiv-Berlin)

bannführer Hermann Krumey, the Litzmannstadt branch (by then termed the
Nebenstelle, or Border Office) of Rapp's agency assumed control of all technical
questions regarding expulsions, including the planning of evacuations, the scheduling of transports in conjunction with RSHA Amt IVD4, and the management of
UWZ camps established within the city for the examination of Polish deportees.
By the beginning of April, twelve UWZ *Aussenstellen* (branch offices) had been
set up in the vicinity of Litzmannstadt, one in each of the Landkreise designated
for ethnic German resettlement as outlined in Greiser's 1 March directive.[28] These
branch offices were to oversee the selection and eviction of Poles, accommodate
the evacuees briefly in local transit camps, and then load them on trains or motorized transport bound for the camps in Litzmannstadt. There, the Poles would
be registered and examined. In accordance with Ehlich's proposals, those considered suitable would be sent to the Altreich either as laborers or for assimilation,
and the rest would proceed to the Generalgouvernement. Though the main office
in Posen still handled basic organizational questions and remained nominally
in charge of operations, the hub of all UWZ activity from the spring of 1940 to
March 1941 was Krumey's Nebenstelle in Litzmannstadt.[29]

SS-Obersturmbannführer
Hermann Krumey, the chief
of the UWZ Border Office in
Litzmannstadt. Krumey was the
de facto leader of the deportation
campaign in Wartheland from
April 1940 on. (Bundesarchiv-
Berlin)

From April 1940 on, Hermann Krumey was perhaps the most important Warthegau official involved in evacuations, more important than Höppner, Ernst Damzog, and even HSSPF Wilhelm Koppe himself. Krumey was a Sudeten German, born in Märisch-Schoenberg in 1905. He was schooled as a pharmacist, and after his release from the Czech army in 1927, he worked as such until 1938. He was an active member of German organizations in the Sudetenland throughout the 1930s, and immediately following the annexation of the region in October 1938, he joined the Allgemeine-SS (General-SS), receiving the rank of Obersturmbannführer. In November 1939, Krumey was assigned to HSSPF Koppe's office in Posen, and he served as Rapp's transport officer until he took control of the UWZ bureau in Litzmannstadt in the spring of 1940. In close and constant contact with Eichmann, Hermann Krumey was, for all intents and purposes, the leader of the deportation campaign in Wartheland during all subsequent actions.[30]

The UWZ system in the Warthegau, particularly the Litzmannstadt office, was in a state of continuous growth and evolution throughout 1940. By the time of the launch of the Zwischenplan in mid-February, the Litzmannstadt bureau had already developed beyond all other branch offices in terms of its size and organizational complexity. Though the agency's operational jurisdiction was still restricted to the city itself, it employed four SS officers as of 19 February and consisted of five individual departments: a racial-screening department, a department for liaison with city officials and the municipal police, a department for administrative matters, a department for transport matters, and a finance department.[31] It also managed a transit camp for deportees.

Just two months later, the staff of the Litzmannstadt bureau had swelled to forty SS personnel and forty-eight paid civilian employees.[32] It is difficult to trace the exact course of the UWZ's maturation over the following months, but by the beginning of February 1941, it had expanded to seven departments, all but one of which were based in Litzmannstadt. In all likelihood, the following organizational structure was in place before the conclusion of the 2.Nahplan:

Department 1—Organizational and Transport Matters

Department 2—Administration

Department 3—Camp Inspection

Department 4—Rasse- und Siedlungsamt (Racial Screening—an independent office as of 1 November 1940)

Department 5—Office for processing applications for exemption from evacuation

Department 6—Fahndungsdienst (Search Service), for the apprehension of fugitive evacuees

Department 7—Medical personnel for the camps

All departments, with the exception of Department 5 and a branch division of the Search Service, both of which were based in Posen, were located in Litzmannstadt. As of late January 1941 (and probably well before), the Litzmannstadt establishment also included four UWZ transit camps, as well as one camp for meticulous racial examinations run by the Rasse- und Siedlungsamt (RuS; Race and Settlement Office).[33] These camps, which constituted the centerpiece of Wartheland's deportation system, will be discussed in detail.

THE 2.NAHPLAN IN ACTION

By the onset of the 2.Nahplan, the bulk of the responsibility for planning and executing evictions and evacuations at the local level had been removed from the hands of the Landräte and Oberbürgermeister and transferred to the UWZ Aussenstellen. During the 1.Nahplan and the Zwischenplan, local civil authorities had played a crucial role in operations, for as one Gestapo officer put it in July 1940, "they alone were in the position to create the complete technical prerequisites" for the deportations.[34] But Rapp's little Staff for the Evacuation of Poles and Jews had by now evolved into a much larger and much more capable organization, and the UWZ Aussenstellen, together with the SS-Ansiedlungsstäbe (SS-AS; SS-Resettlement Staffs, also referred to as SS-Arbeitsstäbe) manned by RKF representatives responsible for the selection of farms for ethnic German settlers and their installation therein, would assume most of the tasks previously handled by civilian officials. Still, the Landräte continued to serve an advisory function in the identification of potential Polish deportees, and perhaps more important, they were required to work closely with UWZ personnel in laying the administrative and technical groundwork for the operation. The latter task included the creation of "Volksdeutsche commissions" to assist in the evacuations, the erection of a transit camp, the provision of office space and materials for authorities involved in the action, the allocation of local police forces to carry out evictions, and the accommodation of police auxiliaries and so-called flying commandos of SS officers for the duration of their stay in the targeted Kreise.[35]

Though the first transports of deportees did not roll to the Generalgouvernement until somewhat later, evictions within the framework of the 2.Nahplan began in mid-March.[36] The entire eviction and evacuation process, from the initial selection of Polish deportees to their transport either to the Generalgouvernement or the Altreich, proceeded as follows. Within villages targeted for Volhynian resettlement, an SS-Ansiedlungsstab identified farms considered suitable for ethnic Germans and then submitted lists of potential deportees to the local UWZ Aussenstelle.[37] Assisted by other German agencies and officials, including the Arbeitsämter and the Landräte, the UWZ reviewed the lists to determine whether the evacuation of the targeted Poles was permissible. Among the factors weighed were the individual's importance to the Gau economy, his or her ethnic background (in other words, whether he or she was of obvious German descent), and additional considerations that will be discussed. The revised lists were then sent back to the SS-AS. With UWZ recommendations in hand, the resettlement staff made its final selection of the farms to be vacated, compiled a final list of evacuees, and turned it over to the Aussenstelle several days before the evacuation was to take place.[38]

An Orpo officer checks his evacuation list as Poles climb onto an open truck. Evicted from their homes in an unidentified town near Litzmannstadt, the Poles' destination is most likely the UWZ camp system within the city. The uniformed man in the background is a Polish policeman. (USHMM, courtesy of the Institute of National Remembrance, USHMM Photo Reference Collection: WS 77870)

The evacuations were managed by the UWZ and were usually carried out by local gendarmerie or Ordnungspolizei battalions stationed in Wartheland.[39] The UWZ and police generally struck before dawn. While as many as fifty uniformed police surrounded the targeted village to prevent escapes, UWZ or other officials, armed with lists of evacuees, approached the designated farmhouses and informed the occupants that they were being evicted. The deportees were allowed to retain one suitcase each with 25 to 30 kilograms of belongings, food sufficient for eight to fourteen days of detainment and travel, and up to 100 reichsmarks, which would be exchanged for zlotys in Litzmannstadt. As in the past, all precious metals, jewelry, artworks, and animals remained behind. After an hour or so, the Poles were loaded onto trucks or buses and transported out. Some went to a local transit camp, others directly to Litzmannstadt, but all eventually found themselves at the UWZ Nebenstelle.[40] If everything went according to plan, the

In an unidentified village near Litzmannstadt, SS men load Polish deportees into a Mercedes bus as onlookers wave goodbye. (USHMM, courtesy of the Institute of National Remembrance, USHMM Photo Reference Collection: WS 77868)

vacated farms were turned over to Volksdeutschen soon after the Poles had left. If no Volksdeutschen stood ready, police officers or NSDAP officials guarded the farms to prevent looting until ethnic German families could be installed.[41] The German settlers were not allowed to witness the evictions, as this might upset them. "Only when the evacuated Polish family is out of sight," Koppe ordered, "should the installation of settlers occur."[42]

Those Polish evacuees who went first to a local transit camp faced a superficial body search and, whenever possible, a superficial racial examination by a representative of the RuS before their transport to Litzmannstadt.[43] Transit camps were often no more than factories or abandoned buildings. In Kutno, for example, a camp was established in a cigarette factory, and in the village of Dobzelin (Kreis Kutno), one was set up in a sugar-production plant.[44] Meticulous body searches and detailed racial, political, and medical examinations awaited all Poles upon their arrival in the Litzmannstadt camps.

By 17 April 1940, three UWZ camps and a delousing station had been established in the western part of the city, all in the vicinity of the railway station

A page from a German photo album. The caption reads, "Treks of evacuated Poles to the internment camp." (USHMM, courtesy of the Institute of National Remembrance, USHMM Photo Reference Collection: WS 51209)

today known as Łódź Kaliska, the point of arrival and departure for the majority of evacuees. The Poles first went to the delousing station at Dessauerstrasse 6-11 and after fumigation proceeded to Lager I, the reception station, situated at Wiesenstrasse 4. There, they underwent medical and political examinations carried out by SD officials, as well as racial exams performed by a staff member of the Rasse- und Siedlungsamt. Those families deemed medically, politically, and racially suitable—"if, in their entire impression, they can be considered racially valuable enough for later acceptance into German Volkstum"—received preferential treatment and could be sent to the Altreich for re-Germanization. It is clear that the racial selection process was based primarily on appearance, that is, Aryan appearance (an indication of so-called valuable blood), though the individual's overall health and political background certainly played a role as well. Moreover, it seems probable that individuals of German ancestry overlooked by UWZ and RuS agents in the field would sometimes enter the Litzmannstadt camps. As the fire wall in the protection of German blood, the racial politicians in Litzmannstadt were responsible for preventing the deportation of all ancestral Germans.[45]

Forced from their homes, Poles board a boxcar for transport to an internment camp.
(USHMM, courtesy of the Institute of National Remembrance, USHMM Photo Reference
Collection: WS 78426)

Some Poles deemed racially valuable flatly refused to go to the Altreich. The
commandant of Lager I noted in mid-May 1940 that a number of Poles had stated
that "under no circumstances" would they become German; they would rather
"drop dead in the Generalgouvernement." A phrase frequently heard in the camps,
he reported, was "Better a beggar than a German" (*Lieber als Bettler, aber niemals
deutsch*).[46] Others simply could not grasp the Nazi concept of race. After a visit to
Mogilno in the later summer or early fall of 1940, an SS-Obersturmführer wrote
with an air of frustration that "it was explained to the Poles time and time again
that because of their racial constitution, they were actually not Poles, but Germans[!]"[47] One can imagine the dumbfounded expressions of the faces of these
Poles when they learned that contrary to their self-perception and despite their
upbringing, national consciousness, and language, they were not, in fact, Poles
but esteemed members of the German Volk.[48]

Those who did opt for assimilation, as well as unmarried individuals who
were considered suitable enough for work in the Altreich but had parents or
siblings who were not, were sent to Lager III at Konstantynów, a suburb of

A German policeman stands guard as a trainload of Warthegau Poles prepares to leave for the UWZ camps in Litzmannstadt. The deportees will make the journey in third-class passenger cars. (USHMM, courtesy of the Institute of National Remembrance, USHMM Photo Reference Collection WS 77869)

Litzmannstadt. All others went to Lager II on Luisenstrasse. There, the evacuees were examined once again, this time to determine whether they qualified for *seasonal* work in Germany proper. But before those who qualified were sent to Lager III, they were presented to the RuS staff, which reserved the right to turn down "crass deviants from the European norm." The so-called deviants and the remaining Poles in the camp were eventually deported to the Generalgouvernement. Lager III, run by the Landesarbeitsamt (Farm Labor Office), was the gateway to the Altreich. There, the Poles—though not those assigned only for seasonal work—were photographed and fingerprinted by the police, issued passports marked "Nationality still unresolved, German?" and eventually loaded onto trains bound for Germany.[49] Except for the delousing, the medical exams, the maintenance of Lager III, and the cost of transport to the Altreich, the entire system was financed by the RKF, primarily through the liquidation of property confiscated from the Polish evacuees.[50]

Those Poles deported to the Generalgouvernement were searched for valuables before transport and were allowed—indeed required—to retain 20 zlotys

Poles arrive at the UWZ camps in Litzmannstadt. This is probably Wiesenstrasse 4, the "reception station." Here they will face medical, political, and racial examinations. Some will perhaps be deemed worthy of "re-Germanization." (USHMM, courtesy of the Jewish Historical Institute, Warsaw, Poland, USHMM Photo Reference Collection: 67367)

per person. They could keep all of the food in their possession, with the exception of perishable items such as raw meat and soft sausage. In early March, Koppe had decreed that their food supply had to suffice for a minimum of two days,[51] but Generalgouverneur Frank protested, threatening that any evacuee who arrived in his jurisdiction without enough provisions for at least eight days would be sent back to Wartheland. Warthegau authorities were evidently forced to comply—despite Krumey's argument, voiced to Eichmann, that Frank's food supply demands would have a disruptive effect on the evacuations. Eichmann, however, assured his subordinate that since virtually all of the deportees were farmers, they could easily provide food for themselves.[52] By mid-April and perhaps due to additional pressure from Frank, the requisite food supply was increased to fourteen days. Eichmann's logic aside, it seems that many Polish evacuees did, in fact, have problems meeting Frank's supply demands, and more than a few did not even have the measly 20 zlotys in cash they were required to take with them to the Generalgouvernement. Therefore, beginning 14 May 1940, German authorities in Litzmannstadt were compelled to furnish 20 zlotys and provisions for fourteen days to each Pole who did not possess such. According to the RKF's

SD and RuSHA officials scrutinize the personal documents of Poles arriving at the UWZ camp system. (USHMM, courtesy of the Institute of National Remembrance, USHMM Photo Reference Collection: WS 77860)

Baggage inspection at the UWZ camps. (USHMM, courtesy of the Institute of National Remembrance, USHMM Photo Reference Collection: WS 90410A)

A group of dejected new arrivals at the UWZ camps. (USHMM, courtesy of the Institute of National Remembrance, USHMM Photo Reference Collection: WS 90413)

Poles interned in Litzmannstadt await their fate. (USHMM, courtesy of the Institute of National Remembrance, USHMM Photo Reference Collection: WS 90412)

The significance of the numbers is unclear, but these Poles may have been selected for either re-Germanization or labor assignment in the Altreich. An SS man stands in the background. (USHMM, courtesy of the Institute of National Remembrance, USHMM Photo Reference Collection: WS 77867)

A scene from a barracks at the UWZ camps. Note the straw bedding and the crucifix on the far wall. The latter may indicate that the building was once a school. (USHMM, courtesy of the Institute of National Remembrance, USHMM Photo Reference Collection: WS 70234)

calculations, 1,401,774 kilograms of foodstuffs and 5,947,780 zlotys (equivalent to 2,973,890 reichsmarks) were handed over to Polish deportees by 15 November 1940.[53] We should assume that these moneys and supplies were, like the operation as a whole, funded primarily through the liquidation of confiscated property.

Department 1 of the UWZ office in Litzmannstadt organized the transports to the Generalgouvernement, as well as all evacuation-related traffic from neighboring Kreise to the camps. As in the case of the Zwischenplan, the coordination of rail transport both to the East and within the Warthegau necessitated close cooperation between the UWZ, the Reichsbahn, the Ostbahn, RSHA Amt IVD4, and the Reich Transport Ministry—a complex task. As Krumey stated in his final report on the 2.Nahplan, as many as twelve transport trains left Litzmannstadt every week during the course of the operation, and anywhere from four to six trains loaded with Polish evacuees arrived. There were nights, he said, in which three incoming transports would appear just as two were pulling out, a situation that complicated the coordination of rail traffic tremendously. Still, Krumey was pleased to report that with the exception of several unavoidable delays, a "frictionless" execution of transports had been the norm.[54]

EVACUATION DEFERMENTS AND EXEMPTIONS

A major responsibility of the UWZ Aussenstellen was to evaluate the evacuation lists submitted by the SS-AS and weed out those individuals who met the criteria for either deferment or exemption from deportation. As in the past, employment in vital industries and occupations, such as those important to the war economy, the infrastructure of Wartheland, and the reconstruction of the Gau, would, in most circumstances, secure the individual in question an evacuation deferment. But since most potential evacuees within the framework of the 2.Nahplan worked in the agricultural sector and tens of thousands of ethnic Germans were available to replace them, deferments based strictly on economic considerations were probably not issued as frequently as in the past. More common at that point, it seems, was the bestowal of outright exemptions from evacuation to persons who, by virtue of their (perceived) racial heritage or their familial connections to German Volkstum, were regarded as instrumental to the rapid Germanization of the province. Although the UWZ camps in Litzmannstadt represented the very last weir for the "protection of German blood," the first lines of defense were the UWZ Aussenstellen. It was their task to ensure that every individual obviously exempt from evacuation never reached the RuS and SD personnel in the Litzmannstadt camps.

A Warthegau native could be excused from deportation for a number of reasons, some clearly in line with Nazi racial ideology and some not. Some were subject to change. For example, as of 18 March 1940, Nazi ethnocrats had concluded that no members of German-Evangelical, German-Catholic, or Polish-Evangelical churches would be deported.[55] The rationale behind this decision was not explained, but these religious affiliations were evidently regarded as somehow in harmony with the psyche of the German people, and membership therefore constituted grounds for acceptance into the ranks of German Volkstum. Though in effect for the first few months of the 2.Nahplan, the granting of blanket exemptions based on Evangelical confession alone was eventually prohibited. On 22 June, Koppe ordered that Evangelical confession would no longer guarantee release from evacuation (he issued no ruling on German-Catholic affiliation); rather, those concerned were to be judged on a case-by-case basis.[56] It is likely that the original guidelines on this matter were allowing too many Poles to escape deportation and consequently slowing the pace of Volhynian German resettlement.

Etched in stone, however, were rules concerning Volksdeutschen, persons of German descent, individuals in German-Polish mixed marriages, those with relatives in the Wehrmacht or living in the Altreich, and foreign nationals.[57] All such persons were exempt from evacuation. Although the ban on deporting foreign nationals was almost certainly instituted in order to avert the possibility of unfavorable foreign policy repercussions, it is clear that the other categories of exemption were meant to facilitate the goals of the Germanization program.

Owing to the precious German blood that flowed through their veins, all Volksdeutschen and people of German ethnic heritage were regarded as essential building blocks in the creation of the racial New Order in the incorporated territories. Therefore, the Nazis sought to prevent their evacuation to the East at all costs. The quest for German blood among the natives of Wartheland began shortly after the conclusion of the Polish campaign. On 28 October 1939, Greiser ordered the creation of a racial classification system geared toward the identification of all ethnic Germans resident in his domain. This system, established at the behest of SS-Obersturmbannführer Dr. Herbert Strickner, an SD specialist in racial affairs based in Posen, was christened the Deutsche Volksliste (DVL; German Ethnic Registry) and placed under the control of Dr. Karl Coulon, chief of Wartheland's Gauamt der NSDAP für Volkstumsfragen. At that time, the DVL

comprised two categories of racial classification, DVL A and DVL B. The DVL
A category was reserved for "known Germans," meaning individuals who had
demonstrated their long-standing commitment to the Volk by belonging to German political, economic, and social organizations before 1 September 1939. The
category DVL B embraced individuals who were of obvious German ethnicity
but had neither expressed such commitment prior to the invasion nor openly
declared their volksdeutsch status during the years of Polish rule. Inclusion in
the Deutsche Volksliste could be secured by filling out a questionnaire and suc-
cessfully passing a police investigation. An NSDAP Kreisleiter (Kreis leader) reviewed all doubtful cases and would consult the Ministry of the Interior if no
final determination regarding an applicant's ethnic status could be reached.[58]
All persons registered in the DVL, be they in category A or B, were exempt from
evacuation.[59] But by no means had all ethnic Germans in Wartheland registered
in the DVL by the launch of the 2.Nahplan. No doubt, many had not done so
because they simply did not realize that they were—at least in terms of National
Socialist racial ideology—Germans. It was the responsibility of the UWZ to identify such persons among potential evacuees and thus prevent the loss of their
prized German blood.

Individuals in German-Polish mixed marriages, those who had relatives serving in the Wehrmacht, and those who had immediate family members living in
the Altreich also qualified for exemptions. Polish spouses of Germans could receive exemptions from evacuation if they had come to adopt German customs
and language, or as Himmler later put it, "if the German part in the marriage has
asserted itself."[60] An additional reason may well have been that their offspring
were half German, though this was never stated. Also unstated was the justification for exempting people with relatives in the Wehrmacht or Altreich. Perhaps
the Nazis viewed these familial connections as a deterrent to any opposition to
the regime, allowing them to rationalize the continued presence of these individuals in the incorporated territories. Whatever the case, the Poles themselves were
responsible for declaring such familial connections. They did so simply by filling out a form stating whether they had parents, siblings, or children of German
citizenship living in the Altreich and/or immediate family members or distant
relatives serving in the Wehrmacht. The UWZ reviewed each form to determine
the validity of the assertions therein and granted exemptions accordingly.[61]

Questions regarding other types of exemptions and deferments arose during the course of the 2.Nahplan. In early June, Höppner noted that a number
of Poles who had saved the lives of Volksdeutschen were scheduled for evacua-

tion. He himself believed that this should not halt their deportation, since "the consolidation of German nationhood," as he phrased it, "is in essence a matter of ethnic and racial cleansing." Acts of heroism, in his view, were irrelevant, but he requested Ehlich's and Eichmann's ruling on the issue all the same.[62] Surprisingly enough, Eichmann deemed Höppner's approach "too radical." Rather, he ordered that policy regarding Poles who had such a "German-friendly" attitude should be determined on a case-by-case basis. As long as they were not politically dangerous, Polish "saviors" were not to be deported immediately; if need be, they could be evacuated toward the end of the operation.[63] A similar approach was taken toward Polish war widows whose husbands had died fighting for Germany during World War I. Himmler evidently considered the question of their fate important enough to give his personal ruling on the matter. He decreed in August that with the exception of those whose family members were involved in anti-German activity or whose farms were needed for Volhynian resettlement, all Polish war widows were exempt from evacuation.[64] Past loyalty to Germany carried weight—but not enough to impede the progress of Himmler's cherished resettlement program.

The handicapped, the sick, and the aged were, insofar as they were not suitable for work or transport (*arbeits-* or *transportsunfähige*), also released from deportation. They were not, however, released from eviction. Instead of being sent east, aged and ailing evictees were accommodated either in the homes of their Polish neighbors or those of their Polish family members living in the Warthegau.[65] This situation led to problems. In the autumn of 1940, Krumey observed that a significant number of old people had been judged unsuitable for transport by police eviction squads and released from evacuation, even though they were perfectly capable of enduring the journey to the Generalgouvernement. He ordered the police to take greater care in evaluating the health of the elderly and to release only those who were truly feeble.[66] The Landrat of Hohensalza also expressed concern over this issue. Writing to his district president in September 1940, he complained about the presence of the many homeless old people incapable of work living in his jurisdiction. Since they could be fed neither by German settlers nor by Poles, they were supported primarily by Nazi welfare organizations, and this, he said, placed "a great financial burden on the Kreis."[67] The Landrat of Posen-Land made a similar complaint the following month. He reported that many sick and elderly Poles were not being evacuated and that their upkeep was costing the local government a good deal of money. The Landrat, for his part, wondered why he was required to accept old and infirm Volksdeutschen in his Kreis but was not allowed to send elderly and sick Poles out.[68] Higher officials eventually took action. Just as the 2.Nahplan was drawing to a close, Greiser announced that on the express orders of the RSHA, all individuals capable of transport, regardless of whether they were old or in poor health, would be included in future evacuations; only those so decrepit that they could not weather the rigors of travel could remain in the Gau.[69]

Evacuation policy regarding sick inmates of the Litzmannstadt camps also caused difficulties within the UWZ establishment. Regulations initially dictated that if a member of a Polish family earmarked for deportation was too ill for transport, that member would remain behind in the camp until he or she recovered, while the rest of the family was sent to the Generalgouvernement. But on 9 May 1940, Eichmann ordered that "the divided evacuation of families" was to be discontinued. If one member of a family of evacuees was sick, the entire family would remain in the camp until their relative recuperated.[70] By the late summer of 1940, however, it had become clear to UWZ authorities that this new policy needed amendment. On 9 August, Rudolf Barth reported to Höppner that as a result of Eichmann's directive, some families had remained in the camps for up to five months. This situation only exacerbated the health problems within the camps, he argued, since such a long internment inevitably led to new outbreaks of illnesses and epidemics. Barth suggested that from then on, Polish families should be transported east even if one member was ill; only mothers with sick children under ten years of age should be allowed to remain behind.[71] Höppner agreed and relayed Barth's proposals to Eichmann, adding that the chief medical officer of the Litzmannstadt camps also recognized the health risks associated with a prolonged detention.[72] Eichmann accepted the logic behind these appeals, but surprisingly, he called for a more liberal policy than that suggested by his subordinates. A parent or relative eighteen or older of a sick child who was fourteen (not ten) or under would be allowed to stay in Litzmannstadt with the youngster until he or she recovered. When the child's health improved, both parties would join the family in the Generalgouvernement.[73]

In light of the obvious fear of epidemics within the Litzmannstadt camps, a question arises: what were the overall health conditions in the UWZ camps? On 5 May 1940, Krumey noted that among the 5,388 people presently interned in the camps, there were ninety-six reported cases of illness, including thirteen lung inflammations, ten cases of scarlet fever, two of diphtheria, and seven heart ailments. But in general, he stated, health conditions were good. To date, only three people had passed away, two elderly persons and a child.[74] Deaths increased dramatically during the summer and into the fall of 1940. On 16 November, an official based at one of the Litzmannstadt camps reported that 410 of the 119,117 Warthegau Poles by then evicted during the course of the 2.Nahplan had perished.[75] This figure, if accurate, probably represents the combined total of camp deaths and deaths that occurred between the time of eviction and arrival in Litzmannstadt.[76] However, Krumey's final report on the 2.Nahplan, issued in late January 1941, reduced this figure by half. According to Krumey, only 216 individuals among the 133,506 evacuated had died during the action. The majority of these were children under fifteen years of age and adults over sixty; neither the causes of death nor the locations where the fatalities occurred were specified.[77] As the unofficial leader of the operation, Krumey may have been privy to more accurate statistics than those cited by the camp functionary, but then again, it is possible—and perhaps probable—that he was merely painting a rosy picture of the 2.Nahplan for his superiors in Berlin.

Death was one way to avoid deportation to the Generalgouvernement, but as has been noted, a Pole—or a Pole redefined as a German—could escape deportation through a number of less lethal channels. Good fortune, such as the luck of living to a ripe old age, employment in a vital enterprise, German familial connections, or German racial heritage (however dubious the latter may have been) could secure an individual an evacuation deferment. Bad fortune, be it an illness or a handicap, could do the same. Another way to escape expulsion was simply to flee at the time of eviction or to avoid one's home entirely during the hours that the UWZ and police normally struck. Much to the chagrin of Nazi deportation authorities, these two methods proved highly effective.

RESISTANCE THROUGH FLIGHT AND OTHER PROBLEMS

Just a few weeks after the inauguration of the 2.Nahplan, Rapp informed his immediate SS-SD superiors in Posen, as well as Ehlich and Eichmann in Berlin, about a growing problem in the field that might well spell doom for the entire operation: the UWZ and the police were consistently failing to apprehend Poles earmarked for evacuation. The activity of the SS-Ansiedlungsstäbe, he stated, triggered the Poles' suspicions that an action was about to take place, causing "disquiet among the entire agrarian population." Poles residing in targeted villages and other villages in the vicinity were leaving their farms at night and returning for just a few hours during the day to tend their livestock. Thus, when the police arrived to carry out evictions, they found only empty homes. The miserable arrest figures of the preceding several weeks led Rapp to predict gloomily that "if [these] conditions persist, only about 20,000 of the approximately 120,000 Poles to be evacuated will be apprehended, while the remaining 100,000 will drift about in the vicinity of their farms." This, he said, brought into question not only the success of the 2.Nahplan but also the success of the fall harvest.[78]

The conditions did persist. On 21 June, Höppner noted with frustration that arrest figures had been declining steadily over the previous weeks. Though the overall success rate of the UWZ's human roundups was above 50 percent (48,580 Poles targeted; 25,735 actually seized), that percentage had dropped to 36 during the actions carried out between 10 and 15 June. It remained to be seen, he said, whether whippings and the threat of executions would lead to better results. Höppner thought that the greatest danger inherent in his agency's glaring failure to meet its arrest quotas was that some 10,000 Poles were presently wandering aimlessly in the forests and fields of the Warthegau. Once the fields were harvested and cold weather set in, gangs of bandits would probably form, and this would threaten the security of the province. The police, Höppner said, had to go after these fugitive Poles. All those apprehended were to be interrogated to determine exactly what had led them to flee their homes in the first place.[79]

The NSDAP *Kreisleitung* (Kreis leadership) of Lentschütz presented a fairly obvious answer to this question: the Poles knew that evacuation commandos would storm their villages between the hours of three and four A.M. and therefore did not sleep at home, preferring to bed down outdoors in the vicinity of their farms. To make matters worse, they often moved their livestock and belongings to the farms of their friends or relatives or simply sold them on the black market.[80] "One must not be surprised," the NSDAP official stated, "if on the day of evacuation only empty homes are found in which all is missing." He also pointed out that there were simply too few police officers at hand to prevent Poles from fleeing evacuation and that the present system of selecting farms for Volksdeutschen was woefully ineffective. In his view, the activity of the SS-Ansiedlungsstäbe, as Rapp had warned earlier, made the Poles suspicious. Whenever an SS-AS representative chalked a number or a mark on a Polish farmhouse, "even the stupidest Pole," the official wrote, knew that he or she would soon be deported and, as a result, was not present when the police arrived. He suggested that the hours of eviction should be moved to midday, since the Poles might then be home working their farms.[81]

The interrogation of Zygmunt Halasiewicz, a resident of the village of Grabow in Kreis Lentschütz who was arrested in November 1940, confirmed the NSDAP official's theory, though in this case, the SS-AS did far more than simply chalk a number on a house. Halasiewicz testified that in April 1940, one day before his village was evacuated, a man in uniform approached his farmhouse and wrote a number on it. As he did so, the official actually told Halasiewicz that he would be evacuated the following day. Halasiewicz and his family immediately fled and took up residence on a nearby farm.[82] UWZ chief Höppner later offered another explanation for the quality of Polish intelligence regarding evacuation actions. On 15 November 1940, he advised Eichmann that the Poles were so well informed not least because almost all German offices in the Warthegau employed Polish personnel due to the scarcity of German workers. Polish mailmen, he proposed, were also to blame.[83]

In late July, a Gestapo officer based in Litzmannstadt would observe that only about 40 percent of Poles who were to be evacuated had been arrested to date. German civilians, he said, bore some of the blame for this problem. It had come to his attention that a number of Volksdeutschen native to Wartheland had warned Poles of an impending action in hopes of purchasing their livestock and belongings at rock-bottom prices. The Poles responded by either selling their possessions or gathering them together and leaving the vicinity. Although the Gestapo, he said, could crack down on the troublesome Volksdeutschen, he conceded that his agency could do nothing to prevent Poles from fleeing.[84]

One example of "subversive" activity on the part of ethnic Germans in the Warthegau occurred in late March 1940. On 28 March, young Arthur Beier, a resident of the town of Brzeziny in Landkreis Litzmannstadt and a member of the Hitler Youth, told the police of his father's recent traitorous shenanigans in a nearby village. Several days earlier, Arthur had accompanied his father, Peter, on a short excursion to purchase eggs from Polish farmers. From each farmer he approached, Herr Beier demanded seventy-five eggs, claiming that they were for the Wehrmacht and gendarmerie. To those who refused or said they had no eggs to sell, he exclaimed, "If you refuse to give me eggs, you will be hanged. You Polish farmers will all be expelled and slaughtered. The Germans will come, all farmers will be driven out, and the Volhynian Germans will move in[!]" Young Beier added that his father treated his family badly and was, in general, "uncouth."[85]

Peter Beier was taken to the local police station to respond to his son's charges. He denied everything but did acknowledge that the Poles in the region hated him simply because he was German. Three Poles, however, confirmed Arthur's story. One reported that Herr Beier had stated explicitly, "All Polish farmers will be expelled and slaughtered, and nobody but Germans will move in. Not one Polish farmer may remain here[!]" The three Poles interrogated avowed that they had not slept at home since Beier made his threats. How the incident of the eggs ended is not recorded. Perhaps Peter Beier suffered the wrath of the police, perhaps not, but after the smoke had cleared, it is likely that young Arthur received a thrashing from his vengeful and "uncouth" father.[86]

While the Gestapo handled ethnic German sedition, the UWZ and it police cohorts took measures to apprehend fugitive Poles. In the late spring or early summer of 1940, a *Fahndungsstelle* (search office) was established in Litzmannstadt and placed under the command of Gendarmeriemeister (Chief of the Gendarmerie) Karl Mollenhauer.[87] Mollenhauer's staff created a card file on all Poles who had escaped the long arm of the UWZ and eventually published a *Fahndungsbuch* (search book) listing the fugitives. Fifteen hundred of these search books were in print by 16 November 1940 and distributed among the various police agencies in Wartheland. From the date of publication to the suspension of evacuations on 15 March 1941, the police managed to arrest 6,213 fugitive Poles and intern them in camps—mediocre results considering the magnitude of the problem.[88] Indeed, in early November 1940, the commander of Police Battalion 101 estimated that 35,000 Poles were on the run in Wartheland. Most, he said, had fled evacuation commandos at the time of eviction; others had returned to the Gau following their deportation to the Generalgouvernement. As of 2 November, 500 had been arrested, 200 of whom were returnees.[89] In a number of instances, the policeman reported, the Poles had gone back to their farms and taken up residence "in the same houses [and] in peaceful harmony" with the new German owners. The Poles, moreover, sometimes resumed control of the farms, assuming the role of "economic leader." The Volksdeutschen often welcomed this, ostensibly because "the Pole knows the conditions better."[90]

The Orpo commander also stated that interrogations of arrested Poles who had returned to the Warthegau after deportation revealed that they knew full well about the punishment that (officially) awaited them. They returned anyway, reasoning that the sympathetic attitude of volksdeutsch settlers, as well as that of German authorities, would help them to avoid the potential consequences of their actions. "In most cases," he conceded, "experience shows that their calculation was not incorrect": the threatened punishment, whether imprisonment or execution, was rarely, if ever, carried out.[91] A VoMi official, SS-Hauptsturmführer Schröder, had complained about this very matter to a DAI representative in Litzmannstadt the previous April. "SS-Gruppenführer Koppe," he asserted, "indeed has a big mouth, but he is too sentimental to stand a few rebellious Poles up against the wall [and shoot them]."[92] Though the Orpo commander did not go as far as to denounce Koppe, he clearly agreed with the tenor of Schröder's complaint, demanding harsh punishment for all Polish fugitives and returnees. He also warned that owing to "the mentality of the Poles," those at large in the Gau represented a serious threat to ethnic German settlers and a grave danger to the German economy. Since they were familiar with their farms and the surrounding countryside, the Poles could easily carry out economic sabotage; preventing such acts would be difficult at best. German officials, he concluded, should immediately take steps to educate all Volksdeutschen about the Poles' rebellious mentality in order to eradicate their sympathetic attitude toward the evacuees.[93]

Resistance through flight, coupled with the unremitting return of Polish evacuees to the Warthegau, was perhaps the most serious operational headache German deportation authorities experienced during the 2.Nahplan, and despite their efforts to solve it, this twofold problem was never overcome. Past mistakes were, from time to time, still cropping up as well. The maximum transport strength of 1,000 evacuees was occasionally surpassed;[94] the SD sometimes failed to supply evacuation lists for the transport leaders;[95] now and then, the Wehrmacht issued travel passes to Poles in the Generalgouvernement, allowing them to return to Wartheland;[96] and Poles were occasionally sent east without money or supplies.[97] But these isolated instances of organizational deficiency were the exceptions, not the rule, and they had little impact on the overall flow of the operation. A far more serious problem—one that held the potential to undermine the success of the demographic project as a whole—was the sluggish pace of ethnic German resettlement.

On 25 April 1940, Greiser decreed that all Volhynian German farmers had to be installed by 1 August at the latest—before the beginning of autumn harvest—in order to preclude the possibility of economic disruptions in Wartheland's agrarian sector.[98] It soon became apparent, however, that the immigrants could not be settled at such a pace. Just two weeks later, Himmler pushed forward the terminus of the Volhynian Action to 31 August 1940 and demanded the installation of at least 100 families per day to meet this goal. He emphasized that conditions in the VoMi transit camps were poor, both in terms of health and atmosphere, implying that morale among the ethnic Germans therein was low. The Volksdeutschen therefore had to be settled as quickly and as "unbureaucratically" (Himmler's word) as possible.[99] At a meeting with SS-Untersturmführer Siegfried Seidl held in Posen on 5 June, Eichmann reiterated Himmler's orders and added that the rate of resettlement would soon be increased to 1,000 families per week.[100] This lofty objective was never realized.

By the late spring of 1940, many Volhynian Germans had been in VoMi camps for up to six months. In an attempt to alleviate their frustration, Himmler addressed a group of 8,000 immigrants in a camp near Litzmannstadt on 4 May: "You must understand that you have to wait. Before you get your farm, a Polack must first be thrown out. Often they are such holes that we first have to put the buildings in order or combine farms ... By summer you will walk on your own land."[101]

A few months earlier, Landrat Vogel of Lentschütz had acknowledged the poor state of many Polish farms—and the poor state of many Volksdeutschen as well—asking UWZ officials "whether or not one can put deloused Volhynian Germans in Polish farms infested with bugs and lice."[102] In fact, Nazi resettlement authorities were somewhat perplexed by the behavior and attitudes of certain elements among the ethnic German immigrants. A member of the SS-Ansiedlungsstab in Turek reported that whereas the Narev and Galician Germans were very diligent, responsible, and orderly, he found that a significant number of Volhynians showed "little pleasure and interest in their farms" and even neglected to harvest their potatoes.[103] In Kreis Samter, a DAI official later noted that 25 percent of the farmers resettled in the district were good workers, 50 percent were only average, and the remainder performed "very poorly." He acknowledged that agricultural training might help to improve the latter group's performance, but if education proved ineffective, there would be no alternative but to take away the idlers' farms, demote the former occupants to the status of landless farmhands, and place them on estates in the Warthegau or the Altreich.[104]

Himmler's orders and promises notwithstanding, there were still 20,000 Volhynian Germans (slackers though many may have been) languishing in VoMi camps at the beginning of October 1940. On 28 October, Eichmann noted that on the basis of available transport trains, only 11,000 more Poles could be evacuated within the framework of the 2.Nahplan, meaning that the resettlement of most of the remaining Volhynians would have to be postponed further still. Their installation was indeed postponed, in many cases indefinitely. As of 1 April 1941, at which point all evacuations to the East had been suspended, 8,640 Volhynian and Galician Germans remained in camps.[105] The Nazis' Volhynian predicament was only exacerbated by the inception of yet another resettlement project, the so-called Chlomeraktion (Cholmer Action) launched on 2 September 1940.

THE CHOLMERAKTION

The Cholmer Action was initiated in order to bring the roughly 30,000 Volksdeutschen residing in the Lublin district of the Generalgouvernement "home to
the Reich." The roots of the operation extended back to December 1939 when
Frank informed Greiser that these 30,000 Germans had "the urgent wish to move
back to suitable settlement land" in Germany. They were, he said, "the most
valuable, purely agrarian Volksdeutschen" and should be treated accordingly.
Upon receiving Frank's message, Greiser contacted Ulrich Greifelt at the RKF
main office in Berlin, requesting Himmler's decision as to whether and in what
manner these ethnic Germans should be resettled in Wartheland.[106] Himmler did
not respond until 9 May 1940, the date he issued RKFDV Anordnung 18/II calling
for the "repatriation" and resettlement of the Germans in question. All would be
bound for the Warthegau.

According to the RFSS, the relocation of the so-called *Cholmerdeutschen*,
referred to as such since most came from the region around the town of Cholm
(Chełm) in the Lublin district, would begin after the corn harvest, therefore in
August 1940. He designated the operation an "exchange resettlement." In theory,
Cholmer Germans and Warthegau Poles would simply swap farms; the Volksdeutschen would be installed on Polish farms in Wartheland, and the Polish
evictees, in compensation for their losses, would receive the vacated German
farms in the Generalgouvernement. The Poles, Himmler stated, would be permitted to retain their household possessions and livestock.[107] A few weeks after
receiving Himmler's directive, German resettlement authorities in Wartheland
determined that the geographic focus of the operation would be Regierungsbezirk
Posen, specifically the four Landkreise of Posen-Land, Schrimm, Schroda, and
Wreschen, all of which comprised planks in the German settlement bridge described in Meyer's Settlement Zone I Order of January 1940.[108]

Throughout the summer of 1940, Wartheland's resettlement and deportation
establishment geared up for the impending Cholmer Action, and as they did,
Himmler's original plan for the operation underwent a number of changes. Although the RFSS-RKFDV had stated in Anordnung 18/II that Polish deportees
would be allowed to bring their movable property to the Generalgouvernement,
Koppe's RKF deputy, SS-Oberführer Hans Döring, quickly protested, arguing
that this liberal policy would lead to a host of logistical difficulties and impede
the smooth and rapid flow of evacuation transports.[109] Evidently, Döring's line

of reasoning was accepted, for the baggage allowance for Poles was eventually restricted to just 30 kilograms per person, no different from that of the 2.Nahplan on the whole.[110] Wartheland's racial politicians also determined that the designated settlement zone for the Cholmer Germans was too narrow. By the end of June, it had been expanded to include nine Landkreise within the Reigierungsbezirke Posen and Hohensalza, only five of which were along the path of Meyer's settlement bridge.[111] But despite the expansion of the settlement zone and despite the continuous problems on the Volhynian resettlement front, Höppner and his SS cohorts in the Warthegau remained confident that they could meet Himmler's August deadline for the inauguration of the Cholmer Action. On 28 June, Höppner reported to Ehlich and Eichmann that he expected all arrangements for the operation to be finalized by 25 July. The exchange resettlement could therefore begin on or around 15 August 1940.[112]

Nevertheless, the launch date of the action was soon postponed, and plans for a genuine exchange resettlement fell by the wayside as well. On 12 July, Höppner learned that EWZ officials in the Generalgouvernement would not complete their registration of the Cholmer German immigrants until the end of August. Due to this unforeseen delay, no transports could roll before the beginning of September.[113] Furthermore, Nazi resettlement authorities decided that an exchange resettlement in the manner of that originally planned would not take place. In late August, operational procedure was redefined as follows. Transport trains, each carrying approximately 120 Cholmer German families (roughly 600 people), their household inventory, livestock, and agricultural machinery, would deliver their cargo to designated villages in the Warthegau. After unloading, the same number of evicted Polish families, each member carrying up to 30 kilograms of personal belongings, would board the empty trains and go directly to the UWZ camps in Litzmannstadt. There, they would undergo racial and political examinations to determine their suitability for re-Germanization or seasonal labor in the Altreich. The very trains that carried them to the camps would be immediately reloaded, this time with already processed Polish evacuees, and then proceed without delay back to the Lublin district of the Generalgouvernement. Their destination was not the villages and farms vacated by the Cholmer German immigrants but rather holding camps within the Generalgouvernement Landkreise of Cholm and Lublin.[114]

Though the Poles deported from Wartheland within the framework of the Cholmer Action had been promised farms in the Generalgouvernement, evidence suggests that relatively few actually received them. Most of the vacated farms, it seems, went to other settler groups, some Polish, some not. Among the second wave of ethnic German immigrants who arrived in Wartheland the previous winter, the Nazis identified numerous Ukrainian and German-Ukrainian families, the former apparently admitted by mistake. On 21 August, Himmler ordered his SS subordinates in Poland to place the Ukrainian families then present in VoMi camps in Wartheland on the evacuated farms in Cholm and Lublin.[115] This move was in accordance with Hans Frank's policy of strengthening the social and demographic position of ethnic Ukrainians (vis-à-vis that of the Poles) within the Generalgouvernement,[116] but it obviously decreased the availability of farms for the Warthegau Poles. The number of vacant farms was decreased—or at least potentially decreased—even further by two other projects then in the works. On the one hand, RFSS Himmler had been toying with the idea of consolidating the Cholmer German farms into a series of large estates that would be placed under the control of SS administrators. On the other, Friedrich-Wilhelm Krüger, the HSSPF of the Generalgouvernement, was considering placing on the same farms 60,000 to 70,000 Poles who had been displaced to create troop-training grounds for the Wehrmacht within his jurisdiction. Therefore, "the farms of the ethnic Germans were thus assigned," as Götz Aly notes, "long before their owners were 'evacuated,' to four very different groups: Ukrainians, Polish Wehrmacht settlers in the Generalgouvernement, Polish settlers from annexed western Poland, and SS-operated large estates."[117] What all of this meant for the Warthegau Poles was summed up in Himmler's 21 August directive: they were simply "at the disposal of the Generalgouverneur." Whether they actually received former German homesteads was the decision of Generalgouvernement authorities alone.[118]

Thus, Polish deportees from the Warthegau initially found themselves in camps, their ultimate fate left to the whim of Frank and his bureaucratic underlings. Their evictions and evacuations were overseen by eleven newly established UWZ Aussenstellen set up within the Landkreise designated for Cholmer German settlement in the western half of Wartheland. All but one of these were under the command of SS officers formally active as Aussenstellen leaders in the eastern districts of the Gau.[119] The first evacuation transport of the Cholmer Action delivered 600 Poles to Lublin on 2 September. Within ten days, 5,761 Poles had been deported for the purpose of Cholmer German resettlement.[120] Pleased with these early results, Krumey optimistically predicted on 13 September that the entire operation would take only sixty days to complete.[121] Time proved otherwise. Because of the limited availability of transport trains, the evacuation pace of early September could not be sustained. Consequently, the last transport of the Cholmer Action did not leave Wartheland until 14 December 1940.[122]

The arrival of this additional contingent of Polish evacuees did not please Hans Frank. In late June, well before the launch of the Cholmer Action, the Generalgouverneur had written to Hans-Heinrich Lammers, the chief of the Reich Chancellery, asserting his refusal to accept any deportees beyond the number— that is, 120,000 for the benefit of the Volhynian German immigrants—specified in the 2.Nahplan. Due to "overpopulation" and "the wretched food supply situation" in the Generalgouvernement, further deportations were, he said, "no longer tenable, considering the catastrophic consequences."[123] Frank's protests carried no weight, since the operation proceeded as planned. Later, after the action was already under way, Frank, along with two of the leading SS officials in the Generalgouvernement, tried to halt the evacuations through an untried tactic: they lied.

During a 27 September conversation between Hermann Krumey and Bruno Streckenbach, the commander of Sipo and the SD in Krakau, the latter asserted that neither he nor HSSPF Krüger had been informed about the population movements then going on around Lublin.[124] This certainly took Krumey by surprise, for the SS- und Polizeiführer of the Lublin district, Odilo Globocnik, had been deeply involved in planning the Cholmer Action throughout the summer of 1940 (as both Streckenbach and Krüger certainly knew). Frank, too, denied all knowledge of the operation, despite the fact that he himself had suggested it in the first place. Obviously disgusted with the duplicity of Generalgouvernement authorities, UWZ chief Höppner took it upon himself to present evidence to his superiors that Frank and his cohorts were lying. On 7 October, he wrote Ehlich and Eichmann, requesting that they examine the introduction, as well as page 142, of a recently published "little book" (*Buchlein*) on the Cholmer Action by SS-Hauptsturmführer Kurt Lück, a Nazi academic expert on German minority groups in the East.[125] Lück's book, *Die Cholmer und Lubliner Deutschen kehren heim ins Vaterland*, speaks for itself: on page 7 is a facsimile of a handwritten note by Generalgouverneur Frank dated 16 August 1940 expressing his unequivocal support for the Cholmer resettlement program. And page 142, as Höppner pointed out, confirms Krüger's knowledge of the operation, noting that the HSSPF, together with Globocnik, was responsible for the delivery of the Cholmer Germans to the Warthegau.[126] The Generalgouvernement's response to this evidence is unrecorded.

Hans Frank remained defiant. He continued his efforts to halt not just the Cholmer Action but all deportations from Wartheland to his jurisdiction. In early November, he informed Arthur Greiser that the Generalgouvernement was overcrowded to the breaking point and that even the Wehrmacht had spoken out against the influx of additional deportees from the west. It was impossible, Frank declared, for the Generalgouvernement to absorb any more Poles and Jews before the end of the war, and therefore, he had instructed his border officials to cease admitting evacuation transports and to send any that subsequently arrived back to the incorporated territories. Greiser was persuaded and agreed to issue no orders for transports beyond those previously approved by the Generalgouverneur. HSSPF Koppe followed Greiser's lead, suggesting that during future operations, the UWZ should consider relocating evicted Poles within Wartheland instead of sending them east. But Höppner, for his part, was undeterred. He notified Ehlich and Eichmann on 6 November that his organization would continue its mission as long as no contradictory instructions came from Berlin.[127] Höppner expressed the same convictions to Koppe, arguing (wrongly) that the Volhynian Action was almost over and that there was no reason to halt the Cholmer Action, since it was an exchange resettlement, meaning that the Generalgouvernement was required to admit no more individuals than it lost through the transfer of Volksdeutschen to the Warthegau.[128] No contradictory orders from Berlin came, and the transports continued to roll. Thus, it seems that a mere SS-Hauptsturmführer had defied not only Frank, an Altkämpfer of the NSDAP, but also Koppe and Greiser, the ranking Nazi officials in Wartheland.

The Cholmer Action drew to a close on 14 December, the date the last of forty-eight transports left Wartheland for Lublin. All told, 28,365 Poles were deported to the Generalgouvernment during the course of the operation, these to create space for the 30,275 Cholmer Volksdeutschen who resettled in the Warthegau. Though characterized as an exchange resettlement, this designation was true only in the sense that Germans from the Lublin region were traded for Warthegau Poles on approximately a one-to-one basis. The Poles in question did not necessarily receive vacated German farms and arrived in the Generalgouvernement just as impoverished as their predecessors had in the past. Lück's glowing depiction of the Cholmer Action, presented in his little book, was far from the truth:

> The resettlers of Polish nationality enjoy the full protection of German authorities [in that] they prosper on the farms assigned to them in the East. So much livestock and inventory is left behind for them that they can immediately set up house again.

Many of them certainly receive better farms than those they gave up in the exchange resettlement. This is based on the law and justice according the great German freedom plan.[129]

This was nonsense. As indicated earlier, the Cholmer Germans were allowed to transport their entire household inventory and all of their livestock to Wartheland, and most probably did just that. The Poles, however, arrived in the Generalgouvernement with a suitcase of belongings and the clothes on their backs. Those few who actually received farms often found it impossible "to set up house again."[130] But it seems the vast majority received nothing. They found themselves not on farms but in camps, and Generalgouvernement officials were authorized to do with them whatever they saw fit.[131]

THE END OF THE 2.NAHPLAN

On 3 December 1940, Höppner informed Krumey that he had just received word from RSHA Amt IVDV that no evacuation trains, including the remaining transports reserved for the Volhynian Action, could travel between 15 December 1940 and 7 January 1941, evidently due to the exigencies of holiday rail traffic. He therefore asked Krumey to take the necessary steps to ensure that the last Poles evicted that year arrived in Litzmannstadt on or before 12 December. A train, he said, would be needed two days later for the purpose of clearing the camps, but if not enough Poles were on hand to fill it to capacity, the transport could be canceled.[132]

Krumey complied. The final evacuation train of 1940 rolled east on 14 December. Three more transports within the framework of the 2.Nahplan traveled to the Generalgouvernement after the holidays, the last leaving Wartheland on 20 January. All in all, the 2.Nahplan—which encompassed both the Volhynian and Cholmer Actions—employed 143 trains. In all, 140 carried a total of 122,984 Poles to Frank's jurisdiction in the east; 3 transports, unconnected to either the Volhynian or the Cholmer Action, evacuated 2,663 Posen Jews in early April 1940.[133] During the operation, 133,506 Poles were evicted from their homes in the Warthegau. Of those entering the UWZ camps who were not deported to the Generalgouvernement, 2,399 were dispatched to the Altreich for re-Germanization and 9,513 as migrant workers; 220 were released from the camps for unspecified reasons; 74 escaped; and if Krumey's tally is to be believed, 216 died either during transport to or within the Litzmannstadt camps.[134]

The UWZ Nebenstelle in Litzmannstadt also took part in the deportation of some 38,000 individuals from other regions of the incorporated territories during the second half of 1940. Within the context of the so-called Saybusch Action, 17,413 Poles evacuated from Landkreis Saybusch (Żywiec) in eastern Upper Silesia traveled through Litzmannstadt and were processed there between 23 September and 14 December.[135] Members of the Nebenstelle oversaw the evacuation of 10,700 Poles from East Prussia, specifically Zichenau, during the Mlawa Action of 10 to 20 November 1940[136] and 6,687 Poles and 3,259 Jews, also from East Prussia, during the Litauer Action of 5 to 17 December. Together with the 125,647 deportees from Wartheland, a grand total of 163,706 people were sent to the Generalgouvernement via organized evacuations during the ten-month operational life span of the 2.Nahplan.[137]

Krumey concluded his final report on the 2.Nahplan by pointing out that if the UWZ had fulfilled all of the requests for individual evacuations submitted by the Landräte, Oberbürgermeister, and other German authorities in Wartheland, another seventy to eighty transport trains would have been needed, but these, he lamented, "were unfortunately not available."[138] It is clear he was referring only to requests regarding the deportation of Poles. Hundreds of thousands of Jews, all slated for eventual expulsion, remained in the Warthegau, the vast majority withering away in the Litzmannstadt ghetto despite earlier promises, based on the Himmler-Frank agreement concluded in the spring, that the evacuation of the ghetto would commence in August 1940, immediately after the conclusion of the Volhynian Action. But as noted, the Volhynian Action ran well behind schedule. This fact, coupled with incorporation of the Cholmer Action into the 2.Nahplan, partly accounts for the failure to clear the ghetto. More important, however, is the fact that Nazi plans for Jewish resettlement changed drastically during the summer of 1940.

In late June 1940, a few days after the surrender of France, RFSS Himmler suddenly and expectedly issued an order halting the imminent deportation of Jews, those of Litzmannstadt included, to the Generalgouvernement.[139] By that point, both Hitler and Himmler were convinced that their so-called Jewish problem could be solved as soon as the war with Great Britain was over by unloading all Jews in Germany's sphere of influence—an estimated 4 million people—on the French colony of Madagascar. This fantastic and wholly unrealistic plan certainly pleased Hans Frank: not only would he be rid of the roughly 1.5 million Jews residing in the Generalgouvernement, he would also no longer have to accept Jewish deportees from other regions under German control. Arthur Greiser, by

contrast, found the Madagascar Plan much less to his liking. He had long been
anxious to evacuate the Litzmannstadt ghetto, and the thought that he would
now have to wait until the end of the war to do so bitterly frustrated him. On 31
July, Greiser and HSSPF Koppe met with Frank and his SS top brass. Emphasizing that "it would be an impossible situation to keep these Jews, packed together
in the ghetto, over the winter," Greiser attempted to convince Frank to accept
the Litzmannstadt Jews as originally planned. Koppe also chimed in, stressing
that "the situation regarding the Jews in the Warthegau worsened day by day"
and pointing out that the ghetto had been created only "on the condition that the
deportation of the Jews would begin by mid-year at the latest." But Frank and
his underlings, basking in the glow of a new racial policy that for once seemed
to favor the Generalgouvernement, flatly rejected Greiser's and Koppe's appeals.
They merely suggested that the Warthegau leadership take steps to ensure that
the Litzmannstadt Jews were on the first transports to Madagascar.[140] Events on
the military front, however, would soon dash the hopes and expectations of Greiser and Frank alike.

The Germans, of course, failed to knock Great Britain out of the war, and the
Madagascar Plan, like the Lublin Reservation scheme before it, was scrapped. As
Götz Aly writes, "The beginning and end of plans to invade Britain mark the time
frame in which the Madagascar Plan is seen as a realistic variant of a 'territorial
final solution,' since at the very least it required the defeating of British naval
supremacy in the Mediterranean."[141] By the end of October 1940, it was clear that
no invasion of Great Britain would take place. The Nazis had reached yet another
cul-de-sac in their search for the elusive territorial solution to the Jewish Question. The Litzmannstadt ghetto therefore remained standing, a stark reminder of
Greiser's shattered dream of a judenfrei Wartheland in 1940.[142]

Deportations from the Warthegau would soon resume, but they would continue to target primarily Poles, just as they had in the past. Although the comprehensive Germanization of Greiser's Mustergau obviously still necessitated the
removal of the region's Jews, they were not included in the evacuation forecast for
1941. A number of factors, some beyond questions of state security or the need to
accommodate ethnic Germans, would dictate that the evacuation of Poles from
Wartheland should, once again, take precedence. The "removal" of Wartheland's
Jews would, however, begin in earnest in the winter of 1941–1942, though the gas
vans of the Chełmno extermination camp—not the evacuation trains of the UWZ
or ships bound for the island of Madagascar—would supply the means.

7

The Short Life of the 3.Nahplan– 1.Teilprogram

There was good reason for unbridled optimism within the ranks of the National Socialist leadership at the beginning of 1941. The previous spring, the German war machine had rolled with surprising ease over Denmark, Norway, Luxembourg, the Low Countries, and France, and the British army had been driven from the continent. German troops moved freely from the English Channel to the Nazi-Soviet line of demarcation in the East. Hitler was now the undisputed lord of northern Europe. Never before had Germany wielded such might.

The much-publicized blitzkrieg victories of 1940 had indeed been astounding. Though the Nazi resettlement and occupation authorities in Poland had not received nearly as much attention in the press as their Wehrmacht counterparts, they certainly believed their lesser-known achievements on the ethnopolitical front had been equally remarkable. In a short article published in the January 1941 issue of *Raumforschung und Raumordnung*, RKF office chief Ulrich Greifelt reminded his readers that whereas the Royal Prussian Colonization Commission had managed to resettle only 170,000 Germans in the Imperial provinces of Posen and West Prussia during its twenty-eight years of peacetime operation, his own organization had in just one year—and "in the middle of a decisive struggle concerning the existence or non-existence of the nation" at that—brought nearly 180,000 Volksdeutschen to the incorporated territories, and thousands more were on the way.[1] Arthur Greiser, too, felt he had cause to gloat. During the first year of his administration, not only had tens of thousands of ethnic Germans found new homes in Wartheland but the Gau had also experienced a significant increase in virtually all spheres of agricultural production, enabling it to deliver 300,000 tons of surplus grain to the Altreich and to manufacture fully one-sixth of all the sugar consumed in Germany.[2] But Wartheland's accomplishments, the Gauleiter

boasted, extended far beyond the realm of agriculture. The very existence of the
Gau was an enormous triumph in itself. The reclamation of and ongoing reconstruction in the East, with Reichsgau Wartheland at its heart, represented "the
greatest and most beautiful task ever confronted by a German generation," the
fulfillment of Germany's historical destiny, and the realization of its long-standing geopolitical aspirations: "As we make the land on the Warthe and the Vistula
the breadbasket of the Greater German Reich and create Lebensraum for millions of German people, we finally end the unhappy chapter in German history
that was characterized by the expression 'People without Space.'"

To be sure, 1940 had been a banner year, and the future looked just as bright.
Before long, Greiser promised, the Warthegau would be capable of producing 1.1
million tons of surplus bread grains every year.[3] And as Greifelt pointed out in
his article, another 200,000 ethnic Germans would be resettled in the coming
months, further promoting the rapid Germanization of the new eastern provinces
of the Reich.[4]

The exhilaration of conquest bred confidence, and the planning of Nazi ethnocrats reflected this. Although the installation of the Volhynian Germans was
far from complete, the RKF and its subordinate agencies embarked on several
new resettlement programs in the wake of the defeat of France. Combined, these
operations would eventually double the number of ethnic German immigrants
in the Altreich and incorporated territories. The provision of housing and employment for the new arrivals, together with a number of initiatives unrelated to
volksdeutsch resettlement, necessitated hundreds of thousands of deportations.
With the exception of Himmler's ephemeral scheme of 30 October 1939, which
had unrealistically called for the expulsion of 1 million individuals in just three
short months, the evacuation plan for 1941 surpassed all its predecessors in terms
of objectives, scale, and organizational complexity. And by any measure, it was
a total failure.

THE 3.NAHPLAN

Well before the Volhynian Action had run its course, preparation began for the
next major resettlement operation—the Bessarabian Action of 1941. In a series of
RFSS-RKFDV directives issued between July and October 1940, Himmler made
known that the ethnic German populations of Lithuania and the Romanian territories of Bessarabia and Bukovina (Buchenland), all recently annexed by the

Soviet Union, would be brought "home to the Reich."[5] A "cleanup" resettlement action was also initiated in the fall of 1940 to "repatriate" those Estonian and Latvian Volksdeutschen who had chosen not to leave their respective homelands with the first wave of immigrants the previous year. Since the two countries had in the meantime officially become Soviet Socialist Republics, evidently the "call of their blood" now sounded much more appealing to these Germans. Between September 1940 and March 1941, roughly 275,000 Volksdeutschen from these various regions emigrated to Germany.[6] The RKF planned to resettle the vast majority in the incorporated territories, though several thousand were destined for the Altreich. Most likely due to the constant delays and organizational headaches on the Volhynian resettlement front, a concrete blueprint for the evacuations necessary to accommodate the new immigrants did not take shape until early January 1941. Hundreds of thousands of deportations unconnected to the resettlement program were planned as well.

Known as the 3.Nahplan, the deportation program for 1941 was designed with far more than the installation of the Baltic and southeastern European Volksdeutschen in mind, and unlike the three previous operations discussed in these pages, the focus of the action extended well beyond the borders of Wartheland. On 8 January, a major conference regarding the forthcoming evacuations took place at the RSHA in Berlin. Chaired by Heydrich, the participants included representatives of the RKF, VoMi, the Wehrmacht, the Reich Transport Ministry, and RSHA IVD4; SS officials from Danzig–West Prussia, Upper Silesia, and the Generalgouvernement; and the leaders of the UWZ-Warthegau, namely, Ernst Damzog, Rolf-Heinz Höppner, and Hermann Krumey. After much deliberation, the lords of the New Order concluded that 1941 would witness the evacuation of 831,000 people from Reich territory to Hans Frank's realm in the East.

A number of disparate issues generated an operational plan of such magnitude. Though most of the participants, it seems, were not yet aware of Hitler's intentions, the invasion of the Soviet Union now loomed large on the horizon. To prepare for the attack, the Wehrmacht sought to establish a network of military training grounds in occupied Poland, an immense project necessitating the immediate expulsion of all Poles residing on or around the seven sites it had selected. Additional evacuations were required to enlarge the farms of ethnic Germans already resident in the incorporated territories (a program called Volksdeutsche Besserstellung [Ethnic German Financial Improvement]), to remove Poles apprehended during "search actions," to create housing for German state officials and their families, and to clear space for the expansion of the Auschwitz concentration camp system in Upper Silesia. The deportation of 60,000 Viennese Jews, a scheme in the works since the autumn of 1939 but continuously postponed due to the exigencies of volksdeutsch resettlement, was included in the 3.Nahplan as well. These various initiatives accounted for nearly half of the expulsions planned for 1941; the accommodation of new German immigrants accounted for the remainder. By the end of the 8 January meeting, Heydrich and his associates had approved the following operational blueprint for the 3.Nahplan:

> For the resettlement of ethnic Germans: Danzig–West Prussia, 100,000 Poles; Wartheland, 148,000 Poles; Upper Silesia, 150,000 Poles, East Prussia: 46,000 Poles
> For Volksdeutsche Besserstellung: 50,000 Poles
> For KZ Auschwitz: 20,000 Poles
> For German state employees: 50,000 Poles
> For the deportation of apprehended Poles: 5,000 Poles
> For troop-training grounds: 202,000 Poles
> For Vienna: 60,000 Jews
> Total: 831,000 evacuees

The first phase of the action, the 3.Nahplan–1.Teilprogram, was scheduled to run from 1 February to 30 April 1941. During this period, 248,500 people would be transferred to the Generalgouvernement, a figure that included 10,000 Viennese Jews. Two trains of 1,000 deportees each would travel daily. The usual supply requirements of warm clothing and rations sufficient for fourteen days applied, though it was now mandatory that every evacuee have at least 60 zlotys in hand at the moment of his or her arrival in the Generalgouvernement. Frank's representatives accepted the objectives of the 3.Nahplan without argument, perhaps because they had no real say in the matter: Hitler, himself, had declared that the reception of these 831,000 deportees was "the most urgent task of the Generalgouvernement for the Reich in the year 1941."[7]

Resigned though they were, Frank and his SS and administrative subordinates were naturally perplexed about the impending influx of nearly a million destitute evacuees into the already overcrowded Generalgouvernement. They met several times during the week following the RSHA conference to discuss the issue, and all agreed that the coming months would be fraught with almost insurmountable difficulties. Stockpiles of food and clothing were not sufficient to meet the needs of so many deportees, and the Reich government, HSSPF Krüger informed Frank, would do little to help. The housing shortage was acute: accommodation possibilities in the Lublin district were almost nonexistent, and one-third of the district of Krakau was closed to resettlement due to the construction of military bases. The district governor of Krakau reported that living conditions were dreadful throughout his jurisdiction and would only grow worse as more deportees arrived. His subordinate district chiefs were in "utter despair," and the local population was "prepared to resist with violence."[8]

Frank conceded that the approaching human tidal wave would place "a hardly bearable increased burden" on the Generalgouvernement, but he reminded his cohorts that there was an immense "foreigner problem" in the incorporated territories and that it must be solved in short order. As Hitler had explained to him in November and again in December 1940, the deportation campaign had to be waged during the war. Bruno Streckenbach, the commander of Sipo and the SD, wholeheartedly agreed, pointing out that "the war affords the opportunity to take relatively rigorous action without regard for world opinion." But the question of exactly how to deal with 831,000 incoming Poles and Jews remained open. Perhaps, Frank queried, a "massive export of workers to the Reich," coupled with labor projects within the Generalgouvernement, such as road construction and the reclamation of marshland, would help to alleviate the problem? Perhaps, another official suggested, all Jews could be driven into ghettos in order to free up housing for Poles? After deliberating these and other proposals over the course of three major conferences held in mid-January 1941, Frank finally asked Eberhard Westerkamp, the head of his Internal Affairs Administration, if the Generalgouvernement would, when all was said and done, be able to cope with the deluge of evacuees. Westerkamp replied that the Generalgouvernement would survive the initial onslaught, despite the obvious hardships. But after the completion of the 3.Nahplan–1. Teilprogram, he advised, a pause of several months would be necessary to allow everyone time to regroup. No doubt to the satisfaction of Frank and his minions, the pause that eventually came would last far longer than several months.[9]

SCHWERPUNKT WARTHELAND: THE BESSARABIAN ACTION AND OTHER PROJECTS

The resettlement of Estonian, Latvian, and Volhynian Germans had centered almost exclusively on Wartheland, but the Bessarabian Action, as the new operation was called, encompassed the incorporated territories in their entirety and East Prussia as well. According to RKF plans, the majority of the Lithuanian Germans would be installed in Danzig–West Prussia and East Prussia, whereas the immigrants from Bessarabia and Bukovina would be scattered throughout West Prussia, Upper Silesia, and the Warthegau. At the beginning of January 1941, Wartheland's share of these incoming Volksdeutschen had been set at only 53,000 individuals. But if the province was no longer the hub of German resettlement, it remained the hotbed of ethnic cleansing in the East. The accommodation of 53,000 immigrants, the construction of military bases, and two initiatives meant to bolster the economic vitality of the Gau (namely, the Volksdeutsche Besserstellung project and the installation of skilled German craftspeople from the Altreich) all necessitated the expulsion of several hundred thousand Poles. A busy year was seemingly in store for the UWZ-Warthegau.

With these various considerations in mind, Koppe and Krumey met in Posen on 6 January to work out a provisional deportation plan for 1941, apparently in preparation for the RSHA conference to be held two days later. They concluded that 330,000 Poles would be deported from Wartheland during the coming year:

> For 42,500 Bessarabian Germans: 132,000 Poles
> For 11,000 Bukovinian Germans: 22,000 Poles
> For military bases: 130,000 Poles
> For Volksdeutsche Besserstellung: 30,000 Poles
> For craftspeople from the Altreich and the deportation of apprehended Poles:
>   16,000 Poles
> Total: 330,000 Poles

The high number of Polish evacuees for the benefit of the Bessarabian Germans, their report explained, was because "small and very small" Polish farms—in many cases, five or six—would have to be combined in order to provide homesteads of an adequate size for the settlers. They added that if additional contingents of Volksdeutschen from Dobruja, Lithuania, and Bukovina eventually found their way to Wartheland, two Poles would be deported for every German immigrant.[10] This evacuation plan was amended to some extent at the RSHA meeting on 8 January and even more so at a railway scheduling conference on 16 January, but before discussing these meetings and their implications for Wartheland, a brief examination of the development of the Volksdeutsche Besserstellung project and the plans for troop-training grounds within the Warthegau is in order.

Although preliminary measures geared toward the realization of the Volksdeutsche Besserstellung program and the establishment of military bases in Wartheland had been taken in late 1940, no evacuations within the framework of the two initiatives had been carried out thus far. Due to limited transport capacity, the various holdups in the resettlement campaign, and perhaps Frank's opposition to any expulsions beyond those outlined in the 2.Nahplan, the UWZ had not been in a position to incorporate further deportations into an operational plan. But by the beginning of 1941, the Wehrmacht's need for training grounds had grown more pressing, and Himmler himself had officially sanctioned the Volksdeutsche Besserstellung scheme. Pressure from the military and the RFSS, then, ultimately forced UWZ officials to take action, despite their reservations about both projects.

The Wehrmacht had chosen Wartheland as the site for three military bases, one of which was to envelop the entire southern half of Kreis Konin, making it by far the largest base in the incorporated territories. SS-Oberscharführer Rudolf Bilharz, the leader of the UWZ Aussenstelle in Konin during the Volhynian Action, first learned about the military's plans for his jurisdiction in mid-May 1940. He asked Höppner for clarification on the matter.[11] After studying the Wehrmacht's proposals and the demography of the region in question, Höppner and his associates in Posen concluded in late June that 80,000 Poles and 4,000 Jews, as well as a significant number of Volksdeutschen, would have to be relocated in order to bring the plans to fruition. The Germans could be resettled in the designated security zone around the base, but Poles and Jews would have to be removed from southern Konin entirely.[12] The evacuation of an additional 84,000 Poles and Jews in the busy summer of 1940 would have stretched the UWZ's transport capacity to the limit, further complicating the resettlement of the Volhynian Germans and perhaps even leading to the cancellation of the Cholmer Action. But on 14 July, SS-Sturmbannführer Dr. Peter Carstens, leader of the SS-Ansiedlungsstab Posen, informed Höppner that the Wehrmacht had decided to postpone its plans for a large-scale Konin base until the end of the war and instead establish only a much smaller base in the region. This new plan, according to Höppner, called for the relocation of all Volksdeutschen and people of German descent living on the site. The Germans, the UWZ chief reasoned, could be resettled in other parts of Kreis Konin, necessitating the deportation of some 1,500 Polish families, an action he then believed could take place within the framework of the 2.Nahplan.[13] Little more was said about the Konin base project until early December 1940.

On 5 December, Bilharz informed Höppner that the Wehrmacht was scheduled to assume control of southern Konin on 1 April 1941. In preparation, the movement of Volksdeutschen from southern to northern Konin, an action being carried out by the SS-Arbeitsstab, was already under way. Since the farms the Volksdeutschen were receiving in the north were generally bigger than the ones they had abandoned in the south, two to three Polish families were being evicted to accommodate each German family. Apparently due to limited transport capacity, the Polish evictees were being sent to the south, where they were to remain until they could be deported.

All of this took Höppner by surprise, and he did not welcome the news. Judging by his report on the matter to his nominal superior, Ernst Damzog, it seems that he was under the impression that plans for even a small Konin base had been scrapped. And judging by his report as well as later developments, it appears that the original plans for a massive base were now back on the table, at a time when the UWZ was in no position to carry out additional deportations. He therefore spoke out against the operation. The fundamental problem with the population exchange, as Höppner pointed out, was that although the Germans were allowed to transport all of their belongings to their new homes, the Poles had to leave everything behind and enter southern Konin completely destitute. He estimated that 10,000 such Poles would soon arrive in the south. These incoming Poles, as well as some 60,000 Polish and Jewish natives of southern Konin, would have to be deported to make room for the proposed military base. The region would become, in effect, a huge transit camp. The entire situation, Höppner argued, added up to a grave security risk. Since many of the Poles in question possessed nothing, there was a good chance that southern Konin would become a "colony of criminals and bands of thieves."[14]

Höppner reiterated his reservations to Eichmann two weeks later. If the Wehrmacht wanted control of the region by 1 April 1941, then the evacuation of southern Konin, now estimated to hold 80,000 people who were supposed to be deported, would have to begin on 15 January, immediately after the holiday transport ban was lifted. The UWZ would require buses, trucks, additional police squads, and eighty evacuation trains over a period of ten weeks to clear the area, all at a projected cost of 1,930,000 reichsmarks.[15] But even if his demands were met, Höppner remained convinced that the Konin project would lead to "an unbelievable state of affairs." There was an imminent danger, he warned, that gangs of thieves and looters would form in the region and eventually break out into neighboring Kreise, threatening the security of a large section of Wartheland.[16]

Though the 1 April deadline for the evacuation of southern Konin was soon postponed by two months, the RSHA made a valiant effort to meet both Höppner's and the Werhmacht's demands. Some 80,000 deportations from the region were incorporated into the 3.Nahplan—75,000 thousand of which were to take place by 1 June 1941—as well as 60,000 more from two other base sites in the Gau.[17] But these plans came largely to nothing. Virtually all of the targeted individuals ultimately remained in Wartheland, and apparently, only one of the two smaller bases was actually constructed.[18] Whether Höppner's fears for the security of southern Konin ever materialized is unrecorded.

The Volksdeutsche Besserstellung project also took shape during the course of the 2.Nahplan. By the late summer of 1940, a substantial number of ethnic German natives of Wartheland had complained to Gau authorities that their economic prosperity was being ignored. Volhynian German immigrants were receiving quality farms of substantial size, but long-standing German residents, they grumbled, were receiving nothing. Their complaints led to action on the part of the SS-Ansiedlungsstäbe, and this came without UWZ consent. On 23 September 1940, an SS-Standartenführer working at Krumey's office in Litzmannstadt notified Koppe's RKF deputy Hans Döring that the SS-AS was, on its own initiative, carrying out evictions and resettlements for the purpose of enlarging the farms of native Volksdeutschen. Poles living on farms adjacent to those owned by Germans were being forced out and left to their own devices. The vacated property was then attached to that of the neighboring Germans. What was to be done with the evicted Poles? The Generalgouvernement, he pointed out, rejected all evacuations unrelated to the Volhynian Action, and moreover, the remainder of the 120 trains allocated by the Reichsbahn for the 2.Nahplan were already reserved. The matter could be resolved, he declared, only by the RFSS.[19]

But no Himmler decision came, at least not immediately. In early November, Höppner complained to Koppe that individual SS-Ansiedlungsstäbe were still working on their own, carrying out evictions for Volksdeutsche Besserstellung without the supervision of any central authority. Since all remaining trains were reserved for the Volhynian and Cholmer Actions, the UWZ simply could not evacuate the evicted Poles until after the conclusion of the 2.Nahplan. For the time being, all that could be done was to leave them to find housing with their families and friends, though this approach, he conceded, would constitute a security risk if appropriate measures were not taken. Sipo had not been able to register those Poles evicted by the SS-AS to date, and consequently, their exact whereabouts was unknown. Höppner therefore asked Koppe to take immediate steps to ensure that all subsequent evictions by the SS-AS were carried out in accordance with a centrally devised plan.[20]

Two days after Höppner penned his report for Koppe, Siegfried Seidl of the UWZ office in Litzmannstadt met with the Aussenstellen leaders to discuss the ongoing work in their respective jurisdictions. He learned that the number of German families earmarked for Besserstellung was substantial—a total of 5,114 spread throughout eighteen Kreise—meaning that an extensive deportation action would eventually have to take place.[21] Himmler evidently learned about the operation soon thereafter. On 21 December 1939, he finally institutionalized the Volksdeutsche Besserstellung project, ordering that the productive capability of the native German rural population of the incorporated territories had to be improved, since the individuals in question felt disadvantaged compared to the new German immigrants. Evicted Poles, he admitted, could not be deported at present; therefore, "it remains up to them to find refuge" with their families and friends.[22]

The following month, the 30,000 Polish evacuations for the purpose of Volksdeutsche Besserstellung that Koppe and Krumey had proposed in their 6 January report were accepted by Heydrich and included in the operational blueprint for the 3.Nahplan.[23] The eviction and deportation process developed was much the same as that for rural evacuations carried out during the 2.Nahplan. The SS-AS selected farms to be seized and submitted deportation lists to the SD. The SD would review the lists and make a final decision regarding the fate of the targeted Poles.[24] Due to the sudden death of the original 3.Nahplan in March 1941, however, few (if any) Polish farmers were actually deported for the purpose of Volksdeutsche Besserstellung.

But in the heady days of January 1941, Nazi resettlement and evacuation specialists in Wartheland and the Reich as a whole were still confident that great things could be accomplished during the coming year. The administrative machinery so carefully assembled in the first sixteen months of the occupation was, they believed, perfectly capable of achieving the goals of the RKF and the Wehrmacht simultaneously. As long as evacuation transports were readily available and the Generalgouvernement remained compliant, there was no cause for restraint. Thus, with their optimistic evacuation plan for the Warthegau in hand, Hermann Krumey and his nominal superiors, Ernst Damzog and Rolf-Heinz Höppner, left for Berlin to attend the 8 January RSHA conference. For the most part, their proposals met with approval. The bid for 30,000 deportations for Volksdeutsche Besserstellung was accepted outright,[25] but the 154,000 deportations needed for the accommodation of ethnic German immigrants were reduced slightly to 148,000. The 130,000 expulsions recommended for the establishment of troop-training grounds, by contrast, were increased to 140,000. An unspecified number of evacuations from Wartheland to secure housing for German state officials and to remove Poles apprehended during search actions were approved as well.[26] But even if we disregard these latter two initiatives and base our calculations only on the concrete figures stated in the minutes of the RSHA meeting, at least 318,000 deportations from the Warthegau alone were incorporated into the original 3.Nahplan of 1941.[27]

During the first stage of the operation—the 3.Nahplan–1.Teilprogram—scheduled to run from 1 February to 30 April 1941, the UWZ-Warthegau would be responsible for the deportation of 109,000 Poles from its jurisdiction. Those present at the conference agreed that 90,000 of these evacuations would be for the benefit of the Bessarabian and Bukovinian Germans. The remaining 19,000 would clear Poles from the three sites selected for military bases: 5,000 from Kreis Sieradsch, 2,000 from Konin, and 12,000 from Obornik. No expulsions within the framework of the Besserstellung project would take place during the 1.Teilprogram.[28] This deportation scheme, however, soon changed—dramatically. At a train-scheduling conference held at Eichmann's office in Berlin on 16 January, Höppner learned that in the week since the RSHA meeting, RFSS-RKFDV Himmler had reduced the total number of evacuations planned for the 1.Teilprogram from 248,000 to only 89,000. Wartheland's share of these was initially placed at 77,000, though Höppner managed to secure an additional 4,000 for Volhynian Germans who had not yet received farms. The following operational plan was approved for Wartheland on 16 January:

February: For Bessarabian/Bukovinian resettlement, 12,000; for the remaining Volhynian Germans, 4,000
March: For resettlement, 16,000; for the Konin base, 2,000; for the Sieradsch base, 5,000
April: For resettlement, 42,000
Total: 81,000 evacuations[29]

The deportation of the 12,000 Poles from the site of the Obornik troop-training grounds, Höppner noted, was canceled; instead, the Poles would remain in the region to serve as workers. He pointed out that this scheme did not include deportations necessary to create space for the Volksdeutschen from southern Konin who were to be transferred to the northern part of the Kreis. Despite Höppner's repeated efforts at the meeting to incorporate these expulsions into the 1.Teilprogram, the RKF representative at the meeting remained undeterred, arguing that the figures set by Himmler could not be altered. Höppner was clearly displeased with the results of the conference, but it was with this operational plan that the UWZ-Warthegau embarked on the 3.Nahplan–1.Teilprogram.[30] And even though the objectives of the action had been significantly curtailed, the results would still fall far short of the Nazis' expectations.

THE 3.NAHPLAN–1.TEILPROGRAM AND ITS DEMISE

The documents do not reveal Himmler's motives for scaling back the goals of the 1.Teilprogram so drastically, but we do know that the RFSS was privy to the highly secret plans for the forthcoming invasion of the USSR.[31] Planning for the conquest of the Soviet Union first moved from the realm of long-term objectives to that of short-term objectives when Hitler announced his intentions to the military top brass at Obersalzberg on 31 July 1940. Expansion toward the east, he declared, would not only secure vital lebensraum for the German people, it would also ensure the greatest possible economic autarky for the Reich, providing the basis for agricultural self-sufficiency, raw materials for German industry and the German war machine, and a huge market for German manufactured goods. Furthermore, the Führer reasoned, the collapse of Russia would bring Great Britain to its knees:

> Britain's hope lies in Russia and the United States. If Russia drops out of the picture, America, too, is lost for Britain because the elimination of Russia would tremendously increase Japan's power in the Far East ... Russia is the factor on which Britain is relying most ... With Russia smashed, Britain's last hope would be shattered. Germany then would be master of Europe and the Balkans. Decision: Russia's destruction must therefore be made part of this struggle. Spring 1941. The sooner Russia is crushed the better ... Resolute determination to eliminate Russia.[32]

The destruction of the USSR, then, would guarantee German hegemony in Europe and facilitate the realization of Hitler's long-standing dream of a Nazi continental empire stretching far into the Soviet Union and encompassing the lush wheat fields of the Ukraine, making the Reich a genuine global power at last.[33]

The Wehrmacht completed the first deployment study for the invasion of the USSR on 5 August 1940,[34] but even before this report was presented to Hitler, German troops had begun moving en masse from west to east. By the end of October, thirty-five divisions had been shifted to the eastern field of operations.[35] Although this initial troop movement took place relatively slowly, the military buildup intensified after Hitler issued Directive No. 21: Operation Barbarossa on 18 December 1940. "The German Wehrmacht," Hitler ordered, "must be prepared to crush Soviet Russia in a rapid campaign, even before the conclusion of the war with England." He placed great emphasis on secrecy: the number of officers involved in preparatory measures would be kept as low as possible, and other authorities were to be notified about the operation as late as possible and only then on a need-to-know basis, their instructions strictly limited to information regarding their individual spheres of responsibility. All preparations for the attack were to be finalized by 15 May 1941.[36]

On 3 February 1941, Hitler and his military chiefs approved a four-step plan for the deployment of additional troops in the East. The first step would commence immediately and end in mid-March, the second would run from mid-March to mid-April, the third from mid-April to 25 April, and the fourth from 25 April to 15 May.[37] According to plans formulated late in the summer of 1940, the German high command intended to have a total of 120 divisions in place for the invasion by the end of the deployment period.[38] However, 153 divisions were eventually assembled for the assault. Such a massive transfer of troops required thousands of transport trains. One historian estimates that roughly 65 trains were needed to move a German infantry division, 100 for a panzer division, and 120 for a Waffen-SS division, which was generally stronger and better equipped than a regular army formation.[39] Franz Halder, the chief of the General Staff, calculated on 19 February that the military would require over 15,000 trains to realize the objectives of the deployment plan.[40] In the coming weeks, tens of thousands of transports would be reserved for the German armed forces, and a portion would come at the expense of the UWZ.

The Wehrmacht's demand for troop transports was in all likelihood the driving force behind Himmler's decision to truncate the goals of the 3.Nahplan–1.Teilprogram. If the operational guidelines of previous actions were followed, the deportation of 248,500 individuals as originally planned would have necessitated a minimum of 248 to 249 transports carrying approximately 1,000 evacuees each.

But due to military activity in the East, the Reichsbahn and Ostbahn were not in a position to allocate so many trains to the deportation program, nor could authorities risk snarling rail traffic with hundreds of transports unrelated to troop deployment. But evidently, a limited operation of only 89,000 evacuations, which would require only 89 transports, was still considered feasible, even though it coincided with the Wehrmacht's deployment program. Time would quickly prove otherwise.

Although Himmler and most likely some of his immediate subordinates within the RSHA were aware of Barbarossa well before the launch of the 3.Nahplan, there is no evidence to suggest that UWZ officials in Wartheland had any concrete information regarding the forthcoming invasion until mid-February 1941. They had, of course, probably noticed that Wehrmacht traffic had been heavier than usual in the late fall of 1940, and they would certainly have observed the rapid escalation of troop movements in the first weeks of February 1941. Nevertheless, in light of Hitler's demand for near-absolute secrecy concerning these measures, we can assume that local deportation authorities were not informed about their purpose.[41] Naturally, even the most unintuitive Nazi could have guessed that something big was on the horizon, but in the days leading up to the first phase of the 3.Nahplan, UWZ functionaries simply went about the prosaic business of preparing for yet another deportation action, fully confident, so it seems, that they would be able to realize the now relatively modest objectives established by their superiors in Berlin. Furthermore, there is no indication that UWZ authorities in the field ever questioned why Himmler had suddenly reduced the evacuation targets of the 3.Nahplan–1.Teilprogram. They may well have been pleased with the new parameters of the operation, believing that they could easily fulfill their orders within the allotted time frame.

Eviction and evacuation procedures were to be much in line with previous actions. Only those individuals on evacuation lists could be seized and transported to the Litzmannstadt camps; those unsuitable for transport would be sent to live with their neighbors or relatives. Evictions would be carried out within one hour, after which a vacated home would be guarded by a constable, an auxiliary policeman, or an NSDAP official until the new owners arrived. The usual baggage allowance of 25 to 30 kilograms per person (half that for children), warm clothes, and one blanket applied; no animals or valuables were permitted. The UWZ did, however, take new steps to ensure that arrest results were better than those of the past. To prevent flight, sabotage, and other forms of opposition, it was now decreed that evacuation squads had to have a complement of at least one policeman

Three young members of the Ordnungspolizei guard a wagon train of Poles bound for an internment camp. It is interesting to note that the men are armed with the Mauser Gewehr 98, the standard German infantry rifle of World War I, not the newer Mauser K98k, introduced in 1935. (USHMM, courtesy of the Institute of National Remembrance, USHMM Photo Reference Collection: WS 51571)

per deportee. But oddly enough, the police were ordered that only active resistance could lead to the use of firearms, and this did not include resistance through flight: fleeing Poles, the guidelines for evacuation explicitly state, could not be fired upon.[42] This quasi-humanitarian order may have been issued to prevent unrest among the Polish population, but it is surprising nonetheless, considering the magnitude of the resistance-through-flight problem in Wartheland.

Unlike previous operations, the resettlement of the Bessarabian and Bukovinian Volksdeutschen did not concentrate on any particular region of the Gau. Rather, the incoming Germans would be placed in homes and on farms spread throughout Wartheland. Ten UWZ offices and Aussenstellen would oversee the evictions and evacuations necessary for the accommodation of the immigrants. Some of these were newly established, but others had been in place since the beginning of the 2.Nahplan; with the exception of the Litzmannstadt Nebenstelle, which handled expulsion-related activity only within the city itself, all were responsible for three to eight Kreise each.[43] As in the past, those evictees suitable for transport would be sent by train, truck, or bus to the Litzmannstadt camps for racial examinations. Poles who did not qualify for labor in the Altreich or "later acceptance into German Volkstum" would then proceed to the General-gouvernement.

Hans Frank and his associates were deeply concerned that hordes of "unpro-ductive elements"—the weak, the old, and the sick, all of whom were potential "welfare cases"—would be evacuated to the Generalgouvernement during the course of the action, thus placing a great financial burden on their jurisdiction. Though the UWZ-Warthegau did not want to jeopardize the operation by pro-voking Frank's wrath, it did aspire to deport from the province as many people deemed unsuitable for work as possible. It apparently resorted to camouflage to do so. In late January 1941, Posen officials asked the UWZ if it could carry out an action to remove a large number of ill Poles from the city. They were informed that though a "closed evacuation" of the sick (meaning a transport composed exclusively of such Poles) was impossible, a few families with "unproductive" members could be included in each transport.[44] This attempt at deception was yet another example of the competition and administrative chaos inherent in the Nazi occupation establishment, as well as within the National Socialist hierarchy as a whole. Officials in the East, being the careerists they were, generally focused their energies on the management and well-being of their personal jurisdictions and paid little attention to the interests of their comrades in other regions. The never-ending tension between Warthegau authorities and those in the General-gouvernement, often detrimental to the regime's overall objectives in occupied Poland, apparently reflected as much.

The first transport of the 3.Nahplan–1.Teilprogram left Litzmannstadt on 5 February 1940—five days behind schedule—bound for the town of Dęblin in the Lublin district of the Generalgouvernement.[45] By that time, British intelligence had established a network of Polish agents in Nazi-occupied territory to monitor rail traffic, supply depots, and warehouse complexes. Many of these agents were recruited from the thousands of Polish railway workers employed by the Reichs-bahn and Ostbahn. Via their contacts, the British learned that on the very day of the launch of the 1.Teilprogram, large formations of German troops, mainly ar-mored, were moving into East Prussia and that there was significant rail conges-tion between Berlin and Warsaw, the major rail line that bisected Wartheland.[46] A Wehrmacht official stationed in Krakau also made note of transport problems on 5 February: "[The following is] making the overall transport situation more difficult: a) the major resettlement program (including, for example, 60,000 Jews from Vienna to the Gen. Gov.); b) not yet registered Air Force material transports for the construction of airports east of the Vistula."[47] Just two days later, another military officer complained that "conditions of the railways on the territory of the Generalgouvernement are now totally unacceptable, by no means satisfactory in meeting the demands of national defense."[48] The conflict between the demands of the resettlement program and the demands of national defense was coming to a head.[49]

To meet the goals of the 1.Teilprogram, which called for 81,000 evacuations from Wartheland by 30 April 1941, the UWZ-Warthegau would need eighty-one transports of 1,000 deportees each. As of 17 Jaunary, Höppner expected that the Reichsbahn would be able to furnish three trains daily for the duration of the operation as a whole, including deportations from Wartheland, the other incorporated territories, and Vienna.[50] Wartheland itself would thus require at least one evacuation transport on nearly every day of the action. But it immediately became clear to UWZ officials that they would probably not receive the requisite amount of rolling stock. After the first transport on 5 February, another train would not leave Litzmannstadt until 13 February, and only four more trains were made available for deportations over the course of the next eight days.[51] On 21 February, Eichmann telegrammed the UWZ offices in Posen, Litzmannstadt, Kattowitz, and Gotenhafen, as well as the Zentralstelle für jüdische Auswanderung in Vienna, to explain the situation. Apparently, the recipients of his message were by now well aware of the cause of the holdup: "Because of obvious military reasons," Eichmann wrote, "the Reichsbahn is no longer in the position to provide the agreed-upon number of evacuation transports for the first phase of the 3.Nahplan." The Reich Transport Ministry would still allocate two trains daily for expulsions until further notice, though this, Eichmann confessed, was a nonbinding accord. In view of these circumstances, he conceded that it was no longer possible to maintain the planned tempo of the 1.Teilprogram. He ordered his subordinates to use the few trains available exclusively for evacuations related to ethnic German resettlement; no deportations were to be carried out for the purpose of military base construction.[52]

The end was in sight, and it came on 15 March 1941. By this date, the Wehrmacht had dispatched 2,500 trainloads of men and material to the East within the framework of the first step of the deployment plan.[53] The UWZ-Warthegau, by contrast, had sent only 19 transports of evacuees to the Generalgouvernement (the single transport of 15 March included), and only 12 since Eichmann's telegram of 21 February.[54] Even this trickle of evacuation transports was apparently too much for the Reichsbahn to bear, and with the second step of the deployment plan scheduled to begin immediately, the train shortage and bottlenecks along the rail lines in the East would only grow worse in the coming weeks. Since the Wehrmacht's preparations for a war of conquest now received absolute priority, the SS resettlement and evacuation campaign, though instrumental to the creation of a racial New Order in annexed western Poland, would have to be put on hold until military objectives were realized. On 15 March, then, the 3.Nahplan–1.Teilprogram was called off. That day, UWZ offices in Wartheland, Danzig–West Prussia, and Upper Silesia, as well as the Zentralstelle in Vienna, received a telegram from SS-Brigadeführer Heinrich Müller, the chief of the Gestapo and Eichmann's superior at RSHA Amt IV. Müller announced that from 16 March 1941 until further notice, "it is not possible to carry out evacuation transports from the incorporated German eastern territories or Vienna." "Instructions concerning the probable time frame of this transitory suspension of evacuation transports," he declared, "cannot be made at this time."[55]

Great plans had come to naught. Although the 1.Teilprogram had called for the evacuation of 89,000 individuals by 30 April 1941, only about 25,000 were actually deported. Instead of expelling 81,000 Warthegau natives, the UWZ had managed to deport only 19,226, a figure that includes 2,140 Jews, before Müller's telegram arrived on 15 March.[56] And instead of receiving the homes and farms they were promised, 256,257 ethnic Germans remained idle in resettlement camps throughout the Altreich and the incorporated territories.[57] The 3.Nahplan–1.Teilprogram was clearly a failure.

AFTERMATH

Müller's directive of 15 March 1941 marked not only the end of the 3.Nahplan–1.Teilprogram but also the end of the Nazi crusade to de-Polonize the incorporated territories via evacuations to the East. The "transitory suspension" of deportations, at least in terms of the expulsion of Polish "undesirables," proved permanent. But UWZ officials had no way of knowing this in the early spring of 1941. Frustrated though they were, they nonetheless believed that the deportation campaign would eventually resume, not in the immediate future perhaps but at some point after the unfavorable transport situation was rectified and the war for new lebensraum was under way. In the meantime, the UWZ still needed to secure accommodations for the hundreds of thousands of Volksdeutschen languishing in

VoMi camps. If it could not do so through evacuations to the Generalgouverne-ment, then another method had to be found.

The mood among SS ethnopoliticians was noticeably gloomy in the immedi-ate wake of the transport halt. On 19 March, four days after Müller's announce-ment, Ulrich Greifelt met with resettlement and evacuation authorities in Berlin to discuss the inauspicious state of affairs in the East and plans for the future. The Reich Transport Minister, Greifelt informed those present, had once again stated that until further notice, "no special trains of any sort"—local rail traffic included—could be allocated exclusively for "resettlement movements" (defined as "the evacuation of Poles and Jews for the resettlement of Volksdeutschen and for Wehrmacht purposes").[58] The minister had, however, suggested that resettle-ment officials work with the various Reichsbahndirektionen in the incorporated territories to determine whether small transports of those ethnic Germans already present in the region could be carried out within the context of normal rail traffic, though he had admitted that such action could take place only in rare cases be-cause regularly scheduled trains were usually filled to capacity. After pondering the situation, Greifelt and his associates agreed that the resettlement of Volks-deutschen would have to be sharply curtailed, and the transport of immigrants from VoMi camps in the Altreich to the incorporated territories would have to be stopped altogether. To provide housing for those Volksdeutschen then residing in transit camps in the East, Poles would still have to be evicted, but the question of exactly how and where the Polish evictees were to be accommodated remained open. By the end of the meeting, the participants concluded that two options ex-isted: either the Poles could be relocated within the eastern Gaue, or they could be delivered to the Altreich to serve as workers. Those unsuitable for labor could be sent to live with other Polish families or housed in the transit camps then oc-cupied by German immigrants. If the camp option were selected, the camps could be cleared of Poles immediately after evacuations resumed.[59]

On the very day of the RKF meeting, Himmler in effect resolved the question regarding the accommodation of evicted Poles for his underlings. "Regardless of present transport difficulties," the RFSS ordered, "the Bessarabian Germans (7,800 persons) still in the Litzmannstadt camp [will] be settled as soon as pos-sible in the Danzig–West Prussia Reichsgau." The UWZ–Danzig was to create space for these Volksdeutschen by housing several Polish families together in one residence and, in accordance with the demands of the war economy, by sending as many Poles as possible to the Altreich as compulsory labor.[60] In the months and years to come, the former approach, one of "internal resettlement" termed

Verdrängung des Polentums (displacement of Polish nationhood), became a
standard—indeed *the* standard—means of accommodating Poles evicted for the
benefit of German immigrants. It was employed with increasing frequency not
only in Danzig–West Prussia but also in the incorporated territories as a whole
and particularly in Reichsgau Wartheland.

Verdrängung des Polentums had been used in Wartheland the preceding autumn, first as a means of quartering the aged, the sick, and others unsuitable for
labor or transport and later to deal with Poles evicted within the context of the
Volksdeutsche Besserstellung project. UWZ agents had long been suspicious of
the reliability of the policy, and they remained skeptical in the aftermath of the
transport halt of 15 March 1941. Other Nazi authorities in the Warthegau questioned the dependability of Verdrängung as well.

On 28 March 1941, the Regierungspräsident of the Litzmannstadt district,
Friedrich Uebelhoer, sent the UWZ two police reports regarding Verdrängung
actions recently carried out in his jurisdiction. The concerns expressed in the
reports were, in his opinion, totally valid. One, an overview of an action that
took place in Kreis Lask on 13 March, stated that fifty Polish families had been
evicted from their farms and left to secure new accommodations by their own
devices. The gendarmerie officer in charge condemned the methods employed,
arguing that the now impoverished evictees would be forced to make ends meet
through smuggling and other forms of criminal activity. Furthermore, since the
Poles had not been sent to any specific location, it would be impossible to monitor
their activity. For these reasons, the officer predicted future security problems in
the region.[61] The other police report described an operation carried out in Kreis
Sieradsch on 22 March. In this instance, 184 Polish families had been evicted
and, as in the prior case, told to seek new accommodations with their families
and friends. The leader of the action noted that this form of "deportation" (his
word) had never before been used within Sieradsch. "Whether it is reliable,"
he warned, "is questionable; moreover, it is to be feared that a large number of
Poles [now] have the opportunity to roam about the countryside without purpose
or plan (security concerns)."[62] In light of the issues raised in these two reports,
Uebelhoer asked the UWZ to take steps "in the interest of the security of the
Regierungsbezirk" to ensure that Poles would not be ejected from their homes
without first assigning them new housing. Poles were not to be allowed to wander
the countryside aimlessly and thus threaten the security of the entire Gau. They
had to be dealt with, he concluded, in some other way.[63]

But owing to the dearth of other options, Verdrängung quickly became the evacuation policy of choice in Wartheland, despite the reservations of those responsible for its implementation. Using this method, the UWZ-Warthegau continued to provide homes and farms for the Bessarabian and Bukovinian Germans throughout 1941 and early 1942. By late January 1942, the UWZ had evicted 82,093 individuals within the context of Verdrängung actions. Including the 19,226 persons deported during the abbreviated 1.Teilprogram, a total of 130,826 Wartheland natives lost their homes as a result of UWZ operations—still termed the 3.Nahplan—between 1941 and 1942. The majority of the evictees remained in the Gau, though 17,084 Poles and 189 Jews seized by the UWZ were handed over to the Arbeitsämter for labor allocation. Only 7,327 Poles were deemed suitable for re-Germanization in the Altreich.[64]

The UWZ adopted the policy of Verdrängung des Polentums ostensibly due to limited rail capacity caused by the Wehrmacht's demand for troop transports, but even if this demand had never arisen, other considerations may have soon halted the evacuations to the East. It is clear that Verdrängung was meant to solve two problems at once: displacement would not only provide housing and employment opportunities for Volksdeutschen still awaiting resettlement, it would also keep Poles at work on the farms and in the factories of the Warthegau. By the spring of 1941, Polish labor had become a hot commodity in both Wartheland and the Reich as a whole. With a two-front war staring them in the face, the Nazis simply could no longer afford to continue their policy of dumping economically valuable Poles in the already overcrowded Generalgouvernement. The needs of the war economy and their impact on deportation policy will be addressed in the final chapter of this work.

CHAPTER

8

Postmortem: Evacuations
versus Expediency

During the first full year of the occupation, Wartheland had managed to deliver a substantial quantity of farm products to the Altreich, an achievement recognized and lauded by central authorities in Berlin. But by the dawn of 1941, agricultural productivity in the province was on the wane. Greiser's promise that his Gau would soon be able to produce 1.1 million tons of surplus grain per year notwithstanding,[1] it had become clear to a number of more astute National Socialists that agricultural exports from the breadbasket of the Greater German Reich could no longer keep pace with the regime's original expectations, not least because of the disruptions in the agrarian sector caused by the ongoing resettlement and deportation campaign. In late December 1940, Julius Claussen, the deputy head of the Reich Ministry for Food and Agriculture, acknowledged as much in a statement that directly contradicted Gauleiter Greiser's rosy economic forecast for the coming year: "Today, problems exist in all areas of food supply. There is a severe shortage in the grain supply ... The Warthegau is unfortunately not in a position to deliver large amounts of grain to the Altreich ... Most Poles residing there must be prepared to leave the country in the near future. The Poles are therefore no longer planting their fields and are trying to sell their property illegally."[2]

Claussen was not alone in his assessment. The chief of the SS-Ansiedlungsstab Planning Office in Litzmannstadt, Alexander Dolezalek, a man with a hands-on understanding of developments in the East, also perceived that evacuation policy was having a negative impact on Wartheland's agrarian economy. On 28 February 1941, Dolezalek outlined his reservations about the expulsion program in a six-page memo entitled "The Polish Question in the Warthegau." Though he did not address the region's declining agricultural output directly, his analysis of the deportation campaign reveals that the failing health of Wartheland's agrarian sector now weighed heavily on the minds of German officials in the district.

Dolezalek began his memorandum by pointing out that intergovernmental resistance against the deportation of Poles to the Generalgouvernement was growing stronger by the day. Indeed, by the time he penned his memo, he and his fellow ethnocrats in Wartheland were well aware that the 3.Nahplan–1.Teilprogram was by no means proceeding according to schedule. More and more transport trains were being allocated to the Wehrmacht, despite the wishes of the SS, and only a trickle of evacuees was actually flowing east. For this reason alone, resettlement authorities must have suspected that the end of the operation was at hand, but other grounds for suspicion not directly related to military developments had emerged as well. Göring had recently demanded an additional 250,000 Polish laborers from the incorporated territories and the Generalgouvernement to work the farms and factories of the Altreich, and the majority, it had been decided, would come from Wartheland.[3] Dolezalek therefore conceded that the resettlement establishment would most likely soon be forced to halt evacuations and retain Poles otherwise marked for expulsion as agrarian and industrial workers. Like other Warthegau Nazis, he assumed that the suspension of transports would be a temporary one. But unlike his counterparts, the planning chief had strong criticism for the way in which evacuations had been carried out to date. When deportations resumed, a major adjustment in policy for the benefit of Wartheland's agrarian economy, he forcefully argued, would have to take place.[4]

A few lines into his memorandum, Dolezalek called for a sweeping reassessment of the deportation campaign. "I am of the opinion," he stated, "that our present deportation policy [will] be disastrous if it does not succeed in resettling the Poles entirely." But that being said, he condemned the manner—and order—in which Poles had been targeted for evacuation during the first seventeen months of the occupation: "Bluntly put ... the best Poles are evacuated. The very best of them, of course, go to the Altreich. But the worst remain in the Warthegau."

Dolezalek's measure for the best and worst Poles was, above all, an economic one, though like deportation policy as a whole, it was justified largely on racial-ideological grounds. He noted correctly that current evacuation initiatives concentrated primarily on those Poles who owned large and middle-sized farms in order to ensure that all ethnic German immigrants received economically viable homesteads. The very best of the evicted Poles were sent to the Reich proper, either to be re-Germanized or to serve as seasonal workers, and those judged racially inferior or politically troublesome were unceremoniously dumped in the

Generalgouvernement. But simple agricultural and industrial workers, that is, individuals who owned no desirable property, were usually allowed to remain in the Gau. The fundamental problem with this scheme, Dolezalek contended, was that "the percentage of productive, upwards-striving, and also externally Nordic people in the large and middle-sized farm-owning class is higher than among agricultural and industrial workers. But exactly these people of higher value are driven out [while those of lesser value remain]."

This policy, as Dolezalek saw it, was fraught with danger. By permitting Poles of "low racial value" to stay on in Wartheland as indispensable workers, the Nazi regime was running the risk that their "racially inferior" blood would eventually mix with that of the German Volk. Furthermore, since the birthrate among Polish farmhands and blue-collar workers was generally higher than among the middle and upper agrarian classes, Polentum would continue to grow in strength and numbers, contrary to the goals of official policy. "I am therefore of the opinion," Dolezalek declared, "that the present resettlement policy must be radically changed. It does not do to send the second-best to the Generalgouvernement, while the inferior remain behind in the Warthegau."

His solution to the problem was fairly straightforward: cease deporting those Poles whose prosperous farms were needed for Volksdeutschen. Rather, keep them in Wartheland to serve as farm labor and evacuate the poorer undesirable workers to the Generalgouvernement instead. If this policy were pursued, the vast majority of allegedly inferior Polish families would be removed, and at the same time, the demographic potential of the lower class would be significantly curtailed. This new approach, Dolezalek noted, could also go far to boost agricultural productivity in the district. Evicted upward-striving Polish farm owners could be placed temporarily on the tiny and generally unhealthy farms abandoned by the evacuated workers; the new owners, owing both to their efficiency and their desire to remain in their home district, would in all likelihood concentrate their ability and efforts to bringing these "gone-to-the-dogs" farms (his words) into order. This, in turn, would facilitate the identification of "especially productive, activist, Nordic elements" among the Polish population. Agricultural productivity had evidently become a gauge for the detection of Aryan blood.

Dolezalek admitted that a number of objections could be raised against his suggestions. Some might argue, he wrote, that due to their natural will to resist foreign domination—something inherent in their Nordic blood—those racially valuable Poles who remained on the small farms would attempt to sabotage the agrarian economy through passive resistance. But all experience, Dolezalek claimed, proved the opposite: a good farm was better for the average Warthegau Pole than a wretched one and much better than the fate that potentially awaited him or her in the Generalgouvernement. Others, he said, might contend that "in the eastern Warthegau, these regulations come too late; all the good Poles have already been removed," and only "inferior elements" who worked tiny farms remained. But this, he countered, was only partially true: among the small farms in the eastern half of the Gau could be found many that were managed very carefully and whose owners were of high racial value. "The size of the farm," he declared, "is no measure of the efficiency of the owner." It was often the case that farmers who succeeded on such small farms distinguished themselves through their great zeal and industry; they possessed "a peculiar efficiency." "For a change in our resettlement policy, it is late," he concluded his memo, "but still not too late."[5]

Even though Dolezalek justified his proposals on the usual racial-ideological grounds, his criterion for evacuation (though he probably would have refused to admit it) was more a matter of economics than one of race. Productivity was now an indication of racial value—a defining characteristic of valuable blood—but not necessarily of *German* racial value. Though a significant number of the productive and upwardly mobile Poles he wanted to retain in Wartheland could, according to the farcical tenets of Nazi racial "science," be considered Germans, Dolezalek all but acknowledged that some Poles were racially valuable just as Poles. This line of reasoning represented a quantum leap in Nazi racial thought, albeit one instigated by economic necessity. The National Socialist regime needed the best workers for the German war economy (in this case, the agrarian sector), whether they were Germans or not. The best Polish agricultural workers were those who owned the best farms. A healthy farm was an indication that the owner was valuable, both racially and economically, and therefore the owner should be exempt from evacuation. Woolly racial theory aside, the new guidelines for deportation that Dolezalek suggested were firmly rooted in economic expediency. The Reich's labor requirements were forcing other Warthegau authorities to take a new look at evacuation policy as well.

IDEOLOGY COMPROMISED: RACIAL POLITICS AND THE DEMAND FOR LABOR

Göring's call in mid-February 1941 for the dispatch of an additional 250,000 Polish workers to the Altreich echoed loudly through the UWZ establishment in the

Warthegau. Since Wartheland was to supply the greater part of this contingent of Reich-bound deportees, the UWZ, as the leading agent of evacuations in the province, would need to play a large role in securing the workforce. On 25 February, Hermann Krumey met with Dr. Storch, a representative of the Arbeitsamt in Litzmannstadt, to discuss how Göring's demands could be met. They agreed that the number of migrant workers normally approved for labor allocation by the AA and the UWZ would not cover the Reich's needs. Long-standing policy dictated as much: since it was forbidden to send racially unsuitable Poles to the Altreich, the majority of those who entered the Litzmannstadt camps were deported to the Generalgouvernement.

During the course of their deliberations, Krumey and Storch brainstormed two options for eliminating the shortage of workers. Both represented a major change in existing policy, for it was now suggested that Poles deemed racially unsuitable could—and should—be placed within the main body of the German Volk in the west. Option A called for families of Polish farmworkers earmarked for evacuation to be divided. The head of the family would either be retained temporarily in Wartheland or evacuated as planned, and the remaining members would be sent to the Altreich as migrant labor. After completion of their labor assignment, the Poles in question would be sent directly to the Generalgouvernement, or if the head of the family had been retained in the Warthegau, the family would be reunited and then all members would be deported together to the East. Under Option B, the entire family in question would be sent to the Reich proper to serve as migrant workers. When their labor was no longer needed, they would be deported directly to the Generalgouvernement.[6] Krumey asked Hans Ehlich of RSHA Amt III in Berlin to weigh these options and pointed out that the labor shortage in the Reich proper was so acute that Greiser himself had suggested that a number of skilled workers from the Warthegau—Germans included—could be sent to the Altreich for assignment.[7] The needs of the war economy were now beginning to undermine even the "constructive" Germanization of the Mustergau of National Socialism.

The movement toward a minor revolution in policy accelerated dramatically over the following week and a half. On 4 March, Rolf-Heinz Höppner, the chief of the UWZ-Posen, convened with Hermann Krumey, SS-Obersturmbannführer Ernst Kendzia (Wartheland's trustee for labor), and Dr. Leopold von Fünke of the Reich Labor Ministry to discuss possible ways to secure more Polish labor in Litzmannstadt for the Reich economy. By this point, Kendzia had already instructed the Arbeitsämter in the district to raise the number of individual Poles and Polish families selected for labor. Presumably on Greiser's orders, he would now go even further and direct the Litzmannstadt Arbeitsamt not only to cease recommending the evacuation of any Pole capable of work[8] but also to remove fit-for-work Polish inmates from the UWZ deportation camps and place them on "a type of labor reserve" (vacant houses within the city) where they would await assignment. Höppner questioned the efficacy of this plan, presumably on the usual racial and security grounds, but ultimately left the decision to Kendzia.

The four also discussed a new order from Greiser concerning Jewish deportations. The expulsion of Wartheland's Jews, banned since April 1940, had been allowed to resume on 7 February.[9] One would imagine that this change delighted Greiser, who had pushed in vain throughout the previous summer for the evacuation of the Litzmannstadt ghetto. The opportunity at least to begin the process was now at hand, but surprisingly enough, Greiser ordered that all Jews capable of work were exempt from evacuation. Such Jews would be assembled in the ghetto and from there assigned labor. Those unfit for work would still be deported, but contrary to guidelines of the past, they were to be sent to the Generalgouvernement even if such an action split apart family units.[10] Greiser's directive further indicated how pressing economic matters had become. It also revealed a recent shift in attitude regarding the continued existence of the Litzmannstadt ghetto.

In the fall of 1940, when it became clear to Warthegau authorities that they would not soon be rid of the Litzmannstadt Jews, extensive efforts were made to transform the ghetto into a self-sustaining unit. Prevailing over "attritionists" who desired "a rapid dying out of the Jews," German "productionists," most notably the Litzmannstadt ghetto manager, Hans Biebow, worked to secure labor contracts for ghetto enterprises in the hope of generating "the greatest possible surplus," allowing the Jews to feed themselves at no cost to the state.[11] The impact of this policy was quickly felt. Though they suffered terribly from hardship and deprivation, the Litzmannstadt Jews were making significant contributions to the German economy by early 1941. The Wehrmacht took notice—and with justification. In its report for the fifteen-month period between October 1940 and December 1941, Wartheland's Rüstungsinspektion (RüI; Armament Inspectorate), a branch of OKW that supervised German military contracts in the province, emphasized that the Jewish population of the Gau constituted "a not to be underestimated labor reservoir." The Litzmannstadt ghetto itself, with its multitudes of skilled craftspeople and diligent workers, had become "the largest workshop in Germany." Fully 90 to 95 percent of ghetto production, including uniforms, fur coats, textile accessories, and wood and metal receptacles, went to the Wehrmacht.[12] The ghetto workers also provided goods and services for the civilian market, manufacturing furniture, gloves, and shoes for domestic consumption and performing tannery, upholstery, and locksmithing for the local population.[13] So extensive was the output that the Oberbürgermeister of the city, Karl Marder, would assert in the summer of 1941 that the ghetto was no longer meant to be "nothing more than a kind of holding or concentration camp"; it was an "*essential element* of the total economy ... a one-of-its-kind large scale enterprise."[14]

Greiser was certainly aware of the growing productive capacity of the Litzmannstadt ghetto in early March 1941. In fact, he was profiting from it personally. Since the previous August, 65 percent of the wages of Jews working for private firms in the ghetto had been seized and placed in a "reconstruction account of the NSDAP" controlled by Greiser's office.[15] Matters of self-interest, then, may well have come into play when the Gauleiter prohibited the deportation of Jews capable of work. But the overriding issue was certainly one of labor and regional production. Jewish industrial labor was needed just as badly as Polish agricultural labor. For the time being, whether they were Jewish or Polish, no individuals fit for work were to be unceremoniously dumped in the Generalgouvernement, despite the regime's long-standing racial-ideological goal of a polenfrei and judenfrei Wartheland.

On 7 March, Höppner had learned that a high-level directive existed that permitted regional authorities in the incorporated territories to send even those Polish families deemed politically suspect to the Altreich for labor assignment. Troubled by this potential threat to German security, he requested Krumey, his nominal subordinate, to provide confirmation.[16] The record does not indicate Krumey's response, but it seems that such an order had, in fact, been distributed. One week later, Höppner notified Hans Ehlich that he had just received an RSHA Amt IVD4 memo issued 7 March containing two Göring directives dated 18 February 1941, one entitled "The Provision of Workers from the Incorporated Eastern Territories to Cover the Labor Needs of the War Economy" and the other "Labor Allocation and Population-, Volkstums- or Racial Policy." "I assume," Höppner wrote,

> that on the basis of the latter mentioned order, misgivings about the dispatch of families as workers to the Altreich are no longer being raised. The families will receive on their papers, so far as they have been evacuated [that is, evicted and scheduled for

deportation to the Generalgouvernement], the stamp "evacuated." Care must be taken that they do not return to the incorporated eastern territories after the conclusion of their labor assignment; rather, [they] will go to the Generalgouvernement.[17]

The UWZ-Posen chief was somewhat more explicit about this fundamental change in labor allocation policy in another telegram sent to Ehlich's office on 27 March, twelve days after the suspension of the 3.Nahplan–1.Teilprogram:

So far as it has been reported to me here, an agreement exists between the Reich Security Main Office and the Reich Labor Ministry that as a result of the Altreich's urgent need for labor and the known Göring directives, the recruitment of Polish families as P-Polen [simply as Poles and racially and, in some cases, politically unsuitable ones at that] for the Altreich is possible, since no consideration is to be taken regarding matters of Volkstum [*Volkstumsgründe*].

Krumey had informed him, Höppner added, that only the UWZ was allowed to carry out the deployment of the non-Germanizable families in question, to ensure they were registered properly. But he had heard, although he could not confirm the information, of cases where the Arbeitsämter had sent Polish families directly to the Altreich on their own accord.[18] Apparently, racially undesirable Poles could now be sent to Germany, but exactly who would manage the labor allocation process—the tried-and-true SS racial experts and security specialists of the UWZ or the state bureaucrats of the Arbeitsämter—remained an open question at that time. Hermann Krumey was confident that it would be the UWZ.

He was in error. Reports of AA officials dispatching Polish families to the Altreich continued to reach the UWZ. On 30 March, Krumey notified Höppner that the Arbeitsamt in Grätz had recently done just that, and it troubled him. "If this becomes the norm," he wrote, "within a short time all service offices in the Warthegau will be sending Polish families to the Altreich." He stressed that the UWZ had to retain control over the process and requested an RSHA ruling on the matter.[19] A ruling came the following day. In a telegram sent to the SD-Abschnitt in Posen, SS-Sturmbannführer Müller of RSHA IIIB stated explicitly that "the allocation of non-Germanizable Polish families in the Altreich obviously has to be carried out by the Arbeitsamt and not by the UWZ. In this respect, SS-Obersturmbannführer Krumey must have made a mistake." Still, Müller instructed the UWZ to register the families in some manner—if only by name—before they were sent west in order to guarantee future control and to ensure that they wound up in the Generalgouvernement after the war. He admitted that it was very doubtful whether the Arbeitsämter were retaining control over the families; "thus the danger exists that unwanted Polish elements will later be able to remain in the Reich."[20]

The UWZ had lost a significant political battle. Since racial and political examinations were apparently no longer a prerequisite for admission into the Altreich, the bureau had been stripped of its original function as a racial filter for culling the Germanic wheat from the Polish chaff. Höppner later expressed his displeasure about this course of action, stating with an air of resignation on 30 May 1941 that "on the whole, these measures deal with things, necessitated by war and deplored by everyone for reasons of race and Volkstum, but which simply have to be accepted during the current state of emergency due to the shortage of workers in the Reich."[21]

The developments of late February and March 1941 indicated that a significant relaxation of racial policy regarding the deployment of Warthegau Poles in the Altreich had transpired. The rigid ethnopolitical guidelines concerning the suitability of Poles for labor assignment in the Reich proper had been tempered as the Nazi regime came to realize the economic value of even its "glaringly racially inferior" and "politically troublesome" Polish subjects. In the past, Polish seasonal workers had to pass a battery of examinations in the UWZ camps before receiving approval for deployment in the Altreich, but it appears that the Nazis—out of economic necessity—were now willing to risk the possible infiltration of Polish blood into that of the German Volk in the West, and assuming Höppner's information was accurate, the Reich Security Main Office itself consented. Naturally, strict regulations, particularly regarding sexual contact between the races (an act punishable by death), were issued to keep Poles and Germans apart,[22] but compared to earlier policy, which sought to erect a clean geographic divide between Reich Germans and racially inferior Warthegau Poles, the new policy was not only far more compromising but also far more dangerous on racial-ideological grounds. Arthur Greiser was also reconsidering the merits of his original racial-political objectives, notably the rapid and comprehensive de-Polonization of his Gau.

On 11 February 1941, Greiser met with his personal adviser, Oberregierungsrat (Senior Civil Servant) Harry Siegmund, and Alexander Dolezalek to discuss whether Wartheland's large estates should be subdivided and parceled out to ethnic German settlers, thousands of whom still lacked jobs and housing.[23] In Greiser's opinion, the answer was categorically "no," and his rationale revealed a marked relaxation in his stance toward the Polish Question:

The task of the Warthegau, as assigned by the Führer and Reichsmarschall [Göring], is the production of grain, grain, and once again grain—a "grain factory." For this reason, the Warthegau was incorporated into the Reich ... For that we need our large estates and for that we need all workers! The workers must, even though they are Poles, remain in the Warthegau. The present agrarian structure cannot be changed. We must bring order to the Warthegau. Order to agricultural production.

Nonetheless, Greiser regarded the preservation of Wartheland's Polish agricultural workforce to be a temporary measure. In response to Dolezalek's adamant assertion that "the long-range objective must under all circumstances be a Gau which is 100 percent German to the last agricultural worker," Greiser concurred wholeheartedly. "That is my goal," he said. "When I finally die, I want to be able [to say] that the Warthegau is German. But since I do not yet intend to die, that could be ten to twenty years." ("Thirty, forty years, Gauleiter! Yes, thirty to forty years," exclaimed his toady, adviser Harry Siegmund.) The comprehensive de-Polonization of Wartheland, then, would have to wait: bringing order to agricultural production necessitated a Polish labor force, regardless of ideological imperatives. The removal of the Warthegau's Polish population could resume with vigor, those present agreed, immediately after the war, but as Greiser's words suggest, the Gauleiter had now conceded that the process might well take twenty years to complete.[24]

At the time of this Dolezalek-Greiser exchange, evacuations, though constrained by troop deployments, were still permitted, but nevertheless, we can see that even Arthur Greiser himself, the man ordered by Hitler to bring the Germanization of Wartheland to a close within ten years, was already backing away from the original objectives of the 3.Nahplan–1.Teilprogram, as well as the deportation campaign as a whole. Greiser's racial mission and his economic mission, both of which were assigned by Hitler in 1939, were simply incompatible, and the Gauleiter evidently recognized that fact. At some point during the course of the 3.Nahplan–1.Teilprogram, Greiser made his sentiments regarding Polish labor official and ordered that no Poles capable of work were to be deported to the Generalgouvernement.[25] Despite the fact that tens of thousands of repatriates from southeastern Europe required housing and employment opportunities and even though the suspension of evacuations was still weeks away, the very leader of Wartheland, long one of the most outspoken advocates of the Reich's Germanizing mission in the East, was leaning toward a policy of economic rationality at the expense of his racist ideological goals, a shift in attitude that was all the more apparent with his impending prohibition on the deportation of "work-capable" Jews discussed earlier. By December 1941, much of the Jewish workforce would be deemed expendable—even as the need for labor increased—but not the Polish workforce. If the Warthegau were to fulfill its primary role as the granary of the Reich, the Poles would have to remain on the land, if not as farm owners then at least as farmworkers. The termination of the 1.Teilprogram on 15 March 1941 may have stemmed directly from the Wehrmacht's demands for troop transports, but due to the pressing need for labor both in the Altreich and in Wartheland itself, economic considerations had already forced the regime to halt the deportation of all Poles judged potentially productive. Military developments aside, a major change in evacuation policy had taken place.

Together, the exigencies of agricultural production and the exigencies of volksdeutsch resettlement made the policy of Verdrängung des Polentums the logical option. Displacing Poles within Wartheland instead of deporting them would meet the housing and employment needs of the ethnic German immigrants and, at the same time, keep the Polish population at work for the benefit of the Gau economy. The Verdrängung, then, was the policy soon adopted and "legalized" officially by Greiser on 10 May 1941.[26] Tens of thousands of Poles were to lose their homes by means of displacement and brought to "suitable work sites" in the province, but only "on the unambiguous understanding," as Greiser's deputy Siegmund told HSSPF Koppe on May 10, "that not one of these Poles leaves the Warthegau."[27]

An examination of the language employed in UWZ memos and directives concerning Verdrängung during the months following the suspension of evacuations suggests that displacement policy was pursued merely as an unwelcome alternative to deportations: if not for the German military's demand for troop transports, such a policy would not have been adopted. In terms of asocial elements or individuals unsuitable for labor, this most likely would have been the case. But the evidence discussed earlier seems to indicate that all Poles capable of work, racially inferior though they may have been, would have been retained in Wartheland (or delivered to the Altreich) even if the evacuations had continued. Directives issued in the wake of the transport halt leave the same impression. Indeed, by the late summer of 1941, Greiser's orders regarding German resettlement and the displacement of Poles were no longer simply implying but explicitly underscoring the importance of retaining the Polish labor force for the Gau economy. For example, on 28 August, Siegmund noted Greiser's response to HSSPF Koppe's recent announcement that a large-scale displacement action would soon be carried out for the benefit of the Bessarabian Volksdeutschen:

So that the Polish workers affected by [the action] *are not lost to the Reichsgau*, the Herr Reichsstatthalter has ordered for the Landräte to support these displacement measures in every way and to such an extent that they accommodate the Poles assigned to them in their Kreise and employ them until bigger projects make necessary the allocation of all Polish workers in the concerned Kreise. If the Landräte are not in the position to do this, then they should work out an agreement with neighboring Kreise [to accommodate and employ the Poles in question]. *In no case may Poles go to the Altreich or to the Generalgouvernement.*[28]

The opening phrase in this quote, "so that the Polish workers affected by [the action] *are not lost to the Reichsgau*" speaks volumes about the new attitude toward the Polish agricultural labor force. Polish workers were remaining in Wartheland not because they could no longer be deported; they were remaining because the Gau economy desperately needed their labor. The loss of Polish workers was the Warthegau's loss, Nazi ideological goals notwithstanding. And as the last sentence in the passage intimates, if Greiser had his way—and in this case, he did not—even the labor requirements of the Altreich were secondary to those of his jurisdiction.[29]

The Rüstungsinspektion for Wehrkreis XXI (Wartheland), too, recognized the vital importance of Polish labor in the Gau, though its concern was primarily industry, not agriculture. As early as October 1940, the RüI was stressing its glaring dependence on Polish workers and the high quality of the work they performed as well. In the fall of 1940, Poles constituted 80 to 95 percent of the workforce in armaments production. Since they were generally "hungry and neglected," Polish workers avidly sought employment opportunities to better their lives. Their performance was "predominantly good." Polish technicians and metalworkers, in particular, regularly demonstrated their capability and diligence. The RüI was not, however, pleased with the performance of Volksdeutschen native to Wartheland or with that of ethnic German immigrants. Many native Volksdeutschen, the RüI complained, were "not conscious of their duty" and had "assumed extraordinarily high pretensions." They were "too good" for manual labor in factories, they had left their old jobs to "hide out" as foremen to avoid hard work, and they were by and large overpaid. Ethnic German immigrants had also "not fully proven their worth": "Their capacity to work and willingness to work does not even approach that of the Poles."[30]

Polish armaments workers may have been better than Volksdeutschen, yet the RüI conceded that their general performance lagged well behind that of

Reich Germans. Evacuations, displacements, low wages, and poor rations were
to blame. Polish workers lived in constant fear of deportation; they were simply
exhausted, often lying awake at night waiting for the police to arrive and expel
them. Displacements were ongoing as well. Poles were constantly moved from
adequate to inferior housing, the latter of which routinely lacked heating or even
kitchen facilities. To make matters worse, Polish workers had little buying power
and could therefore afford little in the way of meats and fats. All of this left them
physically weak, and their job performance suffered accordingly.[31] A later RüI
report, written in January 1942, reiterated these problems. By that time, evacuations to the Generalgouvernement had ceased, but displacements were carried
out with growing regularity. Some Poles, the RüI official wrote, were forced to
move as many as two to four times within a very short period, and many found
themselves farther and farther away from their worksites, with no furniture or
other belongings. They lacked warm clothing, and they did not eat well. Racial
policy, of course, dictated that Poles had to be kept apart from Germans and
treated as a "worker people," which the RüI official readily acknowledged. But
he called upon his readers "to recognize a principle": "If one wants to milk a cow,
one must also feed it." Administering yet another dose of reality, he went on to
take direct aim at the pigheadedness of many within the Nazi hierarchy: "The
widely advocated view, that the Pole may participate in the economic reconstruction of the East merely as *a type of coolie*, is encountering limitations and resistance within the reality of the war economy that cannot be disregarded."[32]

Despite the RüI's remonstrations, displacements continued, low pay and poor
rations persisted, and virtual "coolies" the Poles remained for the duration of the
occupation. They also remained the bedrock of Wartheland's labor force. Despite
the regime's immense efforts to settle Germans in the district, the German population of the Gau stood at only 14 percent at the end of 1941. Some 52 percent of
the German population was native to the province, 10 percent had immigrated
from the Altreich, and the rest were volksdeutsch immigrants. Poles still comprised 80 percent of Wartheland's population on 31 December 1941, even though
approximately 250,000 Poles had been deported to the Generalgouvernement,
some 260,000 more had been dispatched to Germany proper, and several thousand others had been executed in the fall of 1939.[33] If the region were to remain
economically viable and fulfill its mission as the breadbasket of Germany, the
labor of racially inferior Poles simply had to be harnessed in order to keep the
factories and fields of Wartheland producing goods for the Greater German Reich
and the German war economy. And harnessed it was. "Without Poles," Hans-

Erich Volkmann states, "the economy of the Reichsgau would have no doubt collapsed."[34] To be sure, Wartheland's population was overwhelmingly Polish: one could also say that today without the Poles, the Polish economy would collapse!

It seems, then, that the crusade to de-Polonize Wartheland and the incorporated territories as a whole via evacuations to the East was doomed on the basis of hard economic realities alone.[35] The economic value of Poles far outweighed the racial danger that their continued presence in annexed western Poland (or Germany proper) represented for the Reich and the ethnic integrity of the Volksgemeinschaft. But though the deportation program had ground to a halt, the National Socialists did not abandon their racial-ideological objectives in the incorporated territories. The Germanization of the eastern provinces remained a fundamental goal of the regime. Since Poles were to remain in the region, their presence had to be justified on ideological grounds. The Deutsche Volksliste provided a means to accomplish this.

THE DEUTSCHE VOLKSLISTE

Despite Hitler's maxim that "Germanization can only be applied to *soil* and never to *people*," the Nazi regime had pursued a policy of human re-Germanization since the very beginning of the occupation. Through its analysis of evacuation lists supplied by the SS-AS, as well its racial examinations of Polish evictees at the Litzmannstadt camps, the UWZ participated in this process, but ultimately, it declared relatively few "Poles" to be either outright "Germans" or at least suitable for "later acceptance into German Volkstum." Far more Poles became Germans via the Deutsche Volksliste, or German Ethnic Registry. The DVL, as indicated earlier, was initiated in Wartheland in October 1939 in order to identify all ethnic Germans resident in the province. At the time of its inception, this racial classification system contained two categories, DVL A being that reserved for "known Germans" who had actively fought for the German cause during the years of Polish rule and DVL B for those individuals who were of "obvious" German ethnicity but who had demonstrated no such long-standing commitment to the Volk. Tens of thousands of Warthegau natives were registered in the DVL over the following year. By 26 October 1940, 333,700 individuals had been granted volksdeutsch status, 182,500 of whom received the designation DVL A.[36] Still, Nazi ethnopoliticians believed that there was much valuable blood yet to be found among Wartheland's native population. As Egon Leuschner of the Racial

Policy Office of the NSDAP noted in 1940, a significant number of individuals of Deutschstämmigkeit had "gone under into Polentum" over the previous decades. Such people may have believed themselves to be Polish, but in reality, they were only assimilated or Polonized Germans: "Although they themselves claim to think and feel Polish, in their entire way of life, they obviously stand out from the Polish population surrounding them. Cleanliness, sense of order, self-consciousness, honor, righteousness, and frankness ... are the qualities peculiar to them, [as opposed to those] typical of the Polish Volkscharakter [people's character].[37]

The desire to recover this lost "German" blood led to an expansion of Wartheland's racial classification system in late 1940 and was soon followed by the introduction of the Deutsche Volksliste throughout the incorporated territories in early 1941. It seems that considerations of a more practical economic and military nature drove forward the legal and geographic expansion of the DVL as well.

On 12 September 1940, Himmler officially broadened the DVL to include two additional racial categories, and at the same time, he changed the classification system from one of alphabetical to one of numerical designations, with DVL A becoming DVL 1 and so on. The new category DVL 3 denoted individuals of German descent "who over the years have entered into ties with Polentum, but who on the basis of their *conduct* have the qualification[s] to become full-blown members of the German Volksgemeinschaft."[38] Also included in this category were non-Germans who lived in German-Polish mixed marriages in which "the German part of the marriage has asserted itself," as well as those who belonged to the Masurian, Kaschubian, Slonsakian, and Upper Silesian splinter groups. DVL 4 designated ethnic German "renegades" who were politically pro-Polish and anti-Nazi. People belonging to the DVL groups 1 and 2 were considered Volksdeutschen and could therefore remain in the East. But those who received the latter two designations supposedly had to be re-Germanized through an intensive educational program in the Altreich; only after proving themselves worthy could they become "full-blown Germans." Himmler's directive stated that these new regulations now applied to annexed western Poland in its entirety,[39] but it was not until March 1941 that they were codified by the Reich Ministry of the Interior (in collaboration with Himmler and the NSDAP) and officially introduced throughout the eastern provinces.[40]

The perceived need to identify and re-Germanize individuals of German extraction who had "gone under into Polentum" was, of course, justified on the basis of National Socialist racial ideology. Germanness, in the Nazi worldview, lay not in the mind but in the blood. In the blood of every Deutschstämmige—despite the fact that he or she may have spoken Polish, felt Polish, supported the Polish political cause, and thus considered himself or herself to *be* Polish—lay a genuine Aryan who could eventually be reeducated to think and feel German. Though some may well have had their doubts, most Nazi ethnopoliticians involved in the formulation and implementation of the DVL apparently believed that they were being true to their principles in promoting such a policy. Perhaps, then, it was merely a historical coincidence that the DVL fourfold classification system became law throughout the eastern provinces at precisely the same time that the need for Polish labor was so acute, on the one hand, and that the deportation campaign was suspended, on the other. I suggest the contrary.

As of mid-March 1941, deportations to the Generalgouvernement had been put on indefinite hold; moreover, they were also considered by many National Socialists to be detrimental to the German war economy. Nevertheless, Nazi ideological goals still dictated that the eastern provinces were to become a flourishing and purely German region within the foreseeable future. With the deportation program now terminated, the Deutsche Volksliste was used to facilitate this racial metamorphosis. Hundreds of thousands of individuals, even though they were self-consciously Polish and had only the most tenuous connection to German Volkstum, were simply turned into probationary Germans via the DVL, particularly via the third, fairly lenient category of the system. Such racial hocus-pocus increased the German population of annexed Poland with relative ease, de-Polonizing and Germanizing the region simultaneously without the need for resettlements or evacuations. At the same time, it secured manpower not only for the Reich economy but also for the German military, since those who received the designations DVL 1 through DVL 3 qualified for service in the Wehrmacht.[41] The DVL may have corresponded to the ludicrous tenets of Nazi racial ideology, but the timing of its codification and its subsequent widespread application in the incorporated territories lead me to believe that it was employed, either consciously or subconsciously, essentially as an excuse to justify the continued presence of otherwise racially inferior (albeit economically and militarily valuable) Poles in the eastern provinces. The historian Werner Röhr, of the former East Germany, seems to hold the same view: "The DVL was introduced into the entire annexed Polish region in March 1941, therefore at a time when the mass deportations to the Generalgouvernement had to be suspended and when the need for soldiers as well as workers had considerably intensified."[42] Robert L. Koehl is more explicit: "The arrival at standardized regulations on paper for the classification of the population of the annexed Polish territories in 1941 coincided with preparations for *Fall Bar-*

barossa, the invasion of the Soviet Union. The need for soldiers and for workers to replace those called into service encouraged local authorities to swell the third category of the DVL."[43]

The Deutsche Volksliste was, in effect, a pair of rose-colored glasses that, when donned, seemed to reconcile the real world with Nazi utopian ideals. The DVL may have given the appearance that the Germanization of the incorporated territories was proceeding as planned, but appearance belied reality. The vast majority of those who were registered in the latter two categories of the DVL were in all likelihood unalloyed, dyed-in-the-wool Poles who spoke, thought, and felt Polish, despite all dubious ideological justifications to the contrary.[44]

Admittedly, the DVL was not employed in Wartheland to nearly the same extent as it was in the other eastern provinces. In Greiser's Mustergau, the standards for admission were far more rigorous than those in Upper Silesia or Danzig–West Prussia. Still, 494,516 Warthegau natives were registered in the DVL by 1 October 1943, among whom 65,510 received the designation DVL 3 and 18,613 the DVL 4.[45] Only several thousand more were admitted over the course of the following year, bringing the total number of DVL members in the district to 512,500 by the end of 1944.[46] The situation was markedly different in Upper Silesia and Danzig–West Prussia. In Upper Silesia, fully 1,477,000 people were registered in the Volksliste, including 1,040,000 in the third category of the DVL alone. And in Danzig–West Prussia, Nazi authorities managed to identify 976,000 individuals who bore valuable blood, 762,000 of whom were classified as DVL 3.[47] In the latter case, the personality of Gauleiter Albert Forster, who was much less of a racial fanatic than his counterpart in Wartheland, significantly helped to swell the membership of the DVL in his domain. As Herbert Levine argues, Forster was convinced that since his Gau had originally been German territory in its entirety, "the amount of German blood submerged in an apparently Polish population must be very great." This conviction, perhaps coupled with his determination to impress Hitler with the speed with which his province had been Germanized, led to the admission of at least 62.5 percent of the region's population into the DVL by late 1944. Entire villages were sometimes registered in a blanket fashion, with no consideration of individual cases whatsoever. Himmler grumbled about this blatant violation of his DVL guidelines, but since Forster was an Altkämpfer and a favorite of the Führer, he could do nothing.[48]

The DVL 3 category ultimately became "a vast catch-all," as Koehl puts it, for anyone deemed indispensable to the German war effort.[49] "Statistical Germanization" became a widespread practice. Hundreds of thousands of Poles became

Germans simply by registering—or being forcibly registered—in the Deutsche Volksliste, and despite some halfhearted protests by Himmler and a few others, economic and military considerations evidently compelled the Nazi hierarchy to accept this obvious violation of its racial principles.[50] The liberal use of the DVL as well as other trends in the development of Nazi Polenpolitik discussed in these pages seems to constitute grounds for a reevaluation of certain well-established suppositions regarding the nature and evolution of National Socialist racial policy.[51]

A "DE-RADICALIZATION" OF RACIAL POLICY?

With the termination of the 3.Nahplan–1.Teilprogram on 15 March 1941, the Nazi anti-Polish deportation campaign as a whole met an inglorious end. Though the suspension of evacuations was both officially defined and generally regarded as transitory, no more large-scale transports of Polish deportees from the incorporated territories would enter the Generalgouvernement for the duration of the occupation. If, based on its objectives, the 1.Teilprogram can be characterized as a failure, so can the deportation program in its entirety. As has been shown, the Nazis had initially intended to remove millions of individuals from annexed western Poland without delay. In November 1939, Wetzel and Hecht of the Racial Policy Office of the NSDAP estimated that of the roughly 6,336,000 Poles in the incorporated territories, only 1 million at most were candidates for Germanization; the remaining 5,336,000 "genuine" Poles, as well as all Jews, all individuals of Polish-Jewish mixed blood, and all other racial undesirables would have to be deported in short order to the Generalgouvernement, and RFSS-RKFDV Heinrich Himmler wholeheartedly agreed.[52] But according to Eichmann's calculations, only 408,525 Poles and Jews had been deported to the Generalgouvernement by 15 March 1941.[53] The population of Wartheland had borne the brunt of this "limited" ethnic cleansing. Nearly 70 percent of all organized evacuations carried out during the period emanated from the Mustergau of National Socialism. Together, the 1.Nahplan, Zwischenplan, 2.Nahplan, and 3.Nahplan–1.Teilprogram had reduced the Polish and Jewish population of the province by 280,772,[54] but the comprehensive Germanization of Greiser's domain was far from complete. Millions of "racially inferior" Poles and hundreds of thousands of Jews were still in the Warthegau. The Jews would eventually disappear, but the vast majority of the Poles would remain, primarily because the Nazi regime desperately needed their manpower in the so-called breadbasket of the Greater German Reich.

Within the first months of the occupation, Hans-Erich Volkmann asserts, the Nazis faced a major dilemma: the impossibility of bringing the requirements of the war economy into harmony with the goals of Volkstumspolitik.[55] Indeed, though the ideology of Germanization called for the complete elimination of Poles from annexed territory, many in the Nazi regime very quickly came to realize that this was not only unfeasible but also undesirable. A number of historians have acknowledged that practical economic considerations eventually clashed with—and to some degree compromised—anti-Polish, anti-Slavic ideological goals, but with the notable exception of Volkmann, they hold that the clash and compromise transpired only when the fortunes of war turned against the Reich. Ulrich Herbert, the foremost historian of National Socialist foreign labor policy, writes, "The brighter the prospects of victory, the more radically were ideological objectives adhered to and implemented; the worse the war situation, the greater the concessions to economic points of view."[56] In *The Path to Genocide*, Christopher Browning cites with approval Herbert's argument, expressed in a 1987 article, that "from September 1939 to September 1941, there was no conflict between ideological and economic considerations concerning the labor exploitation of Jews, Poles, and Russians. Victory would solve all economic problems, and Jews and Slavs were viewed as a 'burden,' not a source of potential labor" (Browning's words). In the first months of Barbarossa, millions of Russian prisoners of war (POWs) were therefore left to starve and die in open corrals, and the Einsatzgruppen proceeded to exterminate Russian Jews with murderous efficiency. It was not until the fall of 1941 that "fundamental change occurred, leading to a conflict between Vernichtung and Arbeit, between economic interest and ideological primacy." In October 1941—precisely when it became clear that the military collapse of the USSR was not necessarily imminent—severe worker shortages in the Reich compelled Hitler to approve the use of Russian POWs for forced labor (something he had previously rejected), but since most of the prisoners had already perished or were too weak to work, some 1.4 million Russian civilians were sent to Germany in 1942 in their stead.[57] When viewed exclusively in terms of the Russian Question, this argument is sound. But in terms of the Polish Question in the Warthegau, these pages have demonstrated that the conflict between economic interest and ideological primacy began much earlier than September 1941. What is more, the clash ensued not at a time of military setback but at a point when the euphoria of victory was intense and the prospects for a Thousand-Year Reich dominating central Europe seemed very real.

In Wartheland, ideology and pragmatism first locked horns in the autumn of 1939, during the planning stage of the 1.Nahplan. And before the operation had run its course, pragmatism began to prevail. As the Nazis earmarked supposedly dangerous Poles for immediate evacuation, circumstances had forced Rapp's Staff for the Evacuation of Poles and Jews to grant deferments to Polish civil servants, railway personnel, and public utilities workers, as well as many others employed in vital industries, despite the fact that many of these individuals had been deemed racially and politically detrimental to the consolidation of German nationhood. The health of the Wartheland's economy, mainly that of the agricultural sector, remained at the center of evacuation planning in the months to come. SS-Obersturmbannführer Kendzia, the Warthegau's trustee for labor, vehemently argued against the deportation of Polish farmworkers as early as 11 January 1940. The supply of agricultural labor for Wartheland had to be secured, he declared, "since this Gau has great tasks."[58] Reichsmarschall Hermann Göring soon followed suit, asserting on 12 February that the prevailing issue in all "eastern questions" was the need to strengthen the Reich's war potential, particularly in terms of agriculture: "Posen and West Prussia must again become the granary of Germany"; thus, a ready supply of workers had to remain in the incorporated territories, and "it will be for the most part [Polish]."[59] Even the racial fanatic Arthur Greiser voiced essentially the same opinion one year later. Since Wartheland was to be a "grain factory," he contended, all necessary farmworkers had to stay in the district, "even though they are Poles."[60] Such demands for economic rationality were clearly at loggerheads with the official and often-stated racial-ideological objectives of the regime, but it was economic rationality that triumphed in the end. The Poles did remain, even though they were Poles and even though their very presence flew in the face of cherished Nazi racial principles.

A cursory examination of Nazi deportation policy between 1939 and 1941 would lead one to believe that it was driven first and foremost by racial ideology, mainly racial anti-Slavism, and the Nazis certainly justified most of their activity in annexed western Poland on racial grounds. The evidence seems to suggest, however, that utilitarian concerns outweighed issues of race and nationality from the very onset of the deportation campaign—indeed, well before the labor question became so pressing. It appears that the vast majority of Poles evacuated during the period under scrutiny were not expropriated and deported simply because they were Polish; rather, the criteria for evacuation were, in practice, far more dependent upon the possessions of the individual than upon the individual himself or herself.[61] The UWZ deported Poles primarily to secure their property and for the purpose of accommodating ethnic German repatriates. Those Poles with the best properties, not necessarily those considered racially or politically the worst, ultimately emerged as the principal Polish victims of evacuation policy, a fact the SS-AS planning chief, Alexander Dolezalek, pointed out in his memo of February 1941. The dictates of Nazi racial ideology were pushed further aside as the war progressed. When it finally became evident that Polish labor was indispensable, deportation was abandoned in favor of displacement, a practice that enabled the UWZ to continue seizing Polish property for Volksdeutschen while at the same time guaranteeing a regular supply of labor for the German war machine.

This trend raises a theoretical question regarding the historiography of Nazi Germany. "Functionalist" historians such as Hans Mommsen and the late Martin Broszat have argued that a process termed *cumulative radicalization* marked the evolution of Nazi policies, particularly racial policies, between 1933 and 1945. They maintain that Nazi policies generally emerged through improvised and uncoordinated bureaucratic initiatives, not through systematic, long-term planning. Even those policies concerning race and lebensraum, matters central to the National Socialist faith, reflected no highly developed, grand strategic design but were rather ad hoc responses by a fragmentary, "polycratic" regime to immediate political problems and often self-imposed logistical and organizational difficulties. Factionalized and utterly devoid of centralized authority, the Nazi bureaucracy was inherently unstable and incapable of initiating rational, concerted policy. Hitler, the brooding and distant leader, set the ideological tone of policy through his writings, speeches, and public proclamations, but he offered few coherent political objectives and virtually nothing in the way of planning or direction. As the various factions and individuals in the government jockeyed for position through poorly coordinated political action believed to be in accordance with Hitler's will, Nazi policies gradually radicalized, becoming more and more barbarous, inhumane, and irrational, even at the expense of the German economy and the German war effort.[62]

Recent scholarship on the emergence of the Final Solution to the Jewish Question tends to lean toward functionalist views regarding the development of Nazi racial policies. Although there is some debate regarding Hitler's actual role in the decision-making process that ultimately led to the extermination of European Jews, most historians now seem to recognize that Nazi Jewish policy indeed underwent a largely unplanned radicalization between 1933 and 1945.[63] From the anti-Jewish boycott of 1 April 1933 to the Nuremberg Laws of 1935, the forced expulsions of 1938 and 1939, the deportations and ghettoizations between 1939 and 1941, the mass shootings carried out by the Einsatzgruppen on the eastern front, and on to the establishment of industrialized extermination centers in late 1941 and 1942, Nazi Jewish policy steadily intensified. The wheels of radicalization eventually rolled to Auschwitz, but the "road to Auschwitz," as Karl Schleunes argues,[64] was a "twisted" one, each step unplanned but more radical than its predecessor. The Final Solution, then, was an ad hoc policy of last resort implemented only after the failure of all territorial solutions to the Jewish Question, not the consummation of a systematic, premeditated program for total physical annihilation. Furthermore, the wholesale murder of 5 to 6 million European Jews, millions of whom were perfectly capable of work, clearly represents economic irrationality to the extreme; the allocation of the Reich's limited transport capacity and limited manpower to the SS death machine only bolsters this assessment, as well as the functionalist position.

But do functionalist arguments regarding the modus operandi of the Third Reich and the evolution of Nazi racial policy apply to the resettlement and deportation campaign in annexed western Poland? To a certain extent, I think they do. As demonstrated in Chapter Two, the crusade to Germanize the incorporated territories emerged not as the result of long-term planning but rather through a series of ad hoc decisions made in the euphoria of victory that swept Hitler and his regime after the invasion of Poland on 1 September 1939. What is more, Hitler played virtually no role in planning the Germanization and de-Polonization crusade that came to define Nazi Polenpolitik during the first years of the occupation. After issuing his sweeping order for the consolidation of German nationhood on 7 October 1939, Hitler all but disappeared from the scene, leaving his SS and administrative subordinates to bring his lofty political objectives into focus and make them reality. During the various quarrels over the deportation program among Nazi authorities in the East that followed, Hitler took little part. Usually, his underlings settled these disputes on their own, but in the case of the never-ending friction between Generalgouvernement and Warthegau officials, they sometimes did not. Largely the result of Hitler's hands-off leadership, these disagreements often proved detrimental to the smooth implementation of evacuation policy.

Apart from these seemingly valid applications of functionalist theory, the process of cumulative radicalization does not appear to apply to the history of destructive anti-Polish initiatives in Wartheland and the other incorporated territories. Brutal though it was, Nazi Polenpolitik in the eastern provinces apparently grew more rational and less racially motivated as the regime came to realize the military and economic value of its Polish subjects. In effect, it apparently "de-radicalized" as time passed, gradually evolving from the initial unrealistic plans to deport approximately 80 percent of the Polish population in the incorporated territories immediately (coupled with the very real summary executions of thousands of Poles during Operation Tannenberg in September and October 1939) to the point that all Poles capable of work were exempted from evacuation in early 1941. The Nazi regime, by then preparing to fight a two-front war, simply could no longer afford to let a significant portion of its Polish labor force wither and die in the Generalgouvernement. Therefore, evacuations to the East were suspended, and beyond that, hundreds of thousands of Poles soon became Germans—as if by magic—via the DVL, a racial metamorphosis that justified their continued presence in those regions designated to become purely German in a matter of years. Granted, one could argue that the transformation of Poles into Germans was indeed a radical measure, but it was not truly a destructive one in the physical sense of the word. The Poles in question may have been stripped of their Polish nationality—and in the case of the many Polish children taken from their families and raised as Germans, stripped of their Polish self-identity as well[65]—but they did not vanish from Reich territory, as was the original intention of Nazi racial politicians. They remained—indeed, for utilitarian reasons, they had to remain— in the Reich, and by the latter half of the war, the National Socialist hierarchy had, as the vast number of DVL inductees (particularly those in category three) suggests, come to terms with this hard reality.

Regardless of the ideological tenets of Germanization, circumstances forced the Polish Question to the sidelines of the Volkstumskampf in the East. By the summer of 1941, the Jewish Question in Poland, an issue never far from the minds of Nazi ethnocrats (though heretofore tackled only in fits and starts), had moved to the forefront of the "battle for nationality" in the incorporated territories, and as we well know, the Jews—"racial enemy No. 1"—quickly became the primary target of destructive racial-ideological initiatives in the eastern provinces and occupied Europe as a whole. One might contend that the relaxation of the anti-Polish resettlement policy was only a temporary measure and that if the German army had emerged victorious on the eastern front, destructive anti-Polish action, be it in the form of deportation or physical liquidation or both, would have resumed and radicalized with a vengeance. If the Generalplan Ost (GPO) formulated between 1941 and 1942 is any indication, this may have well been the case.

As the launch date for Barbarossa drew nearer in the late spring of 1941, Nazi resettlement and population planners turned their attention farther eastward to Soviet territory. Judging by the astounding success of the Wehrmacht over the previous two years, all expected the conquest of the USSR to be a rapid one, resulting in a vast increase in the amount of lebensraum under German control, as well as a vast increase in the number of unwanted Jews and Slavs, millions of Poles included, in the German sphere of influence. Once the western reaches of the Soviet Union were firmly under the Nazi yoke, the Generalgouvernement would obviously no longer need to serve as a strategic buffer zone against the USSR. It, as well as occupied Soviet territory, would therefore be ripe for Germanization. Through a massive program of German colonization, coupled with the expulsion of most of the region's native inhabitants, the utopian dream of a German Garden of Eden in the East would finally become reality.

On 21 June 1941, the very eve of Barbarossa, Heinrich Himmler ordered his RKF planning chief, Dr. Konrad Meyer, to devise a comprehensive resettlement plan for soon-to-be-conquered Soviet territory, as well as those parts of eastern Europe already under Reich control, including the incorporated territories. Three weeks later, on 15 July, he presented Himmler with a basic outline for such a program, entitled the Generalplan Ost, of which only the cover letter survives.[66] Meyer's plan evidently envisioned a vast expansion, both geographically and demographically, of the resettlement, expropriation, and deportation policies practiced until then in annexed western Poland. The scheme was widely discussed and underwent a number of modifications over the following months. During the fall of 1941, a revised version of the GPO was developed within the RSHA. Like Meyer's original blueprint, the RSHA plan is no longer extant, but a lengthy paper by Dr. Erhard Wetzel of the Racial Policy Office, dated 27 April 1941, revealed the gist of its contents. The RSHA had determined that of the estimated 45 million "foreign" inhabitants of the territory in question, roughly 31 million would be expelled.[67] The deportees would include all Jews, 80 to 85 percent of all Poles, 75 percent of Belorussians, and 65 percent of Ukrainians. Of the 14 million foreigners who remained, 6,200,000 were candidates for Germanization; the rest would apparently serve as workers. These 6,200,000 "Germanizables," combined with the 4,850,000 German colonizers called for by Meyer the following month, would bring the German population of the region to about 11 million individuals. The Germanization of the East, which encompassed a massive program of economic improvement as well as these population transfers, was to be completed within twenty-five years at a cost of 66.6 billion marks, 45.7 billion of which would be devoted to initiatives in the incorporated territories alone.[68] RFSS Himmler was undeterred by the sheer enormity of the program: "I have perused the Generalplan Ost," he wrote to Greifelt on 12 June 1942, "which on the whole pleases me very much. I would like to submit the Generalplan to the Führer at some point."[69]

Meyer later incorporated the GPO in a highly detailed and expanded resettlement and economic improvement scheme termed the Generalsiedlungsplan, which was submitted to Himmler on 23 December 1942. Nazi resettlement plans now embraced occupied Luxembourg and Alsace-Lorraine, as well as Bohemia and Moravia and southeastern Austria.[70] Himmler soon requested that the program be expanded once again to include the Crimean Peninsula, and Meyer responded with a revised Generalsiedlungsplan on 15 February 1943. This document, as Dan Inkelas points out, was to be the last major contribution of the RKF Main Planning Office to the doomed Germanization campaign.[71] The remnants of the German Sixth Army had just surrendered to the Soviets at Stalingrad, a military debacle that marked the beginning of the Nazi retreat from the East.[72]

Due to the steadily deteriorating military situation on the Russian front, virtually nothing came of these grandiose plans for occupied eastern Europe. Only a "probe" resettlement action within the context of the GPO was initiated in the Lublin district of the Generalgouvernement between November 1942 and March 1943, an operation led by Lublin's SS- und Polizeiführer Odilo Globocnik in which evacuation experts of the UWZ-Warthegau took part. The action centered around the town of Zamość, approximately 70 kilometers southeast of the district capital. It was—in terms of its constructive Germanization objectives—an utter failure. Though more than 100,000 of the region's 145,000 native inhabitants were removed from 300 villages during the operation, only 9,000 Volksdeutschen out of 27,000 awaiting resettlement in VoMi camps were actually placed on vacated farms. And though the Nazis intended to settle another 70,000 ethnic Germans in the area, they never managed to do so.[73] Other than the depopulation and resulting economic devastation of the Zamość region, this first and only major step toward the realization of the GPO accomplished little.

It seems, then, that if Himmler and his SS cohorts had had their way, a destructive anti-Polish policy within the framework of the Generalplan Ost and Generalsiedlungsplan would have resumed in the incorporated eastern territories between 1942 and 1943, eventually leading, perhaps, to the complete de-Polonization of the region that had so long been desired. The exigencies of war, however, once again thwarted their plans. The rapidly accumulating defeats on the eastern front certainly went far to prevent any large-scale implementation of the GPO, but as in the case of the earlier deportation schemes, economic considerations most likely played a role as well. The Nazis simply did not have enough German workers to replace the millions of Slavic natives of the East that the more fanatical members of the hierarchy hoped to eradicate. Dr. Hans Ehlich of RSHA Amt IIIB recognized this hard fact in December 1942. In a statement revealing that the outright murder of millions of Slavs was then being discussed in Nazi circles, Ehlich reasoned that the fate of 70 million Slavs in the East could be decided through "neither complete ousting [*restlose Verdrängung*, or comprehensive expulsion] nor total physical annihilation ... because we would never have enough people to even come close to replacing these seventy million."[74] Clearly, if Germany was at last to achieve agricultural self-sufficiency through the exploitation of the annexed and occupied eastern territories, Slavic farmworkers, including the Poles of Wartheland and Danzig–West Prussia, would have to remain on the land; they could not be exterminated or expelled without ceremony en masse. Even if the Wehrmacht had advanced victoriously to the Urals and completely secured the thousands of square kilometers of countryside behind them, this would have been the case.

Military defeat and, even more important, practical necessity prevented the resumption of destructive anti-Polish policy. The Poles still suffered greatly throughout the remaining years of Nazi occupation, but contrary to the regime's original intentions, they did not disappear. Of course, according to orthodox estimates, some 3 million non-Jewish Poles perished during World War II, a death tally that reflects thousands of summary executions as well as the inevitable results of starvation, disease, brutal treatment, and two military drives across Polish territory—one in 1939, the other between 1944 and 1945. But unlike the destruction of Polish Jews, Polish deaths—or at least the vast majority of Polish deaths—did not reflect a concerted, countrywide policy of systematic annihilation. Non-Jewish Poles were not systematically annihilated principally because the Third Reich desperately needed their manpower, and demographic reality suggests that their labor would have remained indispensable even if the Nazis had won World War II. Neither economics nor war, of course, prevented the radicalization of destructive anti-Jewish policy. As John Connelly points out, "The central difference [between the Slavic and] the Jewish case is obvious: the Nazis could imagine the Slavs as useful, the Jews they could not." "For the Nazis," he continues, the Jews were not a race among races. They were the race that destroyed (*zersetzen*) race, the very substance of human existence. There was a uniquely metaphysical dimension in the Nazi hatred of Jews: the Jews were the anti-race; or, as Hitler is supposed to have said to Hermann Rauschning, "the Jew is the anti-man, the creature of another god ... He is a creature outside nature and alien to nature" ... Unlike policies toward the Slavs, or toward any other identifiable human group, policies toward the Jews were an end in themselves ... whereas policies toward Slavs appear as a constant improvisation, in which opportunity and ideology shaped one another.[75]

Close scrutiny reveals another central difference between Nazi Polenpolitik and Judenpolitik: although the process of cumulative radicalization appears generally valid in terms of the evolution of anti-Jewish policy, it does not seem to mark the evolution of anti-Polish policy in the incorporated territories. At the onset of the occupation, Polenpolitik and Judenpolitik were both regarded as key components of a sweeping policy of "ethnic housecleaning" in eastern Europe, but they developed in opposite directions. From late 1939 on, the Nazis gradually came to regard the Poles of the eastern provinces as useful. Their usefulness became increasingly evident as the regime prepared for its face-off with the Soviet Union and even more so as the Allies tightened their grip on Germany's throat. Consequently, Nazi Volkstumspolitik vis-à-vis the Poles in question de-radicalized *in practice* from a policy of deportation to one of displacement, combined with the widespread Germanization of hundreds of thousands of otherwise "racially inferior" Poles. Nazi Judenpolitik, by contrast, radicalized drastically, moving from a policy of deportation to one of comprehensive physical extermination.

In *The Nazi Dictatorship: Problems and Perspectives of Interpretation*, the seminal work on the historiography of Nazi Germany, Ian Kershaw defines the process of cumulative radicalization as "a spiraling radicalization in which the regime lurched from crisis to crisis, burning its boats in a series of *ad hoc* responses to current emergencies and creating a diminishing sense of reality in the pursuit of extravagant objectives."[76] But in the case of anti-Polish Volkstumspolitik in the incorporated territories, the trends discussed in the present work seem to indicate that though the regime certainly did "lurch from crisis to crisis" and certainly did implement "*ad hoc* responses to current emergencies," it did not "burn its boats," nor were its actions marked by "a diminishing sense of reality." *Spiraling radicalization* simply does not define the evolution of Polenpolitik in annexed western Poland. A spiraling *de-radicalization* is a more apt description.

POSTSCRIPT: LATER ACTIVITY OF THE UWZ AND ITS PERSONNEL

By no means did the UWZ's mission in annexed western Poland end with the suspension of the 3.Nahplan–1.Tielprogram on 15 March 1941. Some 250,000 of the roughly 360,000 ethnic Germans who had by then returned to the Reich still remained in VoMi camps awaiting resettlement, including 32,400 Bessarabian, Bukovinian, and Lithuanian Volksdeutschen in Litzmannstadt alone.[77] By November 1944, another 271,000 Germans would arrive in the incorporated territories, mostly as refugees fleeing Soviet territory before the advancing Red Army. Of the 631,485 ethnic German repatriates (or refugees) who entered the eastern provinces during the war, approximately 85 percent (536,931) found their way to Wartheland.[78] The provision of housing and employment for the hundreds of thousands of additional Volksdeutschen preoccupied the UWZ-Warthegau until the collapse of Germany's position in the East in late 1944. Verdrängung des Polentums was the preferred means for doing so.

Between March 1941 and the autumn of 1944, the UWZ organized and, with the help of the police, carried out the evictions of some 550,000 Poles residing in Wartheland within the framework of five operations: the Verdrängung phase of the 3.Nahplan (March 1941 to January 1942), the Erweiterter 3.Nahplan (Expanded 3.Nahplan) of January to December 1942, the so-called Feldarbeiter- or "Z"-Hofbildung Action (Farm Creation Action) of 1942,[79] the displacements of 1943 to create space for Volksdeutschen, and the Aktion Schwarzmeerdeutsche (Black Sea Germans) carried out in 1944 for the purpose of accommodating ethnic German refugees from Soviet territory.[80] The vast majority of these evictees were apparently housed with other Poles; others were concentrated on three *Polenreservate* (Polish reservations) established within the borders of the Gau in the second half of 1942.[81] The Germans also sent a significant number of Warthegau Poles to the Altreich as compulsory workers, some dispatched within the context of UWZ-led actions but most presumably sent by the Arbeitsämter. By December 1944, a grand total of 2,026,000 Polish workers had been dispatched to the Altreich, 1,333,000 from the Generalgouvernement and 693,000 from the incorporated territories. Wartheland's share of the latter was roughly 450,000.[82]

According to Werner Röhr's estimates, the UWZ was directly responsible for the eviction and deportation or displacement of 904,630 Warthegau natives, primarily non-Jewish Poles, during its five years of operation in the province.[83] The lessons learned in Wartheland—particularly the expertise gained during the four organized deportation actions carried out between December 1939 and the spring of 1941—were put to devastating use in the Nazi war of extermination against European Jews. Franz Novak, a transport officer in Eichmann's RSHA Amt IVD4, acknowledged the significance of the first nineteen months of UWZ activity while in investigative detention in 1974: "All this experience in transport techniques, incidentally, was already gained during the evacuation, before Jewish transports, of roughly 500,000 Poles from the areas of the Wartheland and Danzig–West Prussia to the Generalgouvernement."[84]

Beyond providing the experience in transport techniques needed to implement the Final Solution to the Jewish Question, the UWZ also provided crucial manpower. Albert Rapp, the first chief of the UWZ, later commanded Sonderkommando 7A, an SS death squad that operated in the Soviet Union in the spring of 1942.[85] Along with his superior Adolf Eichmann, Hermann Krumey, the leader of the UWZ Border Office in Litzmannstadt, organized the deportation of Hungarian Jews to Auschwitz in 1944.[86] A staff member of Krumey's bureau, Siegfried Seidl, was appointed head of the "model" concentration camp Theresienstadt in 1942.[87] Dieter Wisliceny, the SD leader in Gnesen during the 1.Nahplan, went on to become the "adviser for Jewish Questions" in Slovakia, Salonika, Athens, and Hungary, and he played a leading role in the roundup and transport of Jews from those regions to the deaths camps in Poland.[88] And beginning in late 1941, several members of the UWZ staff in Litzmannstadt participated in the murder of tens of thousands of Jews at the nearby Chełmno (Kulmhof) extermination camp in Kreis Warthbrücken.[89]

Reichsgau Wartheland, Werner Röhr asserts, was seen by the Nazi regime as a testing ground for the New Order. The policies practiced in the district, particularly those involving the physical redistribution of ethnic groups, were largely untried and of an altogether experimental or model character; they served in many respects "as a rehearsal for the further acquisition of Lebensraum in the East."[90] Though the hard realities of the German war economy prevented this rehearsal from ever becoming a full-blown production, the "Warthegau experiment" had catastrophic consequences nevertheless. It left hundreds of thousands of individuals homeless, it left them impoverished, and it very often left them dead. The Umwandererzentralstelle certainly deserves Röhr's designation as "Sipo's principal instrument of terror"[91] in the Mustergau of National Socialism.

Notes

INTRODUCTION

1. Several reports on the pomp and circumstance surrounding Greiser's inauguration day can be found in the *Ostdeutscher Beobachter* (hereafter *OdB*), 3 November 1939. The *OdB*, an official organ of the NSDAP, first appeared in Posen on 1 November 1939, replacing the *Posener Tageblatt*, a German-language daily that had been in existence for seventy-eight years.

2. Dieter Schenk, *Hitlers Mann in Danzig: Albert Forster und die NS-Verbrechen in Danzig-Westpreussen* (Bonn, Germany: Verlag J. H. W. Dietz, 2000), 68.

3. Ian Kershaw, *Hitler 1936–1945: Nemesis* (New York: W. W. Norton, 2000), 250.

4. For a comprehensive overview of the pre-1939 Danzig NSDAP and Greiser's activities therein, see Herbert S. Levine, *Hitler's Free City: A History of the Nazi Party in Danzig, 1925–1939* (Chicago: University of Chicago Press, 1973).

5. Arthur Greiser, *Der Aufbau im Osten* (Jena, Germany: Verlag von Gustav Fischer, 1942), 7.

6. "Geburt und erste Lebenstage des Warthelandes," *OdB*, 26 October 1944. Greiser's official title during the early days of the occupation was Chef der Zivilverwaltung beim Militärbefehlshaber von Posen (Chief of the Civil Administration on the Staff of the Military Commander of Posen).

7. For additional biographical information on Greiser, see Czesław Łuczak, *Arthur Greiser hitlerowski władca w Wolnym Mieście Gdańsku i w Kraju Warty* (Poznan, Poland: PSO, 1997); Ian Kershaw, "Arthur Greiser—Ein Motor der 'Endlösung,'" in Ronald Smelser, Enrico Syring, and Rainer Zitelmann, eds., *Die Braune Elite 2: 21 weitere biographische Skizzen* (Darmstadt, Germany: Wissenschaftliche Buchgesellschaft, 1993), 117–127; Karl Höffkes, *Hitlers politische Generale: Die Gauleiter des Dritten Reiches—Ein biographisches Nachschlagewerk* (Tübingen, Germany: Grabert-Verlag, 1986), 104–105; Greiser's SS officer personnel file, NARA/BDC RG242/A3343/SSO 031A.

8. "Warthegau—Ein lebendiger Ostwall: Die Rede des Gaileiters in Schroda," *OdB*, 6 November 1939.

9. In this book, the term *Poles* will be used to refer to ethnic Poles, generally of the Christian faith, and the term *Jews* will refer to those individuals throughout Poland and Europe as a whole whom the Nazis deemed "Jews," meaning they were targets of specifically anti-Jewish discrimination and ultimately genocide.

10. Referred to in the Nazi lexicon as the "incorporated eastern territories," annexed western Poland included the Reichsgaue Wartheland and Danzig–West Prussia, eastern Upper Silesia, and Regierungsbezirk Zichenau, the latter of which was attached to southern East Prussia. The Generalgouvernement was the name given to the region of eastern Poland occupied by Nazi Germany but not formally annexed to the Reich.

11. In his recent study of German atrocities committed in Poland during the first months of the war, Alexander Rossino also stresses "the decidedly anti-Polish, and not anti-Jewish, animus" of early Nazi extermination policy, arguing that security concerns made ethnic Poles, as opposed to Polish Jews, the primary targets of SS murder squads in the fall of 1939. See Rossino, *Hitler Strikes Poland: Blitzkrieg, Ideology, and Atrocity* (Lawrence: University Press of Kansas, 2003), especially the author's concluding remarks, 233–235.

12. See Robert L. Koehl, *RKFDV: German Resettlement and Population Policy, 1939–1945: A History of the Reich Commission for the Strengthening of Germandom* (Cambridge, MA: Harvard University Press, 1957); Valdis O. Lumans, *Himmler's Auxiliaries: The Volksdeutsche Mittelstelle and the German National Minorities of Europe, 1939–1945* (Chapel Hill: University of North Carolina Press, 1993); Rolf-Dieter Müller, *Hitlers Ostkrieg und die Siedlungspolitik: Die Zusammenarbeit von Wehrmacht, Wirtschaft und SS* (Frankfurt, Germany: Fischer Taschenbuch Verlag, 1991); Dan Inkelas, "Visions of Harmony and Violence: RKF Landscape Planning and Population Policy in Annexed Poland, 1939–1944" (Ph.D. diss., Northwestern University, 1998); Gert Gröning and Joachim Wolschke Bulmahn, *Die Liebe zur Landschaft, Teil III: Der Drang nach Osten. Zur Entwicklung der Landespflege im Nationalsozialismus und während des Zweiten Weltkrieges in den "eingegliederten Ostgebieten"* (Munich, Germany: Minerva Publikation, 1987); Elizabeth Harvey, *Women and the Nazi East: Agents and Witnesses of Germanization* (New Haven, CT: Yale University Press, 2003); Isabel Heinemann, *"Rasse, Siedlung, deutsches Blut": Das Rasse- & Siedlungshauptamt der SS und die rassenpolitische Neuordnung Europas* (Göttingen, Germany: Wallstein Verlag, 2003). Though published roughly a half century ago and based almost exclusively on documents presented at the Nuremberg trials, Koehl's work remains the standard in the field. Also see the discussion of the Final Solution later in this introduction.

13. The work of Götz Aly and Susanne Heim presents a notable exception. See, among others, Aly and Heim, "The Economics of the Final Solution: A Case Study from the General Government," *Simon Wiesenthal Center Annual* 5 (1988): 3–48; Aly and Heim, *Vordenker der Vernichtung: Auschwitz und die deutschen Pläne für eine neue europäische Ordnung* (Frankfurt, Germany: Fischer Taschenbuch Verlag, 1993).

14. The incorporation of Wartheland into the Reich was based on four factors: (1) historical claims—the western part of the district was German territory before 1918; (2) economic considerations—Łódź was (and is) an important industrial and textile center; (3) logistical concerns—the addition of former Russian districts to the province eradicated a territorial "bulge" protruding into annexed western Poland and shortened appreciably the lines of travel, trade, and communication between East Prussia and Upper Silesia; and (4) ethnic German interests—though Łódź had once been situated in Russian, not Prus-

sian, Poland, it had a fairly large German minority. For discussion, see Chapter 3, as well as the October 1939 report by the Reich Ministry of the Interior, "Bericht über das Ergebnis der Grenzziehung Deutschland-Polen," 27 October 1939, APP/Chef der Zivilverwaltung beim Oberbefehlshaber im Militärbezirk Posen/75/1–5.

15. Martin Broszat, *Nationalsozialistische Polenpolitik, 1939–1945* (Stuttgart, Germany: Deutsche Verlags-Anstalt, 1961), 34–35.

16. Ian Kershaw, "Improvised Genocide? The Emergence of the 'Final Solution' in the 'Warthegau,'" *Transactions of the Royal Historical Society*, 6th ser., vol. 2 (1992): 56.

17. Christopher Browning, *The Path to Genocide: Essays on Launching the Final Solution* (Cambridge: Cambridge University Press, 1993), 7, 9.

18. Rossino, *Hitler Strikes Poland*, 234.

19. "Erlass des Führers und Reichkanzlers zur Festigung deutschen Volkstums," 7 October 1939, ND 686-PS, *IMT*, 26: 255–257.

20. Werner Röhr, Elke Heckert, Bernd Gottberg, Jutta Wenzel, and Heide-Marie Grünthal, eds., *Die faschistische Okkupationspolitik in Polen (1939–1945)*, vol. 2 of *Nacht über Europa: Die Okkupationspolitik des deutschen Faschismus (1938–1945)*, Achtbändige Dokumentenedition, ed. Wolfgang Schumann and Ludwig Nestler (Cologne, Germany: Pahl-Rugenstein, 1989); see Röhr's introduction to this collection of documents, 56.

21. Browning, *The Path to Genocide*, 113–114. The timing of the decision to pursue the Final Solution to the Jewish Question, as well as Hitler's actual role in the decision-making process, is a major point of contention among historians of the Third Reich. Since the publication of *The Path to Genocide*, Browning has reevaluated his position and pushed the date of the decision to murder all European Jews—one he firmly believes was made by Hitler—forward to October 1941. He presents his reasoning in his more recent works, *Nazi Policy, Jewish Workers, German Killers* (Cambridge: Cambridge University Press, 2000), 26–57, and *The Origins of the Final Solution: The Evolution of Nazi Jewish Policy, September 1939–March 1942* (Lincoln: University of Nebraska Press, 2004), 309–373.

22. See three works by Browning, *The Path to Genocide*, *Nazi Policy*, and *The Origins of the Final Solution*; Götz Aly, *"Final Solution": Nazi Population Policy and the Murder of European Jews*, trans. Belinda Cooper and Allison Brown (London: Edward Arnold, 1999); Aly and Heim, *Vordenker der Vernichtung*; Aly, "'Jewish Resettlement': Reflections on the Political Prehistory of the Holocaust," in Ulrich Herbert, ed., *National Socialist Extermination Policies: Contemporary German Perspectives and Controversies* (New York: Berghahn Books, 2000), 53–82; Kurt Pätzold, "Von der Vertriebung zum Genozid: Zu den Ursachen Triebkräften und Bedingungen der antijüdischen Politik des faschistischen deutschen Imperialismus," in Dietrich Eichotlz and Kurt Gossweiler, eds., *Faschismusforschung: Positionen, Probleme, Polemik* (Berlin: Akademie-Verlag, 1980), 181–208; Hans Mommsen, "Umvolkungspläne des Nationalsozialismus und der Holocaust," in Helge Grabitz, Klaus Bästlein, and Johannes Tuchel, eds., *Bilanz und Perspektiven der Forschung zu den nationalsozialistischen Gewaltverbrechen* (Berlin: Edition Hentrich, 1994), 58–84; Sybille Steinbacher, *"Musterstadt" Auschwitz: Germanisierungspolitik und Judenmord in Ostoberschlesien* (Munich, Germany: K. G. Saur Verlag, 2000); Peter Longerich, *Politik der Vernichtung: Eine Gesamtdarstellung der nationalsozialistischen Judenverfolgung*

(Munich, Germany: Piper Verlag, 1998); Bogdahn Musial, "The Origins of 'Operation Reinhard': The Decision-Making Process for the Mass Murder of the Jews," *Yad Vashem Studies* 28 (2000): 113–153.

23. Most notably, Broszat, *Nationalsozialistische Polenpolitik*; Czesław Madajczyk, *Die Okkupationspolitik Nazisdeutschlands in Polen, 1939–1945* (Berlin: Akadamie Verlag, 1987). Though valuable, if only because it is the sole in-depth study of Nazi Polenpolitik in the English language, Richard Lukas's more recent work, *The Forgotten Holocaust: The Poles under German Occupation, 1939–44* (New York: Hippocrene Books, 1997), largely ignores the deportation campaign and provides no discussion of the UWZ whatsoever.

24. See, among others, Jerzy Marczewski, *Hitlerowska Koncepcja Kolonizacjno-Wysiedleńczej i jej Realizacja w "Okregu Warty"* (Poznan, Poland: Instytut Zachodni, 1979); Włodzimierz Jastrzębski, *Hitlerowskie wysiedlenia z ziem polskich wcielnych do Rzeszy w latach 1939–1945* (Poznan, Poland: Instytut Zachodni, 1968); and Wacław Szulc's introductions to the two document collections he edited, "Wysiedlanie Ludności w tzw. Kraju Warty i na Zamojszczyźnie Popełnione przy tym Zbrodnie," *Biuletyn Głównej Komisji Badania Zbrodni Hitlerowskich w Polsce 21* (Warsaw: Wydawnictwo Prawnicze, 1970), and *Hitlerowski Aparat Wysiedleńczy w Polsce: Sylwetki Głównych jego "Działaczy"* (Warsaw: Ministerstwo Sprawiedliwości, 1973). Marczewski, whose work represents what is perhaps the most detailed overview of the deportation program in any language to date, presents an English summary of his research in an earlier article, "The Aims and Character of the Nazi Deportation Policy as Shown by Example of the 'Warta Region,'" *Polish-Western Affairs* 10 (1961): 235–262.

25. The same can be said for standard works on the Holocaust. Even the most meticulous study of the policies and administrative processes leading the Shoah, Raul Hilberg's *The Destruction of the European Jews*, 3 vols., 3rd ed. (New Haven, CT, and London: Yale University Press, 2003), devotes only a few pages to the deportation actions in question and fails to even mention the UWZ (see 1: 206ff.). Other general studies of the Final Solution suffer from the same deficiency. See, among others, Lucy Dawidowicz, *The War against the Jews, 1933–1945* (New York: Holt, Rinehart and Winston, 1975); Martin Gilbert, *The Holocaust: A History of the Jews of Europe during the Second World War* (New York: Holt, Rinehart and Winston, 1985); Nora Levin, *The Holocaust: The Destruction of European Jewry, 1933–1945* (New York: Thomas Y. Crowell, 1968); Leni Yahil, *The Holocaust: The Fate of European Jewry, 1932–1945*, trans. Ina Friedman and Haya Galai (New York: Oxford University Press, 1990).

26. In recent years, the so-called Generalplan Ost (GPO; General Plan East) has generated a good deal of interest among historians of the Third Reich. Valuable overviews of the UWZ, at least in terms of its later activities in the Generalgouvernement, are presented in a number of books on the subject. See, for example, Mechthild Rössler and Sabine Schleiermacher, eds., *Der "Generalplan Ost": Hauptlinien der nationalsozialistischen Planungs und Vernichtungspolitik* (Berlin: Akademie Verlag, 1993); Bruno Wasser, *Himmlers Raumplanung im Osten: Der Generalplan Ost in Polen, 1940–1944* (Basel, Switzerland, and Boston: Birkhäuser Verlag, 1993); also the collection of documents in Czesław Madajczyk, ed., *Vom Generalplan Ost zum Generalsiedlungsplan* (Munich, Germany: K.

G. Saur, 1994). The GPO is discussed in some detail in the final chapter of the present volume.

27. See Note 22.

28. With the exception of the material discussed in my own study, "'Absolute Organizational Deficiency': The *1.Nahplan* of December 1939 (Logistics, Limitations, and Lessons)," *Central European History* 2 (2003): 235–273, the only deportation action early in the war that has been painstakingly explored in published sources, most notably in three articles that appeared in the 1980s, is the so-called Nisko Aktion of October 1939. During this operation, five trainloads of Jews—roughly 4,800 individuals—from Kattowitz, Märisch-Ostrau, and Vienna were sent to a transit camp at Nisko on the San River. See Seev Goshen, "Eichmann und die Nisko-Aktion im Oktober 1939," *Vierteljahrshefte für Zeitgeschichte* 27, no. 1 (January 1981): 74–96; Jonny Moser, "Nisko: The First Experiment in Deportation," *Simon Wiesenthal Center Annual* 2 (1985): 1–30; Miroslav Karny, "Nisko in der Geschichte der Endlösung," *Judaica Bohemiae* 23 (1987): 69–84. The Nisko Aktion was no more than an experiment. Owing to both its brevity and its small scale, very little in the way of practical experience could have been—or was, for that matter—actually gained during its course.

CHAPTER 1. THE "POLISH QUESTION" IN GERMAN THOUGHT AND ACTION, 1830–1918

1. The standard work on partitioned Poland is Piotr S. Wandycz, *The Lands of Partitioned Poland, 1795–1918* (Seattle and London: University of Washington Press, 1974).

2. Quoted in Ian F. D. Morrow, "The Prussianization of the Poles," *Slavonic Review* 15 (1936–1937): 159.

3. Martin Broszat, *Zweihundert Jahre deutsche Polenpolitik* (Frankfurt, Germany: Suhrkamp Verlag, 1972), 101.

4. Harry K. Rosenthal, *German and Pole: National Conflict and Modern Myth* (Gainesville: University Press of Florida, 1976), 13–14. Rosenthal wrongly attributes Grolman's memo to 1813. See Broszat, *Zweihundert Jahre deutsche Polenpolitik*, 100; Morrow, "The Prussianization of the Poles," 159.

5. William W. Hagen, *Germans, Poles, and Jews: The Nationality Conflict in the Prussian East, 1772–1914* (Chicago and London: University of Chicago Press, 1980), 89.

6. For detailed population statistics, see ibid., table A1, "Absolute and Relative Changes in the Populations of the Poznanian Nationalities, 1825–1910," 324.

7. Ibid., 89.

8. Flottwell quoted in Richard Tims, *Germanizing Prussian Poland: The H-K-T Society and the Struggle for the Eastern Marches of the German Empire, 1894–1919* (New York: Columbia University Press, 1941), 108.

9. Flottwell's Prussianization policies are discussed in Hagen, *Germans, Poles, and Jews*, 87–91; Broszat, *Zweihundert Jahre deutsche Polenpolitik*, 101–104; Rosenthal, *German and Pole*, 15–17. See also W. F. Reddaway, J. H. Penson, O. Halecki, and R. Dyboski,

eds., *The Cambridge History of Poland: From Augustus II to Pilsudski (1697–1935)* (Cambridge: Cambridge University Press, 1941), 349.

10. Hagen, *Germans, Poles, and Jews*, 91–93; Reddaway, *Cambridge History of Poland*, 351.

11. As will become evident in later discussions, Bismarck's Polenpolitik of the late 1870s and 1880s was, in essence, a revitalization of the earlier policies of Grolman and Flottwell, and there is no doubt that the Iron Chancellor regarded the work of his predecessors in a favorable light. During a speech before the lower house of the Prussian parliament on 28 January 1886, in which Bismarck outlined the principles of his Polenpolitik, he not only discussed the Flottwellian policy of purchasing bankrupt Polish estates and redistributing them to Germans but also quoted at length Grolman's memorandum of March 1832. On the purchase and redistribution of Polish estates, he remarked, "Even though these operations were not in every case carried out with skill or subsequently maintained with the original determination, they nonetheless created a sizeable increase in the German population, as long as the system prevailed in the administration." Though Bismarck did not openly criticize Friedrich Wilhelm IV for abandoning Flottwell's policies, the tenor of his comments on the matter clearly indicated that he did not approve of the thaw in Prussian-Polish relations that resulted. See the transcript of Bismarck's speech of 28 January 1886 in Horst Kohl, ed., *Die Reden des Ministerpräsidenten und Reichskanzlers Fürsten von Bismarck* (Aalen, Germany: Scientia Verlag, 1970), 11: 407–449, especially 412–414. Bismarck also mentioned—with obvious consternation—Friedrich Wilhelm IV's abandonment of Grolman's and Flottwell's policies in his memoirs, *Bismarck: The Man and the Statesman, Being the Reflections and Reminiscences of Otto, Prince von Bismarck*, trans. A. J. Butler (New York and London: Harper and Brothers, 1899), 2: 139.

12. Quoted in Norman Davies, *God's Playground: A History of Poland*, vol. 2, *1795 to Present* (New York: Columbia University Press, 1982), 344.

13. For a detailed overview of the relationship between the events of 1848 and 1849 and the Polish Question, see ibid., 340–346; Reddaway, *Cambridge History of Poland*, 352–364; Hagen, *Germans, Poles, and Jews*, 104–111.

14. Quoted in Hagen, *Germans, Poles, and Jews*, 121.

15. Hagen provides an extended citation in ibid., 123–124. Bismarck addressed his 1848 piece to the *Magdeburger Zeitung*, but the editorial was not published until 1866. See Richard Blanke, *Prussian Poland and the German Empire (1871–1900)* (Boulder, CO: East European Monographs, 1981), 7–8, 14n22.

16. Quoted in Hagen, *Germans, Poles, and Jews*, 125–126.

17. Blanke, *Prussian Poland*, 10.

18. Bismarck on the Poles, quoted by Blanke, ibid., 11. For additional discussion of Bismarck's views on the Polish Question and Germanization, see Otto Pflanze, *Bismarck and the Development of Germany*, vol. 2, *The Period of Consolidation, 1871–1880* (Princeton, NJ: Princeton University Press, 1990), 106–114.

19. Before Napoleon's conquest of the Holy Roman Empire, Germany was composed of over 300 independent states. Their number was reduced to 38 as a result of the settlements concluded in the aftermath of the Napoleonic Wars. The Second Reich was a

union of 18 German states, Prussia being by far the largest, and 1 administrative territory, *Reichsland*, the former French provinces of Alsace and Lorraine.

20. Mary Fulbrook, ed., *German History since 1800* (London: Edward Arnold, 1997), 1.

21. Blanke, *Prussian Poland*, 20–21; Broszat, *Zweihundert Jahre deutsche Polenpolitik*, 134–135.

22. Blanke, *Prussian Poland*, 24. For discussion of the May Laws and the anti-Polish language law, see Hagen, *Germans, Jews, and Poles*, 128–130; Blanke, *Prussian Poland*, 22–24.

23. Many additional measures against the cultural foundations of Polish life were instituted by the Prussian state over the next three decades. These included a ban on Polish-language instruction in Posen's elementary schools; the censorship of Polish newspapers; a ban on the sale of Polish periodicals in railway stations; the Germanization of Polish place-names and, in some cases, even Polish family names; and a 1908 law restricting the use of Polish at public meetings. See Blanke, *Prussian Poland*, 78, 193–195; Hagen, *Germans, Jews, and Poles*, 182–183, 191–192; Morrow, "The Prussianization of the Poles,"162; Tims, *Germanizing Prussian Poland*, 133–150.

24. An insightful analysis of the impact of the Kulturkampf on the Poles and Polish nationalism can be found in Blanke, *Prussian Poland*, 24–33. Geoff Eley provides a short overview of the "struggle for culture" against the Poles in *From Unification to Nazism: Reinterpreting the German Past* (Boston: Unwin Hyman, 1986), 206–208. See also Hans-Ulrich Wehler, *Krisenherde des Kaiserreichs, 1871–1918: Studien zur deutschen Sozial- und Verfassungsgeschichte* (Göttingen, Germany: Vandenhoeck & Ruprecht, 1970), 184–186. For discussion of the Kulturkampf from a Polish perspective, see Wandycz, *The Lands of Partitioned Poland*, 233–236; Józef Feldman, *Bismarck a Polska* (Kraków, Poland: Czytelnik, 1947), 268–301.

25. Hagen, *Germans, Jews, and Poles*, table A1, 324, and table A2, "Rate of Population Growth in Prussia and the Province of Posen, 1825–1910," 325. The population ratios of the national groups in Posen were as follows: in 1871, Poles 61 percent, Germans 35.1 percent, Jews 3.9 percent; in 1890, Poles 63.6 percent, Germans 33.9 percent, Jews 2.5 percent.

26. Robert L. Koehl, "Colonialism inside Germany: 1886–1918," *Journal of Modern History* 25 (1953): 259–260.

27. The catchphrase "the retreat of German nationality" was coined by the journalist Eduard von Hartmann in 1885 and was often employed thereafter to stir German public opinion against the "Slavic menace." See Richard Blanke, "Bismarck and the Prussian Polish Policies of 1886," *Journal of Modern History* 45 (June 1973): 222.

28. Quoted in Blanke, *Prussian Poland*, 47.

29. Wehler, *Krisenherde des Kaiserreichs*, 186.

30. Quoted in Blanke, *Prussian Poland*, 50.

31. Koehl, "Colonialism inside Germany," 261–262. Blanke argues, in *Prussian Poland*, 48, that the deportations were a "one-shot measure" and were as much anti-Semitic as anti-Polish; they should not be regarded as "the opening gun in a comprehensive anti-Polish campaign." But Ely, in *From Unification to Nazism*, 207–208, views the expulsions as part of a "continuous anti-Polish offensive" that began with the Kulturkampf. For

in-depth discussion of the deportations between 1885 and 1887, see Joachim Mai, *Die preussisch-deutsche Polenpolitik, 1885 bis 1887* (Berlin: Rütten & Loening, 1962), 32–74.

32. Koehl, "Colonialism inside Germany," 261.

33. Quoted in Witold Jakóbczyk, "The First Decade of the Prussian Settlement Commissions' Activities (1886–1897)," *Polish Review* 17, no. 1 (1972): 4.

34. Quoted in Hagen, *Germans, Jews, and Poles*, 135.

35. Blanke, *Prussian Poland*, 56–57; Hagen, *Germans, Jews, and Poles*, 135.

36. Koehl, "Colonialism inside Germany," 256–257.

37. One hectare equals 2.47 acres.

38. Jakóbczyk, "The First Decade," 10.

39. Koehl, "Colonialism inside Germany," 267.

40. Jakóbczyk, "The First Decade," 10; Koehl, "Colonialism inside Germany," 267. In 1886, the average cost of a hectare of farmland in the eastern provinces was 556 marks. The figure had risen to 886 marks by 1900 and skyrocketed to 1,451 marks by 1906. See Tims, *Germanizing Prussian Poland*, 154.

41. Tims, *Germanizing Prussian Poland*, 112.

42. The Bromberg Regional Commission alone settled approximately 290 Polish families between 1891 and 1894. See Jakóbczyk, "The First Decade," 8. This "equal opportunity" settlement activity was terminated in 1898.

43. Tims, *Germanizing Prussian Poland*, 115; Koehl, "Colonialism inside Germany," 263.

44. The OMV was also called the H-K-T Society, and the name given to OMV members, Hakatists, was derived from the initials of its three cofounders: Ferdinand von Hansemann, son of a prominent Berlin banker, and the Junker aristocrats Hermann Kenneman and Heinrich von Tiedemann, the owners of two of Posen's largest estates. Bismarck, an outspoken foe of Caprivi, was a charter member of the society. See Tims, *Germanizing Prussian Poland*, 35–40; Blanke, *Prussian Poland*, 180–181.

45. Harry K. Rosenthal, "The Prussian View of the Pole: The Significance of the Year 1894," *Polish Review* 17, no. 1 (1972): 19. It is important to keep in mind, however, that the OMV did not promote the concept of blood in the völkisch-racist sense, as did the Nazis. The organization accepted Germans of Slavic blood and advocated the Germanization of ethnic Poles. See Rosenthal, *German and Pole*, 41.

46. Rosenthal, "The Prussian View of the Pole," 19. Though the organization certainly counted anti-Semites among its members, the Hakatist leaders' attitude toward the Jews was generally favorable, though they were skeptical about the possibility of Jews showing active allegiance to the cause. As Tiedemann wrote in 1895, "Nor do we turn away those Jews who voluntarily apply for membership in our association, since by joining us the Jew of our province avows himself a German and exposes himself to the danger of a commercial boycott by the Poles. To repulse him would be an injury to the German cause." But, he added, "as a matter of fact, only a very few Jews will have the courage to go along with us anyway" (quoted in Tims, *Germanizing Prussian Poland*, 72). Courage had nothing to do with it, but many Jewish businesspeople, particularly in Posen, were indeed highly critical of the OMV program due to its disruptive effect on commerce. Nevertheless, the organization did have Jewish members (though few in number) and by 1911 had come

to the "mature conclusion," as Tims puts it, that the Jews of the Eastern Marches should be considered Germans and that Jewish flight from the East constituted a blow to the mission of the OMV. See Tims, *Germanizing Prussian Poland*, 210–211 (no figures for Jewish OMV membership are provided).

47. Tims, *Germanizing Prussian Poland*, 115–116.

48. Quoted in Koehl, "Colonialism inside Germany," 264. As will become evident in the chapters that follow, Nazi authorities in Reichsgau Wartheland exhibited the same tendency. Loudly calling for the de-Polonization of the "New East," they were nevertheless dependent upon Polish labor from the onset of the occupation and became more so as time passed.

49. Hagen, *Germans, Jews, and Poles*, 274. Such rhetoric naturally annoyed the Junkers, who seemed to prefer Polish labor due to its low cost and its mobility. This situation caused most to leave the ranks of the OMV. By 1900, the organization had lost its original agrarian character and consisted primarily of teachers, government officials, and businesspeople. See Blanke, *Prussian Poland*, 182.

50. Quoted in Tims, *Germanizing Prussian Poland*, 125.

51. Ibid., 126. It is not clear why Prussian authorities did not simply shut down the Polish land banks and resettlement organizations at that time, but we can reason that they believed—albeit wrongly—that the less radical move of merely placing restrictions on the use of Polish property would go far to solve the problem at hand.

52. Broszat, *Zweihundert Jahre deutsche Polenpolitik*, 161.

53. On the 1904 law and its consequences, see Tims, *Germanizing Prussian Poland*, 127–132; Hagen, *Germans, Jews, and Poles*, 186–187.

54. Tims, *Germanizing Prussian Poland*, 152–153.

55. Tims, in ibid., 155–166, explores the debate surrounding the bill, one that clearly violated the right to private property. It passed only after the Junkers were granted a 75 million mark subsidy for employing German instead of Polish workers and assured that their property would not be targeted. Koehl provides the tally of the vote; see his "Colonialism inside Germany," 269.

56. Fearing that the Expropriation Act would antagonize Austrian Poles and weaken their support for the German-Austrian Dual Alliance, the Austrians tried unsuccessfully to persuade the Prussian government to abandon the plan. See Hagen, *Germans, Jews, and Poles*, 188.

57. Ibid., 190.

58. Tims, *Germanizing Prussian Poland*, 177.

59. Hagen, *Germans, Jews, and Poles*, 201.

60. Ibid., 204.

61. Fritz Fischer, *Germany's Aims in the First World War* (New York: W. W. Norton, 1967), 116, 169.

62. Quoted in Hagen, *Germans, Jews, and Poles*, 286.

63. Quoted in Broszat, *Zweihundert Jahre deutsche Polenpolitik*, 183.

64. Fischer, *Germany's Aims*, 116–117, 162–164. The German military high command supported all aspects of Schwerin's plan. Erich Ludendorff, chief of the General Staff of the Eighth Army under Paul von Hindenburg, expressed this in his memoirs written just

after the war: "The inhabitants of Courland and Lithuania were to bring Germany additional manpower ... An increase of the Polish population, which could accrue in the defensive belt, was undesirable, but this grave objection would have to give way to military necessity. The German settlement, which we hoped would take place on a great scale, and the collection of Germans from abroad in those extensive territories, which the Imperial Chancellor had tried to establish as far back as 1915 in certain frontier areas, would in the future provide further increase [of the German population]"; see Ludendorff, *Ludendorff's Own Story: August 1914–November 1918* (New York and London: Harper Brothers, 1919), 2: 140. German World War I policies in the territory beyond the Frontier Strip are meticulously examined in Vejas Gabriel Liulevicius's recent study, *Warland on the Eastern Front: Culture, National Identity and German Occupation in World War I* (Cambridge: Cambridge University Press, 2000).

65. For discussion of the events and deliberations leading to the creation of the Kingdom of Poland, see Fischer, *Germany's Aims*, 198–214, 236–244, 313–316. For a time, it was thought that the kingdom would fall mainly under Austrian influence, but in May 1917, the German government asserted its dominance over the region.

66. Ibid., 200; Hagen, *Germans, Jews, and Poles*, 285. If his postwar memoirs are to be believed, Paul von Hindenburg was highly skeptical about the plan for a Polish buffer state from its very inception. He feared that a semi-independent Kingdom of Poland, despite its position as a German vassal, would continue to serve as a focal point for Polish national sentiment: "I never had the slightest doubt that we could not expect a word of thanks from Poland for freeing her from the Russian knout with our sword and blood, as we had received little recognition for the economic and moral advancement of the Prussian Poles among us. No feeling of gratitude—so far as such a thing exists in politics—would deter a restored, free Poland from seeing *irridenta* in our frontier provinces." His uncertainty about the wartime policy aside, Hindenburg believed that "a victorious Germany would be able to settle the Polish question after the peace." See Hindenburg, *Out of My Life*, trans. F. A. Holt (New York and London: Harper and Brothers, 1921), 2: 4–9.

67. Quoted in M. B. Biskupski, *The History of Poland* (Westport, CT: Greenwood Press, 2000), 49.

68. Richard M. Watt, *Bitter Glory: Poland and Its Fate, 1918 to 1939* (New York: Simon and Schuster, 1979), 71, 76. Of the 2.1 million Germans living in Poland in 1919, 1.1 million resided in the regions of Posen and West Prussia (not including Freistadt Danzig); by 1921 to 1922, approximately two-thirds had emigrated to Germany. See Broszat, *Zweihundert Jahre deutsche Polenpolitik*, 212.

69. For a detailed account and analysis of the 1919 establishment of the German-Polish frontier, see Titus Kormarnicki, *Rebirth of the Polish Republic: A Study in the Diplomatic History of Europe, 1914–1920* (London: William Heinemann, 1957), 325–349. For a general discussion of Germany's territorial losses as dictated by the Treaty of Versailles, see Paul Birdsall, *Versailles Twenty Years After* (New York: Reynal and Hitchcock, 1941), chap. 7. Though Germany certainly lost a significant chunk of its prewar territory with the rebirth of Poland, the largest part of the new Polish state emerged from the territory of the former Russian Empire.

70. Koehl estimates that between 1886 and 1918, the AK settled 288,000 Germans on purchased land in Posen and West Prussia, but since a minimum of one-third were natives of the two provinces, roughly 192,000 real immigrants actually entered the territory during the period in question. See Koehl, "Colonialism inside Germany," 270–271. According to official Prussian figures, the population of Posen was 2,100,000 in 1910, including 1,352,650 Poles, 720,650 Germans, and 26,500 Jews. Although the German population had increased from 556,000 in 1871, its ratio of the total population had decreased from 35.1 percent to 34 percent. The Polish population, by contrast, had risen from 61 percent (966,000) in 1871 to 64.7 percent in 1910. Owing to the Jews' own Ostflucht, the Jewish ratio had declined from 3.9 percent to 1.3 percent during the same period. See Hagen, *Germans, Jews, and Poles*, table A1, 324.

71. See Hagen, *Germans, Jews, and Poles*, table 6, "Distribution of Nationalities among Principal Occupational Groups, 1882–1907," 220, and table 7, "Estimated Distribution of Arable and Forest Land, 1913," 221, as well as commentary, 220–221.

72. According to the first Polish census of 1921, 175,771 Germans remained in West Prussia and 327,846 in Posen, less than half (46 percent) of the 1910 figure. See Richard Blanke, *Orphans of Versailles: The Germans in Western Poland, 1918–1939* (Lexington: University Press of Kentucky, 1993), 32.

73. Actual violations of the minority rights of Polish Germans—guaranteed by the Minority Protections Treaty incorporated into the Versailles settlement—included dispossession and other forms of economic discrimination, the dissolution of German organizations, anti-German Polish school policy, and the refusal to recognize elected German public officials on the grounds that they did not speak Polish (all of which mirrored aspects of Imperial German Polenpolitik). See ibid., 129ff.

74. Harald von Riekhoff, *German-Polish Relations, 1918–1933* (Baltimore, MD: Johns Hopkins University Press, 1971), 384.

75. See Alexander B. Rossino, *Hitler Strikes Poland: Blitzkrieg, Ideology, and Atrocity* (Lawrence: University Press of Kansas, 2003), 22–23, 221ff.

76. Riekhoff, *German-Polish Relations*, 381–382. German-Polish relations during the Weimar period are explored in Volkmar Kellerman, *Schwarzer Adler, Weisser Adler: Die Polenpolitik der Weimarer Republik* (Cologne, Germany: Markus Verlag, 1970).

77. See, for example, Adolf Hitler, *Mein Kampf*, trans. Ralph Mannheim (Boston: Houghton Mifflin, 1943), 236ff., 388–389. Hitler directed his criticism primarily at Imperial efforts to Germanize Poles—to make so-called good Germans out of them through linguistic, educational, and cultural "improvement"—something he regarded as both foolhardy and impossible on racial grounds.

78. Robert L. Koehl, *RKFDV: German Resettlement and Population Policy, 1939–1945: A History of the Reich Commission for the Strengthening of Germandom* (Cambridge, MA: Harvard University Press, 1957), 54.

79. Hitler, *Mein Kampf*, 388 (his emphasis).

80. A number of historians deny or marginalize the basic continuity between Imperial and Nazi policy. Rosenthal, for example, asserts, "The Nazi emphasis on race discredits any claims of continuity from the Hakatists and other German nationalists [of the Imperial

era] to the Nazis." See Rosenthal, *German and Pole*, III. Blanke also rejects the notion of a connection between the colonization policies of the two periods. In an attack on Koehl, who firmly believes Imperial Polenpolitik went far to shape the Nazi resettlement program, Blanke asserts that "only on the most superficial level can one speak of a relationship between the Settlement Law of 1886, with its limited aims and legalistic methods (and the way it was allowed to fail so completely), and National Socialist population transfers." See Blanke, "Bismarck and the Prussian Polish Policies of 1886," 227n43. But in light of the obvious theoretical and practical similarities, it seems to me unreasonable to discredit the apparent historical-political continuity between Imperial and Nazi Germanization schemes. Furthermore, Blanke bases his assessment on but one piece of legislation, the Settlement Law of 1886, not on the thirty-year program as a whole. The ideological basis for anti-Polish action had certainly changed—had certainly "radicalized"—by the Nazi period, but the basic methods remained essentially the same. And if one considers the Land ohne Menschen scheme of World War I, the similarities between the anti-Polish policies of the Second Reich and the Third Reich become all the more striking.

81. Hans-Ulrich Wehler, *The German Empire, 1871–1918*, trans. Kim Traynor (Oxford: Berg Publishers, 1991), 113.

CHAPTER TWO: "RACIAL RESHUFFLING" IN THE EAST: THE GENESIS OF THE PROGRAM

1. Alexander Rossino, *Hitler Strikes Poland: Blitzkrieg, Ideology, and Atrocity* (Lawrence: University Press of Kansas, 2003), 5–8, 22–28, 221–226; Karol Fiedor, Janusz Sobczak, and Wojciech Wrzesiński, "The Image of Poles in Germany and of the German in Poland in the Interwar Years and Its Role in Shaping Relations between the Two States," *Polish-Western Affairs* 19, no. 2 (1978): 204–211, 218–222.

2. Adolf Hitler, *Hitler's Secret Book*, trans. Salvator Attanasio (New York: Grove Press, 1983), 47–48.

3. Hermann Rauschning, the Nazi president of the Danzig Senate (1933–1934) who later broke with the party and fled Germany, reports that Hitler was toying with the concepts of depopulation policy and forced population movements in early 1934. Though he did not mention Poland specifically, Hitler purportedly told Rauschning during a conversation regarding the Slavic "threat" that "we are obliged to depopulate as part of our mission of preserving the German nation ... If you ask me what I mean by depopulation, I mean the removal of entire racial units ... And by 'remove' I don't necessarily mean destroy; I shall simply take systematic measures to dam their great fertility." He went on to say that "we favor the planned control of population movements." See Rauschning, *Hitler Speaks: A Series of Political Conversations with Adolf Hitler on His Real Aims* (London: Thomton Butterworth, 1940), 140.

4. Gerhard Weinberg, *The Foreign Policy of Hitler's Germany: Diplomatic Revolution in Europe, 1933–36* (Chicago and London: University of Chicago Press, 1970), 74.

5. Ibid., 60–62. Though it is highly unlikely, as Weinberg argues, that such a war would have transpired, the German government certainly feared that the possibility existed.

6. For discussion of the German-Polish treaty and the negotiations leading to it, see Weinberg, *The Foreign Policy*, 57–74; Klaus Hildebrand, *The Foreign Policy of the Third Reich*, trans. Anthony Fothergill (Berkeley and Los Angeles: University of California Press, 1973), 32–33; Hans-Adolf Jacobsen, *Nationalsozialistische Aussenpolitik, 1933–1938* (Frankfurt, Germany: Alfred Metzner Verlag, 1968), 403–406; and A. J. P. Taylor's interpretation of the proceedings in *The Origins of the Second World War* (New York: Atheneum, 1983), 80–81.

7. Taylor, *Origins of the Second World War*, 49.

8. John Connelly, "Nazis and Slavs: From Racial Theory to Racist Practice," *Central European History* 32 (March 1999): 11.

9. Richard Blanke, *Orphans of Versailles: The Germans in Western Poland, 1918–1939* (Lexington: University Press of Kentucky, 1993), 186–187.

10. Ibid., 206–207.

11. For in-depth discussion and analysis of the events leading to the invasion, see Gerhard Weinberg, *The Foreign Policy of Hitler's Germany: Starting World War II, 1937–1939* (Chicago and London: University of Chicago Press, 1980), 535ff.; Anton Czubiński, "Poland's Place in Nazi Plans for a New Order in Europe in the Years 1934–1940," *Polish-Western Affairs* 21, no. 1 (1980): 30–41.

12. Christopher Browning, *The Path to Genocide: Essays on Launching the Final Solution* (Cambridge: Cambridge University Press, 1992), 8.

13. For a transcript of the Nazi-Soviet Pact, as well as the Secret Additional Protocol, see U.S. Department of State, *Documents on German Foreign Policy, 1918–1945*, series D (hereafter *DGFP*) (Washington, DC: U.S. Government Printing Office, 1956), 7: docs. 228–229, pp. 245–247. On the Molotov-Ribbentrop Pact and the negotiations that followed, see Gerhard Weinberg, *Germany and the Soviet Union, 1939–1941* (Leiden, Netherlands: E. J. Brill, 1954), 41–61; James E. McSherry, *Stalin, Hitler, and Europe*, vol. 1, *The Origins of World War II, 1933–1939* (Cleveland, OH: World Publishing, 1968), 231–252; McSherry, *Stalin, Hitler, and Europe*, vol. 2, *The Imbalance of Power* (Cleveland, OH: World Publishing, 1970), 5–16.

14. Robert L. Koehl, *RKFDV: German Resettlement and Population Policy, 1939–1945: A History of the Reich Commission for the Strengthening of Germandom* (Cambridge, MA: Harvard University Press), 47–49; Valdis O. Lumans, *Himmler's Auxiliaries: The Volksdeutsche Mittelstelle and the German National Minorities of Europe, 1933–1945* (Chapel Hill: University of North Carolina Press, 1993), 132.

15. Weinberg offers a detailed discussion of the Munich Crisis and the reannexation of the Memelland in *Foreign Policy*, 313–464, 484–486, 536. Nazi volksdeutsch policy in the years preceding the German-Soviet nonaggression treaty is explored in Lumans, *Himmler's Auxiliaries*, 73–130; Blanke, *Orphans of Versailles*, 163ff.

16. "Richtlinien für den auswärtigen Einsatz der Sicherheitspolizei und des SD," 31 July 1939, in Kaszimierz Leszczyński, ed., "Działaność Einsatzgruppen Policji

Bezpieczeństwa na Ziemiach Polskich w 1939 R. w świetle Dokumentów," *Biuletyn Głównej Komisji Badania Zbrodni Hitlerowskich w Polsce* 22 (Warsaw: Wydawnictwo Prawnicze, 1971), doc. 55, pp. 161–164. See also Helmut Krausnick and Hans-Heinrich Wilhelm, *Die Truppe des Weltanschauungskrieges: Die Einsatzgruppen der Sicherheitspolizei und des SD, 1939–1942* (Stuttgart, Germany: Deutsche Verlags-Anstalt, 1981), 36. For discussion of the preparations for Operation Tannenberg, see Rossino, *Hitler Strikes Poland*, 13–57; Michael Wildt, "Radikalisierung und Selbstradikalisierung 1939: Die Geburt des Reichssicherheitshauptamt aus dem Geist des völkischen Massenmords," in Gerhard Paul and Klaus-Michael Mallmann, eds., *Die Gestapo im Zweiten Weltkrieg: "Heimatfront" und besetztes Europa* (Darmstadt, Germany: Primus Verlag, 2000), 16–22.

17. Franz Halder, *Kriegstagebuch: Tägliche Aufzeichnungen des Chefs des Generalstabes des Heeres, 1939–1942*, vol. 1, ed. Hans-Adolf Jacobsen (Stuttgart, Germany: W. Kohlhammer Verlag, 1962), entry for 22 August 1939, 22–26; "Ansprache des Führers vor Oberbefehlshabern an 22.Aug.1939," ND 798-PS, and "Zweite Ansprache des Führers am 22.Aug.1939," ND 1014-PS, International Military Tribunal, *Trial of the Major War Criminals before the International Military Tribunal: Nuremberg, 14 November 1945–1 October 1946*, 42 vols. (hereafter *IMT*) (Nuremberg, Germany: International Military Tribunal, 1947–1949), 26: 338–344, 523–524. See also *DGFP*, 7: docs. 192–193, pp. 200–206.

18. Halder, *Kriegstagebuch*, 25–26.

19. Quoted in Heinz Höhne, *The Order of the Death's Head: The Story of Hitler's SS*, trans. Richard Barry (New York: Ballantine Books, 1971), 336. A detailed analysis of the 22 August 1939 meeting is provided in Winfried Baumgart, "Zur Ansprache Hitlers vor den Führern der Wehrmacht am 22.August 1939: Eine quellenkritische Untersuchung," *Vierteljahrshefte für Zeitgeschichte* 16 (April 1968): 120–149.

20. The career of RFSS Himmler—perhaps the foremost racial ideologue in the Nazi regime and the primary architect of the Final Solution to the Jewish Question—has been the focus of a number of political biographies, as well as general studies of the SS, and it need not be covered here. But see, among others, Peter Padfield, *Himmler: Reichsführer-SS* (New York: Henry Holt, 1990); Richard Breitman, *The Architect of Genocide: Himmler and the Final Solution* (Hanover, NH: Brandeis University Press, 1991); Gerhard Reitlinger, *The SS: Alibi of a Nation, 1922–1945* (New York: Viking Press, 1968); Höhne, *The Order of the Death's Head*.

21. J. Noakes and G. Pridham, eds., *Nazism: A History in Documents and Eyewitness Accounts, 1919–1945*, vol. 2 (New York: Schocken Books, 1988), 928. Tannenberg, the code name for both the section and the operation that ensued, was probably chosen either to commemorate Hindenburg's victory over the Russians (that is, the Slavs) at Tannenberg, East Prussia, in 1914 or to symbolize revenge for the Polish army's triumph over the Teutonic Knights at Tannenberg in 1410. See Breitman, *The Architect of Genocide*, 68.

22. Krausnick and Wilhelm, *Die Truppe des Weltanschauungskrieges*, 34. Short biographies of the Einsatzgruppen leaders can be found in Rossino, *Hitler Strikes Poland*, 29–52; Wildt, "Radikalisierung und Selbstradikalisierung 1939," 17–22.

23. "Amtschefbesprechung am 19.9.39" (Heydrich presiding), 21 September 1939, NARA/T175/239/2728516-19.

24. Charles Sydnor, *Soldiers of Destruction: The SS Death's Head Division, 1933–1945* (Princeton, NJ: Princeton University Press, 1990), 37–38. A number of Ordnungspolizei battalions participated in the operation as well. See Rossino, *Hitler Strikes Poland*, 49, 70–71.

25. See the postwar testimony of Major General Erwin Lahousen regarding a meeting with Hitler, Keitel, and Wilhelm Canaris, held on the "Führer train" in Upper Silesia on 12 September 1939, Lahousen Interrogation, 17 September 1947, NARA/RG238/M1019/40/76–77. Initially defined on 31 July as "the suppression of all anti-Reich and anti-German elements in enemy territory behind the fighting troops," the Einsatzgruppen's mission in Poland was later clarified in a directive issued by the German Eighth Army on 9 September 1939 to include "counter-espionage, apprehension of politically-unreliable individuals, confiscation of arms, safeguarding of important counter-espionage documents, etc." Quoted in Krausnick and Wilhelm, *Die Truppe des Weltanschauungskrieges*, 36.

26. Helmuth Groscurth, *Tagebücher eines Abwehroffiziers, 1938–1940: Mit Weiteren Dokumenten zur Militäropposition gegen Hitler*, ed. Helmut Krausnick and Harold C. Deutsch (Stuttgart, Germany: Deutsche Verlags-Anstalt, 1970), entry for 8 September 1939, 200–201.

27. Christian Jansen and Arno Weckbecker, *Der "Volksdeutsche Selbstschutz" in Polen 1939/40* (Munich, Germany: R. Oldenbourg Verlag, 1992), 61. On the German army's participation in Tannenberg, see Rossino, *Hitler Strikes Poland*, 58ff.; Rossino, "Destructive Impulses: German Soldiers and the Conquest of Poland," *Holocaust and Genocide Studies* 11 (Winter 1999): 351–365. Of the 764 documented mass executions carried out in Poland from 1 September to 24 October 1939, the Wehrmacht committed or participated in 311. See Czesław Madajczyk, *Die Okkupationspolitik Nazideutschlands in Polen, 1939–1945* (Berlin: Akademie-Verlag, 1987), 28.

28. "Vermerk: Amtschef und Einsatzgruppenleiterbesprechung" (21 September 1939), 27 September 1939, NARA/T175/239/2728524–8.

29. For discussion of the prewar anti-Jewish policy of forced expulsion, see Breitman, *The Architect of Genocide*, 46–65; Saul Friedlander, *Nazi Germany and the Jews*, vol. 1, *The Years of Persecution, 1933–1939* (New York: HarperCollins, 1997), 244ff.; Michael Wildt, ed., *Die Judenpolitik des SD, 1935 bis 1938: Eine Dokumentation* (Munich, Germany: R. Oldenbourg Verlag, 1995), 32–64.

30. Emphasis mine. Some members of the Polish ruling class were incarcerated in concentration camps, but Heydrich was apparently employing the term *concentration camps*—in reference to the treatment of the Polish ruling class, though not to that of the lower classes—also as a euphemism for murder, just as the SS would later use the terms *relocation, resettlement*, and *Sonderbehandlung* (special handling) as euphemisms for the extermination of the Jews. His usage of the term for the lower classes probably meant, above all, "transit camps."

31. "Vermerk: Amtschefbesprechung am 7.9.39," 8 September 1939, NARA/T175/239/2728499–502.

32. "Vermerk: Amtschefbesprechung am 14.9.1939," 15 September 1939, NARA/T175/239/2728513–515.

33. Christopher Browning, in *The Path to Genocide*, 8, goes as far as to suggest that these proposals amounted to a concrete blueprint for the "specific" demographic policy—the mass expulsions of Poles and Jews combined with the mass resettlement of eastern European Volksdeutschen—that was later implemented. Although this is within the realm of possibility, I do not believe that Nazi plans were so comprehensive and refined as of 14 September 1939.

34. *DGFP*, 8: doc. 104, p. 105.

35. Halder, *Kriegstagebuch*, entry for 20 September 39, 81–82.

36. "Vermerk: Amtschef- und Einsatzgruppenleiterbesprechung" (21 September 1939), 27 September 1939, NARA/T175/239/2728524–528.

37. On the same day, Heydrich issued even more detailed instructions concerning "the Jewish question in the occupied territories" to his Einsatzgruppen commanders. See Heydrich's Schnellbrief, "Judenfrage im besetzten Gebiet," 21 September 1939, in Kurt Pätzold, ed., *Verfolgung, Vertreibung, Vernichtung: Dokumente des faschistischen Anti-semitismus, 1933 bis 1942* (Frankfurt, Germany: Röderberg-Verlag, 1984), doc. 201, pp. 236–239.

38. Again, the term *concentration camps* in this context was apparently being used both literally and as a euphemism for murder.

39. "Vermerk: Amtschef- und Einsatzgruppenleiterbesprechung" (21 September 1939), 27 September 1939, NARA/T175/239/2728524–2728528. Heydrich's words seem to indicate that the Poles would be deported and then taken back to Reich territory as migrant workers on a seasonal basis. As illustrated in the previous chapter, Imperial German authorities sought to do the same.

40. Ibid.

41. *DGFP*, 8: doc. 131, p. 130.

42. Lumans, *Himmler's Auxiliaries*, 132.

43. Höhne, *The Order of the Death's Head*, 349. Höhne does not explain why Göring did not turn to the Reich Ministry of Labor to tackle the problem, nor why the labor shortage became an SS and police matter at this early date.

44. "Disposition zum Vortrag des Amtschefs der Dienststelle 'Vierjahresplan' im Persönlichen Stab des Reichsführers-SS, SS-Oberführer Greifelt, January 1939," in Dietrich A. Loeber, ed., *Diktierte Option: Die Umsiedlung der Deutsch-Balten aus Estland und Lettland, 1939–1941* (Neumünster, Germany: Karl Wachholtz Verlag, 1972), doc. 2, pp. 4–7; Koehl, *RKFDV*, 44–45.

45. Höhne, in *The Order of the Death's Head*, 349–350, writes: "The propagandists told [the Volksdeutschen] they were answering the call of their blood; in practice, however, the lords of the regime had decided upon their repatriation for a much more prosaic reason: the country of the 'people without space' had insufficient manpower to keep its industry and agriculture running at full blast ... The loss of hundreds of thousands of German workers to the army and the growing requirements of the armaments industry had led Hitler and Göring to adopt Greifelt's solution to the labor problem." I do believe, however, that once the resettlement and expulsion campaign was under way, economic considerations came to take precedence over (virtually) all other concerns, but it was primarily foreign

policy objectives, not economic questions, that led to the decision to repatriate the ethnic Germans in the first place.

46. *DGFP*, 8: doc. 137, pp. 137–139.

47. Ibid., 8: doc. 138, pp. 140–145. Hitler's comments display a firm grasp of facts and figures regarding a "west-to-east" program of German (that is, reichsdeutsch) resettlement, but they reveal few details concerning volksdeutsch resettlement. This, in all likelihood, indicates that he had only very recently decided to repatriate the ethnic Germans and had not, as of that time, given the matter much in the way of careful thought. It also suggests that when he told Brauchitsch on 20 September that "for every German entering the territory, two people would be expelled," he may well have been referring to western Germans, not eastern European Volksdeutschen.

48. Ibid., 8: doc. 153, p. 162.

49. Ibid., 8: doc. 159 (Secret Additional Protocol), p. 166.

50. Lumans, *Himmler's Auxiliaries*, 158.

51. *DGFP*, 8: doc. 158 (Confidential Protocol), p. 165.

52. The new lines of demarcation between the Soviet and German spheres of influence were defined in excruciating detail on 4 October 1939. See ibid., 8: (Supplementary Protocol), doc. 193, pp. 208–212.

53. Though the exact date of their meeting is unclear, Lumans asserts that Hitler summoned Lorenz to the Reich Chancellery "a few days before" 6 October 1939 and appointed him leader of the resettlement program. See Lumans, "Werner Lorenz: Chef der 'Volksdeutschen Mittelstelle,'" in Ronald Smelsner and Enrico Syring, eds., *Die SS: Elite unter dem Totenkopf. 30 Lebensläufe* (Paderborn, Germany: Ferdinand Schöningh, 2000), 339. In light of subsequent developments (which will be discussed), Lorenz's appointment must have taken place at some point shortly before 27 September 1939.

54. Koehl, *RKFDV*, 37–39; Koehl, *The Black Corps: The Structure and Power Struggles of the Nazi SS* (Madison: University of Wisconsin Press, 1983), 186–187; Lumans, *Himmler's Auxiliaries*, 41–87. Lumans provides a lengthy biography of Lorenz in "Werner Lorenz: Chef der 'Volksdeutsche Mittelstelle,'" 332–345.

55. Koehl, *RKFDV*, 49.

56. Within the context of their 21 September discussion regarding Polish and Jewish deportations, Heydrich had told his division heads that "the RFSS will be appointed 'settlement commissioner' for the East." See "Vermerk: Amtschef- und Einsatzgruppenleiterbesrechung" (21 September 1939), 27 September 1939, NARA/T175/239/2728526.

57. The Hitler-Himmler exchange most likely occurred on 27 September or early 28 September when both men were relaxing at the resort town of Zoppot near Danzig. See Breitman, *The Architect of Genocide*, 76.

58. Koehl, *RKFDV*, 49–50.

59. Lammers's letter to von Krosigk, 28 September 1939, NARA/T175/43/2554739.

60. Himmler's note to Greifelt, 4 October 1939, NARA/T175/43/2554737.

61. Greifelt, a veteran of World War I and a Freikorps alumnus, joined the SS as a professional administrator in 1933. As chief of the SS Office of the Four-Year Plan, he had been a member of Himmler's personal staff since 1937. See Koehl, *RKFDV*, 45, 50–51.

62. Alfred Rosenberg, *Das politische Tagebuch Alfred Rosenbergs: 1934/35 und 1939/40*, ed. Hans-Günther Seraphim (Göttingen, Germany: Musterschmidt-Verlag, 1956), entry for 29 September 1939, 80–81.

63. RSHA, "Amtschefsbesprechung am 29.9.1939," 2 October 1939, NARA/T175/239/2728531–533.

64. On the failed Lublin Reservation scheme, see Philip Friedman, "The Lublin Reservation and the Madagascar Plan: Two Aspects of Nazi Jewish Policy during the Second World War," in Ada June Friedman, ed., *Roads to Extinction: Essays on the Holocaust* (New York: Jewish Publication Society of America, 1980): 34–58; Dieter Pohl, *Von der "Judenpolitik" zum Judenmord: Der Distrikt Lublin des Generalgouvernements, 1939–1944* (Frankfurt, Germany: Peter Lang, 1993), 47ff.; Bogdan Musial, *Deutsche Zivilverwaltung und Judenverfolgung im Generalgouvernement: Eine Fallstudie zum Distrikt Lublin, 1939–1944* (Wiesbaden, Germany: Harrassowitz Verlag, 1999), 11off.

65. Ciano met with Hitler and Ribbentrop on 1 October 1939; population transfers were discussed at the conference. See *DGFP*, 8: doc. 176, pp. 184–194.

66. Emphasis mine.

67. For a transcript of the 6 October speech, see Adolf Hitler, *Der grossdeutsche Freiheitskampf: Reden Adolf Hitlers*, vol. 1, *September 1939 bis 10. März 1940* (Munich, Germany: Zentralverlag der NSDAP, Franz Eher Nachf., 1940), 67–100.

68. Madajczyk, *Die Okkupationspolitik Nazideutschlands in Polen*, 444.

69. Hitler, *Die grossdeutsche Freiheitskampf*, 95.

70. See, among countless others, "Die Baltendeutschen in der neuen Heimat," *Ostdeutscher Beobachter* (hereafter *OdB*), 1 November 1939; "Die deutschen Bauern aus Ostpolen werden eingesetzt," *Hohensalzaer Zeitung*, 27–28 April 1940; "Das Schaffen sind wir gewohnt! Mit Galiziendeutschen ins Siedlerdorf," *Hohensalzaer Zeitung*, 17 September 1940; "Der grosse Bauernzug vom Bug zur Warthe," *OdB*, 22 September 1940; "Im Wartheland ist es schöner als in Wolhynien," *OdB*, 13 October 1940; Alfred Kleindienst and Kurt Lück, *Die Wolhyniendeutschen kehren heim ins Reich* (Posen, Poland: Historische Gesellschaft in Posen, 1940); Kurt Lück, *Die Cholmer und Lubliner Deutschen kehren heim ins Vaterland* (Posen, Poland: Historische Gesellschaft in Wartheland/Verlag S. Hirzel in Leipzig, 1940); Hans Johst, *Ruf des Reiches—Echo des Volkes! Eine Ostfahrt* (Munich, Germany: Franz Eher Verlag, 1942).

71. Lammers's letter to Himmler (the draft of the decree is attached), 29 September 1939, NARA/T175/43/2554742–745.

72. Himmler to Lammers, 4 October 1939, NARA/T175/43/2554741.

73. Darré, who considered himself an expert in agricultural affairs, had been a prominent member of the National Socialist hierarchy since his appointment as chief of the SS RuSHA in 1931. In June 1933, six months after the Machtergreifung, he replaced Alfred Hugenberg as Reich minister of food and agriculture. The following year, Darré added the titles Reich peasant führer and leader of the Reich Food Estate, the organization that oversaw the Gleichschaltung of all agricultural activity in Germany, to his portfolio. While with RuSHA, Darré conducted extensive research on agricultural settlement geared toward helping SS men and their families find their "roots in the soil." Due to

poor relations with RFSS Himmler, he resigned from RuSHA in 1938, but as food minister, peasant führer, and a self-proclaimed expert on agrarian settlement, he assumed that his knowledge and position would guarantee him an important post in the agricultural administration of occupied Poland. For an overview of Darré's career, see Anna Bramwell, *Blood and Soil: Richard Walther Darré and Hitler's "Green Party"* (Buckinghamshire, UK: Kensal Press, 1985); J. E. Farquharson, *The Plough and the Swastika: The NSDAP and Agriculture in Germany, 1928–1945* (London: SAGE Publications, 1976); Isabel Heinemann, *"Rasse, Siedlung, deutsches Blut": Das Rasse- & Siedlungshauptamt der SS und die rassenpolitische Neuordnung Europas* (Göttingen, Germany: Wallstein Verlag, 2003).

74. Quoted in Koehl, *RKFDV*, 52.

75. Breitman, *The Architect of Genocide*, 77. This is odd criticism, considering Darré's past work with RuSHA. Himmler discussed his Wehrbauern scheme during a speech before the SS leadership in Posen on 24 October 1939. See Rolf-Dieter Müller, *Hitlers Ostkrieg und die deutsche Siedlungspolitik: Die Zusammenarbeit von Wehrmacht, Wirtschaft und SS* (Frankfurt, Germany: Fischer Taschenbuch Verlag, 1991), doc. 3, pp. 119–121.

76. "Erlass des Führers und Reichskanzlers zur Festigung deutschen Volkstums," 7 October 1939, ND 686-PS, *IMT*, 26: 255–257. According to Darré's Nuremberg testimony, Hitler became angry upon hearing of his criticism of Himmler and forbade him from bothering the RFSS and even entering Poland at all. Hitler probably did lean toward Himmler's side in the matter, but Darré's postwar testimony is obviously exaggerated. See Breitman, *The Architect of Genocide*, 77.

77. Ibid.

78. See "Gesetz über Landbeschaffung für Zwecke der Wehrmacht. Vom 29. März 1935," *Reichsgesetzblatt*, 30 March 1935, part 1, 467–468. Poles and Jews whose property was seized would not, as will be shown, be compensated for their loss "in land and money" as the law stipulated.

79. "Erlass des Führers."

80. Himmler, "Führer Decree, Orders of the Reich Commissioner, *Organization of the Office of the Reich Commissioner* (First Order)," n.d. (mid-October 1939), NO 3078, NARA/M894/14. I shall use the acronyms RKFDV to refer to Himmler's title and RKF to denote the SS-Dienststelle, generally called the Reichskommission für die Festigung deutschen Volkstums. A comprehensive overview of the organization and responsibilities of the RKF is provided by Hans Buchheim, "Rechtstellung und Organisation des Reichskommissars für die Festigung deutschen Volkstums," *Gutachten des Instituts für Zeitgeschichte* (Munich, Germany: Institut für Zeitgeschichte, 1958), 239–279.

81. "Erlass des Führers."

82. For a general discussion of the foundation and organization of the RSHA, see Hans Buchheim, Martin Broszat, Hans-Adolf Jacobsen, and Helmut Krausnick, *Anatomie des SS-Staates* (Munich, Germany: Deutscher Taschenbuch Verlag, 1994), 66ff. On the connections between RSHA and RKFDV policies during the war, see Peter R. Black, *Ernst Kaltenbrunner: Ideological Soldier of the Third Reich* (Princeton, NJ: Princeton University Press, 1984), 139ff.

83. "Erlass Adolf Hitlers über die Gliederung und Verwaltung der Ostgebiete," 8 October 1939, in Herbert Michaelis, Ernst Shraepler, and Günter Schael, eds., *Ursachen und Folgen vom deutschen Zusammenbruch 1918 und 1945 zur staatlichen Neuordnung Deutschlands in der Gegenwart: Eine Urkunden- und Dokumentensammlung zur Zeitgeschichte* (hereafter *UFZ*) (Berlin: Dr. Herbert Wendler, n.d.), doc. 2871/b, 14: 87–89. On the military administration in occupied Poland and its dissolution, see Hans Umbreit, *Deutsche Militärverwaltungen 1938/39: Der militärische Besetzung der Tschechoslowakei und Polens* (Stuttgart, Germany: Deutsche Verlags-Anstalt, 1977), 113ff. See also Martin Broszat, *Nationalsozialistische Polenpolitik, 1939–1945* (Stuttgart, Germany: Deutsche Verlags-Anstalt, 1961), 25–31.

84. Germany had annexed the territory of Freistadt Danzig on 1 September 1939.

85. Madajczyk, *Die Okkupationspolitik Nazideutschlands in Polen*, 35.

86. Rassenpolitisches Amt (Wetzel and Hecht), "Die Frage der Behandlung der Bevölkerung der ehemaligen polnischen Gebiete nach rassenpolitischen Geichtspunkte," 25 November 1939, NARA/T74/9/57/380571ff. The population statistics for Danzig–West Prussia provided by Wetzel and Hecht, as well as those for other regions of occupied Poland presented later, should be regarded as reasonable approximations. The last official census in Poland before the war was conducted in 1931. Despite Wetzel and Hecht's attempts at exactitude, demographic changes since 1931, the population movements caused by the war, the thousands of executions during Operation Tannenberg, the estimated 123,000 Polish fatalities during the September campaign, and the "wild deportations" carried out after 1 September 1939 (discussed in the next chapter) made it impossible for Nazi statisticians to calculate the population and ethnic composition of annexed territory with any precision, and we are in the same position. Postwar historians of the occupation of Poland generally employ statistics compiled by the National Socialists. For example, Jansen and Weckbecker, *Der "Volksdeutsche Selbstschutz" in Polen*, 40, make use of the Rassenpolitisches Amt memo cited here, and Broszat, *Nationalsozialistische Polenpolitik*, 34–37, draws his figures from a Reichsministerium des Innern (RmdI; Reich Ministry of the Interior) report distributed on 13 November 1939. Czesław Madajczyk's footnotes in *Die Okkupationspolitik Nazideutschlands in Polen* are, unfortunately, few and far between, but at least in terms of Danzig–West Prussia, it is clear that he arrives at his population statistics (see Madajczyk, *Die Okkupationspolitik Nazideutschlands in Polen*, 35) via the Polish census of 1931, the Freistadt Danzig census of 1929, and the German census of 1933. The Nazis often employed these same sources in their own calculations; see, for example, Publikationsstelle Berlin-Dahlem, *Die Ostgebiete des Deutschen Reiches und das Generalgouvernement der besetzten polnischen Gebiete in statistischen Angaben* (Berlin: Selbstverlag der Publikationsstelle, 1940), a work based exclusively on the three censuses in question. For a copy of the Polish census of 1931, see Institute for the Study of Minority Problems, *The Polish and Non-Polish Populations of Poland: Results of the Population Census of 1931* (Warsaw: Institute for the Study of Minority Problems, 1932); for analysis, see Henryk Zielinski, *Population Changes in Poland, 1939–1950* (New York: Mid-European Studies Center, 1954).

87. Broszat, *Nationalsozialistische Polenpolitik*, 35. It is worth noting that Broszat's arithmetic does not add up: he asserts that Wartheland's population was only 4.2 million

in the fall of 1939, whereas the actual figure was, as Madajczyk, *Die Okkupationspolitik Nazideutschlands in Polen*, 36, maintains, "over 4.5 million" or—to be more precise (according to Broszat's ethnic breakdown)—4,653,000. For their part, Wetzel and Hecht of the Rassenpolitisches Amt state that Wartheland's total population in November 1939 was 4,202,422, including 3,558,489 Poles, 309,002 Germans, 322,947 Jews, and 11,984 individuals of other nationality. Their statistics for Wartheland, as well as for occupied Poland as a whole, were assembled by a member of Greiser's staff in Posen.

88. Madajczyk, *Die Okkupationspolitik Nazideutschlands in Polen*, 36. Madajczyk places the Jewish population of annexed territory at 600,000; Aly provides a figure of 550,000. See Götz Aly, *"Final Solution": Nazi Population Policy and the Murder of the European Jews*, trans. Belinda Cooper and Allison Brown (London: Edward Arnold, 1999), 5. As will become evident in the chapters that follow, Nazi deportation authorities assumed that the incorporated territories held between 550,000 and 600,000 Jews.

89. See Hans Frank, *Das Diensttagebuch des deutschen Generalgouverneurs in Polen, 1939–1945* (hereafter *Tagebuch*), ed. Werner Präg and Wolfgang Jacobmeyer (Stuttgart, Germany: Deutsche Verlags-Anstalt, 1975), entry for 10 November 1939, 65; also Broszat, *Nationalsozialistische Polenpolitik*, 37.

90. "Erlass Adolf Hitlers über die Verwaltung der besetzten polnischen Gebiete," 12 October 1939, *UFZ*, doc. 2871/c, pp. 89–90.

91. Frank, *Tagebuch*, 7. For an examination of Frank's plans for his jurisdiction and his efforts to realize them, see Martyn Housden, "Hans Frank—Empire Builder in the East, 1939–1941," *Eastern European Quarterly* 24 (1994): 367–393; Housden, *Hans Frank, Lebensraum and the Holocaust* (New York: Palgrave Macmillan, 2003). One should, however, approach Housden's discussion of Polish and Jewish deportations from the incorporated territories to the Generalgouvernement in the latter work (particularly chap. 7) with caution.

92. *Polnische Wirtschaft* (Polish economy) was a German slang term that implied "mismanaged economy" or an absolute lack of productivity and efficiency.

93. "Niederschrift über die Instruktion Adolf Hitlers für Wilhelm Keitel zu den Okkupationszielen im Generalgouvernement [17 October 1939]," 20 October 1939, in Werner Röhr, Elke Heckert, Bernd Gottberg, Jutta Wenzel, and Heide-Marie Grünthal, eds., *Die faschistische Okkupationspolitik in Polen (1939–1945)*, vol. 2 of *Nacht über Europa: Die Okkupationspolitik des deutschen Faschismus (1938–1945)*, Achtbändige Dokumentenedition, ed. Wolfgang Schumann and Ludwig Nestler (Cologne, Germany: Pahl-Rugenstein, 1989), doc. 25, pp. 133–134.

94. Helmuth Groscurth, "Aufzeichnung über die vom Hitler geplante Besatzungspolitik in Polen, 18.10.1939," in his *Tagebücher eines Abwehroffiziers, 1938–1940*, ed. Helmut Krausnick and Harold C. Deutsch (Stuttgart, Germany: Deutsche Verlags-Anstalt, 1970), doc. 24, pp. 381–382. For additional details concerning Hitler's plans for the Generalgouvernement, see Martin Bormann's memorandum regarding a conference with Hitler held on 2 October 1939, ND 172-USSR, *IMT*, 39: 425–429. Hitler later expressed consternation over the existence and status of the Generalgouvernement during a meeting with Mussolini on 18 March 1940. The minutes state: "In a cautious manner, [Hitler] had thought about the creation of a buffer state between Germany and Russia in the territory left over

from Poland, at the same time of course ensuring that danger must never arise again of this state becoming a center of intrigue against Germany. The Führer declared that he would be glad if only the Polish state could stand on its own feet and he no longer had to bear responsibility for it, *for he would rather rule over Negroes than Poles*[!] The culture that had come from Greece and Rome had not penetrated to these regions. There Asia began." *DGFP*, 9: doc. 1, pp. 1–16 (emphasis mine).

95. Groscurth, *Tagebücher eines Abwehroffiziers*, 384.

96. Breitman, *The Architect of Genocide*, 74.

97. It does seem incredible that no one, including Hitler himself, had given careful thought to these matters prior to the invasion of Poland, but the evidence suggests that this was in fact the case. Perhaps the idiosyncratic birth of the resettlement program reflects, at least in part, the character of the Nazi leader. In his summary of the Beerhall Putsch of 1923, Ian Kershaw writes: "Hitler had provided the frenetic pressure for action without delay—a reflection of his 'all or nothing' temperament, but also the need to prevent the dynamism of his movement ebbing away. The half-baked planning, dilettante improvisation, lack of care for detail all bore Hitler's characteristic impulse to act without clear thought for the consequences, and without a fall-back position." See Ian Kershaw, *Hitler 1889–1936: Hubris* (New York: W. W. Norton, 1999), 213. The same, it seems, could be said about Hitler's decisions and actions described in this chapter.

CHAPTER THREE: PIPE DREAMS AND PREPARATIONS

1. These include the memo by Otto Reche, professor of anthropology and ethnology at the University of Leipzig, "Leitsätze zur bevölkerungspolitischen Sicherung des deutschen Ostens," 24 September 1939, in Mechthild Rössler and Sabine Schleiermacher, eds., *Der "Generalplan Ost": Hauptlinien der nationalsozialistische Planungs- und Vernichtungspolitik* (Berlin: Akademie-Verlag, 1993), doc. 10, pp. 351–355 (reprinted and translated in Michael Burleigh, *Germany Turns Eastwards: A Study of Ostforschung in the Third Reich* [Cambridge: Cambridge University Press, 1988], 167–171); the report by the Reich Ministry of the Interior "über die Aufgaben der Zivilverwaltung in den besetzten polnischen Gebieten," 2 October 1939, discussed in Martin Broszat, *Nationalsozialistische Polenpolitik, 1939–1945* (Stuttgart, Germany: Deutsche Verlags-Anstalt, 1961), 20–21; Wissenschaftliche Abteilung der Bundesleitung des VDA/Arbeitsgemeinschaft Ostsiedlung des Reichsstudentenführung (Dolezalek), "Zwölf Thesen zur Umsiedlungsaktion," 11 October 1939, NARA/T81/277/VoMi 175/2398094ff.; memorandum by the historians Albert Brackmann, Theodor Schieder, Werner Trillmich, and Ludwig Petry and the ethnologist Walter Kuhn, "Denkschrift über die Fragen der Eindeutschung Posens und Westpreussens und der damit zusammenhängenden Umsiedlungen," 11 October 1939, discussed in Ingo Haar, *Historiker im Nationalsozialismus: Deutsche Geschichtswissenschaft und der "Volkstumskampf" im Osten* (Göttingen, Germany: Vandenhoeck & Ruprecht, 2000), 11–12. In the 1930s, Germany witnessed a boom in academic research devoted to ethnographic and spatial planning. The interest in the relationship between race and space led to the

creation of two major planning institutions, the Reichsstelle für Raumordnung (RfR) and the Reichsarbeitsgemeinschaft für Raumordung (Reich Working Group for Spatial Order), both of which were directed by Dr. Konrad Meyer, a Berlin professor of farming and agricultural studies who eventually became a prominent member of the RKF. The RfR was, on Hitler's orders, assigned the task of ensuring that "German space is shaped in a way commensurate with the needs of the Volk and the state." The Reichsarbeitsgemeinschaft was to work closely with the RfR by coordinating interdisciplinary university research in the field of spatial planning; its journal, *Raumforschung und Raumordnung*, first published in 1936, is still in print today. See Daniel Inkelas, "Visions of Harmony and Violence: RKF Landscape Planning and Population Policy in Annexed Poland, 1939–1944" (Ph.D. diss., Northwestern University, 1998), 70–72.

2. Rassenpolitisches Amt (Wetzel and Hecht), "Die Frage der Behandlung der Bevölkerung der ehemaligen polnischen Gebiete nach rassenpolitischen Gesichtspunkten," 25 November 1939, NARA/T74/9/57/380571ff.

3. Czesław Madajczyk, *Die Okkupationspolitik Nazideutschlands in Polen, 1939–1945* (Berlin: Akademie-Verlag, 1987), 393. Rapp received a copy of the NSDAP memo on 18 December 1939, one day after the conclusion of the first wave of mass deportations from Wartheland.

4. Richard Breitman, *The Architect of Genocide: Himmler and the Final Solution* (Hanover, NH: Brandeis University Press, 1991), 86.

5. Himmler, "Einige Gedanken über die Behandlung der Fremdvölkischen im Osten," 20 May 1940, NARA/T175/119/2645113ff.

6. Rassenpolitisches Amt (Wetzel and Hecht), "Die Frage der Behandlung."

7. Adolf Hitler, *Mein Kampf*, trans. Ralph Mannheim (Boston: Houghton Mifflin, 1971), 388 (Hitler's emphasis).

8. The authors included neither the 200,000 to 300,000 Kaschubians and Masurians of southeast West Prussia nor the 1 to 1.5 million Upper Silesian Poles (*Wasserpolen*) and Slonsakians in this figure. These ethnic groups were viewed as "intermediary," fundamentally different from Poles and "Polonized" racial Germans. See Burleigh, *Germany Turns Eastwards*, 206–208. For an in-depth discussion of the Masurians, see Richard Blanke, "When Germans and Poles Lived Together: From the History of German-Polish Relations," in Keith Bullivant and Geoffrey Giles, eds., *Germany and Eastern Europe: Cultural Identities and Cultural Differences* (Amsterdam: Rodolphi, 1999), 44–47.

9. Rassenpolitisches Amt" (Wetzel and Hecht), "Die Frage der Behandlung," 6–7, 16–26.

10. Ibid., 27ff.

11. Ibid., 29–31.

12. "Protokoll über die Umsiedlung der deutschen Volksgruppe Estlands in das Deutsche Reich vom 15.Oktober.1939," in Dietrich A. Loeber, ed., *Diktierte Option: Die Umsiedlung der Deutsch-Balten aus Estland und Lettland, 1939–1941* (Neumünster, Germany: Karl Wachholtz Verlag, 1972), doc. 250, pp. 471–476; Valdis O. Lumans, *Himmler's Auxiliaries: The Volksdeutsche Mittelstelle and the German National Minorities of Europe, 1933–1945* (Chapel Hill: University of North Carolina Press, 1993), 161.

13. "Vertrag über die Umsiedlung lettischer Bürger deutscher Volkszugehörigkeit in das Deutsche Reich vom 30.Oktober.1939," in Loeber, *Diktierte Option*, doc. 270, pp. 515–526. For the articles of the German-Soviet resettlement treaty, see AGK/RG838/EWZ-L/75/25–34. See also Andrzej Leśniewski and Roman Nurowski, "Political Background to Population Movements between the Oder and Bug Rivers," in Zachodnia Agencja Prasowa, ed., *Population Movements between the Oder and Bug Rivers, 1939–1950* (Poznan, Poland, and Warsaw: Wydawnictwo Zachodnie, 1961), 19; Hans-Erich Volkmann, "Zur Ansiedlung der Deutschbalten im 'Warthegau,'" *Zeitschrift für Ostforschung* 30, no. 4 (1981): 527–588.

14. Lumans, *Himmler's Auxiliaries*, 161; Der Reichsführer-SS/Reichskommissar für die Festigung deutschen Volkstums, *Der Menscheneinsatz: Grundsätze, Anordnung und Reichtlinien* (hereafter *Der Menscheneinsatz*) (Berlin: Hauptabteilung des RKFDV, 1940), 103, NARA/T81/VoMi 802/2435422ff. I cite the figure presented in *Der Menscheneinsatz*.

15. Lumans, *Himmler's Auxiliaries*, 161–165; *Der Menscheneinsatz*, 103. The Volksdeutschen from eastern Poland and the Baltic Republics were not technically forced to emigrate to the Reich, but they were certainly pressured to do so. The Nazi propaganda machine made no bones about the "fatal changes" that awaited those who remained behind once the USSR assumed full control of their native lands, and this fear of the Soviets—real or imagined—was, as Lumans points out, "the truly decisive factor" that led most to opt for emigration. See Lumans, *Himmler's Auxiliaries*, 160.

16. The agency was initially called the Einwandererzentralstelle Nord-Ost.

17. Götz Aly, *"Final Solution": Nazi Population Policy and the Murder of the European Jews*, trans. Belinda Cooper and Allison Brown (London: Edward Arnold, 1999), 35; Robert L. Koehl, *RKFDV: German Resettlement and Population Policy, 1939–1945—A History of the Reich Commission for the Strengthening of Germandom* (Cambridge, MA: Harvard University Press, 1957), 54; Koehl, *The Black Corps: The Structure and Power Struggles of the Nazi SS* (Madison: University of Wisconsin Press, 1983), 187–188; Lumans, *Himmler's Auxiliaries*, 189–192; Isabel Heinemann, *"Rasse, Siedlung, deutsches Blut": Das Rasse- & Siedlungshauptamt der SS und die rassenpolitische Neuordnung Europas* (Göttingen, Germany: Wallstein Verlag, 2003), 195ff.

18. Koehl, *RKFDV*, 62.

19. Herbert S. Levine, "Local Authority and the SS State: The Conflict over Population Policy in Danzig–West Prussia, 1939–1945," *Central European History* 2 (1969): 350.

20. Koehl, *RKFDV*, 62–63, 73; Levine, "Local Authority and the SS State," 339–342, 350–351; Ruth Bettina Birn, *Die Höheren SS- und Polizeiführer: Himmlers Vertreter im Reich und in den besetzten Gebieten* (Düsseldorf, Germany: Droste Verlag, 1986), 188–196. On Forster's prewar activity as Gauleiter of the Free City of Danzig, see Dieter Schenk, *Hitlers Mann in Danzig: Albert Forster und die NS-Verbrechen in Danzig-Westpreussen* (Bonn, Germany: Verlag J. H. W. Dietz, 2000), 30–125; Herbert S. Levine, *Hitler's Free City: A History of the Nazi Party in Danzig, 1925–39* (Chicago: University of Chicago Press, 1973); Karl Höffkes, *Hitlers politische Generale: Die Gauleiter des Dritten Reiches—Ein biographisches Nachschlagewerk* (Tübingen, Germany: Grabert-Verlag, 1986), 73–75. At the onset of the resettlement program, the higher SS and police leaders of the eastern

provinces officially served as Himmler's RKF deputies within their respective jurisdictions. This changed in the spring of 1940, when Himmler named—or rather, attempted to name—the highest-ranking Nazi official in each province his official RKF deputy. Greiser of Wartheland, as well as Erich Koch of East Prussia, accepted the title; Forster refused, and as a result, the HSSPF of Danzig–West Prussia remained the senior RKF representative in the Gau. See Koehl, *RKFDV*, 73; Hans Buchheim, "Rechtsstellung und Organisation des Reichskommissars für die Festigung deutschen Volkstums," *Gutachten des Instituts für Zeitgeschichte* (Munich, Germany: Institut für Zeitgeschichte, 1958), 248–249.

21. Though Łódź was not renamed Litzmannstadt until early 1940, I will, for the sake of simplicity, henceforth refer to the city as Litzmannstadt. Before it was renamed, the Germans generally called the city Lodsch.

22. Otto Rosenkranz, *Siedlung und Landwirtschaft im Reichsgau Wartheland* (Berlin: Deutsche Landbuchhandlung, Sohrey, 1941), 17–31.

23. Arthur Greiser, *Der Aufbau im Osten* (Jena, Germany: G. Fischer, 1942), 7–8.

24. U.S. Department of State, *Documents on German Foreign Policy, 1918–1945*, series D (1937–1945), 13 vols. (hereafter *DGFP*) (Washington, DC: U.S. Government Printing Office, 1956), 9: doc. 1, p. 7.

25. Greiser was referring to the NSDAP government in Danzig that took control of Danzig–West Prussia and to the fact that Upper Silesia and Regierungsbezirk Zichenau were incorporated into existing Gaue.

26. Congress Poles were those Poles and their descendants who had either emigrated to former German territory from former Russian territory after 1919 or who still resided in former Russian territory annexed to the Reich, for example, the eastern Kreise of Wartheland. Congress Poland was the semi-independent Polish state established at the Congress of Vienna in 1815, a region ruled by the Russian czar under the title "king of Poland." After the November Insurrection of 1830, the state lost what little independence it had.

27. Arthur Greiser, "Die Grossdeutsche Aufgabe im Wartheland," *Nationalsozialistische Monatshefte* 130 (January 1941): 46.

28. Ulrich Schade, *Industrie und Handel im Reichsgau Wartheland* (Berlin: Volk und Reich Verlag, 1942), 11.

29. Aly, *"Final Solution,"* 38.

30. Ibid., 21.

31. The RMdI memo, "Bericht über das Ergebnis der Grenzziehung Deutschland-Polen," 27 October 1939, implies as much. See APP/Chef der Zivilverwaltung beim Oberbefehlshaber im Militärbezirk Posen/75/1–5.

32. Debórah Dwork and Robert Jan van Pelt, *Auschwitz: 1270 to the Present* (New York: W. W. Norton, 1996), 148.

33. Walter Geisler, *Deutscher! Der Osten ruft Dich!* (Berlin: Volk und Reich Verlag, 1941), 22–23. Writing a year earlier, the geographer Dr. Friedrich Lange promoted a similar view, arguing that the Warthegau and the German East in general "has finally found its natural completion." The new annexations, he asserted, created a "dual front" of German cities in the East. Running north to south, the Königsberg-Litzmannstadt-Kattowitz-Ostrau line held the forward position, and behind it to the west, Danzig-Bromberg-Posen-Breslau held

the rear. This geometrical territorial arrangement, he suggested, greatly facilitated trade and commerce, as well as the military defense of the eastern frontier. See Friedrich Lange, *Ostland kehrt heim* (Berlin-Leipzig: Nibelungen Verlag, 1940), 72–73. For additional discussion of Wartheland's economy and infrastructure during the first year of the occupation, see Die Rüstungsinspektion des Werhkreises XXI, "Geschichte des Kreigseinsatz der Rüstungsinspektion des Wehrkreises XXI bis zum 30.September 1940" (presumably October 1940), NARA/T77/619/1807720ff.

34. Wilhelm Zoch, "Neue Ordnung im Osten," *Neues Bauerntum: Fachwissenschaftliche Zeitschrift für das ländliche Siedlungswesen* 3 (March 1940): 85–86.

35. Greiser, "Die Grossdeutsche Aufgabe im Wartheland," 47. At least one Nazi thinker disagreed with Greiser's melting pot idea. In April 1941, Edmond Hahn argued that the incoming Volksdeutschen should not discard their distinct identities, specific knowledge, and specialized skills upon arriving in the incorporated territories. Rather, these valuable characteristics should be preserved, as long as they did not impede in any way the German mission in the region. Hahn envisioned Wartheland as a united "mosaic" of volksdeutsch groups, a *"gärtnerische Leistung"* (horticultural achievement): after all, he wrote, "many types of plants and flowers make for a unified garden." See Hahn, "Land der Zukunft—Wartheland," *Der Deutsche im Osten: Monatsschrift für Kultur, Politik und Unterhaltung* (April 1941): 234–236.

36. Ulrich Greifelt, *Die Festigung deutschen Volkstums als zentrale Ostaufgabe* (undated pamphlet, presumably late 1941 or early 1942), 4, NARA/T74/10/381802ff.

37. Quoted in Kurt Lück, *Der Lebenskampf im deutsch-polnischen Grenzraum* (Berlin: Zentralverlag der NSDAP, Franz Eher, 1940), 76.

38. Greifelt, *Die Festigung deutschen Volkstums,* 4. Greifelt had discussed this idea in greater detail in an article that appeared in *Raumforschung und Raumordnung* in early 1941. The regime, he wrote, had to "organize the relationship between Volkstum and Lebensraum so that the völkisch power (*Kraft*) can be increased most actively and most powerfully." Race and space, then, were indissolubly linked. See Greifelt, "Festigung deutschen Volkstums im deutschen Osten," *Raumforschung und Raumordnung: Monatsschrift der Reichsarbeitsgemeinschaft für Raumordnung* 1 (1941): 4.

39. Darré was the foremost proponent of this view. See his two most famous works, *Das Bauerntum als Lebensquell der nordischen Rasse* (Munich, Germany: J. F. Lehmann, 1938) and *Neuadel als Blut und Boden* (Munich, Germany: J. F. Lehmann, 1935).

40. According to Hermann Rauschning, the Nazi president of Freistadt Danzig's senate from June 1933 until he fell out with the Nazis in November 1934, the province of Posen, in the year before the outbreak of World War I, exported to the rest of the Reich 1,358,000 tons of rye; 1,159,000 tons of barley and malt; 924,000 tons of oats; 2,410,000 tons of potatoes; 1,060,000 tons of sugar; hundreds of thousands of cattle, sheep, and pigs; and a variety of other agricultural products and produce. Rauschning employed these statistics to justify his assertion that the disputed Polish territories "only prospered economically and culturally when they were under predominant German influence—a clear expression of the indisputable geo-political unity of these territories with the German economic space." "These highly developed areas," he added, "cannot permanently maintain their viabil-

ity within the Polish State, with its entirely different economic basis … and these areas will once more experience the painful decline which they experienced before the Prussian era." See Rauschning (writing in 1933), quoted in W. W. Coole and M. F. Potter, eds., *Thus Speaks Germany* (New York: Harper and Brothers, 1941), 260–261.

41. Quoted in Schade, *Industrie und Handel*, 16–17. Göring's dim view of Polish land use was obviously exaggerated.

42. Eberhard Achterberg, "Der deutsche Osten—Aufgabe und Verpflichtung," *Nationalsozialistische Monatshefte* 130 (January 1941): 19.

43. Theodor Oberländer, "Von der Front des Volkstumskampfes," *Neues Bauerntum* 4–5 (April–May 1940): 127–130. For a biography of Oberländer and an overview of his activities both during and after the Nazi years, see Aleksander Drożdżyński and Jan Zaborowski, *Oberländer: A Study in German East Policies* (Poznan, Poland: Wydawnictwo Zachodnie, 1960). Oberländer was a close adviser to Konrad Adenauer on German refugees until a public scandal about his Nazi past drove him from office in 1960.

44. Walter Geisler, *Der Deutsche Osten als Lebensraum für alle Berufsstände* (Berlin, Prag, and Wein: Volk und Reich Verlag, 1942), 12.

45. Schade, *Industrie und Handel*, 22.

46. Egon Leuschner, *Nationalsozialistische Fremdvolkpolitik* (Berlin: Rassenpolitisches Amt der NSDAP, 1940), 26.

47. Oberländer, "Von der Front des Volkstumskampfes," 128.

48. Dr. Kurt Haussmann, "Die Bauernsiedlung in den neuen Ostgauen," *Raumforschung und Raumordnung* 10 (1940): 417.

49. Greiser, *Der Aufbau im Osten*, 9.

50. Hans Ehlich, the leader of RSHA Amt IIIES, defined the term *wild evacuations* as such. See Ehlich's testimony at Nuremberg, 28 October 1947, Case 8, NARA/M894/2/p. 588 (English transcript).

51. Wacław Długoborski, "Die deutsche Besatzungspolitik gegenüber Polen," in Karl Dietrich Bracher, Manfred Funke, and Hans-Adolf Jacobsen, eds., *Nationalsozialistische Diktatur, 1933–1945: Ein Bilanz* (Bonn, Germany: Bundeszentrale für politische Bildung, 1983), 583.

52. RKFDV to Heydrich, Greiser, Forster, Lorenz, Greifelt, etc., 11 October 1939, NARA/M894/15/NO 4613. The day before, the chief of the Gestapo and head of RSHA Amt IV, SS-Gruppenführer Heinrich Müller, had ordered SS-Oberführer Erich Naumann, the commander of Einsatzgruppe VI, to create housing "in the shortest possible time" in Posen for 20,000 Baltic Germans. Naumann was told to select a city quarter and "free" it from the Poles. Most of the evictees were sent to live with other Poles in Posen; the remainder were to be "accommodated" in and around Radom and Kielce in the Generalgouvernement. See Müller to Naumann, 10 October 1939, AGK/Gestapo-Posen/CAMSW 687/29/1. Naumann met with Greiser the same day and learned that the Balts were to receive, as a rule, two-to four-room apartments. Since about 5,000 dwellings were already vacant as a result of flight, Einsatzgruppe VI would have to secure "only" another 1,000 to 2,000 apartments. See Naumann, "Unternehmen Tannenberg—Hier: Unterbringung 20,000 Volksdeutsche aus dem Baltikum," 10 October 1939, AGK/Gestapo-Posen/CAMSW 687/29/2.

53. Müller to Naumann (telegram), 28 October 1939, USHMM/RG15.015M/2/104/1.

54. Himmler's orders notwithstanding, wild evacuations continued—again, primarily from Danzig–West Prussia—until early 1940. This situation was most likely a reflection of Forster's defiance of RFSS-RKFDV authority. Długoborski, in "Die deutsche Besatzungspolitik," 583, estimates that 135,000 individuals were deported during the course of these wild actions, but this was almost certainly an exaggeration. The number was probably somewhat less than 100,000, a figure that included the 50,000 deported from Gdynia alone. See Werner Röhr, Elke Heckert, Bernd Gottberg, Jutta Wenzel, and Heide-Marie Grünthal, eds., *Die faschistische Okkupationspolitik in Polen (1939–1945)*, vol. 2 of *Nacht über Europa: Die Okkupationspolitik des deutschen Faschismus (1938–1945)*, Achtbändige Dokumentenedition, ed. Wolfgang Schumann and Ludwig Nestler (Cologne, Germany: Pahl-Rugenstein, 1989), table 4, 356.

55. Undisciplined, fanatical, and fervently anti-Polish, the Volksdeutsche Selbstschutz even perplexed Heydrich, who later complained about "certain intolerable and uncontrollable acts of revenge" perpetrated by these ethnic Germans. See Heydrich's "Aktenvermerk" to Himmler, 2 July 1940, published in Helmut Krausnick, "Hitler und die Morde in Polen: Ein Beitrag zum Konflikt zwischen Heer und SS um die Verwaltung der besetzten Gebiete," *Vierteljahrshefte für Zeitgeschichte* 11 (April 1963): 206–209. But as Heinz Höhne asserts, Heydrich was certainly troubled far more about discipline than humanitarian concerns; see Höhne, *The Order of the Death's Head: The Story of Hitler's SS*, trans. Richard Barry (New York: Ballantine Books, 1971), 341–342. For additional discussion of the Selbstschutz, see Christian Jansen and Arno Weckbecker, *Der "Volksdeutsche Selbstschutz" in Polen 1939/40* (Munich, Germany: R. Oldenbourg Verlag, 1992); Peter R. Black, "Rehearsal for 'Reinhard'? Odilo Globocnik and the Lublin *Selbstschutz*," *Central European History* 2 (1992): 204–226.

56. See Piotr Wandycz, *The Lands of Partitioned Poland, 1795–1918* (Seattle: University of Washington Press, 1974), 65–131. The Nazis regarded Congress Poles as a greater threat to the consolidation of German nationhood than so-called Prussian Poles. On the one hand, these Poles were seen as more Slavic and less Germanized than their Prussian counterparts. On the other, those who had emigrated westward had supposedly taken advantage of Germany's defeat in World War I, moving into the region after the German withdrawal and, in many cases, seizing former German property as well. As Walter Geisler stated in 1941, "It goes without saying that the Poles were removed from the former Reich areas who came after 1919 … This had to be the first act of re-righting the wrong [done] to the expelled German *Volksgenossen*, who can again find a sphere of activity in their old eastern German homeland." He also argued that even Prussian Poles did not like these immigrants; twenty years of Polish rule could not bridge the cleft between them. See Geisler, *Deutscher! Der Osten ruft Dich!* 58. Wetzel and Hecht added that politically and ethnically speaking, Congress Poles were far more conscious of their national identity than the long-standing Polish residents of the annexed territories; therefore, they would have to be deported almost without exception. See Rassenpolitisches Amt (Wetzel and Hecht), "Die Frage der Behandlung," 21.

57. RFSS-RKFDV, "Anordnung 1/II," 30 October 1939, in Szymon Datner, Janusz Gumkowski, and Kazimierz Leszczyński, eds., *Wysiedlanie ludności ziem Polskich wcielonych do Rzeszy: Biuletyn Głównej Komisji Badania Zbrodni Hitlerowskich w Polsce 12* (hereafter *Biuletyn 12*) (Warsaw: Wydawnictwo Prawnicze, 1960), doc. 1, pp. 4F–6F.

58. Hans Frank, *Das Diensttagebuch des deutschen Generalgouverneurs in Polen, 1939–1945,* ed. Werner Präg and Wolfgang Jacobmeyer (Stuttgart, Germany: Deutsche Verlags-Anstalt, 1975), entry for 31 October 1939, 52.

59. Creutz's memo called for the "temporary sheltering of the ethnic Germans—to be expected within the next few weeks—from the Baltic and Volhynia." Since the first transport of Estonian Germans arrived on 18 October, the memo was most likely issued before this date. See "General Orders and Directives of the Reich Commissioner for the Strengthening of Germanism," NO 4059, Nuernberg Military Tribunals, *Trials of War Criminals before the Nuernberg Military Tribunals under Control Council Law no. 10, Nuernberg, October 1946–April 1949,* 15 vols. (hereafter *TWC*) (Washington, DC: U.S. Government Printing Office, 1949–1953), 4: 873. Dan Inkelas, for his part, dates the Creutz memo 9 December 1939, the same day Himmler announced that in the future, the resettlement and reconstruction of the incorporated territories would be guided by *Anordnungen* (orders) and *Allgemeine Anordnungen* (general orders) issued by the RKFDV. See Inkelas, "Visions of Harmony and Violence," 128.

60. Aly, for example, assumes the figure of 1 million deportees included the Litzmannstadt Jews. See Aly, *"Final Solution,"* 37. See also Christopher Browning, *Nazi Policy, Jewish Workers, German Killers* (Cambridge: Cambridge University Press, 2000), 7.

61. Greiser directive, 1 November 1939, APP/Reichsstatthalter-Wartheland/2/10–11. Damzog had been the leader of Einsatzgruppe V during Operation Tannenberg. For biographical information on Damzog, see Alexander B. Rossino, *Hitler Strikes Poland: Blitzkrieg, Ideology, and Atrocity* (Lawrence: University Press of Kansas, 2003), 46–47.

62. No provenance, "Besprechung beim Stadtkommissar am 1.November 1939 in der Frage der Balten-Ansiedlung," 1 November 1939, AGK/Gestapo-Posen/CAMSW 687/29/122–123. The report called for the eviction and internment of 7,000 Poles by 5 December. It provided a breakdown of targeted Polish families according to occupational groups: 450 families from the intelligentsia, 350 from industry and trade, 900 from the artisan sector, and 300 from the city bureaucracy. With the exception of the intelligentsia, Poles from these groups were to be ousted in order to provide employment for Baltic Germans trained in the same occupations.

63. HSSPF Wilhelm Koppe soon took notice of this problem. In a letter to the Schupo written at some point in November 1939, he ordered that the police had to take greater care to ensure that they arrested only individuals specified on evacuation lists. Those who had been mistakenly arrested and interned had to be released from the camp, and this, he implied, required a lot of paperwork. See Koppe to Kommando der Schupo, November 1939 (no specific date), AGK/Greiser Trial/36/536.

64. See the 8 November 1939 report on conditions in Lager Glowno (signature illegible), USHMM/RG15.015M/3/188/3–6. The report states that a representative of the Posen

city administration, Oberinspektor Otto, became commandant of the camp on 5 November. Presumably, he dictated or at least approved the memo. The figures cited earlier concerning the arrival of the first contingent of evacuees were specified in this report. Archiwum Państwowe Łódź contains a handwritten record listing the numbers of individuals entering Glowno on a daily basis between 1 November 1939 and May 1940. See "Tägliche Eingänge von evakuierten Personen aus verschieden Kreise, 1939-1940," APL/UWZ-L/11a/1-205. Discrepancies exist between this record and the 8 November 1939 report. For example, the handwritten log records that 131 individuals, not 217, entered the camp on 5 November 1939 and 146, not 222, on 7 November. Whatever the actual numbers, the handwritten record provides an invaluable overview of the scale of evacuations from the Posen region during the first seven months of the operation, particularly in terms of evictions carried out before the onset of the 1.Nahplan.

65. "Niederschrift über die am 8.11.1939 stattgefundene Besprechung beim Generalgouverneur Polen in Krakau," *Biuletyn 12*/doc. 3/11F-14F. For Himmler's orders announcing the "repatriation" of the Baltic Germans and the Volksdeutschen from Volhynia, Galicia, and the Narev region, see RFSS-RKFDV, "Anordnung 9/II," 3 November 1939, and "Anordnung 2/VI," 30 October 1939, respectively, in *Der Menscheneinsatz*, 13-14, 22.

66. Greiser, "Rundschreiben an alle Parteidienststellen, Staatsdienststellen, Landräte, usw.," 4 December 1939, AGK/Greiser Trial/13/176.

67. See Koppe's SS personnel file, NARA/BDC RG242/A3343/SSO 200A; also T. Friedmann, ed., *Der Höhere SS- und Polizeiführer beim Reichsstatthalter in Posen im Wehrkreis XXI, Wilhelm Koppe: SS-Obergruppenführer und General der Polizei: Dokumentensammlung* (Haifa: Institute of Documentation in Israel for the Investigation of Nazi War Crimes, 1997).

68. Virtually all of the deportation plans and orders issued at that time employed 28 February 1940 as the termination date for the first stage of organized evacuations. In fact, 1940 was a leap year; the various Nazi authorities in question may well have overlooked this.

69. Ernst Damzog informed his subordinates about the annexation of the Łódź region on 10 November. The incorporated territory in question included the city of Litzmannstadt and the Landkreise Litzmannstadt, Lask, Lentschütz, and Kutno. See Damzog's memorandum, 10 November 1939, USHMM/RG15.015M/2/104/5. See also "Lodsch im Reichsgau Wartheland," *OdB*, 12 November 1939.

70. HSSPF-Posen, "Abschiebung von Juden und Polen aus Reichsgau 'Warthe-Land,'" 10 November 1939, USHMM/RG15.015M/95/8-14. In verbal orders issued the same day, Koppe backpedaled somewhat, stating that economic considerations could perhaps play a role in the operation but "only insofar as they do not constitute an interruption in achieving the objectives of the mission." See Rapp, "Abschiebung von Juden und Polen: Mündliche Anordnung des Höhere SS- und Polizeiführer, SS-Gruppenführer Koppe, vom 10.11.39," 12 November 1939, USHMM/RG15.015M/95/4-7. An Orpo directive, also issued 10 November 1939, stressed the "political moment" as well, declaring that it was especially urgent to deport Poles "who have fought Deutschtum in an especially rigorous manner"; it was the responsibility of Schupo and the gendarmerie to identify and apprehend

such Poles. See "Auszugweise Abschrift aus dem Tagesordnungen des Befehlshaber der Ordnungspolizei, Nr. 1–18," no. 11, 10 November 1939, AGK/Befehlshaber-Orpo/CAMSW 717/1/1–10.

71. HSSPF-Posen, "Ansiedlung von Baltendeutschen und Wolhyniendeutschen und Evakuierung von Juden und Polen," 11 November 1939, NARA/T81/286/VoMi 321.

72. See Rapp's SS personnel file, NARA/BDC RG242/A3343/SSO-007B. His participation in Operation Tannenberg comes to light through an Einsatzgruppe VI memo he signed on 2 October 1939; see APP/Chef der Zivilverwaltung beim Oberbefehlshaber im Militärbezirk Posen/54/53–55. For Heydrich's order proclaiming the Einsatzgruppen henceforth stationary, see Der Chef der Sicherheitspolizei und des SD (gez. Best), "Unternehmen Tannenberg," 6 October 1939, *Biuletyn* 21/doc. 50/157. The special Tannenberg section of the Sipo Hauptamt (Main Office) (after 27 September 1939, the RSHA) was dissolved on 17 October; see RSHA (gez. Heydrich), "Unternehmen Tannenberg—Hier: Auflösung des Sonderreferates," 17 October 1939, *Biuletyn* 22/doc. 52/158–159. On 20 November, the *Gruppenstab* (roughly meaning "board of directors") of Einsatzgruppe VI (of which Rapp was apparently a member) was officially assigned to Damzog's office. Einsatzkommando 11/VI was assigned to the Staatspolizeistelle (State Police Office) in Hohensalza, EK 14/VI to the Staatspolizeistelle in Litzmannstadt, and EK 15/VI to the Staatspolizeistelle in Posen. See the directive of the Chef der Sipo und des SD (gez. Best), 20 November 1939, *Biuletyn* 22/doc. 61/173–174.

73. I have no reliable data concerning the exact size of the Jewish populations of Posen, Gnesen, and Hohensalza in November 1939. According to the Polish census of 1931, approximately 7,000 Jews then lived in the (Polish) province of Poznań, a region that included the cities of Gniezno (Gnesen) and Inowrocław (Hohensalza). The total population of the province was then 2,107,000; in all, .3 percent of the people registered their religion as Jewish, and .2 percent registered as Yiddish or Hebrew. See Franciszek Kubiczek, ed., *Historia Polski w Liczbach* (Warsaw: Główny Urząd Statystyczny, 1994), 160, 164.

74. HSSPF-Posen, "Geheim! Abschiebung von Juden und Polen aus dem Reichsgau 'Warthe-Land,'" 12 November 1939, USHMM/RG15.015M/2/99/1–5.

75. Rapp, "Abschiebung von Polen und Juden aus dem Reichsgau 'Wartheland,'" 16 November 1939, AGK/UWZ-L/5/15–19.

76. Polski Związek Zachodni and Twarzystwo Powstańców i Wojaków, respectively.

77. For additional information on targeted Polish groups, see the report by the SD-Führer of Einsatzgruppe II (Schäfer), "Polnische politische Organisationen," 5 October 1939, USHMM/RG15.007M/8/96/1–8; Der Führer des SD-Einsatzkommando 14/VI, "Listenmässige Erfassung aller reichsfeindlichen Elemente," 5 October 1939, AGK/Gestapo-Posen/CAMSW 687/19/2. The former report, which deals primarily with the Radom region of the Generalgouvernement, presents a detailed discussion of the Polish Socialist Party, the National Democratic Party, and the Party of National Unity. The latter simply states that "anti-Reich elements" included the leaders of Polish political parties and organizations, the Catholic clergy, Polish civil servants, and Polish academics.

78. On 13 December 1939, SS-Sturmbannführer Dr. Helmut Bischoff of the Gestapo-Posen ordered preparations to begin for the evacuation of the Catholic clergy. The objective

of the action, he stated, was to remove up to 80 percent of the clergy from Wartheland. He demanded a list of all priests, monks, and nuns in the province by 30 December 1939. See Gestapo-Posen (gez. Bischoff), "Abschiebung von Polen und Juden," 13 December 1939, APP/Landrat-Schrimm/100/37–40. I assume the deportation of the clergy soon took place, though I have found no documentation regarding it.

79. Rapp, "Abschiebung von Polen und Juden." 16 November 1939,

80. Rapp (draft), "Überprüfung der Beamten, Angestellten und Arbeiter polnischer Volkszugehörigkeit in Zusammenhang mit den geplanten Evakuierungsmassnahmen," 16 November 1939, USHMM/RG10.015M/2/144/1–2.

81. See OdB, 15 November 1939; also Rapp, "Gesuche um Genehmigung von Umzügen und Abwanderungen," 17 November 1939, USHMM/RG15.015M/1/4/4–5.

82. Rapp telegram to Best, "Abschiebung von Polen und Juden—Erkennungsdienstliche Massnahme," 16 November 1939, USHMM/RG15.015M/2/99/6–7.

83. Additional problems arose regarding the survey of anti-German Poles in Wartheland. Significant numerical discrepancies existed between the evacuation lists compiled by Rapp's staff—which employed materials such as census reports and statistical data concerning the social and occupational structure of the Polish population—and those compiled by local authorities and Sipo officials in the field. Rapp attributed these inconsistencies to side effects of the September campaign, specifically the structural displacement caused by uncontrolled population movements in the wake of advancing German troops. To ensure that evacuations went smoothly despite this conundrum, he argued that a "dual calculation" should guide the operation. His staff would supply approximate figures regarding the number of deportees from any particular area, and local functionaries would supplement these through their investigations in the field. See Rapp, "Festlegung der für die Abschiebung in Frage kommenden Personenzahl," 17 November 1939, USHMM/ 15.015M/1/96/1–2.

84. Economic officials included representatives from the Treuhandstelle-Ost and the SS-Bodenamt, two newly created agencies responsible for the confiscation of Polish and Jewish property. On 19 October, Göring, acting in his capacity as plenipotentiary of the Four-Year Plan, established the Haupttreuhandstelle-Ost (HTO; Central Trust Agency for the East), a bureau charged with the registration, confiscation, and redistribution of property in the incorporated territories. This act, which completely disregarded RKFDV authority, specifically that of Sipo and the SD, naturally irritated Himmler. In fact, the RFSS had established his own agency, the Zentralbodenamt (ZBA; Central Land Office), several days earlier to seize property for the German immigrants. Eventually, it was agreed that the HTO would handle the confiscation of urban commercial and industrial property, and the ZBA would handle that of agricultural assets. See Koehl, RKFDV, 59–61; Greifelt testimony, 16 February 1948, TWC, 4: 978–979.

85. Rapp, "Niederschrift über die am 23.November 1939—16 Uhr—unter Leitung von SS-Sturmbannführer Rapp durchgeführte Besprechung über die Behandlung der jüdischen und polnischen Vermögenswerte, die im Züge der Evakuierungsmassnahmen der Beschlagnahme zu Gunsten des Reiches verfallen," 25 November 1939,

USHMM/RG15.015M/2/107/10–14. For a complete transcript of the meeting, see USHMM/RG15.015M/2/107/17–35.

86. Rapp, "Rückstellungsanträge und Fürsprache für evakuierte Juden und Polen," 3 December 1939, USHMM/RG15.015M/2/101/4 (Rapp's emphasis).

87. Rapp, "Abschiebung von Juden und Polen: Mündliche Anordnung des Höhere SS- und Polizeiführer, SS-Gruppenführer Koppe von 10.11.39," 12 November 1939, USHMM/RG15.015M/1/95/4–7.

88. HSSPF-Posen (signed Rapp), "Abschiebung von Juden aus dem Reichsgau 'Wartheland,'" 24 November 1939, AGK/UWZ-L/5/45–46.

89. Rapp, "Durchführung der Evakuierung," 18 November 1939, NARA/T81/286/VoMi 321/2409565ff.

90. HSSPF-Posen, "Merkblatt für die Durchführung der Evakuierung von Juden und Polen," 22 November 1939, APP/Landrat-Jarotschin/20/2.

91. Koppe, "Inventuraufnahme in Wohnungen polnischer oder jüdischer Flüchtlinge or Ausgewiesener," 24 November 1939, NARA/T81/286/VoMi 321/2409558ff.

92. Rapp, "Richlinien über die Durchführung der Polen- und Judenevakuierung und deren Abtransport an die endgültigen Bestimmungsorte," 22 November 1939, NARA/T81/286/VoMi 321/2409562ff.

93. Rapp, "Durchsuchung der Lagerinsassen vor Abgang des Transports zum endgültigen Bestimmungsort," 22 November 1939, NARA/T81/286/VoMi 321/2409561ff.

94. Rapp, "Transportanweisung für das Begleitkommando der Evakuierungszüge," 22 November 1939, USHMM/RG15.015M/3/188/23–24; see also Rapp's supplemental order of the same date, USHMM/RG15.015M/3/188/21.

95. No provenance, no title, no date, APP/Landrat-Schrimm/100/31.

96. Rapp, "Transportanweisung."

97. Krumey, "Bericht zu Aufstellung der Abtransporte," 22 November 1939, USHMM/RG15.015M/2/104/13.

98. Heydrich (telegram), "Raeumung in den neuen Ostprovinzen," 28 November 1939, Biuletyn 12/doc. 4/15F–17F; Heydrich (telegram), "Raeumung im Warthegau," 28 November 1939, USHMM/RG15.015M/2/99/2. Heydrich provided no stipulations regarding the ethnic mix of the 80,000 deportees; he simply stated "Poles and Jews." The Fernplan he alluded to has not been found in the archives, but Aly believes he has discovered a rudimentary version in the Bundesarchiv-Koblenz. He dates this document, entitled "Long-Term Plan for Resettlement in the Eastern Territories," to late November 1939 and claims that it was probably issued by RSHA Amt III. In a nutshell, it states that the basic goal of the resettlement program was the "de-Polonization" and "de-Jewing" of the incorporated territories. All Jews and those Poles who stood out as political leaders were to be deported. Remaining Poles would undergo a racial screening; those judged racially sound would be used as agricultural labor in the Altreich. Skilled Polish workers in annexed territory would be gradually replaced by Germans. A certain number of unskilled Poles would remain in the region as menial laborers. All those not of economic use to the Reich would be deported. See Aly, "Final Solution," 40, 54nn44–45.

CHAPTER FOUR: THE 1.NAHPLAN: LOGISTICS, LIMITATIONS, AND LESSONS

1. Könekamp's emphasis. The Deutsches Ausland-Institut was a research institution devoted to both the study and the support of ethnic Germans living abroad. In February 1937, it, along with other think tanks involved in Volkstumspolitik, fell under the jurisdiction of VoMi chief Werner Lorenz. See Valdis O. Lumans, *Himmler's Auxiliaries: The Volksdeutsche Mittelstelle and the German National Minorities of Europe, 1933–1945* (Chapel Hill: University of North Carolina Press, 1993), 64.

2. Deutsches Ausland-Institut, "Umsiedlung der Polen aus dem neuen Reichsgebiet: Auszug aus dem Bericht von Dr. Könekamp—Polenfahrt vom 29.11 bis 9.12.39," December 1939, NARA/T81/273/VoMi 140/2393478ff. It should be pointed out that despite his overall favorable review of the evacuation process, Könekamp did concede that problems existed. For example, all individuals present in the designated homes at the time of eviction, including household personnel, were arrested, with those not included on the evacuation lists later having to be released. And in Litzmannstadt, a volksdeutsch civil servant, apparently working for the Nazis, found his own name on an evacuation list.

3. Aly states: "In view of the German crimes, its one of the greatest achievements of historians since World War II to have made the victims' perspective their own. Thus the view from the perpetrators' perspective is bound to be upsetting. But the subject matter—the decision-making process leading to the Holocaust—forces us to look inside the minds of the administrators and planners. *What to the victims must have seemed the horrible efficiency of the bureaucracy of death appeared very different in the eyes of the perpetrators. In the contemporary view of the deporters, the same story was seen as an unbroken series of defeats, an inability even to approach their goals, once established*" (emphasis mine). See Götz Aly, *"Final Solution": Nazi Population Policy and the Murder of the European Jews*, trans. Belinda Cooper and Allison Brown (London: Edward Arnold, 1999), 59. Here, Aly refers to the "de-Jewing" of the Reich and the various unrealistic deportation objectives connected with it. But his observations regarding the perpetrators' gloomy view of their so-called achievements is also valid in terms of the 1.Nahplan. Nazi functionaries, in this case, may have met their numerical objectives, but they were by no means pleased with the manner in which they did so.

4. Richter, "Bericht über die im Lodsch von 12.Dezember bis 16.Dezember durchgeführte Evakuierung von Polen und Juden," 16 December 1939, USHMM/RG15.015M/3/218/27–35.

5. The Ordnungspolizei (Orpo) encompassed all uniformed police forces, including the Schutzpolizei (municipal police), the rural gendarmerie (equivalent to county troopers), and Orpo police battalions (units with military training, equipment, and organization), as well as the Volksdeutsche Selbstschutz. (I would like to thank Peter Black, senior historian at the Center for Advanced Holocaust Studies, U.S. Holocaust Memorial Museum, for clarification on this matter.) See Christopher Browning, *Ordinary Men: Reserve Police Battalion 101 and the Final Solution in Poland* (New York: HarperCollins, 1992), 3–4.

6. SS-Obersturmbannführer Hermann Krumey, Rapp's transport officer at that time, served as the liaison man between the Staff for the Evacuation of Poles and Jews and the Reichsbahn. See "Aktenvermerk über die Referentenbesprechung bei SS-Sturmbannführer Rapp am 1.Dezember 1939," 1 December 1939, USHMM/RG15.015M/2/105/1–2.

7. Evacuation trains consisted primarily of unheated freight and cattle cars; coaches were provided for German escorts and sometimes for the sick and elderly. More "luxurious" travel accommodations were provided for one shipment of evacuees originating from Lankdreis Schrimm. It consisted of one passenger car with first- and second-class seats for forty-five people, thirteen with third-class seats for fifty people each, and ten freight cars for forty people each. This situation was, however, by no means the norm. See APP/Landrat Schrimm/100/32 (no provenance and no date but presumably December 1939).

8. See the extract from the "Erlass des Chefs des Distrikts Radom im Generalgouvernement für die besetzten Gebiete," 4 December 1939, in Kurt Pätzold, ed., *Verfolgung, Vertreibung, Vernichtung: Dokumente des faschistischen Antisemitismus, 1933 bis 1942* (Frankfurt, Germany: Röderberg-Verlag, 1984), doc. 219, pp. 251–252.

9. See the handwritten camp records, "Tägliche Eingänge von evakuierten Personen aus verschiedenen Kreisen, 1939–1940," APL/UWZ-L/11a/1–205. The total number of individuals who entered Glowno by 30 November was 2,767; some were no doubt released due to mistaken arrests. An additional 10,496 Polish evacuees, primarily from Posen, entered the camp between 1 and 17 December. Eleven evacuation trains stood at the disposal of Warthegau authorities on 1 December, three of which left Glowno that same day. All of these, according to the original travel plan, were bound for Lublin. See "Fahrplanordnung" for 1 to 12 December 1939, USHMM/ RG15.015M/3/197/1.

10. Zugwachtmeister und Transportführer Howein, "Bericht über den Verlauf des Evakuierten-Transportes I," 7 December 1939, USHMM/RG15.015M/3/202/2–3. For an example of an evacuation list, see APP/Landrat Schrimm/100/42. Lists included the name, date and place of birth, address, and occupation of each deportee, as well as his or her destination.

11. Zugwachtmeister und Transportführer Nehrkorn, "Bericht über den Evakuiertentransport am 1.12.39, 1:30 Uhr, von Glowno nach Ostrowiec," 7 December 1939, USHMM/ RG15.015M/3/202/3.

12. Haupwachtmeister und Transportführer Dünzl, "Fahrtverlauf des Abtransportes der aus dem Kreis Dietfurt evakuierten Polen nach Minsk-Mazow," 10 December 1939, AGK/Reichsstatthalter-Wartheland/293/13–16. Georg Hansen provides a discussion of the Germanization of place-names in Wartheland in his article "Damit wurde der Warthegau zum Exerzierplatz des praktischen Nationalsozialismus: Eine Fallstudie zur Politik der Einverleibung," in Christoph Klessmann, ed., *September 1939: Krieg, Besatzung, Widerstand in Polen* (Göttingen, Germany: Vandenhoeck & Ruprecht, 1989), 55–72. For more on transport problems during the 1.Nahplan, see "Beanstandungen bei den Dienststellen des Generalgouvernements auf Grund der Transportberichte, die durch den Transportführer einzureichen waren" (no provenance but presumably Rapp), 17 January 1940, USHMM/ RG15.015M/3/207/1–2.

13. Rapp, "Evakuierung der Polen und Juden—Transportmeldewesen," 4 December 1939, USHMM/RG15.015M/3/97/2–3.

14. Rapp, "Verantwortung der Transportführer für ihren Transportzug," 7 December 1939, USHMM/RG15.015M/1/96/3–5; Rapp to all Landräte and Oberbürgermeister, "Begleitkommandos der Evakuierungstransporte," 7 December 1939, USHMM/RG15.015M/3/197/4–5.

15. The camp records indicate that 3,233 Poles were taken to Glowno between 1 and 7 December, enough to fill three transports. See "Tägliche Eingänge von evakuierten Personen aus verschiedenen Kreise, 1939–1940," APL/UWZ-L/11a/1–205.

16. Strickner to Rapp, "Schwierigkeiten bei der Evakuierung," 8 December 1939, USHMM/RG15.015M/3/195/3.

17. Rapp, "Abtransport der Evakuierten," 8 December 1939, USHMM/RG15.015M/3/188/35.

18. Richter had first complained about the disappearance of this file in early December. In an undated report, he explained that a large card file had been compiled by the Gestapo during the first week of the September campaign and turned over to the SD on 9 September 1939. "What has happened to the lists," he said, "is unknown … only a fraction of them is still available." Beginning on 28 November, the SD, he stated, began formulating a new evacuation list with the objective of registering 15,000 members of the Polish intelligentsia. See Richter's report on the situation in Litzmannstadt (no date but presumably early December 1939), USHMM/RG15.015M/3/218/13–14.

19. Richter, "Bericht über die in Lodsch vom 12.Dezember bis zum 16.Dezember durchgeführte Evakuierung von Polen und Juden," 16 December 1939, USHMM/RG15.015M/3/218/27–35.

20. Ordensjunker Walther, "Auszugweise den Tätigkeitsbericht des Vorkommandos in Gnesen vom 18.12.1939," 18 December 1939, USHMM/RG15.015M/3/212/2.

21. See the affidavit of Dr. Hans Burckhardt, the Regierungspräsident of the district of Hohensalza, which lists all of the Landräte and Oberbürgermeister who operated in his jurisdiction, 4 September 1945, AGK/Greiser Trial/27/67–72.

22. One originated from Hohensalza and three from Litzmannstadt. See "Bericht über die vorbereitenden Massnahmen und die Durchführung der Evakuierung von Polen und Juden aus dem Reichsgau Wartheland in der Zeit von 1. bis 17.Dezember.1939 (no provenance but presumably Krumey), 19 January 1940, USHMM/RG15.015M/3/208/17–33; Krumey, "Bericht über die vorbereitenden Massnahmen der Evakuierung sowie über die Durchführung derselben aus den kreisfreien Städten und Landkreisen im Reichsgau Wartheland," 14 January 1939, USHMM/RG15.015M/3/208/13–16.

23. Rapp, "Erfahrungsbericht über die Umsiedlung von Polen und Juden aus dem Reichsgau 'Wartheland,'" 26 January 1940, NARA/T81/286/VoMi 322/2409574ff.

24. Der Reichsstatthalter-Warthegau to the Reich Ministry of the Interior (signed Coulon), "Evakuierungsmassnahmen im Reichsgau Wartheland" (draft), c. 9 February 1940, AGK/Reichsstatthalter-Warthegau/297/83–90.

25. Christopher Browning, *Nazi Policy, Jewish Workers, German Killers* (Cambridge: Cambridge University Press, 2000), 9–10. Icchak Rubin estimates that approximately 5,800 Jews were deported from Litzmannstadt during both the 1.Nahplan and the Zwischenplan; I regard this figure as far too low. See Icchak Rubin, *Żydki w łodzi pod Niemecką Okupacą 1939–1945* (London: Kontra, 1988), 180.

26. DAI, "Umsiedlung der Polen aus dem neuen Reichsgebiet: Auszug aus dem Bericht von Dr. Könekamp—Polenfahrt vom 29.11 bis 9.12.39," December 1939, NARA/T81/273/2393478ff.

27. Rapp's two comprehensive reports on the 1.nahplan were: "Abschiebung von Juden und Polen aus dem Warthegau: Erfahrungen aus dem bisherigen Ablauf der Aktion und Planung für die zukünftigen Transporte," 18 December 1939, in Szymon Datner, Janusz Gumkowski, and Kazimierz Leszczyński, eds., *Wysiedlanie ludności ziem Polskich wcielonych do Rzeszy:Biuletyn Głównej Komisji Badania Zbrodni Hitlerowskich w Polsce 12* (hereafter *Biuletyn 12*) (Warsaw: Wydawnictwo Prawnicze, 1960), doc. 8, pp. 22F–31F; "Erfahrungsbericht über die Umsiedlung von Polen und Juden aus dem Reichsgau 'Wartheland,'" 26 January 1940, NARA/T81/286/VoMi 322/2409574ff. Unless otherwise noted, all that follows in this section refers exclusively to these two documents.

28. In a 6 January 1940 circular to all Regierungspräsidenten, Landräte, and Oberbürgermeister in the Gau, HSSPF Koppe was careful to point out that the problems outlined here had occurred only in a few instances, implying that most Warthegau bureaucrats had done their best to follow the regulations that he and his subordinates had set. See HSSPF Koppe, "Herreichung eines Erfahrungsberichtes und der in den bisherigen Anordnungen des Höheren SS- und Polizeiführers Warthe geforderten Gesamtaufstellungen und Unterlagen," 6 January 1940, USHMM/RG15.015M/1/96/6–7.

29. Petzel (General der Artillerie and Wehrkreisbefehlshaber), "Wehrmacht und Polizei," 3 February 1940, USHMM/RG15.015M/3/166/1. Though beyond the scope of this study, Rapp's observations regarding the variations in performance and behavior between younger and older German bureaucrats, on the one hand, and younger and older German soldiers, on the other, raise interesting questions about generational attitudes toward racial policy that deserve further exploration and analysis.

30. See, for example, HSSPF Wartheland, copy of 17 December 1939 report by the Gendarmerieabteilung Dobra, in Kreis Turek, "Evakuierungstransport nach Bochnia," 10 January 1940, USHMM/RG15.015M/3/202/8–9. In this case, Polish railway workers, presumably in the Generalgouvernement, refused to provide coal and water for an evacuation train, thus delaying its journey. Although 9,298 Germans comprised the leading personnel of the Ostbahn in early 1940, the system was staffed by 36,640 Polish workers. By late 1943, the Ostbahn employed 145,000 Poles and a few thousand Ukrainians, but it was still run by only 9,000 Germans. See Raul Hilberg, *The Destruction of the European Jews*, 3rd ed. (New Haven, CT, and London: Yale University Press, 2003), 1: 200. In addition and much to the consternation of Rapp, the Ostbahn, as well as the Wehrmacht, sometimes requisitioned evacuation trains for its own purposes. As a result, only five of the first eleven transports from the Warthegau returned to pick up more evacuees and then only after six to seven days. Thus, no evacuation trains were available between 3 and 5 December, and only two or three were available between 6 and 8 December. See Rapp, "Stellungsnahme zum Bericht des Herrn Regierungspräsidenten von Hohensalza betreffend Evakuierung," 9 January 1940, USHMM/RG15.015M/2/100/4–6; Krumey, "Bericht über die vorbereiten Massnahmen und die Durchführung der Evakuierung von Polen und Juden aus dem Reichsgau Wartheland in der Zeit von 1. bis 17. Dezember 1939," USHMM/RG15.015M/3/208/17–23.

31. See the extract from the 29 December 1939 report to Hans Frank "über das Schicksal der Vertriebenen nach ihrer Ankunft im 'Generalgouvernement,'" in Kurt Pätzold, ed., *Verfolgung, Vertriebung, Vernichtung: Dokumente des faschistischen Antisemitismus, 1933 bis 1942* (Frankfurt, Germany: Röderberg-Verlag, 1984), doc. 222, p. 254.

32. Polish Ministry of Information, *The Black Book of Poland* (New York: G. P. Putnam's Sons, 1942), 195.

33. Martin Broszat, *Nationalsozialistische Polenpolitik, 1939–1945* (Stuttgart, Germany: Deutsche Verlags-Anstalt, 1961), 43.

34. See the report on the 4 January 1940 meeting in Berlin concerning future deportation of Poles and Jews from the incorporated territories (Eichmann presiding), 8 January 1940, *Biuletyn 12*/doc. 12/37F–39F. As pointed out earlier, Rapp had officially ordered that deportation trains could—indeed should—be overloaded. The consequences of this order constituted but one of many problems that caused friction between Warthegau and Generalgouvernement authorities.

35. Heinrich Himmler, "Rede vor Gauleitern und Parteifunktionären am 29.2.1940," in Bradley K. Smith and Agnes F. Peterson, eds., *Geheimreden 1933 bis 1945 und andere Ansprachen* (Frankfurt, Germany: Propyläen Verlag, 1974), 137.

36. For other reports concerning transport deaths, see Polish Ministry of Information, *The Black Book of Poland*, 170ff.

37. Gestapo-Posen (gez. Bischoff), "Behandlung von Juden, die sich entgegen dem Umsiedlugsbefehl auf dem Gebiet des Deutschen Reiches befinden," 13 December 1939, APP/Landrat-Schrimm/100/35. This directive was transmitted verbally to the Jewish Council of Elders in each community in the Warthegau. According to its wording, it was aimed at the Polish population as well.

38. Der Polizeipräsident-Posen to the RFSS, "Erteilung von Wiedereinreisegenehmigung an evakuierte Polen durch militärische Dienststellen," 2 January 1940, AGK/Reichsstatthalter-Warthegau/299/40.

39. Landrat Konin, "Evakuierung," 6 January 1940, AGK/Reichsstatthalter-Warthegau/299/24.

40. Report of 26 January 1940, NARA/T81/VoMi 322/2409574ff. The "pestering" of Volksdeutschen sometimes occurred from afar. On 21 February 1940, the Regierungspräsident of Posen reported that a number of Poles had sent postcards to the ethnic Germans living in their former homes, informing the new occupants that they would soon return and that they held the Volksdeutschen responsible for the safekeeping of their property and valuables in the meantime. See Regierungspräsident-Posen, "Lagerbericht 16.Januar 1940–15.Februar 1940," 21 February 1940, APP/Reichsstatthalter-Warthegau/1828/93–114.

41. Hans Frank, *Das Diensttagebuch des deutschen Generalgouverneurs in Polen, 1939–1945*, ed. Werner Präg and Wolfgang Jacobmeyer (Stuttgart, Germany: Deutsche Verlags-Anstalt, 1975), entry for 19 January 1940, 93.

42. Der Reichsstatthalter, "Vermerk: Umsiedlung von Polen und Juden," 9 February 1940, AGK/Reichsstatthalter-Warthegau/297/81–82. Though execution supposedly awaited evacuees upon their return, I have found no evidence to indicate that many executions were actually carried out. In fact, some of the deportees who returned to Kreis Gos-

tingen in January 1940 were allowed to stay temporarily; others were simply sent back east without punishment. See the report by Commander of the Gendarmerie-Posen, "Bericht vom 16.Januar 1940," 16 January 1940, USHMM/RG15.015M/3/170/1.

43. Rapp, "Abschiebung von Polen und Juden aus dem Reichsgau 'Wartheland,'" 4 January 1940, AGK/Greiser Trial/13/32–33.

44. Wetzel and Hecht, "Die Frage der Behandlung der Bevölkerung der ehemaligen polnischen Gebiete nach rassenpolitischen Gesichtspunkten," 25 November 1939, NARA/ T74/9/57/38057ff. The problem of ethnic identification was compounded by the fact that large numbers of Poles were claiming to be Volksdeutschen in order to avoid deportation. In a 15 January 1940 letter to SS-Sturmbannführer Kasper Schwarzhuber, an officer based at Lager Glowno, Rapp brought this problem to light and stated unequivocally that an "independent confession is in no way a ticket for membership in German Volkstum or for an exemption from evacuation." See Rapp to Schwarzhuber, 15 January 1940, USHMM/ RG15.015M/3/188/39.

45. Report of 26 January 1940, NARA/T81/VoMi 322/2409574ff.

46. Report of 18 December 1939, *Biuletyn 12*/doc. 8/25F.

47. Ibid., 26F.

48. Ibid., 31F.

49. Oberlandesgerichtspräsident (gez. Froböss), "Evakuierung von ehemals polnischen Justizbediensten, die vorübergehenden Dienstleistung eingestellt," 6 December 1939, USHMM/RG15.015M/4/271/1–2.

50. For a large file of deferment requests by Jarotschin authorities, see APP/Landkreis Jarotschin/22. For the school commissioner's petition, see "Evakuierung polnischer Lehrkräfte," 19 December 1939, APP/Landkreis Jarotschin/22/4–25.

51. See, respectively, the letter from the Staatsarchiv to the Polizeipräsident-Posen, 17 November 1939, AGK/Reichsstatthalter-Warthegau/297/36–39; Apothekerkammer Wartheland to the Umsiedlungsamt-Posen, 2 March 1940, APP/SS-Ansiedlungsstab-Posen/101/8; Der Reichsstatthalter, "Vermeidung der Evakuierung polnischer Dienstkräfte," 1 October 1940, USHMM/RG15.015M/4/269/5–6; Dr. Spreng, "Zurückstellung des in wichtigen Betrieben unentberhlichen Personals von der Evakuierung," 8 January 1940, USHMM/ RG15.015M/4/268/6.

52. Rapp, "Zurückstellung von Angestellten und Arbeiter der Reichsbahndirektion Posen," 1 December 1939, USHMM/RG15.015M/4/268/1–2.

53. Der Präsident der Reichsbahndirektion Posen to Greiser, "Abschieben von polnischen Eisenbahnern," 30 December 1939, AGK/Reichsstatthalter-Warthegau/293/ 18–19v.

54. Hilberg, *The Destruction of the European Jews*, 1: 200 (no statistics provided for Wartheland itself).

55. Der Reichsstatthalter (gez. Dr. Spreng), "Zurückstellung des in der Wirtschaft unentbehrlichen Personals von der Evakuierung," 18 December 1939, AGK/Greiser Trial/36/525–526.

56. No provenance, no date (apparently issued by Dr. Spreng of Greiser's staff on 8 January 1940), USHMM/RG15.015M/4/268/7.

57. HSSPF Koppe, "Abschiebung von Juden und Polen aus den Reichsgau 'Wartheland,'" 10 November 1939, USHMM/RG15.015M/1/95/8–14; HSSPF-Posen, "Geheim! Abschiebung von Juden und Polen aus dem Reichsgau 'Warthe-Land,'" 12 November 1939, USHMM/RG15.015M/2/99/1–5.

58. The discrepancy of 10,000 is unexplained. Rapp stated that the missing reports were, for the most part, those from small or *judenfrei* (free of Jews) districts. Incidentally, just five days earlier, Rapp had described the total number of potential evacuees suggested by local civilian officials as "three times too high." He wanted to reduce the number to 220,000 in order to meet Koppe's demand for 300,000 deportation by the end of February 1940 (300,000 minus the 80,000 evacuated during the 1.Nahplan). See "Gesamtplanung der Evakuierungstransporte," 13 December 1939, USHMM/RG15.015M/3/197/6–7.

59. Report of 18 December 1939, *Biuletyn 12*/doc. 8/26F–31F

60. Ibid., 30F–31F.

61. Ibid., 31F.

CHAPTER FIVE: VOLKSDEUTSCHEN, POLES, AND JEWS: AN
ORDERING OF PRIORITIES

1. Chef der Sipo und des SD (gez. Heydrich), "Räumung in den Ostprovinzen," 21 December 1939, AGK/UWZ-L/5/ 83–84.

2. Chef der Sipo und des SD (gez. Heydrich), "Räumung in den Ostprovinzen," 21 December 1939, in Szymon Datner, Janusz Gumkowski, and Kazimierz Leszczyński, eds., *Wysiedlanie ludności ziem Polskich wcielonych do Rzeszy: Biuletyn Głównej Komisji Badania Zbrodni Hitlerowskich w Polsce 12* (hereafter *Biuletyn 12*) (Warsaw: Wydawnictwo Prawnicze, 1960), doc. 9, p. 32F.

3. Götz Aly, *"Final Solution": Nazi Population Policy and the Murder of the European Jews*, trans. Belinda Cooper and Allison Brown (London: Edward Arnold, 1999), 64–66.

4. Eichmann note concerning a meeting with Gestapo chief Heinrich Müller, 6 October 1939, quoted in Christopher Browning, *Nazi Policy, Jewish Workers, German Killers* (Cambridge: Cambridge University Press, 2000), 7

5. See Seev Goshen, "Eichmann und die Nisko-Aktion im Oktober 1939," *Vierteljahrshefte für Zeitgeschichte* 27, no. 1 (January 1981): 74–96; Jonny Moser, "Nisko: The First Experiment in Deportation," *Simon Wiesenthal Center Annual* 2 (1985): 1–30; Miroslav Karny, "Nisko in der Geschichte der Endlösung," *Judaica Bohemiae* 23 (1987): 69–84.

6. For an overview of Eichmann's career before 21 December 1939, see David Cesarani, *Becoming Eichmann: Rethinking the Life, Crimes, and Trial of a "Desk Murderer"* (Cambridge, MA: Da Capo Press, 2006), 36–81; Hans Safrian, *Eichmann und seine Gehilfen* (Frankfurt, Germany: Fischer Taschenbuch Verlag, 1997), 9–86; Heinz Höhne, *The Order of the Death's Head: The Story of Hitler's SS*, trans. Richard Barry (New York: Ballantine Books, 1971), 378ff. In addition, Hannah Arendt's *Eichmann in Jerusalem: A Report on the Banality of Evil* (New York: Viking Press, 1964) remains a noteworthy work on Eichmann's life.

7. See Karl Heinz Roth, "'Generalplan Ost'—'Gesamtplan Ost,' Forschungsstand, Quellenprobleme, neue Ergebnisse," in Mechthild Rössler and Sabine Schleiermacher, eds., *Der "Generalplan Ost": Hauptlinien der nationalsozialistischen Planungs- und Vernichtungspolitik* (Berlin: Akademie-Verlag, 1993), 85n64; also Ehlich's testimony at Nuremberg, 28 October 1947, Case 8, NARA/M894/2/572ff.

8. Nazi ethnocrats initially expected 120,000 immigrants: 65,000 from Volhynia; 46,000 from Galicia; and 9,000 from the Narev region. Some 36,000, primarily women, children, the elderly, and the sick, were supposed to arrive by train, and 84,000 were to make the journey by road. See Koppe, "Umsiedlung Wolhynien and Galizien," 21 December 1939, USHMM/RG.15.015M/2/130/1–3.

9. For the articles of the German-Soviet resettlement treaty, signed on 3 November 1939, see AGK/RG838/EWZ-L/75/25–34. The treaty imposed strict limitations on the property Volksdeutschen could transport out of Soviet territory. Although the settlers were allowed to take livestock with them, this was restricted to no more than two horses, a pair of oxen, one cow, one pig, five sheep or goats, and ten birds per family. The transport of carrier pigeons, interestingly enough, was banned. Additional regulations placed restrictions on currency, precious metals, jewelry, artworks, arms, occupational machinery, and even personal sewing machines.

10. One camp with facilities for 30,000 immigrants was established within the city itself, and the other two were set up in the suburbs of Żgierz and Pabianice. The suburban camps could accommodate 20,000 and 15,000, respectively. See Chef der Sipo und des SD, EWZ-Nordost, Posen, "Aktenvermerk: Organisation und personalle Fragen bei der Erfassung der Wohlhynien- und Galiziendeutschen," 4 December 1939, AGK/CAMSW167/RuSHA/1/1–3.

11. Lumans claims the first resettlement teams entered the Soviet zone on 9 December, crossing at Przemyśl; see Valdis O. Lumans, *Himmler's Auxiliaries: The Volksdeutsche Mittelstelle and the German National Minorities of Europe, 1933–1945* (Chapel Hill: University Press of North Carolina, 1993), 163. But according to Koppe, "Umsiedlung Wolhynien and Galizien," they did so on 8 December.

12. Aly, *"Final Solution,"* 42.

13. Lumans, *Himmler's Auxiliaries*, 163–164. Lumans claims 10,000 ethnic Germans died on the journey, citing the Nazi propaganda publication (commissioned by the Reichsführer-SS) *Der Treck der Volksdeutschen aus Wolhynien, Galizien und dem Narew-Gebiet* (Berlin: Volk und Reich Verlag, 1941), 9. There probably were many deaths, but the figure of 10,000 is almost certainly an exaggeration.

14. Heinrich Himmler, "Rede vor Gauleitern und Parteifunktionären am 29.2.40," in *Geheimreden 1933 bis 1945 und andere Ansprachen*, ed. Bradley K. Smith and Agnes F. Peterson (Frankfurt, Germany: Propyläen Verlag, 1974), 137.

15. Greiser later stated that more than 75 percent of all workers among the Volhynian, Galician, and Narev German immigrants were farm owners, agricultural administrators, and farmhands. See Der Reichsstatthalter, "Ansiedlung von Wolhynien- und Galiziendeutschen," 1 March 1940, AGK/Greiser Trial/36/549.

16. Chef der Sipo und des SD, "2.Nahplan," 21 December 1939, USHMM/RG15.015M/2/99/10–16. It is not clear exactly why Heydrich shifted the focus of the deportation

campaign back to Jews, but it seems reasonable to assume that his new orders were intended to meet Himmler's demand, stated in RKFDV Anordnung 1/II of 30 October 1939, for the expulsion of the entire Jewish population of the incorporated territories. Adolf Eichmann, the SD expert on the Jewish Question who had just been appointed chief of RSHA Amt IVR, may have had some say in the matter as well.

17. As discussed in the following chapter, the Nazis intended to create a deep belt of German farms along the eastern border of the incorporated territories to serve as a defensive barrier—an Ostwall—of "German flesh and blood" against the Slavic population of the East. Apparently, the deportation of the 10,000 Danzig–West Prussian Poles was geared toward the realization of this scheme.

18. It is interesting that Heydich seemed more concerned with providing employment for Poles rather than for the thousands of Volksdeutschen who would begin arriving just two days later.

19. Koppe, "Räumung in den Ostprovinzen: Hier—Umsiedlung der Juden," 14 January 1940, USHMM/RG15.015M/2/98/1–4.

20. Chef der Sipo und des SD, "2.Nahplan."

21. Ibid.

22. Within a week of the meeting, Warthegau officials had concluded that the figure of 200,000 Jewish evacuees was far too low. Rather, a grand total of 317,000 Jews were to be expelled from the Gau: 280,000 from Litzmannstadt and 37,000 from Hohensalza; Posen, for its part, was declared "practically judenfrei." See "Bericht über die Besprechung am 11.Januar 1940 10 Uhr," 11 January 1940, USHMM/RG15.015M/2/146/9–15.

23. See the "Vermerk" on the RSHA conference of 4 January, 8 January 1940, Biuletyn 12/doc. 12/37F–39F. One must keep in mind that this report did not represent concrete orders for action; it was merely a summary of the topics discussed at the meeting. But if the participants' calculations and suggestions had been incorporated into a revised 2.Nahplan, the operation would have targeted 200,000 Jews from Wartheland, 120,000 to 125,000 from Upper Silesia, 30,000 from East Prussia (primarily from Zichenau), and 2,000 from Danzig–West Prussia; 90,000 Poles would also be deported—80,000 from the Warthegau and, as originally planned, 10,000 from Danzig–West Prussia.

24. Ibid.

25. Hans Frank, Das Diensttagebuch des deutschen Generalgouverneurs in Polen, 1939–1945, ed. Werner Präg and Wolfgang Jacobmeyer (Stuttgart, Germany: Deutsche Verlags-Anstalt, 1975), entry for 19 January 1940, 95. At least one Warthegau official, incidentally, would make a complaint of a similar nature. On 18 January 1940, the Regierungspräsident of Posen protested that the Polizeipräsident of Gotenhafen had, on his own initiative, deported Poles from his jurisdiction to Posen on the grounds that the Poles in question were Posen natives and did not belong in Danzig–West Prussia. See Regierungspräsident-Posen (Bleschke), "Zuzug von Polen aus dem Reichsgau Danzig-Westpreussen," 18 January 1940, APP/Landrat-Grätz/23/1. This situation is yet another illustration of the competition and administrative chaos within the Nazi establishment. It seems that many officials in the East, being first and foremost careerists who wanted to

advance within the ranks of the Nazi hierarchy, focused their activities and attention almost exclusively on the management of their own narrow jurisdictions and were little interested in what went on elsewhere or the success of occupation policy as a whole.

26. RSHA IVD4-IIIES, "Besprechung am 30.Januar.1940," 30 January 1940, *Biuletyn 12*/doc. 22/66F–75F.

27. Überprüfungsstelle (SS-Untersturmführer Strickner), "Arbeitsanweisung für Abteilung III (Evakuierungslisten)," 6 January 1940, AGK/Greiser Trial/36/523.

28. Martin Broszat, *Nationalsozialistische Polenpolitik, 1939–1945* (Stuttgart, Germany: Deutsche Verlags-Anstalt, 1961), 122.

29. Der Reichsstatthalter (Dr. Coulon) to all Landräte and Stadtkommissare, "Evakuierungen," 5 January 1940, AGK/Reichsstatthalter-Warthegau/293/22–22v. On 18 January, Rapp confirmed that the scope of the 2.Nahplan would be enlarged to include Polish "a-social elements" and Poles convicted of crimes. Still, evacuation was to be no replacement for punishment. A plan, he said, had to be worked out with the Generalgouvernement whereby the punishment of offenders would be carried out in the East following their expulsion from the Warthegau. See Rapp, "Evakuierung rechtkräftig verurteiler Polen vor Strafsverbüssung," 18 January 1940, USHMM/RG15.015M/3/209/8–9.

30. Koppe, "Räumung in den Ostprovinzen: Hier—Umsiedlung der Juden," 14 January 1940.

31. This figure was soon raised to 120,000.

32. RSHA IIIES-IVR, "Vermerk! Zwischenlösung zum 2.Nahplan," 17 January 1940, USHMM/RG15.015M/8/103/3–5.

33. In German, the "Amt für die Umsiedlung der Polen und Juden" (the name is sometimes rendered "Amt für die Umsiedlung von Polen und Juden"). The evolution from "staff" to "office" indicated that Rapp's agency now employed more personnel than before and had grown in terms of its managerial and organizational capability.

34. Evidently, these branch offices had been previously established to handle the evacuation of Jews from the cities in question.

35. HSSPF Koppe, "Umsiedlung der Polen und Juden: Hier—Zwischenplan," 20 January 1940, AGK/UWZ-L/5/105–108. It seems that these new orders surprised SD officials in Wartheland. On 20 January, SS-Obersturmführer Rudolf Barth, the leader of the Litzmannstadt branch of Rapp's office, was still operating under the assumption that the 2.Nahplan—the comprehensive evacuation of Jews—remained in effect. See Barth to Rapp, "Vorbereitung für zukünftige Judenevakuierungen," 20 January 1940, USHMM/RG15.015M/2/99/34–36.

36. Seidl, "Besprechung zwischen SS-H'Stuf. Eichmann und SS-Hauptscharführer Seidl am 22. und 23.Januar 1940 in Berlin—Kurfürstenstrasse 116," 25 January 1940, USHMM/RG15.015M/2/107/44–45.

37. Krumey, "Bericht über die am 26.und 27.1.1940 in Leipzig stattgefunde Fahrplanbesprechung," 30 January 1940, USHMM/RG15.015M/1/96/14–15.

38. Siedl, "Besprechung zwischen SS-H'Stuf. Eichmann und SS-Hauptscharführer Seidl"; also see Aly, *"Final Solution,"* 67.

39. Rapp, "Evakuierung von Polen," 29 February 1940, USHMM/RG15.015M/3/198/6–7.

40. The final report on the 2.Nahplan includes data on the Zwischenplan. See UWZ-Posen, Dienststelle-Litzmannstadt (gez. Krumey), "Abschlussbericht über die Aussiedlung im Rahmen der Wolhynien-, Galizien- und Cholmerdeutschen (2.Nahplan) im Reichsgau Wartheland, 1940," c. 20 January 1941, NARA/T81/286/VoMi 323/2409604ff. I am unaware of an independent final report on the Zwischenplan.

41. RSHA IVD4-IIIES, "Besprechung am 30.Januar 1940," 30 January 1940, 68F–69F.

42. Major der Schupo und Verbindungsoffizier (signature illegible), "Bericht: Mündliche Besprechung über besonders zu beachtende Punkte bei der Abschiebung von Polen und Juden," 31 January 1940, USHMM/RG15.015M/96/16–17. This report, which covered a series of meetings held in late January between the Schupo officer and a number of Landräte and Oberbürgermeister, indicated that almost all of the local officials concerned had complained that many Poles evacuated in December had since returned to the Warthegau. It was agreed that these individuals would be sent back to the Generalgouvernement, either at their own expense or on the forthcoming transports.

43. RSHA IVD4-IIIES, "Besprechung am 30.Januar 1940," 30 January 1940, 69F.

44. Often brutal and undisciplined, the vast majority of the Warthegau Volksdeutsche Selbstschutz had been disarmed by order of the RFSS on 14 December 1939. Thereafter, they were to be outfitted with weapons by the Ordnungspolizei only when necessary. See Befehlshaber-Orpo (Posen), "Tagesordnung vom 27.12.39," AGK/Befehlshaber-Orpo/RG717/1/23–26. Still, select units of the Warthegau Selbstschutz continued to operate (apparently with their own weapons) until April 1940; see Christian Jansen and Arno Weckbecker, Der "Volksdeutsche Selbstschutz" in Polen 1939/40 (Munich, Germany: R. Oldenbourg Verlag, 1992), 195.

45. Rapp, "Evakuierungstransporte im Rahmen des Zwischenplans," 6 February 1940, USHMM/RG15.015M/1/96/23–25.

46. Major der Schupo und Verbindungsoffizier, "Bericht: Mündliche Besprechung."

47. Rapp, "Evakuierungstransporte im Rahmen des Zwischenplans," 16–17. This transport almost certainly carried inmates from Lager Glowno who had been evicted during the previous weeks. Ostbanhof-Posen was—and still is—situated very near the site of the camp.

48. See the report sent to Koppe by the Office for the Resettlement of Poles and Jews regarding the evictions of 10 February in Posen, "Meldebogen für die Räumungsaktionen," 11 February 1940, APL/UWZ-L/16I/1–3. The condition of the homes was evaluated either as "good," "inferior," or "poor—uninhabitable." Archiwum Państwowe Łódź contains many additional police reports regarding evictions and arrests carried out during the Zwischenplan, which can be found in the records of the UWZ-Litzmannstadt/16I/1–71 and 16II/1–101. The reports indicate that the evictions generally followed along the same lines as the action discussed earlier. However, most evictions in February 1940 occurred in the morning: the police usually struck at about 6:30 A.M., and the homes were, as a rule, cleared by 7:30 A.M. Beginning in March, the trend shifted to the evening hours. The reports also discuss the confiscation of valuables. In most cases, the police seized nothing whatso-

ever (apparently because the Poles had nothing worth taking), though now and again they managed to secure titles and certificates and particularly bankbooks.

49. Amt für die Umsiedlung von Polen und Juden (signed Blenk), "Statistik über die Güte der zu evakuierenden Wohnungen," 20 January 1940, USHMM/RG15.015M/1/7/14. Some 26.3 percent were declared average.

50. VoMi-Posen, "Protokoll über die Besprechung der Abteilungsleiter vom 13.Februar 1940," APP/VoMi-Posen/23/87–89.

51. See "Polizeiverordnung über die Wohn- und Aufenthaltsrechte der Juden," *Lodscher Zeitung*, 9 February 1940. The geographic parameters of the ghetto had been set the previous day.

52. Raul Hilberg, *The Destruction of the European Jews*, 3rd ed. (New Haven, CT, and London: Yale University Press, 2003), 1: 223–224, 230.

53. The map entitled "Die Wohngebiete der Juden und Polen," published in the 11–12 February 1940 issue of the *Lodscher Zeitung*, illustrates the new ethnic layout of the city.

54. VoMi-Posen, "Protokoll über die Besprechung der Abteilungsleiter vom 16.Februar 1940," APP/VoMi-Posen/23/92–95. Generalgouverneur Frank had other grievances as well. On 22 February, Greiser reported that Frank was once again complaining about the arrival of "illegal" transports (that is, transports not scheduled for the Zwischenplan) of Poles and Jews in his domain. The RFSS, Greiser stated, had ordered that all such transports had to cease, since they would "bring increasing disorder to the entire organization of the evacuations." Anyone who violated this order was answerable to the RFSS. See Greiser's letter to the Regierungspräsidenten of the Warthegau (gez. Melhorn), 22 February 1940, APP/Landrat-Grätz/37/6.

55. VoMi-Posen, "Protokoll über die Besprechung der Abteilungsleiter vom 5.März 1940," APP/VoMi-Posen/23/118–119. The minutes stated Rapp had ordered that "only a-social elements" could be evacuated during the operation, but unless he was extending the definition of *a-social* to include "political undesirables," this almost certainly represented a misunderstanding of his orders. The "a-social problem" was, as one Nazi saw it, particularly acute in Posen. On 5 March, Oberbürgermeister Scheffler informed HSSPF Koppe that immediately after the conclusion of the Zwischenplan, he wanted to deport "a-social" Polish families who were presently residing in dugouts, "holes in the ground," and shanties within the city. An estimated 1,060 families (4,423 people), he said, were then living in such conditions, and an additional 911 families (4,550 people) were living in the old forts and barracks surrounding Posen. The evacuation of these people was most urgent, he argued, since almost all were "a-socials." (Generally speaking, the term was applied to anyone who exhibited "un-German" behavior, be he or she a beggar, a prostitute, a criminal, or simply a "work-shy" individual; living in a hole in the ground was obviously something no good German would ever do.) See Scheffler's letter to Koppe, 5 March 1940, USHMM/RG15.015M/3/153/1–2.

56. Krumey, "Vermerk über eine Besprechung bei der Reichsbahn-Direktion Posen am Vormittag des 15.2.1940 über Ferngespräche mit der RBD-Bahnrat Kukielka," 16 February 1940, AGK/Reichsstatthalter-Warthegau/297/92–93.

57. Döring circular to all Regierungspräsidenten, Landräte, and Oberbürgermeister in the Warthegau, 21 February 1940, USHMM/RG15.015M/3/198/5.

58. See the draft of Rapp's telegram to Eichmann, "Zuteilung von 5 neuen Transportzügen," 7 March 1940, USHMM/RG15.015M/1/96/37–38.

59. See the "Aktenvermerk" regarding Eichmann's telephone call (signature illegible), 11 March 1940, USHMM/RG15.015M/3/197/27.

60. Quoted in Aly, *"Final Solution,"* 98 and 103n78.

61. See the updated transport schedule for the "second part" (22 February 1940 to 15 March 1940) of the Zwischenplan. All of the twenty-nine transport lists were checked, implying that they did, in fact, proceed east according to plan; see USHMM/RG15.015M/3/197/24 (undated). Incidentally, VoMi agents were, at least for a while, operating under the assumption that the transport halt would last until the beginning of March. See VoMi-Posen, "Protokoll über die Besprechung der Abteilungsleiter vom 23.Februar. 1940," APP/VoMi-Posen/23/105.

62. UWZ-Posen, Dienststelle-Litzmannstadt (gez. Krumey), "Abschlussbericht über die Aussiedlung."

63. We do know that 1,200 Jews from Kreis Konin were transported to Litzmannstadt on 3 March 1940, and 421 subsequently arrived in Krakau on March 7. See Christopher Browning, *The Origins of the Final Solution: The Evolution of Jewish Policy, September 1939–March 1942* (Lincoln: University Press of Nebraska, 2004), 64.

64. Der Reichsstatthalter (gez. Coulon), "Evakuierungen," 5 January 1940, AGK/Reichsstatthalter-Warthegau/293/22–22v.

65. No provenance, "Bericht über die Besprechung am 11.Januar 1940 10 Uhr," 11 January 1940, USHMM/RG15.015M/2/146/9–15.

66. As of 11 January 1940, plans for the evacuation of all Jews from the incorporated territories were still in effect.

67. "Bericht über die Besprechung am 11.Januar 1940 10 Uhr," 11 January 1940, USHMM/RG15.015M/2/146/9–15. Kendzia also served as the leader of Wartheland's *Landesarbeitsamt* (Agricultural Labor Office).

68. Ibid.

69. Ibid. (emphasis mine). As of 30 January 1940, Warthegau officials had offered to send an additional 20,000 Polish officers to the Altreich. Their offer notwithstanding, Heydrich decreed that "it is necessary to take without compromise *all* Poles from the eastern Gaue who are eligible [to serve] as farm hands [in the Reich proper]." The number of Polish farmhands needed in the Altreich was now placed at 1 million. See "Besprechung am 30.Januar 1940," *Biuletyn* 12/doc. 22/70F. Exactly how many Poles from the incorporated territories were immediately sent west is undocumented, but by July 1940, 126,000 had been transported to the Altreich. See Werner Röhr, Elke Heckert, Bernd Gottberg, Jutta Wenzel, and Heide-Marie Grünthal, eds., *Die faschistische Okkupationspolitik in Polen (1939–1945)*, vol. 2 of *Nacht über Europa: Die Okkupationspolitik des deutschen Faschismus (1938–1945)*, Achtbändige Dokumentenedition, ed. Wolfgang Schumann and Ludwig Nestler (Cologne, Germany: Pahl-Rugenstein, 1989), table 6, 130 (no figures provided for Wartheland itself).

70. "Sitzung über Ostfragen unter dem Vorsitz des Ministerpräsidenten Generalfeldmarschall Göring" (gez. Dr. Gramsch), 12 February 1940, International Military Tribunal, *Trial of the Major War Criminals before the International Military Tribunal, Nuremberg, 14 November 1945–1 October 1946*, 42 vols. (hereafter *IMT*) (Nuremberg, Germany: International Military Tribunal, 1947–1949), doc. 305-EC, 36: 299–307.

71. Browning, *The Origins of the Final Solution*, 62.

72. "Sitzung über Ostfragen unter dem Vorsitz des Ministerpräsidenten Generalfeldmarschall Göring." The record of the conference does not indicate how the others reacted to Himmler's arguments, but Frank left the meeting believing Göring had prevailed. No evacuations to the Generalgouvernement, he now assumed, could take place without his personal approval. What is more, he was convinced that for all intents and purposes, the regime's sweeping program of "ethnic distribution" had been scrapped. Three weeks later, he wrote: "In general, the great resettlement ideas have been given up. The idea that one could gradually transport 7 ½ million Poles to the Generalgouvernement has been fully abandoned. It is now only a question of the transfer of some 100,000–120,000 Poles, some 30,000 Gypsies, and a still to be determined number of Jews from the Reich, because the final goal shall be to make the German Reich free of Jews." However, three months later, Hitler reaffirmed Himmler's control over all matters related to resettlements and deportations and ratified the RFSS memo entitled "Some Thoughts on the Treatment of the Alien Population in the East," which reiterated the goal of deporting the entire Polish population of the incorporated territories (with the exception of 1 million "Poles" who could be "re-Germanized"). For discussion of Himmler's memo, written in May 1940, see the following chapter. Frank is quoted—and his interpretation of the Carinhall meeting is discussed—in Browning, *The Origins of the Final Solution*, 62–63.

73. See Koppe's letter to the Regierungspräsidenten (to be relayed to all Landräte and Oberbürgermeister in their jurisdictions), 24 January 1940, AGK/Reichsstatthalter-Warthegau/293/24.

74. Kendzia, "Einschaltung bei der Evakuierungen," 9 January 1940, AGK/Greiser Trial/36/515–516.

75. See Der Reichsführer-SS/Reichskommissar für die Festigung deutschen Volkstums, *Der Menscheneinsatz: Grundsätze, Anordnung und Richtlinien* (hereafter *Der Menscheneinsatz*) (Berlin: Hauptabteilung des RKFDV, 1940), 104, 110, NARA/T81/VoMi 802/2435422ff. One must also keep in mind that not all of this minute ethnic German industrial labor force was resettled in Wartheland; some of the skilled workers were placed in the Altreich, and others found homes in Silesia and Danzig–West Prussia. According to *Der Menscheneinsatz*, 24,096 of the Baltic German immigrants and 62,848 of those from Volhynia, Galicia, and the Narev region were considered "active workers." In terms of the former, 5,324 of those who received employment by 31 March 1940 were placed in the agricultural sector; 6,726 were employed in the industrial sector; and the remainder were employed primarily as merchants, doctors, bureaucrats, and health-care workers. In the case of the latter, 48,062 were farmers; 9,968 were industrial workers; and the rest were free professionals, utility and healthcare workers, and household helpers.

76. Die Rüstungsinspektion des Wehrkreises XXI, "Geschichte des Kreigseinsatzes der Rüstungsinspektion des Wehrkreises XXI. Teil II. 1/10/40–31/12/41" (presumably January 1941), NARA/T77/620/1807804ff.

77. Die Rüstungsinspektion des Wehrkreises XXI, "Geschichte des Kreigseinsatz der Rüstungsinspektion des Wehrkreises XXI. Teil III. 1/1/42–31/5/42" (presumably June 1942), NARA/T77/620/1807931ff.

78. RSHA IVD4-IIIES, "Bespechung am 30.Januar 1940," 30 January 1940, 66F–75F.

79. UWZ-Posen, Dienststelle-Litzmannstadt (gez. Krumey), "Abschlussbericht über die Aussiedlung."

80. Browning, *The Origins of the Final Solution*, 65.

81. Walter Hewel of the German Foreign Office reported that on 12 March 1940, Hitler remarked that "the Jewish question really was a space question which was difficult to solve, particularly for him, since he had no space at his disposal. Neither would the establishment of a Jewish state around Lublin ever constitute a solution as even there the Jews lived too close together to be able to attain a somewhat satisfactory standard of living." See ibid., 68.

82. Christopher Browning, *The Path to Genocide: Essays on Launching the Final Solution* (Cambridge: Cambridge University Press, 1992), 9.

CHAPTER SIX: THE 2.NAHPLAN

1. See Dr. Rüdiger, "Bericht über die bisherigen Arbeiten der Kommission des DAI für die Dokumentation der Umsiedlungen," 21 April 1940, NARA/T81/373/DAI 164/5108801ff. Rüdiger pointed out that the last line has a double meaning.

2. Rapp, "Abschiebung von Juden und Polen aus dem Warthegau: Erfahrungen aus dem bisherigen Ablauf der Aktion und Planung für die zukünftigen Transporte," 18 December 1939, in Szymon Datner, Janusz Gumkowski, and Kazimierz Leszczyński, eds., *Wysiedlanie ludności ziem Polskich wcielonych do Rzeszy: Biuletyn Głównej Komisji Badania Zbrodni Hitlerowskich w Polsce Biuletyn Głównej Komisji Badania Zbrodni Hitlerowskich w Polsce 12* (hereafter *Biuletyn 12*) (Warsaw: Wydawnictwo Prawnicze, 1960), doc. 12, p. 31F.

3. Though Nazi racial experts certainly recognized a distinction between Volhynian, Galician, and Narev Germans, they generally employed the term *Volhynian Germans* to refer to all three groups. For the sake of simplicity, I will do the same unless otherwise noted.

4. Daniel Inkelas, "Visions of Harmony and Violence: RKF Landscape Planning and Population Policy in Annexed Poland, 1939–1944" (Northwestern University: Ph.D. diss., 1998), 83–89.

5. Ibid., 106.

6. According to Meyer, the Wartheland bridge would run from the Kreise of Birnbaum and Neutomischel (later renamed Grätz) in the west; eastward through Posen-Land, Schrimm, Wreschen, Konin, and Kolo; and on to the industrial region of Litzmannstadt.

7. RFSS-RKFDV, Planungshauptabteilung (Meyer), "Planungsgrundlagen für den Aufbau der Ostgebiete" (undated), NARA/T74/15/109/386668ff. Karl Heinz Roth dates the memorandum 24 January 1940; see his "'Generalplan Ost'—'Gesamtplan Ost'": Forschungsstand, Quellenprobleme, neue Ergebnisse," in Mechthild Rössler and Sabine Schleiermacher, eds., *Der "Generalplan Ost": Hauptlinien der nationalsozialistischen Planungs- und Vernichtungspolitik* (Berlin: Akademie Verlag, 1993), 90–91n217.

8. According to Greiser, the placement of the volksdeutsch families would proceed as follows: Wielum, 1,500; Lask, 1,600; Sieradsch, 1,700; Turek, 1,900; Lodsch-Land, 800; Lentschütz, 1,300; Kutno, 1,500; Gostynin, 2,000; Leslau, 1,700; Konin, 2,100; and Nessau, 400.

9. Der Reichsstatthalter (gez. Greiser), "Ansiedlung von Wolhynien und Galizien-deutschen," 1 March 1940, APP/Landrat-Schrimm/206/28–34.

10. Rüdiger, "Bericht über die bisherigen Arbeiten der Kommission." Rüdiger soon learned from his coworker, Dr. Walter Quiring, a DAI official stationed at the EWZ office in Litzmannstadt, that the Umwanderung-Zentrale had been established. See the two-page supplement later attached to the Rüdiger report discussed previously, NARA/T81/373/DAI 164/5108657ff.

11. RSHA IIIES (Ehlich), "Errichtung von Umwanderungszentralstellen" (undated), USHMM/RG15.007M/8/103/6–13. At that time, Ehlich wanted to dispatch UWZ advisers to the SD-Abschnitten in Allenstein (for Zichenau), Thorn (for Danzig–West Prussia), Kattowitz (for Upper Silesia), and Hohensalza and Litzmannstadt (for Wartheland). None were necessary at the SD-Leitabschnitt in Posen, he argued, since the forthcoming evacuations would take place in the eastern part of the Warthegau. Each SD-Abschnitt was to establish at least one camp for the purpose of examining Poles. The contents of Ehlich's memo (or one similar to it) were discussed at the RSHA meeting of 30 January 1940 (see the discussion later in this chapter), though Aly claims that Heydrich did not receive Ehlich's proposals until 2 February; Götz Aly, *"Final Solution": Nazi Population Policy and the Murder of the European Jews*, trans. Belinda Cooper and Allison Brown (London: Edward Arnold, 1999), 47.

12. Rassenpolitisches Amt (Wetzel and Hecht), "Die Frage der Behandlung der Bevölkerung der ehemaligen polnischen Gebiete nach rassenpolitischen Gesichtspunkten," 25 November 1939, NARA/T74/9/57/388057iff.

13. These racially valuable Polish parents—or, as the Nazis viewed them, Polonized Germans—were to undergo a process of re-Germanization once in the Altreich. Not until they proved their loyalty to the Reich could they be used as human building blocks in the creation of a New Order in the East. As Ulrich Griefelt made clear in late 1941, "only the best" Germans—that is, those who were unquestionably German in mind, body, and blood—could serve as racial pioneers. See Ulrich Greifelt, *Die Festigung deutschen Volkstums als zentrale Ostaufgabe* (pamphlet, undated but presumably late 1941 or early 1942), p. 4, NARA/T74/10/381802ff.

14. Himmler, "Einige Gedanken über die Behandlung der Fremdvölkischen im Osten," 20 May 1940, NARA/T175/119/2646113ff. Himmler believed that it was from "Nordic elements" among the Polish masses that the Polish ruling class tended to recruit itself. See, for example, RFSS-RKFDV (gez. Greifelt) order to the Higher SS- and Police Leaders, 3

July 1940, in Der Reichsführer-SS/Reichskommissar für die Festigung deutschen Volkstums, *Der Menscheneinsatz: Grundsätze, Anordnung und Reichtlinien* (hereafter *Der
Menscheneinsatz*) (Berlin: Hauptabteilung des RKFDV, 1940), 54–55, NARA/T81/VoMi
802/2435422ff. The goal of the racial selection process as defined in this directive was "on
the one hand, to supply racially-valuable families for German labor allocation and, on the
other, to deprive Polish Volkstum of those families determined to be Nordic."

15. RFSS, memo of 28 May 1940, NARA/M894/14/NO-1881 (English transcript).

16. The Madagascar project will be discussed in greater detail later in this and the
next chapter.

17. Quoted in Aly, *"Final Solution,"* 89.

18. Quoted in Christopher Browning, *The Path to Genocide: Essays on Launching
the Final Solution* (Cambridge: Cambridge University Press, 1992), 17–18.

19. HSSPF-Posen (Döring), "Schreiben des RFSS vom 20.5.40," 29 May 1940,
USHMM/RG15.015M/2/251/1–3.

20. Indeed, Himmler asserted on 3 July 1940 that measures then under way to secure
the labor of re-Germanizable Poles—which he called "a problem of great ethno-political
importance"—should "not be carried out according to labor allocation requirements."
Granted, the economy, he implied, would certainly benefit from these measures, but the
overriding goal was simply to complete the process of re-Germanization as quickly as possible. See RFSS-RKFDV (gez. Greifelt) order to the Higher SS- and Police Leaders.

21. See the Gestapo-Berlin telegram (apparently to Gestapo-Posen) relayed to Koppe's
RKF deputy, SS Oberführer Hans Döring, 5 January 1940, USHMM/RG15.015M/2/146/1.

22. Rapp, "Vermerk über die Besprechung vom 30.1.40 in Berlin, Reichsicherheitshauptamt, für die Höhere SS- und Polizeiführer, Inspekteure der Sicherheitspolizei und des
SD und Sacharbeiter für die Evakuierung in den Ostgebieten," 1 February 1940, USHMM/
RG15.015M/2/109/1–3; RSHA IVD4-IIIES, "Besprechung am 30.Januar 1940," 30 January
1940, *Biuletyn* 12/doc. 22/66F–75F.

23. Chef der Sicherheitspolizei und des SD (gez. Dr. Best), "Errichtung einer Umwandererzentralstelle," 24 April 1940, AGK/UWZ-L/1/13–14. Rapp's "Office" operated under
the designation Umwanderungsstelle from 21 March 1940 until it was renamed Umwandererzentralstelle on 24 April. See Gestapo Staatspolizeistelle Hohensalza, "Zuständigkeitsregelung zur Durchführung der Evakuierungen von Fremdstämmigen im Warthegau," 17
July 1940, USHMM/RG15.015M/2/102/1–4. The agency was occasionally referred to as the
Umwandererstelle as well. Unless otherwise noted, I will henceforth refer to Rapp's "Office" or the Umwanderungsstelle as the UWZ.

24. Krumey, "Abschlussbericht über die Aussiedlungen im Rahmen der Ansetzung
der Wolhynien-, Galizien- und Cholmerdeutschen (2.Nahplan) im Reichsgau Wartheland,
1940," c. 20 January 1941, NARA/T81/286/VoMi 323/2409604ff (Krumey's emphasis).

25. Aly, *"Final Solution,"* 52.

26. See Wacław Szulc, ed., *Hitlerowski Aparat Wysiedleńczy w Polsce: Sylwetki
Głównych jego "Działaczy"* (Warsaw: Ministerstwo Sprawiedliwości, 1973), 39.

27. Chef der Sicherheitspolizei und des SD, UWZ-Posen (gez. Damzog), "Errichtung einer Umwandererzentralstelle," 21 May 1940, AGK/UWZ-L/1/18; Höppner's SS per-

sonnel file, NARA/BDC RG242/A3343/SSO-104A. Evidently, there was some confusion about this change in command. One day after Höppner's appointment, Ehlich contacted Posen, claiming that as he understood it, Hermann Krumey (the leader of the UWZ office in Litzmannstadt), not Höppner, was to take over command of the Posen office. Ehlich requested an immediate clarification on this matter. See RSHA Amt IIIB to UWZ-Posen (gez. Ehlich), 22 May 1940, USHMM/RG15.015M/1/49/1–2. Höppner responded on 1 June, stating that for administrative reasons, Damzog did not think it was possible for Krumey to serve as chief; Krumey, it was implied, held a crucial position as leader of the Litzmannstadt office, and moreover, the Posen main office would not be moved to Litzmannstadt. Thus, Höppner retained his position. See UWZ-Posen (Höppner), "SS-Obersturmbannführer Krumey," 1 June 1940, USHMM/RG15.015M/1/49/2–3. This correspondence did not explain why Posen should remain the central headquarters of the UWZ when the focus of deportation activity had by then shifted to Litzmannstadt; I can only surmise that the UWZ main office remained in Posen because Posen was the capital and administrative center of the Warthegau.

28. As of 1 April 1940, the UWZ Aussenstellen and their leaders were as follows: Gostynin, SS-Untersturmführer Joseph Peters; Lask, SS-Hauptsturmführer Karl Bitz; Lenschütz, SS-Obersturmführer Arthur Harder; Leslau and Nessau, SS-Untersturmführer Wilhelm Wassermann; Litzmannstadt-Land, SS-Obersturmführer Rudolf Barth; Koło (Warthbrücken), SS-Oberscharführer Reinhold Steinberg; Konin, SS-Oberscharführer Rudolf Bilharz; Kutno, SS-Obersturmführer Erwin Mieschel; Sieradsch, SS-Untersturmführer Wilhelm Schmidtsiefen; Turek, SS-Untersturmführer Paul Schweichel; and Wielun, SS-Obersturmführer Gustaw Hütte.

29. Der Inspekteur der Sicherheitspolizei und des SD, Umwanderungsstelle (gez. Rapp), "Aussiedlung von Polen im Zuge des Wolhynienplans," 1 April 1940, USHMM/RG15.015M/2/130/43–49. Rudolf Barth led the Litzmannstadt Nebenstelle during the Zwischenplan. After Krumey assumed control, Barth became his subordinate.

30. See Krumey's SS personnel file, NARA/BDC RG242/A3343/SSo-221A, as well as his testimony at Nuremberg (affidavit), 30 September 1947, NARA/M894/16/NO-5364 (English transcript).

31. Rudolf Barth, "Aufbau der heisigen Aussenstelle," 19 February 1940, USHMM/RG15.015M/1/12/7–8.

32. "Verzeichnes der eingezogenen bezw. kommandierten SS-Führer, -Unterführer, und Männer, die zum Teil Tagegelder erhalten"; "Verzeichnis der von der Dienststelle bezahlten Mitarbeiter und Mitarbeiterinnen," 19 April 1940, USHMM/RG15.015M/1/23/1–2.

33. UWZ-Litzmannstadt, "Dienststelleneinteilung," 4 February 1941, USHMM/RG15.015M/6/10–17; Krumey, "Abschlussbericht" on the 2.Nahplan.

34. Gestapo Staatspolizeistelle Hohensalza, "Zuständigkeitsregelung zur Durchführung der Evakuierungen von Fremdstämmigen im Warthegau," 17 July 1940, USHMM/RG15.015M/2/102/1–3.

35. Krumey, "Bericht über die Besprechung am Sonntag 4.2.40 in der hiesigen Dienststelle," 4 February 1940, USHMM/RG15.015M/2/101/16–17; a series of reports on meetings between UWZ officials and the Landräte, 6 February 1940, USHMM/RG15.015M/2/100/

5–33 and 2/107/3–6; Rapp, "Merkblatt über die technischen Vorbereitungen für die durchzuführenden Arbeiten im Rahmen der Wolhynienaktion," 18 March 1940, USHMM/RG15.015M/2/130/36–40.

36. Krumey's final report on the 2.nahplan, NARA/T81/286/VoMi 323/2409604ff, indicates that the first transport of Polish evacuees left Litzmannstadt on 5 May 1940, even though the official launch date for the operation—as Aly states, in *"Final Solution,"* 51,—was 1 April 1940. Evictions and the delivery of Poles to the Litzmannstadt camps as well as the installation of Volksdeutschen, however, were already under way by 1 April. See, for example, "Aktenvermerk—Verlauf der Evakuierung und Ansiedlung am 20.3.40," NARA/T81/286/VoMi 510/2419820ff., and "Bericht über die ersten Ansiedlungstag" (undated), NARA/T81/286/VoMi 333/2409921ff. Both reports are of unknown provenance, though one was issued in Litzmannstadt. They indicate that evictions and resettlements began on 20 March 1940 and were carried out in Landkreis-Litzmannstadt for the benefit of Volhynian Germans. According to the former report, the action took place in the village of Mokradolna.

37. On Koppe's orders, only the best properties were to be selected. See HSSPF Koppe, "Mehrpunkte für die Arbeitsstäbe der Kreise im Bezug auf Vorbereitung und Ablauf der Ansiedlung von Wolhynien- un Galiziendeutschen," 2 March 1940, USHMM/RG15.015M/2/130/26–32.

38. Ehlich's testimony at Nuremberg, 28 October 1947, Case 8, NARA/M894/p. 577ff. (English transcript). See also UWZ-Litzmannstadt (Krumey), "Aktenvermerk über eine Besprechung mit dem Leiter des städtischen Einsatz, SS-Oberstuf. Hübner: Einsatz der städtischen Bevölkerung—Cholmeraktion," 30 October 1940, USHMM/RG15.015M/2/118/5. In her recent *Women and the Nazi East*, Elizabeth Harvey has brought to light the participation of German women in the evacuation process. Members of the Bund deutscher Mädel, the NS-Frauenschaft, and the women's Arbeitsdienst occasionally took part in the selection of Polish homes to be cleared, the evictions themselves, the seizure and distribution of movable Polish property, and the cleaning of the homes and farms before they were turned over to ethnic German settlers. See Harvey, *Women and the Nazi East: Agents and Witnesses of Germanization* (New Haven, CT, and London: Yale University Press, 2003), 152–157.

39. By the autumn of 1940, three Orpo battalions were involved in the evacuations from Wartheland: Battalion 44, based in Posen, and Battalions 101 and 132, stationed in Litzmannstadt. See Gendarmeriemeister Mollenhauer's report to Krumey, 16 November 1940, APL/UWZ-L/1/201–202.

40. Rapp, "Merkblatt über die technischen Vorbereitungen"; Ehlich's testimony at Nuremberg, 28 October 1947.

41. Der Inspekteur der Sipo und des SD (UWZ), "Merkblatt für den Polizeibeamte zur Durchführung der Evakuierungen von polnischen Hofbesitzern," 9 May 1940, NARA/T81/295/VoMi 510/2419818ff.

42. Koppe, "Mehrpunkte für die Arbeitsstäbe der Kreise." For an example of an eviction action, see UWZ Aussenstelle Warthbrücken (Steinberg), "Bericht über die am 6. und 7.Mai dieses Jahres durchgeführte Polenevakuierung und Ansiedlung der Wolhyniendeutschen in Kreis Warthbrücken—Gemeinde Tonningen," 8 May 1940, USHMM/

RG15.015M/3/223/11–12. In this case, the Poles were interned in a transit camp before their transport to Litzmannstadt. Steinberg noted that there was a "desperate mood" among the Poles at the camp. The women believed their children would be taken from them and sent to the Altreich and that their husbands would be "locked up," leaving them (the women) "to their fate." Steinberg thought it necessary to explain the situation in order to calm the crowd and facilitate an orderly transport. He did so, he reported, "in the Russian language," an indication that Steinberg spoke no Polish. But owing to the linguistic similarities between Polish and Russian, as well as to the fact that these evacuees were most likely Congress Poles, most probably understood his words.

43. Rapp, "Aussiedlung von Polen im Zuge der Wolhynienplans," 10 April 1940, AGK/UWZ-L/5/130–132.

44. UWZ Aussenstelle Kutno (Mieschel), "Tätigskeit-Situationsbericht der hiesigen Aussenstellen von 5.IV.40," 5 May 1940, USHMM/RG15.015M/3/215/5–6.

45. In actuality, the UWZ-RuS establishment deemed only 2,399 "Poles" fit for re-Germanization during the course of the 2.Nahplan and only another 7,327 during the 3.Nahplan (21 January 1941 to 20 January 1942). See Krumey, "Abschlussbericht" on the 2.Nahplan; Krumey, "Abschlussbericht über die Aussiedlungen im Rahmen der Ansetzung der Bessarabiendeutschen (3.Nahplan) vom 21.1.1941–20.1.1942 im Reichsgau Wartheland," c. 20 January 1942, NARA/T81/286/VoMi 325/2409652ff. On 7 October 1940, Höppner noted that the "percentage of Poles selected [for re-Germanization] is extraordinarily low—between 1% and 5%." See Höppner, "Politische Überprüfung rassisch ausgesuchte Familien," 7 October 1940, USHMM/RG15.015M/3/254/3. Evidently, this came as some surprise to Höppner, since Himmler (as well as Wetzel and Hecht) had earlier predicted that up to 1 million Poles in the incorporated territories would qualify for re-Germanization. Egon Leuschner of the Racial Policy Office of the NSDAP concurred with Himmler, asserting in 1940 that a significant number of individuals of German ethnicity had "gone under into Polentum" over the past century. It was the Reich's task, he argued, to recover this "lost German blood" for the good of the German racial community. See Egon Leuschner, *Nationalsozialistische Fremdvolkpolitik* (Berlin: Rassenpolitisches Amt der NSDAP, 1940), 34–35. For discussion of the RuSHA's participation in the racial examination of Poles, see Isabel Heinemann, *"Rasse, Siedlung, deutsches Blut": Das Rasse- & Siedlungshauptamt der SS und die rassenpolitische Neuordnung Europas* (Göttingen, Germany: Wallstein Verlag, 2003), 251–259.

46. Sammellager Wiesenstrasse (gez. Lorenz), "Aktenvermerk," 15 May 1940, USHMM/RG15.015M/4/261/10.

47. See the fragment of a memorandum by SS-Oberführer Tensfeld, "Umwanderung (Umsiedlungsfragen, Evakuierung)" (undated), USHMM/RG15.015M/4/259/23.

48. It should be pointed out that incoming ethnic German immigrants were subject to a rigorous screening process very similar to the one applied to Poles. The EWZ served as the main processing center for the classification and geographic placement of volksdeutsch immigrants. Its bureaus in the field, usually based in VoMi camps, were staffed by representatives of the Ministries of Finance and the Interior, the Reich Health Office, and the Reich Labor Office and, even more important, by agents of RuSHA and Sipo and the

SD. RuSHA agents conducted racial examinations (under the guise of strictly medical exams), measuring skulls and facial angles, studying body structure, eye and hair color, and the like. A racial and medical composite of each immigrant family was submitted, along with political and criminal reports compiled by Sipo-SD representatives, to an EWZ panel that passed final judgment on the resettlers and classified them accordingly. The two most common classifications were "O-cases" (Ost), meaning that the family was worthy enough to receive property and assume the role of German colonists in the East, and "A-cases" (Altreich), indicating that they could serve as workers in Germany proper but would not receive their own farm or shop (instead, they were issued Reich bonds in compensation for the property they had left behind). A third category, "S-cases" (*Sonderfälle* [special cases]), was assigned to those deemed of doubtful racial and/or political qualifications. These individuals or families either remained in VoMi camps (many were eventually put to work in the Altreich despite their questionable ethnicity) or were deported to the Generalgouvernement; in some instances, they were sent back to their country of origin. See Heinemann, "*Rasse, Siedlung, deutsches Blut*," 232–250; Valdis O. Lumans, *Himmler's Auxiliaries: The Volksdeutsche Mittelstelle and the German National Minorities of Europe, 1933–1945* (Chapel Hill: University of North Carolina Press, 1993), 189–192; Robert L. Koehl, *RKFDV: German Resettlement and Population Policy, 1939–1945—A History of the Reich Commission for the Strengthening of Germandom* (Cambridge, MA: Harvard University Press, 1957), 104ff.

49. Along with the 2,399 "re-Germanizable" Poles sent from Litzmannstadt to the Altreich during the 2.Nahplan, 7,513 were sent as workers. See Krumey, "Abschlussbericht" on the 2.*Nahplan*.

50. For discussion of the camp system and evaluation process, see Barth, "Auswahl von Arbeitskräften im Rahmen der Aussiedlungsaktion," 1 April 1940, USHMM/ RG15.015M/2/109/16–17; Der Inspekteur der Sicherheitspolizei und des SD, Umwanderungsstelle (gez. Rapp), "Aussiedlung von Polen im Zuge des Wolhynienplans"; Krumey, "Anweisung für das Lager Litzmannstadt," 17 April 1940, AGK/UWZ-L/16/64–66. As stated earlier, the RuS conducted racial examinations in its own camp beginning 1 November 1940. After that point, RuS personnel were no longer subordinate to the UWZ. An additional holding camp for Polish evacuees, commanded by SS-Hauptsturmführer Hermann Kagel, was established on Gniesenaustrasse by 4 May 1940, apparently to supplement the capacity of Lager II. As of that date, the commandants of the other camps were SS-Obersturmbannführer Erich Lorenz (Lager I), SS-Oberscharführer Ernst (Lager II), and SS-Obersturmführer Wacker (Lager III). As camp inspector, SS-Sturmbannführer Kasper Schwarzhuber oversaw the camp system as a whole. See the "Aktenvermerk," 4 May 1940, USHMM/RG15.015M/1/156. The camps were guarded by the SS-Wachtbataillon Lodsch (SS-Guard Battalion), staffed by 200 men from the SS-Abschnitt 43 based in Litzmannstadt. All were members of the Allgemeine-SS, but while on duty, they were considered Hilfspolizei (Auxiliary Police) and received orders from the Kommando der Schutzpolizei (Municipal Police Command) under Litzmannstadt's Schupo commander, Hauptmann Kreuzhofen. See Polizeipräsident-Lodsch (Schäfer), "Wachtbataillon für Umsiedlungslager," 2 April 1940, AGK/UWZ-L/142/1–2.

51. Koppe, "Mehrpunkte für die Arbeitsstäbe der Kreise."

52. See the "Aktenvermerk" regarding Eichmann's telephone conversation with Krumey, 8 March 1940, USHMM/RG15.015M/2/130/33.

53. *Der Menscheneinsatz*, 117.

54. Krumey, "Abschlussbericht" on the 2.*Nahplan*.

55. Seidl, "Wolhynieneinsatz-Konin," 19 March 1940, USHMM/RG15.015M/3/214/1.

56. Krumey, "Bedingungen für Rückstellung bei Evakuierungen," 24 June 1940, USHMM/RG15.015M/4/252/8.

57. UWZ-Posen, "Verantwortlichkeit der Aussenstellenleiter bei der Durchführung der Evakuierungen," 24 April 1940, AGK/UWZ-L/16/80.

58. Martin Broszat, *Nationalsozialistische Polenpolitik, 1939–1945* (Stuttgart, Germany: Deutsche Verlags-Anstalt, 1961), 121–122; Robert L. Koehl, "The Deutsche Volksliste in Poland, 1939–1945," *Journal of Central European Affairs* 15 (1956): 357. The DVL system was expanded to include two additional categories at the beginning of 1941 and introduced throughout the incorporated territories soon thereafter. The DVL is discussed in further detail in the final chapter.

59. Seidl, "Wolhynieneinsatz-Konin."

60. RFSS-RKFDV, "Erlass für die Überprüfung und Assonderung der Bevölkerung in den eingegliederten Ostgebiete," 12 September 1940, *Der Menscheneinsatz*, 91–93.

61. For an example of this questionnaire, see AGK/UWZ-L/15/277.

62. Höppner to Ehlich and Eichmann, "Aussiedlung im Kreise Wielun," 1 June 1940, USHMM/RG15.015M/3/158/2–3.

63. Seidl, "Aktenvermerk für SS-Hauptsturmführer Höppner: Unterredung zwischen SS-Hauptsturmführer Eichmann und SS-Untersturmführer Seidl am 5.6.40 in Posen," 6 June 1940, USHMM/RG15.015M/3/161/2–3. See also RSHA IIIB2 to the SD-Leitabschnitt Posen, "Aussiedlung im Kreise Wilun [*sic*]," 10 June 1940, USHMM/RG15.015M/3/158/4–5.

64. RSHA IIIB, "Evakuierung von Kriegswitwen," 20 August 1940, USHMM/RG15.015M/3/163/3–4.

65. UWZ-Posen, "Verantwortlichkeit der Aussenstellenleiter"; Krumey, "Bedingungen für Rückstellung bei Evakuierungen."

66. Krumey, "Evakuierung von kranken und schwächlichen Personen," 10/12/40, AGK/UWZ-L/16/127.

67. Landrat-Hohensalza to the Regierungspräsident of Hohensalza, "Evakuierung," 16 September 1940, USHMM/RG15.015M/3/195/7.

68. SD-Hauptaussenstelle Posen, "Auswirkungen der Umsiedlung im Landkreisen Posen," 19 October 1940, USHMM/RG15.015M/3/195/4–5.

69. Der Reichsstatthalter, "Umsiedlung volksdeutscher Rückwanderer aus dem Lubliner und Cholmer Land," 19 December 1940, AGK/CAMSW 775/Kommando der Schutzpolizei-Kalisch/130/11–11v.

70. Höppner, "Getrennte Evakuierung von Familien," 10 May 1940, USHMM/RG15.015M/3/150/2.

71. Barth to Höppner, 9 August 1940, USHMM/RG15.015M/3/150/8.

72. Höppner to Eichmann, 12 August 1940, USHMM/RG15.015M/3/150/3–4.

73. Eichmann, "Getrennte Evakuierung von Familien," 30 August 1940, USHMM/RG15.015M/3/150/1.

74. UWZ-Ltizmannstadt (Krumey) to Damzog, 5 May 1940, USHMM/RG15.015M /3/188/11–12.

75. Durgangslager-Flottwellstrasse (Litzmannstadt), report of 16 November 1940, AGK/UWZ-L/15/69.

76. Indeed, another report states that between 1 June and 31 December 1940, only 68 people had died in the camps themselves. See "Statistik der Krankenheitsfälle von 1.6.40 bis zum 31.13.40 in den Polenlagern der Umwandererzentralstelle in Litzmannstadt," in Czesław Łuczak, ed., *Położenie Ludności Polskiej w tzw. Kraju Warty w Okresie Hitlerowskiej Okupacji—Documenta Occupationis 13* (hereafter *Documenta Occupationis 13*) (Poznan, Poland: Instytut Zachodni, 1990), doc. III-28, 140–141.

77. Krumey, "Abschlussbericht" on the 2.Nahplan.

78. Rapp to Koppe, Damzog, Ehlich, and Eichmann, "Wolhynienaktion," 20 April 1940, USHMM/RG15.015M/2/ 130/73–75. A report by the UWZ Aussenstelle in Gostingen brings this problem into perspective. Between 18 and 22 May, four actions were carried out in the Kreis: 5,157 Poles were targeted, but only 1,780 were seized. The first action had a success rate of 75 percent, but the results of the latter three were poor, apparently because the Poles came to understand that their deportation was imminent and fled. The report also noted that the Volhynian Germans refused to eat food left behind in the vacated homes because they feared it was poisoned. See UWZ Aussenstelle Gostingen (Peters), "Aussiedlung von Polen," 25 May 1940, USHMM/RG15.015M/3/213/13–14.

79. Höppner, "Massnahmen zur Verhinderung der Flucht von Polen, die zur Evakuierung vorgesehen sind," 21 June 1940, in Wacław Szulc, ed., "Wysiedlanie Ludności Polskiej w tzw. Kraju Warty i na Zamojszczyźnie oraz Popełnione przy tym Zbrodnie," *Biuletyn Głównej Komisji Badania Zbrodni Hitlerowskich w Polsce 21* (hereafter *Biuletyn 21*) (Warsaw: Wydawnictwo Prawnicze, 1970), doc. 20, pp. 82–87. The overall results of eviction and evacuation actions carried out by the end of June 1940 were as follows: 59,997 Poles targeted and 30,038 seized. See the series of "Aktenvermerke," all signed by Seidl, AGK/UWZ-L/80/2–12. AGK/UWZ-L/15–80 includes many reports by the UWZ Aussenstellen regarding police dragnets in their respective jurisdictions. The success rate varied, but in *no* case did the Germans manage to arrest all of the Poles earmarked for evacuation. Sometimes, the results were truly miserable. SS-Oberscharführer Reihold Steinberg of the Kalisch Aussenstelle, for example, reported on 19 June that of the 186 families sought during a recent action, only 46 were arrested. See Barth's note to Krumey, 19 June 1940, AGK/UWZ-L/46/8.

80. As early as 11 March 1940, it was reported that a substantial number of Poles who feared they would soon be evacuated slaughtered their livestock and sold the meat on the black market, not just for the money but also because they believed that their actions would endanger Germany's food supply. See Befehlshaber der Ordnungspolizei-Posen, "Tagesordnung Nr. 32," 11 March 1940, AGK/Befehlshaber-Orpo/CAMSW 717/2/38–41.

81. NSDAP Kreisleitung Lentschütz, "Evakuierung der Polen und Ansiedlung der Rückwanderer aus Ostpolen" (undated), NARA/T81/295/VoMi 510/2419832ff.

82. Gend. Posten Grabow, Kreis Lentschütz, interrogation of Zygmunt Halasiewicz, 19 November 1940, USHMM/RG15.040M/2/358/276/112.

83. Höppner, "Geheimtätigkeit der Polen im Kreis Schroda," 15 November 1940, USHMM/RG15.015M/2/143/9–10.

84. Gestapo Staatspolizeileitstelle-Litzmannstadt, "Nationale Opposition—Polentum," 25 July 1940, USHMM/RG15.015M/3/169/5.

85. No provenance, interrogation of Arthur Beier, 28 March 1940, APL/UWZ-L/1/64.

86. No provenance, interrogations of Peter Beier and Konstantin, Stanisław, and Janina Domanski, 28 March 1940, APL/UWZ-L/1/65–68.

87. Plans for the creation of this office were on the table as of 29 April 1940. See HSSPF Koppe, "Fahndung nach geflüchten polnischen Bauernfamilien," 8 May 1940, AGK/Reichsstatthalter-Warthegau/297/103.

88. UWZ-Litzmannstadt, Mollenhauer's report on a staff meeting held 22 June 1940, APL/UWZ-L/1/123; Mollenhauer to Krumey, 16 November 1940; Polizei und Fahndungsabteilung (Mollenhauer), report for Krumey, 17 December 1941, APL/UWZ-L/1/281.

89. Some evacuated Poles returned to Wartheland more than once—and were arrested more than once. For example, the Polish farmer Ignac Olszewski of Kreis Lask was evacuated on 23 June 1940, processed in Litzmannstadt, and then deported to the Generalgouvernement. Four weeks later, he returned to his village in the Warthegau, where he worked throughout the autumn as a hand on various farms. Shortly before Christmas, he was arrested, sent back to the Litzmannstadt camps, and again deported to the Generalgouvernement. He remained there for only two weeks before returning to Wartheland, where he again worked as a farmhand until his second arrest on 13 March 1941. His punishment—if there was one—is unrecorded. See Gend. Posten Belchatow, Landkreis Lask, interrogation of Ignac Olszewski, 14 March 1941, USHMM/RG15.040M/2/358/274/4.

90. Polizei-Bataillon 101 (gez. Asmus), report on recent actions to apprehend fugitive Poles, 2 November 1940, *Documenta Occupationis 13*, doc. III-24, pp. 136–137. On the same day this report was issued, Krumey noted that many fugitive Poles were active on their former farms as workers; since their labor was cheap, the new owners did not report their presence to the police. See Krumey, "Ergebnis bei der Fahndung," 2 November 1940, in Czesław Łuczak, ed., *Wysiedlenia Ludności Polskiej na tzw. Ziemiach Wcielonych do Rzesyzy 1939–1945—Documenta Occupationis 8* (hereafter *Documenta Occupationis 8*) (Poznan, Poland: Instytut Zachodni, 1969), doc. 50, pp. 72–73. One Polish woman, for example, stated under interrogation that after spending two months on the run following the evacuation of their village, she and her family found work in September 1940 on the farm of Helmut Dombrowski, presumably an ethnic German. They were paid little: she earned only 15 reichsmarks per month and her son 17.50, but they did receive free housing and heat, as well as 150 kilograms of rye for flour. Dombrowski, she said, knew of their fugitive status but needed farmhands and therefore did not report their presence to the police. But by February 1941, Dombrowski no longer needed workers, so he turned in the woman and her family and demanded their evacuation. They were arrested on 21 February 1941. See Gendarmerieposten Wojkow, Kreis Sieradz, interrogation of Franciszka Olszewska, 21 February 1941, USHMM/RG15.040M/2/358/277/38.

91. Asmus's report, 2 November 1940, *Documenta Occupationis 8*, doc. III-24, pp. 136–137.

92. DAI, "Bericht Dr. Quiring Nr. 9," 19 April 1940, NARA/T81/490/DAI 749.

93. Asmus's report, 2 November 1940, *Documenta Occupationis 8*, doc. III-24, pp. 136–137. The record does not state whether Asmus's suggestions became policy. Examples of the sympathetic attitude of ethnic Germans toward Poles can be found in Harvey, *Women and the Nazi East*, 173–174, 214–215.

94. Höppner, "2.Nahplan—Transportstärken," 25 June 1940, USHMM/RG15.015M/3/203/3.

95. No provenance, "Polentransporte," 30 September 1940, USHMM/RG15.015M/3/156/6.

96. Krumey, "Aussenstellenleiterbesprechung—Statistische Aufstellung," 28 October 1940, USHMM/RG15.015M/2/108/1.

97. Seidl, "Missstände bei Durchführung der bisherigen Umsiedlungsaktion," 29 April 1940, USHMM/RG15.015M/3/179/5–6.

98. Greiser, "Erlass betreffend die beschleunigte Ansetzung von volksdeutschen Umsiedlern," 25 April 1940, APP/Landrat-Schrimm/206/17–19.

99. RFSS-RKFDV, letter to Greifelt, 10 May 1940, USHMM/RG15.015M/2/130/80–82.

100. Seidl, "Aktenvermerk für SS-Hauptsturmführer Höppner," 4.

101. Quoted in Aly, *"Final Solution,"* 62.

102. See the notes on the meeting between Vogel and UWZ officials, 7 February 1940, USHMM/RG15.015M/2/131/15–17. One immigrant expressed displeasure over the state of his new farm, writing that "the main room is cold and dirty, and it stinks. The walls are covered with kitsch. The furniture is, with a few exceptions, good. The courtyard is filled with garbage. It is a rich farm, but everything is somehow shabby and chaotic—in short, Polish." But he found faith in Hitler and was therefore undeterred: "We thought about the Führer, what he expects of us and what we owe him. We thought about our task in the East and that we had resolved not to give up. And so we gained courage." Quoted in Debórah Dwork and Robert Jan van Pelt, *Auschwitz: 1270 to the Present* (New York: W. W. Norton, 1996), 154.

103. SS-Arbeitsstab Turek, "Inspektion im Kreis Turek," 4 October 1940, APP/SS-Ansiedlungsstab Posen/110/4–6.

104. Unknown provenance (presumably a DAI observer), Report on Conditions in Kreis Samter to Councilor (Ratsherr) Götz of the Deutsches Ausland-Institut in Stuttgart, 19 June 1941, NARA/T81/415/DAI/5159829ff.

105. Aly, *"Final Solution,"* 63.

106. Greiser (gez. Siegmund), telegram to Greifelt, 21 December 1939, USHMM/RG15.015M/2/115/1. At that point, the Lublin region was still set aside for a Judenreservat; therefore, the Volksdeutschen would have to be resettled.

107. RFSS-RKFDV, "Anordnung 18/II," 9 May 1940, *Der Menscheneinsatz*, 41.

108. UWZ-Posen, "Umsiedlung der Cholmer Deutschen," 29 May 1940, USHMM/RG15.015M/2/115/5.

109. Höppner, "Umsiedlung der Cholmerdeutschen," 17 June 1940, USHMM/RG15.015M/2/115/9.

110. SS-Polizeiführer Lublin, Umsiedlungsstab (gez. Holst), "Umsiedlung der Volksdeutschen aus dem Gebiet ostwärts des San und der Weichsel ohne Stadt Warschau," no date (presumably late August 1940), AGK/UWZ-L/15/32–40.

111. Seidl, "Aktenvermerk über die Besprechung mit dem Leiter der Ansiedlungsstabes am heutigen Tage," 27 June 1940, USHMM/RG15.015M/2/115/11. The Kreise now designated for Cholmer German settlement were Birnbaum, Gnesen, Neutomischel, Obornik, Posen-Land, Scharnikau, Schrimm, Schroda, and Wreschen. Three more were later added to the mix, namely, Dietfurt, Samter, and Wollstein. See UWZ-Posen, "Liste der Aussenstellen der UWZ und Namen der Aussenstellenleiter vom 12.9.40," 11 September 1940, USHMM/RG15.015M/1/15/8.

112. Höppner, "Ansiedlung der Cholmer Deutschen," 28 June 1940, USHMM/RG15.015M/2/115/21–24.

113. Seidl, "Aktenvermerk: Besprechung mit dem Ansiedlungsstab," 12 July 1940, USHMM/RG15.015M/2/115/38.

114. SS-Polizeiführer Lublin, Umsiedlungsstab (gez. Holst), "Umsiedlung der Volksdeutschen."

115. RFSS-RKFDV (gez. Greifelt), "Vorgang: Ansiedlung von Ukrainiern im Generalgouvernment," 21 August 1940, USHMM/RG15.015M/2/119/1–3. The precise number of the Ukrainian families in question (described as farmers) is not stated.

116. See Aly, *"Final Solution,"* 104n81.

117. Ibid.

118. RFSS-RKFDV (gez. Greifelt), "Vorgang."

119. UWZ-Posen, "Liste der Aussenstellen." The jurisdiction of some UWZ branch offices included more than one Kreis. One Aussenstelle in the eastern part of the province, that in Gostingen, remained active, still involved in evacuations connected to Volhynian resettlement. Evacuations in other Kreise for the benefit of Volhynian Germans continued, but they were now carried out primarily by flying commandos based in Litzmannstadt.

120. Krumey, "Abschlussbericht" on the 2.Nahplan.

121. Krumey, "Vermerk über die augenblicklich laufenden Evakuierungen im Rahmen der Ansiedlung der Wolhynien und Cholmerdeutschen," 13 September 1940, USHMM/RG15.015M/2/130/102.

122. Krumey, "Abschlussbericht" on the 2.Nahplan.

123. Aly, *"Final Solution,"* 91.

124. Krumey to Eichmann, "Bericht—Entwicklung der Cholmer Aktion," 27 September 1940, AGK/UWZ-L/15/52–53.

125. Höppner to Ehlich, "Cholmer Umsiedlung," 7 October 1940, USHMM/RG15.015M/2/115/52; Höppner to Eichmann, 7 October 1940, USHMM/RG15.015M/2/115/53.

126. Kurt Lück, *Die Cholmer und Lubliner Deutschen kehren heim ins Vaterland* (Posen, Poland: Historische Gesellschaft im Wartheland/Verlag S. Hirzel in Leipzig, 1940), 7, 142.

127. Höppner, "Blitzfernschrieben" to Ehlich and Eichmann, 6 November 1940, *Biuletyn 12*/doc. 50/113F-114F. Frank's telegram to Greiser is attached.

128. Höppner, "Aktenvermerk" for Ehlich, Eichmann, and Damzog regarding his 4 November 1940 meeting with Koppe, AGK/Greiser Trial/36/557–558.

129. Lück, *Die Cholmer und Lubliner Deutschen*, 148–150.

130. See, for example, the interrogation of Wojciech Trzcinka, a Pole who returned to Wartheland after his deportation during the Cholmer Action and was subsequently arrested. Trzcinka and his wife were lucky enough to receive a farm in the Generalgouvernement, but upon arrival, they discovered that "everything had been taken away." They found nothing to eat and nothing with which to set up house. Each had only the 20 zlotys given to them in the Litzmannstadt camps, and once this had been spent, they found themselves flat broke with no source of additional income. Therefore, they decided to return to Wartheland. See Gendarmerieposten Piaskowice, Landkreis Lenschütz, "Selbstevakuierung und Flucht aus dem Gouvernement des Trzcinka Wojciech," 29 November 1940, USHMM/RG15.040M/2/378/276/134.

131. For a brief synopsis of all organized Polish evacuations to the Lublin district (the Cholmer Action included) carried out between 1939 and 1941, see Janina Kiełboń, *Migracje ludności w dystrykcie lubelskim w latach, 1939–1944* (Lublin, Poland: Państwowe Muzeum na Majdanku, 1995), 24–38. Valuable statistical data on each operation can be found therein.

132. Höppner, "Fahrplan für weitere Züge," 3 December 1940, USHMM/RG15.015M/2/130/122–123.

133. Browning, *The Origins of the Final Solution*, 67.

134. Krumey, "Abschlussbericht" on the 2.Nahplan.

135. The Saybusch Action was implemented to create space for 4,125 ethnic German farmers from eastern Galicia. For an overview of the operation, see Sybille Steinbacher, *"Musterstadt" Auschwitz: Germanisierungspolitik und Judenmord in Ostoberschlesien* (Munich, Germany: K. G. Saur Verlag, 2000), 132–136.

136. Though Krumey's "Abschlussbericht" mentions only Poles, Browning states that at least one of the eleven trains employed during the Mlawa Action carried Jews. See Browning, *The Origins of the Final Solution*, 97.

137. Krumey, "Abschlussbericht on the 2.Nahplan.

138. Ibid.

139. Frank was aware of this order by 25 June 1940; see Browning, *The Path to Genocide*, 18. UWZ chief Rolf-Heinz Höppner evidently did not learn of it until 7 July; see "Besprechung der Evakuierungsangelegenheiten im Warthegau zwischen SS-H'Stuf. Höppner und IVD4 am 9.7.1940," 9 July 1940, USHMM/RG15.015M/2/115/36. Höppner had only recently presented Eichmann with a contingency plan for evacuation of the Litzmannstadt ghetto. Developed by the SD-Abschnitt in Litzmannstadt, the plan was based on the assumption that the action would begin in August and that two trains per day would be available for the operation. It was expected to last for seven months, until February 1941. See Höppner to Eichmann, "Meldungen aus dem Abschnittsgebiet Litzmannstadt," 27 June 1940, and the attached plan, "Meldungen aus dem Abschnittsgebiet, 6/24/40, USHMM/RG15.015M/2/129/2–3.

140. Hans Frank, *Das Diensttagebuch des deutschen Generalgouverneurs in Polen, 1939–1945*, ed. Werner Präg and Wolfgang Jacobmeyer (Stuttgart, Germany: Deutsche Verlags-Anstalt, 1975), entry for 31 July 1940, 261–263. The Greiser-Frank meeting is quoted and discussed in Browning, *The Origins of the Final Solution*, 84–85.

141. Aly, *"Final Solution,"* 92–93.

142. For an in-depth investigation of the Madagascar Plan of 1940, including its deeper historical roots, see Hans Jansen, *Madagaskar-Plan: Die beabsichtigte Deportation der europäischen Juden nach Madagaskar* (Munich, Germany: Herbig Verlag, 1997). Browning provides valuable analysis in *The Origins of the Final Solution*, 81–89.

CHAPTER SEVEN: THE SHORT LIFE OF THE 3.NAHPLAN–1.TEILPROGRAM

1. Ulrich Greifelt, "Festigung deutschen Volkstums im deutschen Osten," *Raumforschung und Raumordnung* 1 (January 1941): 3.

2. Whether Greiser's statistics are accurate is unknown, but Czesław Łuczak does assert that in light of its substantial deliveries of farm products to Germany proper during the first stage of the occupation, Wartheland indeed "earned its designation as the Kornkammer" of the Greater German Reich. See Łuczak, "Die Agrarpolitik des Dritten Reiches im Okkupierten Polen," *Studia Historiae Oeconomicae* 17 (1982): 196.

3. Arthur Greiser, "Die Grossdeutsche Aufgabe im Wartheland," *Nationalsozialistische Monatshefte* 130 (January 1941): 43, 50.

4. Greifelt, "Festigung deutschen Volkstums im deutschen Osten," 3.

5. RFSS-RKFDV, "Anordnung 19/III" (Lithuania), 22 July 1940; "Anordnung 21/II" (Bessarabia/northern Bukovina), 20 August 1940; "Anordnung 21/I" (southern Bukovina/Dobruja), 31 October 1940; see Der Reichsführer-SS/Reichskommissar für die Festigung deutschen Volkstums, *Der Menscheneinsatz: Grundsätze, Anordnung und Reichtlinien* (hereafter *Der Menscheneinsatz*) (Berlin: Hauptabteilung des RKFDV, 1940), 37–38, 36–37, 37–38, respectively, NARA/T81/VoMi 802/2435422ff. The Red Army occupied Lithuania on 15 June 1940 and Estonia and Latvia on 17 June. On 28 June, the USSR moved against Romania, seizing the territories of northern Bukovina and Bessarabia. All of these actions took place in accordance with the Nazi-Soviet agreements of August and September 1939. Two days before the Soviets seized northern Bukovina and Bessarabia, Molotov approved Ribbentrop's request to resettle the Volksdeutschen living therein; on 5 September 1940, the agreement became official via yet another resettlement treaty between Germany and the USSR. On 7 September, Romania ceded southern Dobruja to Bulgaria, in line with the Craiova Accord. Romania and Germany subsequently signed a treaty to resettle the Dobrujan and southern Bukovinian Germans, as well as others scattered throughout Romania, on 20 October. See Götz Aly, *"Final Solution": Nazi Population Policy and the Murder of the European Jews*, trans. Belinda Cooper and Allison Brown (London: Edward Arnold, 1999), 97–99, 108–109; Valdis O. Lumans, *Himmler's Auxiliaries: The Volksdeutsche Mit-*

telstelle and the German National Minorities of Europe, 1933–1945 (Chapel Hill: University of North Carolina Press, 1993), 171–175.

6. According to Aly, from Bessarabia came 93,548 Volksdeutschen; North Bukovina, 43,531; South Bukovina, 52,107; Dobruja, 15,603; the Romanian interior, 9,732; Lithuania, 50,700; Estonia and Latvia, 12,000. See Aly, *"Final Solution,"* 108. Figures provided by Lumans, in *Himmler's Auxiliaries*, 165ff, differ only slightly.

7. Westerkamp, "Bericht über die Besprechung betreffend Umsiedlung von Polen und Juden in das Generalgouvernement im Reichsicherheitshauptamt am 8.Januar 1941," 13 January 1941, Nuernberg Military Tribunals, *Trials of War Criminals before the Nuernberg Military Tribunals under Control Council Law no. 10, Nuernberg, October 1946–April 1949*, 15 vols. (hereafter *TWC*) (Washington, DC: U.S. Government Printing Office, 1949–1953), 4: 873, doc. 22323-PS, 29: 487–491. As the Wehrmacht also demanded military bases within the Generalgouvernement, approximately 180,000 individuals were slated for internal resettlement within Frank's jurisdiction. All told, then, over 1 million people were to be deported to or relocated within the Generalgouvernement in 1941. Since the 3.Nahplan encompassed not only Wartheland but also Danzig–West Prussia, Upper Silesia, and East Prussia, the RSHA soon established two additional UWZ offices, one in Danzig (but based in Gotenhaufen) and another in Kattowitz. Franz Ambromeit, the Sipo supervisor of evacuations in Danzig–West Prussia since the beginning of 1940, assumed control of the former, and Rudolf Barth, previously Krumey's deputy at the UWZ-Litzmannstadt, was appointed leader of the latter. See Chef der Sipo und des SD, "Errichtung einer Umwandererzentralstelle in Danzig," 23 January 1941, APB/Umwandererzentralstelle-Danzig/1/1–2; RSHA Amt 1B1, "Errichtung einer Umwandererzentralstelle in Kattowitz," 14 February 1941, USHMM/RG15.007M/103/36–37. Eichmann's creation, the Zentralstelle für jüdische Auswanderung in Vienna, was to handle the deportation of Jews from the city. On the expansion of the Auschwitz concentration camp system and ethnic redistribution in East Upper Silesia, see Sybille Steinbacher, *"Musterstadt" Auschwitz: Germanisierungspolitik und Judenmord in Ostoberschlesien* (Munich, Germany: K. G. Saur Verlag, 2000).

8. Hans Frank, *The Diensttagebuch des deutschen Generalgouverneurs in Polen, 1939–1945* (hereafter *Tagebuch*), ed. Werner Präg and Wolfgang Jacobmeyer (Stuttgart, Germany: Deutsche Verlags-Anstalt, 1975), entries for 11 January 1941 and 15 January 1941, 318–321, 326–329, respectively. See also the extract from Frank's diary, "Besprechung von Fragen der Einsiedlung von Polen und Juden in das Generalgouvernement," 15 January 1941, *TWC*, doc. 2233-PS, 29: 481–487; and Aly, *"Final Solution,"* 139.

9. Frank, *Tagebuch*, entries for 11 January 1941, 318–321, 13 January 1941, 321–322, and 15 January 1941, 326–329; *TWC*, doc. 2233-PS, 29: 481–487. Streckenbach is quoted in Aly, *"Final Solution,"* 140. For additional discussion of the Generalgouvernement's preparations for the influx of deportees, see Regierung des Generalgouvernements, Der Staatssekretär (Bühler), "Evakuierung von Polen und Juden ab 1.II.1941," 17 January 1941, USHMM/RG11.001M/91/1447-1/340/1–8.

10. Krumey, "3.Nahplan," 6 January 1941, in Szymon Datner, Janusz Gumkowski, and Kazimierz Leszczyński, eds., *Wysiedlanie ludności ziem Polskich wcielonych do Rzeszy: Biuletyn Głównej Komisji Badania Zbrodni Hitlerowskich w Polsce Biuletyn*

Głównej Komisji Badania Zbrodni Hitlerowskich w Polsce 12 (hereafter *Biuletyn 12*) (Warsaw: Wydawnictwo Prawnicze, 1960), doc. 62, pp. 127F–128F.

11. Bilharz, "Einsatz von Wolhyniendeutschen im Kreis Konin," 19 May 1940, USHMM/RG15.015M/2/121/1–2.

12. Höppner, "Übungsplatz für Kreis Konin" (undated), USHMM/RG15.015M/2/121/11; Höppner, "Truppenübungsplatz im Kreis Konin," 28 June 1940, USHMM/RG15.015M/2/121/7.

13. Höppner, "Schiessplatz Konin" (presumably 18 July 1940), USHMM/RG15.015M/2/121/16.

14. Höppner, "Schiessplatz im Kreise Konin," 5 December 1940, USHMM/RG15.015M/2/122/4. Interestingly, Höppner failed to call attention to the fact that moving Poles from northern to southern Konin and then later deporting them to the Generalgouvernement constituted a double resettlement. Such an action, at least in principle, flew in the face of the 5 January 1940 agreement between the RSHA and the Reich Labor Ministry.

15. Höppner to Eichmann, "Truppenübungsplatz Konin," 20 January 1940, USHMM/RG15.015M/2/122/17; "Aktenvermerk: Überschlag für die Kosten der Aussiedlung von Polen aus dem Gelände des Schiessplatzes in Konin," 20 December 1940, USHMM/RG15.015M/2/122/16.

16. Höppner, "Errichtung eines Schiessplatzes in Konin," 23 December 1940, USHMM/RG15.015M/2/122/20.

17. Westerkamp, "Bericht über die Besprechung," 13 January 1941, 488. Krumey, "Vermerk über die nach der Haupttagung in Berlin stattgefundene Besprechung Reichssicherheitshauptamt IVD4 am 8.Januar 1941," 10 January 1941, USHMM/RG15.015M/3/199/4–6.

18. The base was established in Kreis Sieradsch in the eastern part of Wartheland. See Krumey, "Abschlussbericht über die Aussiedlungen im Rahmen der Ansetzung der Bessarabiendeutschen (3.Nahplan) vom 21.1.1941–20.1.1942 im Reichsgau Wartheland," c. 20 January 1942, NARA/T81/386/VoMi 325/2409652ff.

19. "Besserstellung der Volksdeutschen durch Zuteilung von polnischen Bauernhöfen" (signature illegible), 23 September 1940, USHMM/RG15.015M/2/134/4. For a detailed description of the Volksdeutsche Besserstellung scheme, see "Richtlinien für die Befreidigung des dringstens Landbedarfes gaueingessessener Volksdeutscher" (no provenance), 3 September 1940, APP/Landrat-Scharnikau/160/1–3.

20. Höppner, "Aktenvermerk" for Koppe, 7 November 1940, AGK/UWZ-L/182/1–2.

21. Seidl, "Besprechung mit den Aussenstellenleitern am 9.November 1940," 10 November 1940, USHMM/RG.15.015M/2/109/9–13.

22. RFSS-RKFDV, "Anordung 9/IV," 21 December 1939, discussed and quoted in Aly, *"Final Solution,"* 136.

23. Höppner to Döring, "Umsiedlung zur Besserstellung von volksdeutschen Familien," 20 January 1941, AGK/UWZ-L/182/5–7.

24. "Durchführung des Verfahrens zur Befreidigung des dringendstens Landbedarfs der gaueingessessen Volksdeutschen" (no provenance), 18 February 1941, APP/Landrat-Schrimm/160/48–51. The memo reveals, interestingly enough, that local officials in Kreis Schrimm evidently attempted to dupe the SD, requesting that the SS-AS submit a list of

approximately double the number of farms actually needed for Besserstellung so as to ensure that enough farms would be available for the project even if the SD rejected some proposed.

25. Heydrich approved 50,000 evacuations for Volksdeutsche Besserstellung for the incorporated territories in their entirety; 30,000 of these were for the Warthegau alone. See Höppner to Döring, "Umsiedlung zur Besserstellung."

26. Some 50,000 evacuations were granted for the former action and 5,000 for the latter. The minutes of the meeting do not state from which Gaue the deportees would originate, though we can assume that most, if not all, of the 5,000 evacuations recommended for the removal of apprehended Poles would come from Wartheland. The expulsions proposed by Koppe and Krumey for the purpose of creating space for skilled craftspeople from the Altreich were not addressed at the conference.

27. Westerkamp, "Bericht über die Besprechung," 8 January 1941, 488. On the basis of a statistical overview of the 3.Nahplan compiled by Alexander Dolezalek on 10 January 1941, Aly asserts that Heydrich reduced Krumey and Koppe's request for 330,000 deportations by 20 percent, to 268,000, on 8 January (apparently at some point after the RSHA meeting held earlier that day). Aly does not explain the discrepancy between this figure and that specified in the minutes of the meeting, and I have not examined Dolezalek's memo, but in light of later developments (which will be discussed), Heydrich may well have taken such action. See Aly, "Final Solution," 137 and 147n23.

28. Westerkamp, "Bericht über die Besprechung," 8 January 1941, 488. See also Krumey, "Vermerk über die nach Haupttagung," 4. The figure of only 2,000 evacuations for the construction of the Konin base would seem to indicate that the project had been scaled back, but this was not the case: as Krumey stated, 73,000 expulsions from Konin were scheduled for April and May 1941. In his report, the realist Krumey pointed out that "on the basis of past experience," it was probable that the 90,000 deportations planned for volksdeutsch resettlement would not be realized within the designated time frame. He was correct.

29. Höppner noted that the UWZ might need to carry out an additional 10,000 evacuations from the Konin site in February. A Wehrmacht decision on the matter was pending.

30. Höppner, "Aktenvermerk: In Berlin am 16.1.41 im Reichssicherheitshauptamt Amt IVD4 stattgefundene Farhplankonferenz," 17 January 1941, USHMM/RG15.015M/3/199/8–10.

31. Barton Whaley asserts that Himmler first learned of Operation Barbarossa at least as early as 1 January 1941. But since Whaley himself claims that Heydrich was informed about the impending invasion on 18 December 1940, it seems highly likely that the RFSS was clearly aware of Hitler's plans by 18 December as well. See Whaley, Codeword BARBAROSSA (Cambridge, MA: MIT Press, 1973), 137, 270. Richard Breitman states that Himmler "gave a strong hint" that he knew of Barbarossa as early as 11 July 1940, in other words, before Hitler announced his plans to the high command. See Breitman, The Architect of Genocide: Himmler and the Final Solution (Hanover, NH: Brandeis University Press, 1991), 128.

32. Quoted in Jürgen Förster, "Hitler's Decision in Favour of War against the Soviet Union," in Horst Boog, Jürgen Förster, Joachim Hoffmann, Ernst Klink, Rolf-Dieter Müller, and Gerd Veberschär, eds., and Dean S. McMurray, Ewald Osers, and Louise Willmott, trans. *Germany and the Second World War*, vol. 4, *The Attack on the Soviet Union* (Oxford: Clarendon Press, 1998), 26.

33. Ibid., 24 ff.

34. Aly, "*Final Solution*," 96.

35. Eugen Kreidler, *Die Eisenbahnen im Machtbereich der Achsenmächte während des Zweiten Weltkrieges: Einsatz und Leistung für die Wehrmacht und Kriegswirtschaft* (Göttingen, Germany: Musterschmidt, 1975), 115. The regime also took steps to improve the rail network within the Generalgouvernement at that time. Beginning in October 1940, the *Ottoprogram* was initiated, a large-scale construction project geared toward the creation of railway links to the Soviet border. According to the original plans, the objectives of the program were to be realized by 1 May 1941. See Kriedler, *Der Eisenbahn*, 115; Alfred C. Mierzejewski, *The Most Valuable Asset of the Reich: A History of the German National Railway*, vol. 2, *1933–1945* (Chapel Hill: University of North Carolina Press, 2000), 89ff.

36. "Weisung Nr. 21 (Fall Barbarossa)," in Erhard Moritz, ed., *Fall Barbarossa: Dokumente zur Vorbereitung der faschistischen Wehrmacht auf die Aggression gegen die Sowjetunion (1940/41)* (Berlin: Deutscher Militärverlag, 1970), doc. 36, pp. 140–144.

37. "Aus dem Protokoll der Besprechung Hitlers mit führenden Offizieren des OKW, des OKH, und des OKL über die Operationen gegen die Sowjetunion und die Heranziehung der Satellitenstaaten, 3.Februar 1941," in Moritiz, *Fall Barbarossa*, doc. 40, pp. 162–166. The deployment plan changed somewhat after the onset of the Balkan campaign in early April 1941.

38. "Aus dem Aktenvermerk über eine Besprechung beim Chef des Stabes des Befehlshabers des Ersatzheeres über Aufstellung und Aufmarsch deutscher Truppen zur Vorbereitung der Aggression gegen die Sowjetunion, 5.September 1940," in Moritz, *Fall Barbarossa*, doc. 66, pp. 229–232.

39. Kreidler, *Der Eisenbahnen*, 302.

40. He later increased this figure to 17,000. See ibid., 117.

41. Even Otto Dietrich, Hitler's press secretary, did not catch wind of the forthcoming invasion until the beginning of March 1941, and even then, he was convinced that his information was erroneous. He reported that talk of an impending clash continued to spread in German political and diplomatic circles throughout the spring of 1941, "but in spite of the thickening rumors I still believed, on the basis of all that Hitler has said in speeches and private statements, that Germany would never undertake aggressive action against Russia." It was not until the night of 21–22 June, Dietrich claimed, that he realized the rumors were true. See Dietrich, *Hitler*, trans. Richard and Clara Winston (Chicago: Henry Regnery, 1955), 65–66. Though sharing information on a need-to-know basis had long been a hallmark of Nazi rule, Hitler officially institutionalized secrecy within the regime via his Fundamental Order of 25 September 1941. In brief, the order stated that German officials were to be made aware of no classified information beyond that "absolutely necessary for

the execution of their tasks." For a copy of the order, see Der Führer und Reichskanzler, "Grundsätzlicher Befehl," 25 September 1941, USHMM/RG15.029M/1/2.

42. UWZ-Litzmannstadt, "Merkblatt für die Evakuierung von polnischen Hofbesitzern," January 1941, NARA/T81/ 295/VoMi 510/241981off. Whether this order was followed to the letter is unknown, but it is worth noting that according to a series of police reports on evacuations in Kreis Kempen issued during the 1.Teilprogram, the evacuation squads *never* had cause to fire their weapons. See the reports issued by the Gendarmerie-Kempen, AGK/CAMSW 701/Gendarmerie-Kempen/3/1ff.

43. As of 4 February 1941, the UWZ-Warthegau offices, or Aussenstellen, and their leaders were as follows: Posen Stadt-Land (Bilharz), Lissa (Harder), Altburgund (Hahn), Kempen (Hütte), Gnesen (Koch), Kutno (Mieschel), Leslau Stadt-Land (Peters), Jarotschin (Schmidtsiefen), Litzmannstadt-Land (Skarabis), and Litzmannstadt-Stadt (Püschel). See UWZ-Litzmannstadt, "Dienststellenleitung, der UWZ Aussenstellen," 4 February 1941, USHMM/RG15.015M/1/6/16–17.

44. SS-Oberscharführer R. (only the initial provided), "Aktenvermerk für SS-Sturmbannführer Höppner," 6 February 1941, USHMM/RG15.015M/3/151/1.

45. Krumey, "Abschlussbericht" on the 3.Nahplan, c. 20 January 1942.

46. F. H. Hinsley, *British Intelligence in the Second World War: Its Influence on Strategy and Operations* (New York: Cambridge University Press, 1979), 1: 438, 455; Whaley, *Codeword BARBAROSSA*, 48.

47. Quoted in Aly, *"Final Solution,"* 141.

48. Ibid.

49. Although the resettlement program and, with it, the construction of the human Ostwall along the eastern border of the incorporated territories were considered by many to be instrumental to the defense of the Reich, it is clear that the Wehrmacht officers in question viewed national defense in strictly military terms.

50. Höppner, "Aktenvermerk," 17 January 1941.

51. Krumey, "Abschlussbericht" on the 3.Nahplan.

52. RSHA Amt IVD4 (gez. Eichmann), "3.Nahplan—1.Teilprogram," 21 February 1941, USHMM/RG15.015M/2/122/35–36. Several days later, Eichmann instructed UWZ officials to once again consider evacuations for troop-training grounds. See ibid., 41–42. No such evacuations, however, were ever carried out, though the Germans eventually evicted some 20,000 Poles from the base sites and resettled them within Wartheland. See Krumey, "Abschlussbericht" on the 3.Nahplan.

53. Kreidler, *Die Eisenbahnen*, 118.

54. Krumey, "Abschlussbericht" on the 3.Nahplan.

55. Müller, "3.Nahplan—1.Teilprogram," 15 March 1941, *Biuleytn 12*/doc. 69/138F–139F. In all probability, UWZ officials in the Warthegau had received word of the impending transport halt several days earlier. Indeed, we can be certain that the UWZ-Danzig was aware of the suspension at least as early as 11 March. On that day, Franz Abromeit, the leader of the Gotenhafen office, informed his subordinates that for "transport-technical reasons," all deportations from Danzig–West Prussia to the Generalgouvernement had to

be stopped; the duration of the interruption, he said, was unknown. The last evacuation transports from Abromeit's jurisdiction would roll on 12–13 March. See Abromeit, "3.Nahplan, 1.Teilprogram," 11 March 1941, APB/UWZ-D/97/14. If the leader of the UWZ-Danzig knew of the halt on 11 March, officials in Wartheland, where a much larger operation was under way, most likely knew as well.

56. Of these, 19,001 were sent to the Generalgouvernement on the nineteen transports that left Litzmannstadt between 5 February and 15 March 1941; 225 were deported by means of regular rail traffic. See Krumey, "Abschlussbericht" on the 3.Nahplan. On 7 February 1941, the UWZ-Warthegau received permission to resume expelling Jews. See "Richtlinien zur Durchführung der Evakuierungsaktionen in eingegliederten Ostgebieten," 7 February 1941, AGK/UWZ-L/1/38/41. Two of the nineteen transports from Wartheland were composed exclusively of Jews. Of the 25,000 individuals deported within the context of the operation, approximately 9,000 were Jews, including 2,140 from Wartheland and 5,000 from Vienna. See Christopher Browning, *The Path to Genocide: Essays on Launching the Final Solution* (Cambridge: Cambridge University Press, 1992), 22; Aly, *"Final Solution,"* 149. The remainder were probably among the 10,504 people evacuated from Danzig–West Prussia between 15 November 1940 and 15 March 1941. See Werner Röhr, Elke Heckert, Bernd Gottberg, Jutta Wenzel, and Heide-Marie Grünthal, eds., *Die faschistische Okkupationspolitik in Polen (1939–1945)*, vol. 2 of *Nacht über Europa: Die Okkupationspolitik des deutschen Faschismus (1938–1945)*, Achtbändige Dokumentenedition, ed. Wolfgang Schumann and Ludwig Nestler (Cologne, Germany: Pahl-Rugenstein, 1989), table 4, 356–357.

57. Aly, *"Final Solution,"* 149.

58. It is clear that transport problems in the East were particularly acute at that time. On 21 March, Höppner learned from the RSHA Amt IIIB (presumably Ehlich) that Polish evictees could not even be taken by means of local rail traffic to Litzmannstadt for racial exams. See Höppner's telegram to Krumey, "Fortsetzung der Ansetzung von Umsiedlern," 21 March 1941, USHMM/RG15.015M/2/146/37–38.

59. RFSS-RKFDV (gez. Greifelt), "Umsiedlung im Osten/Evakuierung von Polen und Juden. Bezug: Besprechungen am 19.März 1941," 26 March 1941, NARA/T81/295/VoMi 510/2419815ff. As Aly points out, the Nazis planned to house a significant number of "unproductive" Bessarabian Germans in the camps as well. See Aly, *"Final Solution,"* 154–155.

60. Quoted and discussed in Aly, *"Final Solution,"* 155.

61. Gendarmerie Abteilung Belchatow, Kreis Lask, "Sicherheit im Bezirk der Gend. Abtlg. Belchatow," 18 March 1941, USHMM/RG15.015M/2/126/4. The date of this action, 13 March, two days before the termination of the 1.Teilprogram, may well be a further indication that the UWZ-Warthegau was aware of the impending suspension of evacuation transports.

62. Gendarmerie, Kreis Sieradz, "Evakuierung in Gemeinden Brezeznio und Zloczew, Kreis Sieradz," 22 March 1941, USHMM/RG15.015M/2/126/3–3v.

63. Der Regierungspräsident, "Evakuierungen im Regierungsbezirk Litzmannstadt," 28 March 1941, USHMM/RG15.015M/2/126/2.

64. Krumey, "Abschlussbericht" on the 3.Nahplan, c. 20 January 1942.

CHAPTER EIGHT: POSTMORTEM: EVACUATIONS VERSUS
EXPEDIENCY

1. Arthur Greiser, "Die Grossdeutsche Aufgabe im Wartheland," *Nationalsozialistische Monatshefte* 130 (January 1941): 50.

2. Quoted in Götz Aly, *"Final Solution": Nazi Population Policy and the Murder of the European Jews*, trans. Belinda Cooper and Allison Brown (London: Edward Arnold, 1999), 136. (Claussen made his statement on 26 December 1940 during a conference with a representative of the Armament Economy Office.) As Wacław Długoborski points out, Wartheland's waning agricultural production was also the result of the volksdeutsch settlers' unfamiliarity with the agrarian conditions of western Poland; ethnic German resettlement, he writes, "was as a rule accompanied by a drop in agricultural production as these Germans adapted to the new unknown conditions only slowly and with difficulty." See Długoborski, "Economic Policy of the Third Reich in Occupied and Dependent Countries, 1938–1945: An Attempt at a Typology," *Studia Historiae Oeconomicae* 15 (1980): 186. No detailed statistics concerning agricultural production in Wartheland are available, but Czesław Łuczak claims that in comparison to the first stage of the occupation, production of wheat, potatoes, and sugar beets in the province dropped markedly between 1941/1942 and 1943/1944. See Łuczak, "Die Agrarpolitik des Dritten Reiches im okkupierten Polen," *Studia Historiae Oeconomicae* 17 (1978): 199.

3. Krumey, "Arbeitskräftebedarf im Altreich," 25 February 1941, USHMM/RG15.015M/2/146/23–24. Göring's demands and Wartheland's response will be discussed later in the chapter.

4. SS-Ansiedlungsstab, Planungsabteilung (Dolezalek), "Polenfrage im Warthegau," 28 February 1941, NARA/T81/287/VoMi 338/2409315ff. The following discussion refers exclusively to this document, which is also the source of the quotes in these passages.

5. Ibid.

6. The Generalgouvernement, Krumey stated, refused to accept entire Polish families if the family head was not present.

7. Krumey, "Arbeitskräftebedarf im Altreich."

8. Indeed, at some point during the course of the 3.Nahplan–1.Teilprogram, Greiser ordered that no Poles capable of work were to be deported to the Generalgouvernement. See Krumey, "Abschlussbericht über die Aussiedlungen im Rahmen der Ansetzung der Bessarabiendeutschen (3.Nahplan) vom 21.1.1941–20.1.1942 im Reichsgau Wartheland," c. 20 January 1942, NARA/T81/286/VoMi 325/2409652ff.

9. The UWZ directive "Richtlinien zur Durchführung der Evakuierungsaktionen in eingegliederten Ostgebieten," 7 February 1941, AGK/UWZ-L/1/38–41, allowed the deportation of Jews to resume.

10. Höppner, "Aussuchen arbeitseinsatzfähiger Polen in Litzmannstadt," 7 March 1941, USHMM/RG15.015M/2/146/26–27.

11. Christopher Browning, *The Origins of the Final Solution: The Evolution of Nazi Jewish Policy, September 1939–March 1942* (Lincoln: University of Nebraska Press, 2004),

118–120. Also see Browning, *The Path to Genocide: Essays on Launching the Final Solution* (Cambridge: Cambridge University Press, 1992), 34–36. *Attritionist* and *productionist* are his terms.

12. Rüstungsinspektion des Wehrkreises XXI, "Geschichte des Kriegeinsatzes der Rüstungsinspektion des Wehrkreises XXI. Teil II. 1/10/40–31/12/41" (presumably January 1942), NARA/T77/620/180784ff.

13. Browning, *The Path to Genocide*, 43.

14. Quoted in Browning, *The Origins of the Final Solution*, 120 (emphasis mine).

15. Ibid., 118.

16. Höppner to Krumey, 7 March 1941, USHMM/RG15.015M/4/259/38.

17. Höppner, "Bereitstellung von Arbeitskräften aus den eingegliederten Ostgebieten zur Deckung des Kräftebedarfs der Kreigswirtschaft," 14 March 1941, USHMM/RG15.015M/4/259/39–40. Höppner's request for information dealt specifically with 4,000 Polish families to be selected and removed from the UWZ camps by the Litzmannstadt Arbeitsamt in cooperation with Kendzia's office.

18. Höppner, "Arbeitseinsatz von polnischen Familien," 27 March 1941, USHMM/RG15.015M/2/146/44–45. I have not had the opportunity to examine the two Göring directives to which Höppner referred, nor have I discovered a documented agreement between the RSHA and the Labor Ministry regarding the recruitment of "racially unsuitable" families for labor in the Altreich. Moreover, I am unaware of any secondary source that examines either the Göring directives or the RSHA–Labor Ministry agreement. Göring's orders as well as a written accord (assuming the agreement was put into writing) between the RSHA and the Labor Ministry may well be lost. Therefore, I am basing my argument on Höppner's interpretation of Göring's directives (which he clearly had in hand) and his statement regarding the RSHA–Labor Ministry agreement (which he assumed existed).

19. Krumey, "Vermittlung von polnischen Familien in das Altreich," 30 March 1941, USHMM/15.015M/4/259/43.

20. RSHA IIIB (Müller) to SD-Abschnitt Posen (Höppner), "Arbeitseinsatz von polnischen Familien," 31 March 1941, USHMM/RG15.015M/2/146/50.

21. See Höppner to the RuSHA-Litzmannstadt, "Evakuierung," 30 May 1941, USHMM/RG15.015M/2/146/59–60.

22. See Ulrich Herbert, *Hitler's Foreign Workers: Enforced Foreign Labor in Germany under the Third Reich*, trans. William Templer (Cambridge: Cambridge University Press, 1997), 75ff., 108ff.; Diemut Majer, *"Non-Germans" under the Third Reich: The Nazi Judicial and Administrative System in Germany and Occupied Eastern Europe, with Special Regard to Occupied Poland, 1939–1945*, trans. Peter Thomas Hill, Edward Vance Humphrey, and Brian Levin (Baltimore, MD: Johns Hopkins University Press, 2003), 149–154, 180–183.

23. Himmler and Konrad Meyer, the chief of the RKF Planungshauptabteilung, had originally intended to subdivide Wartheland's large estates, among other reasons to facilitate the establishment of a land-based peasantry. See Aly, *"Final Solution,"* 130. As indicated in Chapter One, plans for subdividing large estates in the East had originated during

the Imperial era. Since their operation required a large force of Polish agricultural workers, Imperial authorities were convinced that "large estates Polonize," and leading Nazi racial politicians were basically of the same opinion.

24. SS-Ansiedlungsstab (Dolezalek), "Der Gauleiter und sein persönlicher Referent Oberregierungsrat Siegmund über die zukünftige Siedlung im Warthegau (Grossgrundbesitzfrage)," 12 February 1941, NARA/T81/286/VoMi 318/2409327ff.

25. The exact date of this directive is unknown, but Krumey referred to it in his "Abschlussbericht" on the *3.Nahplan*, c. 20 January 1942, NARA/T81/386/VoMi 325/2409652ff. Krumey stated that "fundamentally, no Poles capable of work were deported." Although this may have been true as a matter of principle, his statistical breakdown of the operation indicates that a number of fit Poles were sent east (perhaps before Greiser's order was issued).

26. See Krumey, "Arbeit der Umwandererzentralstelle vom 1.10.40 bis jetzt," 8 September 1941, AGK/UWZ-L/26/1–3.

27. Siegmund to Koppe, "Geheim! Evakuierung von Polen zum Zwecke der Ansiedlung von Buchenland- und Bessarabiendeutschen," 10 May 1941, AGK/Reichsstatthalter-Warthegau/346/139–139v.

28. Siegmund to Ministerialdirektor Jäger, 28 August 1941, AGK/Reichsstatthalter-Warthegau/346/186 (emphasis mine).

29. By the end of the war, some 450,000 Warthegau Poles had been dispatched to the Altreich for compulsory labor. See Czesław Łuczak, *Pod Niemieckim Jarzmem (Kraj Warty 1939–1945)* (Poznan, Poland: Wydawca, 1996), 77.

30. Rüstungsinspektion der Wehrkreises XXI, "Geschichte des Kriegeinsatzes der Rüstungsinspektion des Wehrkrieses XXI bis zum 30.September 1940" (presumably October 1940), NARA/T77/619/1807720ff. Similar criticism would be leveled at future contingents of ethnic German immigrants. In 1944, SS officials in the Warthegau complained that many Russian Volksdeutschen had forgotten how to work, were lazy and promiscuous, and were sadly lacking in German-language skills. See Doris I. Bergen, "The 'Volksdeutschen' of Eastern Europe, World War II, and the Holocaust: Constructed Ethnicity, Real Genocide," *Yearbook of European Studies* 13 (1999): 82.

31. Rüstungsinspektion der Wehrkreises XXI, "Geschichte des Kriegeinsatzes der Rüstungsinspektion des Wehrkrieses XXI bis zum 30.September 1940."

32. Rüstungsinspektion des Wehrkreises XXI, "Geschichte des Kriegeinsatzes der Rüstungsinspektion des Wehrkreises XXI, Teil II, 1/10/40–31/12/41" (presumably January 1942), NARA/T77/620/180784ff (his emphasis).

33. Ibid. On Polish workers sent to the Altreich, see Rüstungsinspektion des Wehrkreises XXI, "Geschichte des Kriegeinsatzes der Rüstungsinspektion des Wehrkreises XXI, Teil III, 1/1/42–31/5/42" (presumably January 1942), NARA/T77/620/1807931ff. According to this report, 261,607 Polish workers had been sent to Germany proper between October 1939 and the end of December 1941. Of these, approximately 100,000 were employed in the industrial sector.

34. Hans-Erich Volkmann, "Zwischen Ideologie und Pragmatismus: Zur nationalsozialistischen Wirtschaftspolitik im Reichsgau Wartheland," in Ulrich Haustein, Georg

Strobel, and Gerhard Wagner, eds., *Ostmitteleuropa: Berichte und Forschungen* (Stuttgart, Germany: Ernst Klett, 1981), 438.

35. The incorporated territories did, of course, lose roughly 700,000 Poles via the allocation of workers to the Altreich, but since the Poles in question—many of whom were considered racially and politically undesirable—did not disappear from Reich territory as was initially planned, by no means did this fulfill the regime's original ideological objectives.

36. See "333,700 Volksdeutsche im Gau," *Ostdeutscher Beobachter*, 26 October 1940.

37. Egon Leuschner, *Nationalsozialistische Fremdvolkpolitik* (Berlin: Rassenpolitisches Amt der NSDAP, 1940), 34–35. Leuschner, a lieutenant of the Racial Policy Office's leader, Dr. Walter Gross, was sent to the Warthegau in late 1939 or early 1940 to take part in the development of the DVL. See Robert L. Koehl, "The Deutsche Volksliste in Poland, 1939–1945," *Journal of Central European Affairs* 15 (1956): 357–358.

38. Emphasis mine.

39. RFSS/RKFDV, "Erlass für die Überprüfung und Aussonderung der Bevölkerung in den eingegliederten Ostgebieten," 12 September 1940, in Der Reichsführer-SS/Reichskommissar für die Festigung deutschen Volkstums, *Der Menscheneinsatz: Grundsätze, Anordnung und Reichtlinien* (hereafter *Der Menscheneinsatz*) (Berlin: Hauptabteilung des RKFDV, 1940), 91–93, NARA/T81/VoMi 802/2435422ff.

40. "Verordnung über die Deutsche Volksliste und die deutsche Staatsangehörigkeit in den eingegliederten Ostgebieten," 4 March 1941, *Reichsgesetzblatt* 1941, Teil I, 118–120.

41. Werner Röhr, Elke Heckert, Bernd Gottberg, Jutta Wenzel, and Heide-Marie Grünthal, eds., *Die faschistische Okkupationspolitik in Polen (1939–1945)*, vol. 2 of *Nacht über Europa: Die Okkupationspolitik des deutschen Faschismus (1938–1945)*, Achtbändige Dokumentenedition, ed. Wolfgang Schumann and Ludwig Nestler (Cologne, Germany: Pahl-Rugenstein, 1989), 61. Furthermore, on 19 May 1943, Hitler ordered that all *deutschstämmige Ausländer* (foreigners of German stock) serving in the Wehrmacht, the Waffen-SS, the German Police, or Organization Todt were to receive German citizenship; exceptions were to be determined on an individual basis. See "Erlass des Führers über den Erwerb der deutschen Staatsangehörigkeit durch Einstellung in die deutsche Werhmacht, die Waffen-SS, die deutsche Polizei oder die Organisation Todt vom 19.Mai 1943," 25 May 1943, *Reichsgesetzblatt* 1943, Teil I, 315.

42. Werner Röhr, "Forschungsprobleme zur deutschen Okkupationspolitik im Spiegel der Reihe 'Europa unterm Hakenkreuz,'" in *Europa unterm Hakenkreuz: Analysen, Quellen, Register*, ed. Werner Röhr (Heidelberg, Germany: Verlag Heidelberg, 1996), 271.

43. Koehl, "The Deutsche Volksliste in Poland," 359.

44. There is, to my knowledge, no documentary evidence that links the creation and implementation of the DVL with the de facto end of evacuations. The apparent cause-and-effect relationship between the two discussed here represents my interpretation of the political developments in question. It seems to represent Röhr's and Koehl's interpretations as well.

45. "Übersicht über den Stand der Deutschen Volksliste im Reichsgau Wartheland vom 1.Oktober 1943: Regierungsbezirke Posen, Hohensalza und Litzmannstadt," APP/Reichsstatthalter-Warthegau/594/44.

46. See Röhr et al., *Die faschistische Okkupationspolitik in Polen*, table 17, "Die 'Deutsche Volksliste' im annektieren Polen (Stand 1944)," 385.

47. Ibid. The liberal use of the DVL in industrial Upper Silesia was largely the reflection of local authorities' desire to keep the mines and factories in their jurisdiction operating at full capacity. See Robert L. Koehl, *RKFDV: German Resettlement and Population Policy 1939–1945—A History of the Reich Commission for the Strengthening of Germandom* (Cambridge, MA: Harvard University Press, 1957), 118, 121; Czesław Madajczyk, *Die Okkupationspolitik Nazideutschlands in Polen, 1939–1945* (Berlin: Akademie-Verlag, 1987), 506ff.

48. Herbert S. Levine, "Local Authority and the SS State: The Conflict over Population Policy in Danzig–West Prussia, 1939–1945," *Central European History* 2 (1969): 341ff. In postwar testimony, a member of VoMi described the application of the DVL in Danzig–West Prussia: "During the process of Germanizing Poles on the basis of the Ethnic Register, there were many cases where whole villages or towns were compulsorily entered in the register according to fixed quotas laid down by Forster. For example, a [Nazi] local branch leader or mayor was instructed to enter eighty percent of his village in the register although it was at least 80 percent Polish. When the local branch leader refused, he was reported by the district leader to the Gauleiter, then the Gauleiter himself came to the village and gave the branch leader such a dressing down in an inn in front of all the Germans and the Poles that the branch leader promptly sat down, lined up all the Poles and simply entered them in the Ethnic Register ... I reported this incident to Heinz Bruckner [VoMi]. Bruckner simply said that he had passed on my information to Himmler but that Forster allowed no one to interfere with his ethnic policy but based his position on Hitler's support." Quoted in J. Noakes and G. Pridham, eds., *Nazism: A History in Documents and Eyewitness Accounts, 1919–1945* (New York: Schocken Books, 1988), 2: doc. 663, p. 948.

49. Koehl, "The Deutsche Volksliste in Poland," 366.

50. One could argue that the vast number of individuals granted DVL 3 status could have—and would have—been declared Poles again after they were no longer needed for the war effort; that is, if Germany had succeeded in defeating the USSR in short order (as Hitler expected), the German status of the people in question would have been revoked, and they would have been deported as originally planned. Indeed, it is likely that the racial experts would have eventually reevaluated individual cases; according to a Himmler directive of 9 February 1942, the RMdI, in cooperation with the office of the RFSS, reserved the right to revoke the citizenship of DVL 3s on an individual basis if their Germanization or re-Germanization proved to be a failure. See RFSS/RKFDV, "Allgemeine Anordnung Nr 12/0 über die Behandlung der in die Deutsche Volksliste eingetragenen Personen," 9 February 1942, USHMM/RG.15.029(Landrat Wollstein)/1/6/36–39. But considering the sheer size of the DVL 3 population in the incorporated territories, it seems improbable that the Nazis would ever have simply revoked the German status of the majority of DVL 3s in blanket fashion. One must keep in mind that according to both Himmler's guidelines and Nazi racial theory (nonsensical and at loggerheads with reality though both may have been), those registered as DVL 3s, with the exception of non-Germans in German-Polish mixed marriages, were Deutschstämmige—individuals of German ethnicity, of German blood that had to be retained for the good of the Volk, who had unfortunately "gone under"

NOTES TO PAGES 211–212

into Polentum over the previous decades. The "discovery" of this lost German blood not only helped to swell the ranks of both the Wehrmacht and the labor force of the new Reichsgaue, it also dramatically increased the "German" population of annexed territory, thus furthering the goals of the Germanization campaign. I imagine that at least in the case of Danzig–West Prussia, a man such as Albert Forster would have fought tooth and nail against the removal of his 762,000 recently discovered DVL 3 Germans among the Polish masses.

51. For a valuable overview and analysis of the legal intricacies of the Deutsche Volksliste, see Majer, "*Non-Germans*" *under the Third Reich*, 123–127, 238–246. On RuSHA's involvement in the DVL program, see Isabel Heinemann, "*Rasse, Siedlung, deutsches Blut*": *Das Rasse- & Siedlungshauptamt der SS und die rassenpolitische Neuordnung Europas* (Göttingen, Germany: Wallstein Verlag, 2003), 260–282. Doris Bergen demonstrates how "newly minted ethnic Germans" often benefited directly from the destruction of eastern European Jews. Citing a few examples from the Generalgouvernement and Hungary, she shows how some individuals, be they (formerly) Polish, Ukrainian, or Hungarian, used their new status as Germans to seize the property of murdered Jews, arguing that sheer greed exacerbated anti-Semitism in the regions in question: "Given the difficulties of defining Volksdeutsche, those who aspired to membership found the easiest way to prove themselves good Germans was to show that they were good Nazis. And the most effective way to establish Nazi credentials was by endorsing and actively implementing attacks on the enemies of the Reich. Enlisting in the SS, participating in pogroms, and laying claim to Jewish property could all be means to that end." See Bergen, "The 'Volksdeutschen' of Eastern Europe," 77–78, as well as her earlier article, "The Nazi Concept of 'Volksdeutsche' and the Exacerbation of Anti-Semitism in Eastern Europe, 1939–1945," *Journal of Contemporary History* 29, no. 4 (October 1994): 569–582; also Klaus-Peter Friedrich, "Kollaboration und Antisemitismus in Polen unter deutscher Besatzung (1939–1944/45): Zu verdrängten Aspekten eines schwierigen deutsch-polnisch-jüdischen Verhältnisses," *Zeitschrift für Geschichtswissenschaft* 45, no. 9 (1997): 828–829. Although it is probable that similar incidents occurred in Wartheland, I have found no evidence at all to pass judgment. Moreover, given the dearth of housing and employment opportunities for true ethnic German immigrants, as well as the more rigorous DVL admission standards in the province, it seems unlikely that this form of Polish collaboration in the genocide of Warthegau Jews occurred with any frequency.

52. Rassenpolitisches Amt (Wetzet and Hecht), "Die Frage der Behandlung der Bevölkerung der ehemaligen polnischen Gebiete nach rassenpolitischen Gesichtspunkten," 25 November 1939, NARA/T74/9/57/ 38057ff.; Himmler, "Einige Gedanken über die Behandlung der Fremdvölkischen im Osten," 20 May 1940, NARA/T175/119/2646113ff.

53. RSHA IVB4 (Eichmann), "Ausstellung 'Die grosse Heimkehr,'" 3 April 1941, AGK/EWZ-L/838/2/4.

54. Krumey, "Abschlussbericht" on the 3.Nahplan, c. 20 January 1942.

55. Volkmann, "Zwischen Ideologie und Pragmatismus," 430.

56. Ulrich Herbert, *A History of Foreign Labor in Germany, 1880–1980: Seasonal Workers/Forced Laborers/Guest Workers*, trans. William Templer (Ann Arbor: University of Michigan Press, 1990), 177.

57. Browning, *The Path to Genocide*, 73. Herbert detects a correlation between the decision to exploit Russian labor and the intensification of Jewish slaughter in the East, arguing that the use of Russian forced labor allowed the Nazis to step up the extermination of Russian and Polish Jews with no consideration of their potential economic value.

58. Kendzia, "Bericht über die Besprechung am 11.Januar 1940, 10 Uhr," 11 January 1940, USHMM/RG15.015M/2/146/9–15.

59. "Sitzung über Ostfragen unter dem Vorsitz Generalfeldmarschall Göring" (gez. Dr. Gramsch), 12 February 1940, International Military Tribunal, *Trial of the Major War Criminals before the International Military Tribunal, Nuremberg, 14 November 1945–1 October 1946*, 42 vols. (Nuremberg, Germany: International Military Tribunal, 1947–1949), 36: doc. 305-EC, 299–307.

60. SS-Ansiedlungsstab (Dolezalek), report on meeting with Greiser, 12 February 1941.

61. Martin Broszat, *Nationalsozialistische Polenpolitik, 1939–1945* (Stuttgart, Germany: Deutsche Verlags-Anstalt, 1961), 88.

62. See, for example, Hans Mommsen, "Hitlers Stellung im nationalsozialistischen Herrschaftssystem, in Gerhard Hirschfeld and Lothar Kettenacker, eds., *Der "Führerstaat": Mythos und Realität* (London: Publications of the German Historical Institute, 1981), 43–72; Mommsen, "National Socialism: Continuity and Change," in Walter Laqueur, ed., *Fascism: A Reader's Guide* (Berkeley: University of California Press, 1976), 179–210; Martin Broszat, *The Hitler State: The Foundation and Development of the Internal Structure of the Third Reich*, trans. John W. Hiden (New York: Longman Group, 1981), particularly the final chapter; Broszat, "Hitler und die Genesis der 'Endlösung': Anlass der Thesen von David Irving," *Vierteljahrshefte für Zeitgeschichte* 25 (1977): 737–775. *Cumulative radicalization* is Mommsen's term.

63. For examples, see Note 21 in the Introduction to this book. Christopher Browning, one of the foremost proponents of the radicalization theory (and one who argues—convincingly, in my opinion—that Hitler played a central role in the decision-making process) provides an overview of recent scholarship in *Nazi Policy, Jewish Workers, German Killers* (Cambridge: Cambridge University Press, 2000), 26–32. For a more detailed discussion of the literature, see Ian Kershaw (who also leans toward the functionalist position), *The Nazi Dictatorship: Problems and Perspectives of Interpretation* (London: Arnold, 2000), chap. 5.

64. Karl Schleunes, *The Twisted Road to Auschwitz: Nazi Policy towards the Jews, 1933–1939* (Chicago: University of Illinois Press, 1970).

65. On the kidnappings, see Richard C. Lukas, *Did the Children Cry? Hitler's War against Jewish and Polish Children, 1939–1945* (New York: Hippocrene Books, 2001), 105–126; Gitta Sereny, *The Healing Wound: Experiences and Reflections, Germany, 1938–2001* (New York: W. W. Norton, 2002), 25–52.

66. Aly, *"Final Solution,"* 189–190; Daniel Inkelas, "Visions of Harmony and Violence: RKF Landscape Planning and Population Policy in Annexed Poland, 1939–1944" (Ph.D. diss., Northwestern University, 1998), 200. For a transcript of the cover letter, see Czesław Madajczyk, ed., *Vom Generalplan Ost zum Generalsiedlungsplan* (Munich, Germany: K. G. Sauer Verlag, 1994), doc. 2, pp. 14–15.

67. Wetzel, for his part, regarded these figures as far too low, asserting that the actual "foreign" population of the region was approximately 60 million; 46 to 51 million people, then, would have to be deported to achieve the goals of the plan.

68. Wetzel, "Stellungnahme und Gedanken zum Generalplan Ost des Reichsführers SS," 27 April 1942, in Madajczyk, *Vom Generalplan Ost zum Generalsiedlungsplan*, doc. 16, pp. 50–81; Meyer, "General Plan East—Legal, Economic and Territorial Principles for the Reconstruction of the East," 28 May 1942, NARA/M894/14 (English transcript); Inkelas, "Visions of Harmony and Violence," 202–205.

69. Himmler, "Generalplan Ost—Rechtliche, wirtschaftliche und räumliche Grundlagen des Ostaufbaus," 12 June 1942, in Madajczyk, *Vom Generalplan Ost zum Generalsiedlungsplan*, doc. 27, pp. 133–134. Himmler noted that before he could submit the proposals to Hitler, he would need a comprehensive resettlement scheme embracing all former plans regarding the incorporated territories, as well as plans for Bohemia and Moravia, Alsace-Lorraine, Upper Carniola (part of occupied Yugoslavia), and Southern Styria (the southeastern Austrian region around Graz). Meyer responded with the Generalsiedlungsplan, which will be briefly discussed.

70. Meyer, "Ostraum ingesamt: Material zum Generalsiedlungsplan—Flächen und Bevölkerungsberechnung, Unterlagen für einen Generalsiedlungsplan—Grundzahlen und Karten," 23 December 1942, in Madajczyk, *Vom Generalplan Ost zum Generalsiedlungsplan*, doc. 71, pp. 235–255.

71. Inkelas, "Visions of Harmony and Violence," 208.

72. For a detailed discussion of the GPO and subsequent Germanization plans, see Helmut Heiber, "Der Generalplan Ost," *Vierteljahrshefte für Zeitgeschichte* 6 (1957): 281–325; Madajczyk, "Generalplan Ost," *Polish-Western Affairs* 3, no. 2 (1962): 390–443; the collection of essays in Mechthild Rössler and Sabine Schleiermacher, eds., *Der "Generalplan Ost": Hauptlinien der nationalsozialistischen Plangungs- und Vernichtungspolitik* (Berlin: Akademie-Verlag, 1993); Bruno Wasser, *Himmlers Raumplanung im Osten: Der Generalplan Ost in Polen, 1940–1944* (Basel, Switzerland, and Boston: Birkhäuser, 1993); Götz Aly and Susanne Heim, *Vordenker der Vernichtung: Auschwitz und die deutschen Pläne für eine neue europäsche Ordnung* (Frankfurt, Germany: Fischer Taschenbuch Verlag, 1995), 394–440; Heinemann, *"Rasse, Siedlung, deutsches Blut,"* 359–376.

73. Bruno Wasser, "Die 'Germanisierung' im Distrikt Lublin als Generalprobe und erste Realisierugsphase der 'Generalplan Ost,'" in Rössler and Schleiermacher, *Der "Generalplan Ost,"* 290. See Wasser's *Himmlers Raumplanung im Osten*, 133ff., as well.

74. Ehlich, "Die Behandlung des fremden Volkstums, Referat des SS-Standartenführers Dr. Ehlich, Reichssicherheitshauptamt, auf der Tagung des volkspolitischen Reichsreferats der RSF am 10./11.Dezember 1942 in Salzburg," in Rössler and Schleiermacher, *Der "Generalplan Ost,"* doc. 2, p. 49. As early as January 1941, with the invasion of the USSR still months away, Himmler told his SS leaders that "the inevitable war with Bolshevism" could serve as a means to destroy 30 million Slavs, thus facilitating German colonization. See Inkelas, "Visions of Harmony and Violence," 199–200.

75. John Connelly, "Nazis and Slavs: From Racial Theory to Racist Practice," *Central European History* 32 (January 1999): 32.

76. Kershaw, *The Nazi Dictatorship*, 77.

77. Aly, *"Final Solution,"* 159; Czesław Łuczak, "Die Ansiedlung der deutschen Bevölkerung im besetzten Polen (1939–1945)," *Studia Historiae Oeconomicae* 13 (1978): 194.

78. Łuczak, "Die Ansiedlung der deutschen Bevölkerung," 201.

79. The "Z"-Hofbildung Action was initiated in 1942 at Göring's behest in order to provide agricultural workers for the Altreich. By Jerzy Marczewski's estimate, as many as 155,230 Poles (171,947 according to Röhr) were evicted for this purpose, as well as for the purpose of consolidating small farms in the Gau (presumably for Volksdeutsche Besserstellung), but ultimately, only 38,168 were actually sent to Germany proper. The remainder were simply "resettled" internally within Wartheland. See Marczewski, "The Aims and Character of the Nazi Deportation Policy as Shown by Example of the 'Warta Region,'" *Polish-Western Affairs* 10 (1961): 256–257.

80. Röhr et al., *Die faschistische Okkupationspolitik in Polen*, Table 4, 356–357.

81. The Polenreservat scheme is outlined in Krumey's memo, "Bericht—Monat Juli 1942," 5 August 1942, in Wacław Szulc, ed., "Wysiedlanie Ludności Polskiej w tzw. Kraju Warty i na Zamojszczyźnie oraz Popełnione przy tym Zbrodnie," *Biuletyn Głównej Komisji Badania Zbrodni Hitlerowskich w Polsce 21* (Warsaw: Wydawnictwo Prawnicze 1970), doc. 23, pp. 113–114. Three reservations were established, a large one in Kreis Kalisch and two smaller ones in Ostrowo and Wielun. See "Erfahrungsbericht über die Errichtung von Polenreservaten in den Kreisen Kalisch, Ostrowo, und Wielungen [*sic*]" (no provenance, undated), AGK/Reichsstatthalter-Warthegau/73/4–6. The scheme had been on the table since at least March 1941. Krumey originally saw reservations as a lesser evil than merely displacing Poles, reasoning that they were easy to guard, would supply a ready source of manpower for enterprises in their respective vicinities, and would simplify the later transport of Poles to the Generalgouvernement when evacuations resumed. See Krumey, "Aktenvermerk über eine Besprechung mit Pg. Dietz von Landesarbeitsamt-Posen/UWZ-Litzmannstadt am 21.März 1941," 21 March 1941, USHRI/RG15.015M/2/146/40–41. By the end of 1942, 5,134 Poles had been interned on these three reservations. See Krumey, "Abschlussbericht über dir Arbeit der Umwandererzentralstelle im Rahmen des erweiterten 3.Nahplanes (Ansetzung der Reste der Umsiedlergruppen, Besserstellung der Volksdeutschen und Landzulagen) im Reichsgau Wartheland für das Jahr 1942," 31 December 1942, NARA/T81/286/VoMi 331/2409839ff.

82. Röhr et al., *Die faschistische Okkupationspolitik in Polen*, table 6, 360; Łuczak, *Pod Niemieckim Jarzmem*, 77.

83. Röhr et al., *Die faschistische Okkupationspolitik in Polen*, table 4, 356–357.

84. Quoted in Aly, *"Final Solution,"* 65.

85. See Rapp's SS personnel file, NARA/BDC/RG242/A3343/SSO–007B, as well as the transcript of his trial for war crimes held in Essen between 1965 and 1966, in Irene Sagel-Grande, H. H. Fuchs, and C. F. Rüter, eds., *Justiz und NS-Verbrechen: Sammlung deutscher Strafurteile wegen nationalsozialistischer Tötungsverbrechen, 1945–1966* (Amsterdam: University Press Amsterdam, 1979), 20: Case 588, 719–815.

86. Hans Safrian, *Eichmann und seine Gehilfen* (Frankfurt, Germany: Fischer Taschenbuch Verlag, 1997), 293–311.

87. Aly, *"Final Solution,"* 8.

88. Safrian, *Eichmann und seine Gehilfen,* 209ff.

89. Aly, *"Final Solution,"* 8. Rolf-Heinz Höppner, Rapp's successor as office chief of the UWZ-Posen, suggested to Eichmann on 16 July 1941 that since many of the Jews of the Warthegau, specifically implying those in the Litzmannstadt ghetto, would probably not survive the coming winter due to the scarcity of food, the most "humane solution" to the Jewish Question would to "finish off the Jews unfit for labor through some fast-acting means." The gassings at Chełmno began the following December. See Höppner, "Lösung der Judenfrage," 16 July 1941, AGK/Greiser Trial/36/568–568v. The participation of many UWZ personnel in the Holocaust reflected a trend: just as UWZ deportation specialists ultimately employed the knowledge they had gained in annexed Poland in the roundup and transport of European Jews to the death camps, many staff members of the Nazi T-4 euthanasia program, responsible for the extermination of over 70,000 physically handicapped and mentally impaired individuals between 1939 and 1941, devoted their expertise in mass gassing to the physical annihilation of Jews within the murder factories themselves, including Chełmno, Bełżec, Sobibor, and Treblinka. See Michael Burleigh, *Ethics and Extermination: Reflections on Nazi Genocide* (Cambridge: Cambridge University Press, 1997), 126–127; Henry Friedlander, "Step by Step: The Expansion of Murder, 1939–1941," in Omer Bartov, ed., *The Holocaust: Origins, Implementation, Aftermath* (London: Routledge, 2000), 68–71. For an in-depth examination of the connections between the T-4 program and the Final Solution, see Henry Friedlander, *The Origins of Nazi Genocide: From Euthanasia to the Final Solution* (Chapel Hill: University of North Carolina Press, 1995).

90. Röhr et al., *Die faschistische Okkupationspolitik in Polen,* 26.

91. Ibid., 56.

Bibliography

ARCHIVAL SOURCES

Archiwum Głównej Komisji Badania Zbrodni Hitlerowskich w Polsce—
Instytutu Pamięci Naradowej (AGK), Warsaw

CAMSW 167, Rasse- und Siedlungsamt, Aussenstelle—Litzmannstadt
CAMSW 687, Geheime Staatspolizei, Staatspolizeileitstelle—Posen
CAMSW 701, Gendarmerie Kreis Kempen
CAMSW 717, Befehlshaber der Ordnungspolizei—Posen
CAMSW 775, Kommando der Schutzpolizei—Kalisch
CAMSW 838, Chef der Sicherheitspolizei und des SD, Einwandererzentralstelle—Litzmannstadt
Najwyszy Tribunał Naradowy, Proces Artura Greisera (Greiser Trial)
Reichsstatthalter im Warthegau
Umwandererzentralstelle—Posen, Dienststelle Litzmannstadt

Archiwum Państwowe Bydgoszcz (APB), Bydgoszcz, Poland

Umwandererzentralstelle—Danzig

Archiwum Państwowe Łódź (APL), Lodz, Poland

Umwandererzentralstelle—Posen, Dienststelle Litzmannstadt

Archiwum Państwowe Poznań (APP), Poznan, Poland

Befehlshaber der Ordnungspolizei—Posen
Chef der Zivilverwaltung beim Oberbefehlshaber im Militärbezirk Posen
Der Reichsstatthalter im Reichsgau Wartheland
Landratsamt Grätz
Landratsamt Jarotschin
Landratsamt Scharnikau
Landratsamt Schrimm
SS-Ansiedlungsstab—Posen
Volksdeutsche Mittelstelle—Posen

U.S. Holocaust Memorial Museum Archive (USHMM), Washington, DC

RG 11.001M, Records from the "Osobyi" Archive in Moscow

RG 15.007M, Reichssicherheitshauptamt

RG 15.015M, Chef der Sipo und des SD, Umwandererzentralstelle—Posen

RG 15.029M, Landrat Wollstein

RG 15.040M, Umwandererzentralstelle Poznań, Service Branch in Łódź

U.S. National Archives and Records Administration (NARA), College Park, MD

BDC RG 242 A3343, Personnel Records of SS Officers

M 894, Trials of War Criminals before the Nuernberg Military Tribunal: Case 8 ("The RuSHA Case")

RG 238, World War II War Crimes Records

T 74, Reich Commissioner for the Strengthening of Germandom

T 77, Records of the German Armed Forces High Command (OKW, Oberkommando der Wehrmacht)

T 81, Deutsches Ausland-Institut

T 175, Reich Leader of the SS and Chief of German Police

PUBLISHED PRIMARY SOURCES

Achterberg, Eberhard. "Der deutsche Osten—Aufgabe und Verpflichtung." *Nationalsozialistische Monatshefte* 130 (January 1941): 16–20.

Bismarck, Otto von. *Bismarck: The Man and the Statesman, Being the Reflections and Reminiscences of Otto, Prince von Bismarck.* Trans. A. J. Butler. New York and London: Harper and Brothers, 1899.

Coole, W. W., and M. F. Potter, eds. *Thus Speaks Germany.* New York: Harper and Brothers, 1941.

Darré, R. Walther. *Das Bauerntum als Lebensquell der nordischen Rasse.* Munich, Germany: J. F. Lehmann, 1938.

———. *Neuadel als Blut und Boden.* Munich, Germany: J. F. Lehmann, 1935.

Datner, Szymon, Janusz Gumkowski, and Kazimierz Leszczyński, eds. *Wysiedlanie ludności ziem Polskich wcielonych do Rzeszy: Biuletyn Głównej Komisji Badania Zbrodni Hitlerowskich w Polsce 12.* Warsaw: Wydawnictwo Prawnicze, 1960.

Dietrich, Otto. *Hitler.* Trans. Richard and Clara Winston. Chicago: Henry Regnery, 1955.

Frank, Hans. *Das Diensttagebuch des deutschen Generalgouverneurs in Polen, 1939–1945.* Ed. Werner Präg and Wolfgang Jacobmeyer. Stuttgart, Germany: Deutsche Verlags-Anstalt, 1975.

Friedmann, T., ed. *Der Höhere SS- und Polizeiführer beim Reichsstatthalter in Posen im Wehrkreis XXI, Wilhelm Koppe: SS-Obergruppenführer und General der Polizei—Dokumentensammlung.* Haifa: Institute of Documentation in Israel for the Investigation of Nazi War Crimes, 1997.

Geisler, Walter. *Der Deutsche Osten als Lebensraum für alle Berufsstände.* Berlin, Prague, and Vienna: Volk und Reich Verlag, 1942.

———. *Deutscher! Der Osten ruft Dich!* Berlin: Volk und Reich Verlag, 1941.

Greifelt, Ulrich. "Festigung deutschen Volkstums im deutschen Osten." *Raumforschung und Raumordnung: Monatsschrift der Reichsarbeitsgemeinschaft für Raumordnung* 1 (January 1941): 2–6.

Greiser, Arthur. *Der Aufbau im Osten.* Jena, Germany: G. Fischer, 1942.

———. "Die Grossdeutsche Aufgabe im Wartheland." *Nationalsozialistische Monatshefte* 130 (January 1941): 46–50.

Groscurth, Helmuth. *Tagebücher eines Abwehroffiziers, 1938–1940.* Ed. Helmut Krausnick and Harold C. Deutsch. Stuttgart, Germany: Deutsche Verlags-Anstalt, 1970.

Hahn, Edmond. "Land der Zukunft—Wartheland." *Der Deutsche im Osten: Monatsschrift für Kultur, Politik und Unterhaltung* (April 1941): 234–236.

Halder, Franz. *Kriegstagebuch: Tägliche Aufzeichnungen des Chefs des Generalstabes des Heeres, 1939–1942.* Edited by Hans-Adolf Jacobsen. 2 vols. Stuttgart, Germany: W. Kohlhammer Verlag, 1962.

Haussmann, Dr. Kurt. "Die Bauernsiedlung in den neuen Ostgauen." *Raumforschung und Raumordnung: Monatsschrift der Reichsarbeitsgemeinschaft für Raumordnung* 10 (1940): 416–418.

Himmler, Heinrich. *Geheimreden 1933 bis 1945 und andere Ansprachen.* Ed. Bradley K. Smith and Agnes F. Peterson. Frankfurt, Germany: Propyläen Verlag, 1974.

Hindenburg, Paul von. *Out of My Life.* Trans. F. A. Holt. New York and London: Harper and Brothers, 1921.

Hitler, Adolf. *Der grossdeutsche Freiheitskampf: Reden Adolf Hitlers.* Vol. 1, *September 1939 bis 10. März 1940.* Munich, Germany: Zentralverlag der NSDAP, Franz Eher Nachf., 1940.

———. *Hitler's Secret Book.* Trans. Salvator Attensio. New York: Grove Press, 1961.

———. *Mein Kampf.* Trans. Ralph Mannheim. Boston: Houghton Mifflin, 1971.

Hohensalzaer Zeitung, 1940.

Institute for the Study of Minority Problems. *The Polish and Non-Polish Populations of Poland: The Results of the Population Census of 1931.* Warsaw: Institute for the Study of Minority Problems, 1932.

International Military Tribunal. *Trial of the Major War Criminals before the International Military Tribunal, Nuremberg, 14 November 1945–1 October 1946.* 42 vols. Nuremberg, Germany: International Military Tribunal, 1947–1949.

Johst, Hans. *Ruf des Reiches—Echo des Volkes! Eine Ostfahrt.* Munich, Germany: Franz Eher Verlag, 1942.

Kleindienst, Alfred, and Kurt Lück. *Die Wolhyniendeutschen kehren heim ins Reich.* Posen, Poland: Historische Gesellschaft in Posen, 1940.

Kohl, Horst, ed. *Die Reden des Ministerpräsidenten und Reichskanzlers Fürsten von Bismarck.* Aalen, Germany: Scienta Verlag, 1970.

Lange, Friedrich. *Ostland kehrt heim.* Berlin-Leipzig: Nibelungen Verlag, 1940.

Leszczyński, Kaszimierz, ed. "Działaność Einsatzgruppen Policji Bezpieczeństwa na Ziemiach Polskich w 1939 R. w świetle Dokumentów." *Biuletyn Głównej Komisji Badania Zbrodni Hitlerowskich w Polsce 22*. Warsaw: Wydawnictwo Prawnicze, 1971.

Leuschner, Egon. *Nationalsozialistische Fremdvolkpolitik*. Berlin: Rassenpolitisches Amt der NSDAP, 1940.

Litzmannstädter Zeitung (Lodscher Zeitung), 1940–1941.

Loeber, Dietrich A., ed. *Diktierte Option: Die Umsiedlung der Deutsch-Balten aus Estland und Lettland, 1939–1941*. Neumünster, Germany: Karl Wachholtz Verlag, 1972.

Lück, Kurt. *Die Cholmer und Lubliner Deutschen kehren heim ins Vaterland*. Posen, Poland: Historische Gesellschaft im Wartheland/Verlag S. Hirzel in Leipzig, 1940.

———. *Der Lebenskampf im deutsch-polnischen Grenzraum*. Berlin: Zentralverlag der NSDAP, 1940.

Łuczak, Czesław, ed. *Połeżenie Ludności Polskiej w tzw. Kraju Warty w Okresie Hitlerowskiej Okupacji. Documenta Occupationis 13*. Poznan, Poland: Instytut Zachodni, 1990.

———, ed. *Wysiedlenia Ludności Polskiej na tzw. Ziemiach Wcielonych do Rzeszy, 1939–1945. Documenta Occupationis 8*. Poznan, Poland: Instytut Zachodni, 1969.

Ludendorff, Erich. *Ludendorff's Own Story, August 1914–November 1918*. New York and London: Harper Brothers, 1919.

Madajczyk, Czesław, ed. *Vom Generalplan Ost zum Generalsiedlungsplan*. Munich, Germany: K. G. Sauer Verlag, 1994.

Michaelis, Herbert, Ernst Schraepler, and Günther Schael, eds. *Ursachen und Folgen vom deutschen Zusammenbruch 1918 und 1945 bis zur staatlichen Neuordnung Deutschlands in der Gegenwart: Eine Urkunden- und Dokumentensammlung zur Zeitgeschichte*. 29 vols. Berlin: Dr. Herbert Wendler, n.d.

Moritz, Erhard, ed. *Fall Barbarossa: Dokumente zur Vorbereitung der faschistischen Wehrmacht auf die Aggression gegen die Sowjetunion (1940/41)*. Berlin: Deutscher Militärverlag, 1970.

Noakes, J., and G. Pridham, eds. *Nazism: A History in Documents and Eyewitness Accounts, 1919–1945*. 2 vols. New York: Schocken Books, 1988.

Nuernberg Military Tribunals. *Trials of War Criminals before the Nuernberg Military Tribunals under Control Council Law no. 10, Neurnberg, October 1946–April 1949*. 15 vols. Washington, DC: U.S. Government Printing Office, 1949–1953.

Oberländer, Theodor. "Von der Front des Volkstumskampfes." *Neues Bauerntum* 4–5 (April–May 1940): 127–130.

Ostdeutscher Beobachter, 1939–1940.

Pätzold, Kurt, ed. *Verfolgung, Vertreibung, Vernichtung: Dokumente des faschistischen Antisemitismus, 1933 bis 1942*. Frankfurt, Germany: Röderberg-Verlag, 1984.

Publikationsstelle Berlin-Dahlem. *Die Ostgebiete des Deutschen Reiches und das Generalgouvernement der besetzten polnischen Gebiete in statistischen Angaben*. Berlin: Selbstverlag der Publikationsstelle, 1940.

Rauschning, Hermann. *Hitler Speaks: A Series of Political Conversations with Adolf Hitler on His Real Aims*. London: Thomton Butterworth, 1940.

Reichsgesetzblatt, 1935, 1941, 1943.

Röhr, Werner, Elke Heckert, Bernd Gottberg, Jutta Wenzel, and Heide-Marie Grünthal, eds. *Die faschistische Okkupationspolitik in Polen (1939–1945)*. Vol. 2 of *Nacht über Europa: Die Okkupationspolitik des deutschen Faschismus (1938–1945)*, *Achtbändige Dokumentenedition*. Ed. Wolfgang Schumann and Ludwig Nestler. Cologne, Germany: Pahl-Rugenstein, 1989. [Schumann and Nestler's multivolume work was published under the title *Europa unterm Hakenkreuz: Die Okkupationspolitik des deutschen Faschismus (1938–1945)*, between 1988 and 1996.]

Rosenberg, Alfred. *Das politische Tagebuch Alfred Rosenbergs: 1934/35 und 1939/40*. Ed. Hans-Günther Seraphim. Göttingen, Germany: Musterschmidt-Verlag, 1956.

Rosenkranz, Otto. *Siedlung und Landwirtschaft im Reichsgau Wartheland*. Berlin: Deutsche Landsbuchhandlung, Sohrey, 1941.

Sagel-Grande, Irene, H. H. Fuchs, and C. F. Rüter, eds. *Justiz und NS-Verbrechen: Sammlung deutscher Strafurteile wegen nationalsozialistischer Tötungsverbrechen, 1945–1966*. 22 vols. Amsterdam: University Press Amsterdam, 1979.

Schade, Ulrich. *Industrie und Handel im Reichsgau Wartheland*. Berlin: Volk und Reich Verlag, 1942.

Szulc, Wacław, ed. *Hitlerowski Aparat Wysiedleńczy w Polsce Sylwetki Głównych jego "Działaczy."* Warsaw: Ministerstwo Sprawiedliwości, 1973.

———, ed. "Wysiedlanie Ludności Polskiej w tzw. Kraju Warty i na Zamojszczyźnie oraz Popełnione przy tym Zbrodnie." *Biuletyn Głównej Komisji Badania Zbrodni Hitlerowskich w Polsce 21*. Warsaw: Wydawnictwo Prawnicze, 1970.

U.S. Department of State. *Documents on German Foreign Policy; 1918–1945*. Series D (1937–1945). 13 vols. Washington, DC: U.S. Government Printing Office, 1949–1957.

Wildt, Michael, ed. *Die Judenpolitik des SD, 1935 bis 1938: Eine Dokumentation*. Munich, Germany: R. Oldenbourg, 1995.

Zoch, Wilhelm. "Neue Ordnung im Osten." *Neues Bauerntum: Fachwissenschaftliche Zeitschrift für das ländliche Siedlungswesen* 3 (March 1940): 84–87.

SECONDARY LITERATURE

Aly, Götz. *"Final Solution": Nazi Population Policy and the Murder of the European Jews*. Trans. Belinda Cooper and Allison Brown. London: Edward Arnold, 1999.

———. "'Jewish Resettlement': Reflections on the Political Prehistory of the Holocaust." In *National Socialist Extermination Policies: Contemporary German Perspectives and Controversies*, ed. Ulrich Herbert. New York: Berghahn Books, 2000.

Aly, Götz, and Susanne Heim. "The Economics of the Final Solution: A Case Study from the General Government." *Simon Wiesenthal Annual* 5 (1988): 3–48.

———. *Vordenker der Vernichtung: Auschwitz und die deutschen Pläne für eine neue europäsche Ordnung*. Frankfurt, Germany: Fischer Taschenbuch Verlag, 1995.

Arendt, Hannah. *Eichmann in Jerusalem: A Report on the Banality of Evil*. New York: Viking Press, 1964.

Baumgart, Winifried. "Zur Ansprache Hitlers vor den Führern der Wehrmacht am 22. August 1939: Eine quellenkritische Untersuchung." *Vierteljahrshefte für Zeitgeschichte* 16 (April 1968): 120–149.

Bergen, Doris I. "The Nazi Concept of 'Volksdeutsche' and the Exacerbation of Anti-Semitism in Eastern Europe, 1939–1945." *Journal of Contemporary European History* 29, no. 4 (October 1994): 569–582.

———. "The 'Volksdeutschen' of Eastern Europe, World War II, and the Holocaust: Constructed Ethnicity, Real Genocide." *Yearbook of European Studies* 13 (1999): 70–93.

Birdsall, Paul. *Versailles Twenty Years After.* New York: Reynal and Hitchcock, 1941.

Birn, Ruth Bettina. *Die Höheren SS- und Polizeiführer: Himmlers Vertreter im Reich und in den besetzten Gebieten.* Düsseldorf, Germany: Droste Verlag, 1986.

Biskupski, M. B. *The History of Poland.* Westport, CT: Greenwood Press, 2000.

Black, Peter R. *Ernst Kaltenbrunner: Ideological Soldier of the Third Reich.* Princeton, NJ: Princeton University Press, 1984.

———. "Rehearsal for 'Reinhard'? Odilo Globocznik and the Lublin *Selbstschutz.*" *Central European History* 2 (1992): 204–226.

Blanke, Richard. "Bismarck and the Prussian Polish Policies of 1886." *Journal of Modern History* 45 (1973): 211–239.

———. *Orphans of Versailles: The Germans in Western Poland, 1918–1939.* Lexington: University Press of Kentucky, 1993.

———. *Prussian Poland and the German Empire (1871–1900).* Boulder, CO: East European Monographs, 1981.

———. "When Germans and Poles Lived Together: From the History of German-Polish Relations." In *Germany and Eastern Europe: Cultural Identities and Cultural Differences,* ed. Keith Bullivant and Geoffrey Giles. Amsterdam: Rodolphi, 1999.

Bramwell, Anna. *Blood and Soil: Richard Walther Darré and Hitler's "Green Party."* Buckinghamshire, UK: Kensal Press, 1985.

Breitman, Richard. *The Architect of Genocide: Himmler and the Final Solution.* Hanover, NH: Brandeis University Press, 1991.

Broszat, Martin. *The Hitler State: The Foundation and Development of the Internal Structure of the Third Reich.* Trans. John W. Hiden. New York: Longman Group, 1981.

———. "Hitler und die Genesis der 'Endlösung': Anlass der Thesen von David Irving." *Vierteljahrshefte für Zeitgeschichte* 25 (1977): 737–775.

———. *Nationalsozialistische Polenpolitik, 1939–1945.* Stuttgart, Germany: Deutsche Verlags-Anstalt, 1961.

———. *Zweihundert Jahre deutsche Polenpolitik.* Munich, Germany: Franz Ehrenwirth Verlag, 1963.

Browning, Christopher. *Nazi Policy, Jewish Workers, German Killers.* Cambridge: Cambridge University Press, 2000.

———. *Ordinary Men: Reserve Police Battalion 101 and the Final Solution in Poland.* New York: HarperCollins, 1992.

———. *The Origins of the Final Solution: The Evolution of Nazi Jewish Policy, September 1939–March 1942.* Lincoln: University of Nebraska Press, 2004.

————. *The Path to Genocide: Essays on Launching the Final Solution*. Cambridge: Cambridge University Press, 1992.

Buchheim, Hans. "Rechtsstellung und Organisation des Reichskommissars für die Festigung deutschen Volkstums." In *Gutachten des Instituts für Zeitgeschichte*. Vol. 1. Munich, Germany: Institut für Zeitgeschichte, 1958.

Buchheim, Hans, Martin Broszat, Hans-Adolf Jacobsen, and Helmut Krausnick. *Anatomie des SS-Staates*. Munich, Germany: Deutscher Taschenbuch Verlag, 1994.

Burleigh, Michael. *Ethics and Extermination: Reflections on Nazi Genocide*. Cambridge: Cambridge University Press, 1997.

————. *Germany Turns Eastwards: A Study of Ostforschung in the Third Reich*. Cambridge: Cambridge University Press, 1988.

Cesarani, David. *Becoming Eichmann: Rethinking the Life, Crimes, and Trial of a "Desk Murderer."* Cambridge, MA: Da Capo Press, 2006.

Connelly, John. "Nazis and Slavs: From Racial Theory to Racist Practice." *Central European History* 32 (January 1999): 1–33.

Czubiński, Anton. "Poland's Place in Nazi Plans for a New Order in Europe in the Years 1934–1940." *Polish-Western Affairs* 21, no. 1 (1980): 19–46.

Davies, Norman. *God's Playground: A History of Poland*. 2 vols. New York: Columbia University Press, 1982.

————. *Heart of Europe: A Short History of Poland*. Oxford: Oxford University Press, 1984.

Dawidowicz, Lucy. *The War against the Jews, 1933–1945*. New York: Holt, Rinehart and Winston, 1975.

Długoborski, Wacław. "Die deutsche Besatzungspolitik gegenüber Polen." In *Nationalsozialistische Diktatur, 1933–1945: Ein Bilanz*, ed. Karl Dietrich Bracher, Manfred Funke, and Hans-Adolf Jacobsen. Bonn, Germany: Bundeszentrale für politische Bildung, 1983.

————. "Economic Policy of the Third Reich in Occupied and Dependent Countries, 1938–1945: An Attempt at a Typology." *Studia Historiae Oeconomicae* 15 (1980): 179–212.

Drożdżyński, Aleksander, and Jan Zaborowski. *Oberländer: A Study in German East Policies*. Poznan, Poland: Wydawnictwo Zachodnie, 1960.

Dwork, Debórah, and Robert Jan van Pelt. *Auschwitz: 1270 to the Present*. New York: W. W. Norton, 1996.

Eley, Geoff. *From Unification to Nazism: Reinterpreting the German Past*. Boston: Unwin Hyman, 1986.

Farquharson, J. E. *The Plough and the Swastika: The NSDAP and Agriculture in Germany, 1928–1945*. London: SAGE Publications, 1976.

Feldman, Jósef. *Bismarck i Polska*. Kraków, Poland: Czytelnik, 1947.

Fiedor Karol, Janusz Sobczak, and Wojciech Wrzesński. "The Image of Poles in Germany and of the German in Poland in the Interwar Years and Its Role in Shaping Relations between the Two States." *Polish-Western Affairs* 19, no. 2 (1978): 203–228.

Fischer, Fritz. *Germany's Aims in the First World War*. New York: W. W. Norton, 1967.

Förster, Jürgen. "Hitler's Decision in Favour of War against the Soviet Union." In *Ger-*

many and the Second World War. Vol. 4, *The Attack on the Soviet Union,* ed. Horst
Boog, Jürgen Förster, Joachim Hoffmann, Ernst Klink, Rolf-Dieter Müller, and Gerd
Veberschär; trans. Dean S. McMurray, Ewald Osers, and Louise Willmott. Oxford:
Clarendon Press, 1998.

Friedlander, Henry. *The Origins of Nazi Genocide: From Euthanasia to the Final Solution.*
Chapel Hill: University of North Carolina Press, 1995.

————. "Step by Step: The Expansion of Murder, 1939–1941." In *The Holocaust: Origins,
Implementation, Aftermath,* ed. Omer Bartov. London: Routledge, 2000.

Friedlander, Saul. *Nazi Germany and the Jews.* Vol. 1, *The Years of Persecution, 1933–1939.*
New York: HarperCollins, 1997.

Friedman, Philip. "The Lublin Reservation and the Madagascar Plan: Two Aspects of
Nazi Jewish Policy during the Second World War." In *Roads to Extinction: Essays
on the Holocaust,* ed. Ada June Friedman. New York: Jewish Publication Society of
America, 1980.

Friedrich, Klaus-Peter. "Kollaboration und Antisemitismus in Polen unter deutscher
Besatzung (1939–1944/45): Zu verdrängten Askpekten eines schwierigen deutsch-
polnisch-jüdischen Verhältnisses." *Zeitschrift für Geschichtswissenschaft* 45, no. 9
(1997): 818–834.

Fulbrook, Mary, ed. *German History since 1800.* London: Arnold, 1997.

Gilbert, Martin. *The Holocaust: A History of the Jews of Europe during the Second World
War.* New York: Holt, Rinehart and Winston, 1985.

Goshen, Seev. "Eichmann und die Nisko-Aktion im Oktober 1939." *Vierteljahrshefte für
Zeitgeschichte* 27, no. 1 (January 1981): 74–96.

Gröning, Gert, and Joachim Wolschke Bulmahn. *Die Liebe zur Landschaft. Teil III: Der
Drang nach Osten: Zur Entwicklung der Landespflege in National-sozialismus und
während des Zweiten Weltkrieges in den "eingegliederten Ostgebieten."* Munich, Germany: Minerva Publikation, 1987.

Haar, Ingo. *Historiker im Nationalsozialismus: Deutsche Geschichtswissenschaft und der
"Volkstumskampf" im Osten.* Göttingen, Germany: Vandenhoeck & Ruprecht, 2000.

Hagen, William. *Germans, Jews and Poles: The Nationality Conflict in the Prussian East,
1772–1914.* Chicago: University of Chicago Press, 1980.

Hansen, Georg. "Damit wurde der Warthegau zum Exerzierplatz des praktischen Nationalsozialismus: Eine Fallstudie zur Politik der Einverleibung." In *September 1939:
Krieg, Besatzung, Widerstand in Polen,* ed. Christoph Klessmann. Göttingen, Germany: Vandenhoeck & Ruprecht, 1989.

Harvey, Elizabeth. *Women and the Nazi East: Agents and Witnesses of Germanization.*
New Haven, CT: Yale University Press, 2003.

Heiber, Helmut. "Der Generalplan Ost." *Vierteljahrshefte für Zeitgeschichte* 6 (1957): 281–
325.

Heinemann, Isabel. *"Rasse, Siedlung, deutsches Blut": Das Rasse- & Siedlungshauptamt
der SS und die rassenpolitische Neuordnung Europas.* Göttingen, Germany: Wallstein
Verlag, 2003.

Herbert, Ulrich. *A History of Foreign Labor in Germany, 1880–1980: Seasonal Workers/ Forced Laborers/Guest Workers*. Trans. William Templer. Ann Arbor: University of Michigan Press, 1990.

———. *Hitler's Foreign Workers: Enforced Foreign Labor in Germany under the Third Reich*. Trans. William Templer. Cambridge: Cambridge University Press, 1997.

———, ed. *National Socialist Extermination Policies: Contemporary German Perspectives and Controversies*. New York: Berghahn Books, 2000.

Hilberg, Raul. *The Destruction of the European Jews*. 3 vols. 3rd ed. New Haven, CT, and London: Yale University Press, 2003.

Hildebrand, Klaus. *The Foreign Policy of the Third Reich*. Trans. Anthony Fothergill. Berkeley and Los Angeles: University of California Press, 1973.

Hinsley, F. H. *British Intelligence in the Second World War: Its Influence on Strategy and Operations*. 2 vols. New York: Cambridge University Press, 1979.

Höffkes, Karl. *Hitlers politische Generale: Die Gauleiter des Dritten Reichs—Ein biographisches Nachschlagewerk*. Tübingen, Germany: Grabert-Verlag, 1986.

Höhne, Heinz. *The Order of the Death's Head: The Story of Hitler's SS*. Trans. Richard Barry. New York: Ballantine Books, 1971.

Housden, Martyn. "Hans Frank—Empire Builder in the East, 1939–1941." *East European Quarterly* 24 (1994): 367–393.

———. *Hans Frank, Lebensraum and the Holocaust*. New York: Palgrave Macmillan, 2003.

Inkelas, Daniel. "Visions of Harmony and Violence: RKF Landscape Planning and Population Policy in Annexed Poland, 1939–1944." Ph.D. diss., Northwestern University, 1998.

Jacobsen, Hans-Adolf. *Nationalsozialistische Aussenpolitik, 1933–1938*. Frankfurt, Germany: Alfred Metzner Verlag, 1968.

Jakóbczyk, Witold. "The First Decade of the Prussian Settlement Commission's Activities (1886–1897)." *Polish Review* 17, no. 1 (1972): 3–13.

Jansen, Christian, and Arno Weckbecker. *Der "Volksdeutsche Selbstschutz" in Polen 1939/40*. Munich, Germany: R. Oldenbourg Verlag, 1992.

Jansen, Hans. *Madagaskar-Plan: Die beabsichtigte Deportation der europäischen Juden nach Madagaskar*. Munich, Germany: Herbig Verlag, 1997.

Jastrzębski, Włodzimierz. *Hitlerowskie wysiedlenia z ziem polskich wcielnych do Rzeszy w latach, 1939–1945*. Poznan, Poland: Instytut Zachodni, 1968.

Karny, Miroslav. "Nisko in der Geschichte der Endlösung." *Judaica Bohemiae* 23 (1987): 69–84.

Kellermann, Volkmar. *Schwarzer Adler, Weisser Adler: Die Polenpolitik der Weimarer Republik*. Cologne, Germany: Markus Verlag, 1970.

Kennedy, Robert M. *The German Campaign in Poland, 1939*. Washington, DC: Department of the Army, 1956.

Kershaw, Ian. "Arthur Greiser—Ein Motor der 'Endlösung.'" In *Die Braune Elite 2: 21 weitere biographische Skizzen*, ed. Ronald Smelser, Rainer Zitelmann, and Enrico Syring. Darmstadt, Germany: Wissenschaftliche Buchgesellschaft, 1993.

——. *Hitler 1889–1936: Hubris*. New York: W. W. Norton, 1999.

——. *Hitler 1936–1945: Nemesis*. New York: W. W. Norton, 2000.

——. "Improvised Genocide? The Emergence of the 'Final Solution' in the 'Warthegau.'" *Transactions of the Royal Historical Society*, 6th ser., vol. 2 (1992): 51–78.

——. *The Nazi Dictatorship: Problems and Perspectives of Interpretation*. London: Arnold, 2000.

Kiełboń, Janina. *Migracje ludności w dystrykcie lubelskim w latach, 1939–1944*. Lublin, Poland: Państwowe Muzeum na Majdanku, 1995.

Koehl, Robert L. *The Black Corps: The Structure and Power Struggles of the Nazi SS*. Madison: University of Wisconsin Press, 1983.

——. "Colonialism inside Germany: 1886–1918." *Journal of Modern History* 25 (1953): 255–272.

——. "The Deutsche Volksliste in Poland, 1939–1945." *Journal of Central European Affairs* 15 (1956): 354–366.

——. *RKFDV: German Resettlement and Population Policy, 1939–1945—A History of the Reich Commission for the Strengthening of Germandom*. Cambridge, MA: Harvard University Press, 1957.

Kormanicki, Titus. *Rebirth of the Polish Republic: A Study in the Diplomatic History of Europe, 1914–1920*. London: William Heinemann, 1957.

Krausnick, Helmut. "Hitler und die Morde in Polen: Ein Beitrag zum Konflikt zwischen Heer und SS um die Verwaltung der besetzten Gebiete." *Vierteljahrshefte für Zeitgeschichte* 11 (April 1963): 196–209.

Krausnick, Helmut, and Hans-Heinrich Wilhelm. *Die Truppe des Weltanschauungskrieges: Die Einsatzgruppen des Sicherheitspolizei und des SD, 1938–1942*. Stuttgart, Germany: Deutsche Verlags-Anstalt, 1981.

Kreidler, Eugen. *Die Eisenbahnen im Machtbereich der Achsenmächte während des Zweiten Weltkrieges: Einsatz und Leistung für die Wehrmacht und Kriegswirtschaft*. Göttingen, Germany: Musterschmidt, 1975.

Kubiczek, Franciszek, ed. *Historia Polski w Liczbach*. Warsaw: Główny Urząd Statystyczny, 1994.

Leśniewski, Andrzej, and Roman Nurowski. "Political Background to Population Movements between the Oder and Bug Rivers." In *Population Movements between the Oder and Bug Rivers, 1939–1950*, ed. Zachodnia Agencja Prasowa. Poznan, Poland, and Warsaw: Wydawnictwo Zachodnie, 1961.

Levin, Nora. *The Holocaust: The Destruction of European Jewry, 1933–1945*. New York: Thomas Y. Crowell, 1968.

Levine, Herbert S. *Hitler's Free City: A History of the Nazi Party in Danzig, 1925–39*. Chicago: University of Chicago Press, 1973.

——. "Local Authority and the SS State: The Conflict over Population Policy in Danzig–West Prussia, 1939–1945." *Central European History* 2 (1969): 331–355.

Liulevicius, Vejas Gabriel. *Warland on the Eastern Front: Culture, National Identity and German Occupation in World War I*. Cambridge: Cambridge University Press, 2000.

Reitlinger, Gerald. *The SS: Alibi of a Nation, 1922–1945*. New York: Viking Press, 1968.

Röhr, Werner, ed. *Europa unterm Hakenkreuz: Analysen, Quellen, Register*. Heidelberg, Germany: Verlag Heidelberg, 1996.

Rosenthal, Harry K. *German and Pole: National Conflict and Modern Myth*. Gainesville: University Press of Florida, 1976.

———. "The Prussian View of the Pole: The Significance of the Year 1894." *Polish Review* 17, no. 1 (1972): 13–20.

Rossino, Alexander B. "Destructive Impulses: German Soldiers and the Conquest of Poland." *Holocaust and Genocide Studies* 11 (Winter 1999): 351–365.

———. *Hitler Strikes Poland: Blitzkrieg, Ideology, and Atrocity*. Lawrence: University Press of Kansas, 2003.

Rössler, Mechthild, and Sabine Schleiermacher, eds. *Der "Generalplan Ost": Hauptlinien der nationalsozialistischen Planungs- und Vernichtungspolitik*. Berlin: Akademie-Verlag, 1993.

Rubin, Icchak. *Żydki w Lodzi pod Niemecką Okupacą, 1939–1945*. London: Kontra, 1988.

Rutherford, Phillip T. "'Absolute Organizational Deficiency': The *1.Nahplan* of December 1939 (Logistics, Limitations, and Lessons). *Central European History* 36, no. 2 (2003): 235–273.

Safrian, Hans. *Eichmann und seine Gehilfen*. Frankfurt, Germany: Fischer Taschenbuch Verlag, 1997.

Schenk, Dieter. *Hitlers Mann in Danzig: Albert Forster und die NS-Verbrechen in Danzig-Westpreussen*. Bonn, Germany: Verlag J. H. W. Dietz, 2000.

Schleunes, Karl. *The Twisted Road to Auschwitz: Nazi Policy towards the Jews, 1933–1939*. Chicago: University of Illinois Press, 1970.

Sereny, Gitta. *The Healing Wound: Experiences and Reflections, Germany, 1938–2001*. New York: W. W. Norton, 2002.

Smelser, Ronald, and Enrico Syring, eds. *Die SS: Elite unter dem Totenkopf. 30 Lebenläufe*. Paderborn, Germany: Ferdinand Schöningh, 2000.

Smelser, Ronald, Rainer Zitelmann, and Enrico Syring, eds. *Die Braune Elite 2: 21 weitere biographische Skizzen*. Darmstadt, Germany: Wissenschaftliche Buchgesellschaft, 1993.

Steinbacher, Sybille. *"Musterstadt" Auschwitz: Germanisierungspolitik und Judenmord in Ostoberschlesien*. Munich, Germany: K. G. Sauer Verlag, 2000.

Sydnor, Charles. *Soldiers of Destruction: The SS Death's Head Division, 1933–1945*. Princeton, NJ: Princeton University Press, 1990.

Taylor, A. J. P. *The Origins of the Second World War*. New York: Atheneum, 1983.

Tims, Richard. *Germanizing Prussian Poland: The H-K-T Society and the Struggle for the Eastern Marches of the German Empire, 1894–1919*. New York: Columbia University Press, 1941.

Umbreit, Hans. *Deutsche Militärverwaltungen 1938/39: Die militärische Besetzung der Tschechoslowakei und Polens*. Stuttgart, Germany: Deutsche Verlags-Anstalt, 1977.

Volkmann, Hans-Erich. "Zur Ansiedlung der Deutschbalten im 'Warthegau.'" *Zeitschrift für Ostforschung* 30, no. 4 (1981): 527–558.

———. "Zwischen Ideologie und Pragmatismus: Zur nationalsozialistischen Wirtschafts-politik im Reichsgau Wartheland." In *Ostmitteleuropa: Berichte und Forschungen*, ed. Ulrich Haustein, Georg Strobel, and Gerhard Wagner. Stuttgart, Germany: Ernst Klett, 1981.

Wandycz, Piotr. *The Lands of Partitioned Poland, 1795–1918.* Seattle: University of Washington Press, 1974.

Wasser, Bruno. *Himmlers Raumplanung im Osten: Der Generalplan Ost in Polen, 1940–1944.* Basel, Switzerland, and Boston: Birkhäuser, 1993.

Watt, Richard M. *Bitter Glory: Poland and Its Fate, 1918 to 1939.* New York: Simon and Schuster, 1979.

Wehler, Hans-Ulrich. *The German Empire, 1871–1918.* Trans. Kim Traynor. New York: St. Martin's Press, 1991.

———. *Krisenherde des Kaiserreichs, 1871–1918: Studien zur deutschen Sozial- und Verfassungsgeschichte.* Göttingen, Germany: Vendenhoeck & Ruprecht, 1970.

Weinberg, Gerhard L. *The Foreign Policy of Hitler's Germany: Diplomatic Revolution in Europe, 1933–1936.* Chicago and London: University of Chicago Press, 1970.

———. *The Foreign Policy of Hitler's Germany: Starting World War II, 1937–1939.* Chicago and London: University of Chicago Press, 1980.

———. *Germany and the Soviet Union, 1939–1941.* Leiden, Netherlands: E. J. Brill, 1954.

Whaley, Barton. *Codeword BARBAROSSA.* Cambridge, MA: MIT Press, 1973.

Wildt, Michael. "Radikalisierung und Selbstradikalisierung 1939: Die Geburt des Reichssicherheitshauptamt aus dem Geist des völkischen Massenmords." In *Die Gestapo im Zweiten Weltkreig: "Heimatfront" und besetztes Europa*, ed. Gerhard Paul and Klaus-Michael Mallmann. Darmstadt, Germany: Primus Verlag, 2000.

Yahil, Leni. *The Holocaust: The Fate of European Jewry, 1932–1945.* Trans. Ina Friedman and Haya Galai. New York: Oxford University Press, 1990.

Zielinski, Henryk. *Population Changes in Poland, 1939–1950.* New York: Mid-European Studies Center, 1954.

Index

326 *Index*

S-cases, 276n48
Scheffler, Gerhard, 122, 267n55
Schroda, 1, 2, 3, 165
Schulaufsichtsgesetz, 19
Schulenburg, Friedrich Werner von der,
    45–46, 48, 49
Schutzstaffel (SS), 2, 9
Schwarzhuber, Kasper, 276n50
Schwerin, Friedrich von, 30
SD (Sicherheitsdienst), 41
search
    body searches, 85, 95, 146
    by National Socialists, 11
    of persons and luggage, 85
    Search Service, 143
    UWZ search office, 82–83
    for weapons or valuables, 84, 85, 114,
        149–150
Second Reich
    foundation of, 5
    Germanization of Polish provinces, 5–6
    Poland's rebirth, 31
    Posen as German nation-state, 17–18
secrecy of plans
    1.Nahplan, 80
    3.Nahplan–1.Teilprogram, 184, 185, 186
    consolidation of German nationhood,
        55, 56
    Hitler's Fundamental Order, 287n41
    Umsiedlung, 48
Secret Additional Protocol, 40
security concerns
    cleansing and safeguarding of German
        regions, 79
    clergy as threat, 14, 15, 17
    criminal activity, 192
    evacuation based on danger of individuals,
        81–82
    housing with families and friends,
        181–182, 192
    Kreis Konin, 180–181
    nobility as threat, 14, 15, 17
    priority in 1.Nahplan, 98
    Prussia, 13–14
    resettlement vs. national defense
        programs, 188–189
    risks of worker deferments, 129
    during 2. Nahplan, 116–117
    Zwischenplan evictions, 122, 124–125
    See also criminal activity

Seidl, Siegfried, 118, 119, 164, 182, 222
Selbstschutz, 43, 74, 75, 250n55
settlement, belts of, 53. *See also* resettlement
Settlement Law (Ansiedlungsgesetz), 22–23
Settlement Zone I Order, 134–135
Sicherheitsdienst (SD), 41
Sicherheitspolizei (Sipo), 41, 42
sick people, exempt from deportation, 157–
    158, 188
Siegmund, Harry, 202, 202–203
Sipo (Sicherheitspolizei), 41, 42
Soviet Union. *See* Russia
Spiraling radicalization, 220
SS (Schutzstaffel), 2, 9
SS-Ansiedlungsstab (SS-AS), 144, 154, 160–
    161, 181
SS-Bodenamt, 254n84
SS-Einsatzgruppen, 9
Stalin
    division of Poland, 48
    German-Soviet nonaggression treaty, 40, 41
    invasion of Poland, 45
    relations with Germany, 49, 62
statistical Germanization, 210–211
Streckenbach, Bruno, 77–78, 86
Strickner, 93
Sudeten Crisis, 40–41

T-4 euthanasia program, 299n89
Tannenberg, 42, 43, 242n86
teacher deferments, 106
territorial organization of occupied Poland,
    58–62, 59 (map)
3.Nahplan
    Kreis Konin evacuation, 181
    overview, 174–175
    planning, 175–176
    purpose of, 9, 175
3.Nahplan–1.Teilprogram
    aftermath, 190–193, 211
    baggage allowance, 176, 186
    failure of, 190, 203–204, 211
    overcrowding of Generalgouvernement,
        176–177
    project planning, 176, 183–184
    resettlement vs. national defense
        programs, 188–189
    resistance-through-flight problem, 186–187
    Russian invasion, impact on deportations,
        184–186